SO-BAC-052

# In Praise of
# Adi Da (The Da Avatar)

Adi Da is the greatest Spiritual Master ever to walk the earth. Seeing this, attending to this truth, we need not walk in the dark any longer. Adi Da is the God-Man. He reveals the ultimate truth residing in the human heart and at the heart of all religions.

THE REV. THOMAS AHLBURN
Senior Minister, The First Unitarian Church,
Providence, Rhode Island

There exists nowhere in the world today, among Christians, Jews, Muslims, Hindus, Buddhists, native tribalists, or any other groups, anyone who has so much to teach, or speaks with such authority, or is so important for understanding our situation.

HENRY LEROY FINCH
Professor of Philosophy;
author, *Wittgenstein—The Early Philosophy*
and *Wittgenstein—The Later Philosophy*

Adi Da provides a way in which Oneness may be experienced by anyone who is bold enough to follow his teachings. It is important to understand that his vision is neither Eastern nor Western, but it is the eternal spiritual pulse of the Great Wisdom which knows no cultural, temporal, or geographical locus.

LARRY DOSSEY, M.D.
author, *Healing Words; Space, Time, and Medicine;
Beyond Illness;* and *Recovering the Soul*

I regard the work of Adi Da and his devotees as one of the most penetrating spiritual and social experiments happening on the planet in our era.

JEFFREY MISHLOVE, PH.D.
host, *Thinking Allowed* public television series
author, *The Roots of Consciousness*

$M$y relationship with Adi Da as His devotee over the past 21 years has only confirmed my certainty of His Realization and the Truth of His impeccable Teaching.

RAY LYNCH
composer, *The Sky of Mind*; *Deep Breakfast*; *No Blue Thing*;
*Nothing Above My Shoulders but the Evening*

$A$di Da is a great teacher with a dynamic ability to awaken in his listeners something of the Divine Reality in which he is grounded, with which he is identified, and which in fact, he is.

He is a man of both the East and the West; perhaps in him they merge and are organized as the One that he is.

ISRAEL REGARDIE
author, *Psychology, Magic & Mysticism*;
*The Golden Dawn*

$A$di Da is a man who has truly walked in Spirit and given true enlightenment to many.

SUN BEAR
founder, The Bear Tribe Medicine Society

# THE HEART'S SHOUT

**ADI DA (THE DA AVATAR)**
The Mountain Of Attention, California, 1995

# THE HEART'S SHOUT

Perfect and Urgent Wisdom
From The Living Heart of Reality,
The Incarnate Divine Person,

## ADI DA
(THE DA AVATAR)

THE DAWN HORSE PRESS
MIDDLETOWN, CALIFORNIA

NOTE  TO  THE  READER

All who study Adidam (the Way of the Heart) or take up its practice should remember that they are responding to a Call to become responsible for themselves. They should understand that they, not Avatara Adi Da or others, are responsible for any decision they may make or action they take in the course of their lives of study or practice.

The devotional, Spiritual, functional, practical, relational, cultural, and formal community practices and disciplines referred to in this book are appropriate and natural practices that are voluntarily and progressively adopted by each student-novice and member of Adidam and adapted to his or her personal circumstance. Although anyone may find them useful and beneficial, they are not presented as advice or recommendations to the general reader or to anyone who is not a student-novice or a member of Adidam. And nothing in this book is intended as a diagnosis, prescription, or recommended treatment or cure for any specific "problem", whether medical, emotional, psychological, social, or Spiritual. One should apply a particular program of treatment, prevention, cure, or general health only in consultation with a licensed physician or other qualified professional.

© 1996 The TDL Trust Pty Ltd, as trustee for The TDL Trust. All rights reserved. No part of this book may be copied or reproduced in any manner without permission from the publisher.

The TDL Trust Pty Ltd, as trustee for The TDL Trust, claims perpetual copyright to this book, to the entire Written (and otherwise recorded) Wisdom-Teaching of Adi Da (The Da Avatar) and to all other writings and recordings of Adidam.

Printed in the United States of America

Produced by Adidam
in cooperation with the Dawn Horse Press

International Standard Book Number: 1-57097-019-X

Library of Congress Catalog Card Number: 96-83384

# CONTENTS

ADI DA, THE DA AVATAR     11
*An Introduction by His devotees*

THE MOST PERFECT TEACHING, THE MOST PERFECT TEACHER     25
*An Introduction to* The Heart's Shout

## PART I
## I Have Come To Reveal The Joy Of Being
### 29

SECTION 1. THE LIBERATING RELATIONSHIP     31
    1. The Divine Physics of Evolution     32
    2. Dreaming and Waking     37
    3. Coming into the Presence of Very God,     42
       *by Frank "Cheech" Marrero*
    4. On Spiritual Transmission     49
    5. The Great Relationship     51
    6. Aham Da Asmi     58

SECTION 2. THE GIFT OF "RADICAL" UNDERSTANDING     65
    7. The Columbia Experience     66
    8. A Heart-Awakened Insight     71
    9. The Dreaded Gom-Boo, or The Impossible Three-Day     75
       Thumb-and-Finger Problem
    10. From Charlie's Place to Adidamashram:     81
       How Adi Da Awakened My Heart, *by Brian O'Mahony*
    11. Self-Understanding     89

SECTION 3. WHAT ARE YOUR CONCLUSIONS ABOUT REALITY?     99
    12. The Asana of Science     100
    13. Free Inquiry and Scientific Materialism     108
    14. You Do Not Know What a Single Thing Is     112
    15. The Divine Trickster Talks Wild,     120
       *by the Adidam Writers Guild*

SECTION 4. THE TRUTH ABOUT GOD     127
    16. The Parental Deity and the One to Be Realized     128
    17. The Tacit Obviousness of God     133
    18. God Is Guru     139
    19. The Red Sitting Man, *by Annie Rogers*     142
    20. Beyond the Cultic Tendency in Religion     145
    21. God Is The Deep Of the world     148

SECTION 5. THE SEVEN STAGES OF LIFE                                    153
            AND THE GREAT TRADITION
    22. The Seven Stages of Life, *by the Adidam Writers Guild*        154
    23. The Religious Ambivalence of the West                          166
    24. Exoteric Christianity and the Universal Spiritual Message      173
        of Jesus
    25. Moving Beyond the Techniques of East and West                  180
    26. I Am Here to Complete the Great Tradition of Mankind           185

PART II

# Live With Me

The Foundation of Practice in the Way of the Heart

189

SECTION 1. ISHTA-GURU-BHAKTI YOGA                                      191
    27. The Testament and the Means of Freedom Itself                  192
    28. Divine Distraction                                             197
    29. The Master Is the Means                                        201
    30. "That Is My Work", *by Elizabeth Lowe*                         204
    31. Surrender the Faculties of the Body-Mind to Me                 210
    32. The Way That I Offer to You and to All                         215
    33. The Essence of Devotion                                        220

SECTION 2. SERVICE AND self-DISCIPLINE                                 223
    34. To Serve Me you Must Actively Transcend all ego-serving work   224
    35. Money, Food, and Sex                                           227
    36. Diet and Fasting                                               238
    37. The Secret of How to Change                                    243

SECTION 3. THE PRACTICE OF LOVE AND SEXUALITY                          245
    38. Ecstatic Living                                                246
    39. The Wound of Love                                              248
    40. Sex Is a Heart-Matter                                          253
    41. Right Celibacy Is Yogic, self-Transcending, and Happy          259
    42. Remember the Mystery in Which You Live                         261

SECTION 4. THE CALL TO COMMUNITY                                       265
    43. The Religious Necessity of Community                           266
    44. Cooperative, Human-Scale Community and the Integrity           267
        (Religious, and Altogether) of Civilization
    45. A New Human Order                                              273

SECTION 5. DEATH AND THE MEANING OF LIFE                          277
   46. The Heart of Understanding                    278
   47. There Is No Individual self That Dies          279
   48. This Liberating Impulse                         282
   49. The Only Way Out, *by Frans Bakker, M.D., and Tom Closser*
     291
   50. The Understanding That Overcomes Suffering      301

SECTION 6. DIVINE ENLIGHTENMENT                                   309
   51. The Great Event in the Vedanta Temple          310
   52. What Is to Be Realized?                         316
   53. "Crazy Wisdom"                                  318
   54. There Is Simply The "Bright" Itself             322
   55. The Man of Understanding                        325

EPILOGUE
## The Avatar Since Eternity
331

AN INVITATION TO ADIDAM                                           333

REGIONAL CENTERS OF ADIDAM                                        348

THE SACRED LITERATURE OF ADI DA (THE DA AVATAR)                   349

GLOSSARY                                                          363

AN INVITATION TO SUPPORT ADIDAM, THE WAY OF THE HEART             371

FURTHER NOTES TO THE READER                                       373

INDEX                                                             377

**Adi Da (The Da Avatar)**
**The Mountain Of Attention, 1995**

# Adi Da,
# the Da Avatar

*An Introduction by His devotees*

There is a State of Being that is completely, unequivocally, permanently, infinitely Happy and Free—a State that cannot be lost under any conditions, in this world or after death. Such a State is not just imaginary. It is the underlying Truth of existence. In various times and places, great saints and sages have tasted this Happiness to some degree. But now this Truth, this Joy, has <u>perfectly</u> emerged in the world for the first time, and has become the actual possibility of all human beings.

In November 1939, on Long Island, New York, a baby was born who was not an ordinary child. But no one knew this. No one knew that this child—named by His parents "Franklin Albert Jones"—had Work to accomplish that was great and sublime beyond description. This Work, which began at His birth, continues today, and will continue beyond His human lifetime, forever. The One born as Franklin Jones is Adi Da, the Da Avatar, whose Presence in the world is an outpouring of Divine Grace and Compassion never seen before.

# The "Bright"

During His infancy, Adi Da was perfectly aware of everything around Him. He saw that people were not happy, that each person presumed himself or herself to be separate from everyone else, each struggling to find his or her own separate joy. Adi Da found this remarkable—it was not His experience at all. He knew only Oneness, only Blissfulness. His consciousness was not yet identified with a bag of flesh and skin. As He describes in His Spiritual Autobiography, *The Knee of Listening*, Adi Da lived in an entirely different State of Awareness—as "Infinitely and inherently Free Being", a sphere of Radiance and Love that He called the "Bright". Adi Da was inseparable from the Bliss and Joy of the "Bright". He knew Himself to be the very Source of It, the true and

"For His first two years, Adi Da enjoyed the
undiminished Bliss of His Real Condition."

"Bright" Condition of everything. How could a baby have known this? What Adi Da describes as His earliest experience is more than the experience of an ordinary human infant. The One who appeared in the world as "Franklin Jones" Exists eternally—before this birth and forever. Adi Da's description of His own "Bright" Condition is the confession of the Divine Being, the ultimate Truth and Reality, appearing in human form.

For His first two years, Adi Da enjoyed the undiminished Bliss of His Real Condition. Then during His second year, something very mysterious occurred. As Adi Da was crawling across the linoleum floor one day, His parents let loose a new puppy they were giving Him—and in the instant of seeing the puppy and seeing His parents, Adi Da's infinite Awareness suddenly changed. He made the spontaneous choice to be an "I", an apparently separate person relating to apparently separate others.

# "Forgetting" the "Bright"

What had happened? Adi Da had relinquished the "Bright", out of a "painful loving", a sympathy for the suffering and ignorance of human beings. He was responding to the great impulse behind His birth—the impulse to make the "Bright" known to every one. But the only way that Adi Da could fulfill this purpose was to intentionally "forget" the "Bright" and experience life from the ordinary human point of view—and then, in the midst of that limited condition, to find the way to recover the "Bright".

This was Adi Da's early-life ordeal, and it was a perilous, desperate affair. He did not know how it would turn out. He had no "method" for recovering the "Bright". But He embraced every aspect of human life, both great and ordinary, in order to reveal the complete Truth of existence, the Truth that can set everyone Free. Adi Da did this through a most intense ordeal that lasted for His first thirty years.

In the course of this ordeal, Adi Da always risked everything for the Truth. He could not bear to place any limitations on His quest to recover the "Bright". In this disposition, Adi Da not only thoroughly explored the realms of ordinary human experience, but He also passed through every possible kind of psychic and Spiritual awakening—and with extraordinary speed. It was as though these awakenings were already, in some sense, thoroughly familiar to Him. But Adi Da was not satisfied. He had the intuition of some "incredible knowledge". He knew that the ultimate Truth had to be greater than any of these experiences, any of these visions, any moment of revelation. The hidden force of the "Bright" Itself was always alive in Him, leading Him toward the perfect fulfillment of His quest.

**Adi Da (The Da Avatar)**
**Adidamashram, 1994**

# God-Realization

Many individuals throughout history have been acknowledged as "God-Realized" or "Enlightened", or in union with the Divine in some sense. Different religious traditions mean different things when they speak of the ultimate goal of religion. But it can be said, in the general sense, that God-Realization is the Condition in which God, or the Divine Self, has been "made Real". It is the State in which God (or the Divine) has become the living Reality of one's existence—rather than a great Being or Power apart from oneself. In the same way, to be Enlightened is to be profoundly Awakened to God, Truth, or Reality, to the point that even the body becomes radiant with Spiritual Force.

Throughout history, remarkable men and women have lived their lives as an heroic ordeal directed to attaining God, Truth, or Reality. Some of them—the greatest saints, yogis, and sages—attained various degrees of Enlightenment, or God-Realization. But Adi Da had nothing to attain. He is the "Bright" of God, the Perfect Descent of the Divine. And the State of most perfect God-Realization that Adi Da has brought into the world is a Realization never known before. It is the Realization of the "Bright", the all-surpassing Divine Enlightenment that Adi Da has now made possible for all beings.

The Great Mystery of Who Adi Da is and what He has come to give is not a claim to be believed, but a Secret to be discovered at heart. People of all kinds have already experienced this overwhelming, joyous surprise and have become devoted to Adi Da as their beloved Spiritual Master and Divine Liberator. Once the depth of that Secret is revealed, nothing is ever the same again.

# The Immense Bond of Guru-Love

The bond between Spiritual teacher and disciple that Adi Da's devotees have discovered in His company is more fundamental than any other, more intimate than family ties, more passionate than any relationships with lovers and friends. It has been treasured in all religious traditions throughout time. To be accepted as the disciple of a saint or a being of true Spiritual Realization has always been regarded as the most precious Grace, the very means of one's own Awakening to Truth. Why is this? Because the time-proven way to learn anything great is to go to a master, to imbibe that skill, that art, that wisdom in the company of one who knows it through and through and can transmit its secrets to worthy disciples. In the case of a true Spiritual Master, what is transmitted is not merely esoteric knowledge, but the very Power and Condition of the Master's own Spiritual Realization.

There is a secret law, operating in every dimension of our lives, that explains how the relationship between the disciple and the Spiritual Master works. Avatara Adi Da has powerfully expressed this secret in a few words: "You become what you meditate on." That is to say, you duplicate in body and in mind the qualities of whatever object or condition you consistently give your attention to. Everyone observes how consistent dwelling on negative thoughts disturbs and depresses the whole body and may even cause disease. In the same way, positive thought and action enlivens the being. The great leap in human growth into the dimension of Spiritual Realization requires that we give to a Spiritually Realized Being our constant love and attention, meditatively, actively, day in and day out. Then the great law, "you become what you meditate on", becomes our greatest advantage.

To give one's attention to Avatara Adi Da, to meditate on Him through all thought, feeling, and action, is to begin to duplicate <u>Him</u>, to Realize the Divine State of the "Bright" Itself. The more this process magnifies, the more one forgets the limited body-mind-self. The heart responds to Adi Da through sheer <u>attraction</u>, through the very same principle that brings all love-relationships, all friendships into being. But attraction to Adi Da is not mere attraction to a human individual who seems to answer one's need for love and self-fulfillment. It is Attraction to the Free Condition, the unbounded State of Happiness that Avatara Adi Da Transmits. For His potential devotee, Adi Da becomes the Attractive Center of the universe, and the passion to Realize His Divine Condition grows greater than any other urge.

Adi Da, like other Westerners of His generation, grew up with no knowledge of the Guru-devotee relationship. He discovered "the Immense Bond of Guru-Love" as spontaneously as He discovered everything else in the process of His Re-Awakening. His first Teacher was an American— Swami Rudrananda (also known as "Rudi"). Rudi, who taught in New York City, guided Adi Da in the initial stages of His Spiritual growth, and, later, passed Adi Da on to his own Gurus in India. These great Realizers—Swami Muktananda and Swami Nityananda—were instrumental in Adi Da's Awakening to higher Spiritual Realizations.

Adi Da's Gurus were extraordinary beings. They were Siddhas, Yogis alive with Spiritual Force, who constantly transmitted their Spirit-Power to Him. He loved them and submitted to their instruction and their discipline with limitless devotion and heart-felt gratitude. But Adi Da was not the usual disciple, just as He was not an ordinary, or even an extraordinary, man. His Realization was already absolute, but it was "latent in the heart", not yet fully active. He was in the process of recovering the "Bright", His native State of Being, and that was the process that each of His Gurus

**Adi Da meditating in Bombay, August 1969,
with pictures of His Gurus Swami Muktananda (right)
and Swami Nityananda (left)**

served in Him. All kinds of Spiritual Realizations are described in the traditions, and Adi Da passed through all of them—visions, trances, mystical raptures, "cosmic consciousness", states of profound meditation and Transcendental knowledge. But in the closing phases of His ordeal of Spiritual Realization, Adi Da's overwhelming impulse to the Truth drove Him into territory unknown to His Gurus, unknown in the annals of Spiritual literature. His ultimate Re-Awakening to the "Bright" occurred on the basis of a unique and all-encompassing insight, a "radical understanding" that places mankind's whole history of Spiritual seeking and Realization in a new light—and leads beyond all of it.

# "Radical" Understanding

"Radical" understanding is the bedrock of Adi Da's Teaching. Normally, when we say we "understand", we are indicating that we have figured out a concept, grasped how something works, intuited the nature of the object (or person), or become sympathetic with someone's feelings. When Adi Da speaks of "'radical' understanding", or just "understanding", He is not using the word in the conventional sense. He is referring to a most profound and liberating insight—a direct awareness of the single root-cause behind all un-Happiness. He is pointing to something we are always doing, an activity that is actually holding back the flood-gates of Divine Bliss, Joy, Happiness, and Love. What is that Happiness-preventing activity exactly? What is it that we are doing that is keeping us from Realizing the "Bright" right now?

Adi Da was moved to discover for Himself what the underlying answer to these questions was.

Through the most rigorous observation of Himself in every possible circumstance—talking, reading, dreaming, eating, at the movies, at a party, walking alone—this primal activity more and more stood out in His awareness. He saw that we are always <u>contracting</u>—recoiling from existence, physically, emotionally, mentally, psychically. This self-contraction, Adi Da came to see, is our constant, though largely unconscious, response to the uncontrollable, unknowable world in which we find ourselves. It is a fearful reaction to the fact that we know we are going to die. And its effects are devastating. The self-contraction, Adi Da realized, is the source of fear, sorrow, anger, desire, guilt, competitiveness, shame, and all the mayhem of this world. Even ordinary pleasurable moments are governed by the same seed-activity. It became awesomely obvious to Adi Da that <u>everything</u> we do is a form of search, an effort to be free of the self-inflicted pain of self-contraction. But this effort cannot succeed, because the search itself is a form of the self-contraction. And so seeking for release, for freedom, cannot lead us to the Happiness we desire. Perfect Truth, or unqualified Happiness, Adi Da saw, only appears when the activity of self-contraction is "radically" understood, and therefore spontaneously ceases—revealing the simplicity, the Joy of Being that is always already the case.

This understanding may seem simple to grasp. But to truly live it is <u>most</u> profound. As Adi Da discovered, the self-contraction is programmed into the very cells of the body. Thus, even after this fundamental intuition arose in Him, Adi Da could not instantaneously correct the fault—because He had submitted to all the limits of human existence. But Adi Da's unique understanding, once it was basically established, accelerated His entire course of Divine Re-Awakening. It proved to be a kind of "muscle", an insight that gave Him the key to every experience, high and low.

As He moved closer to the great resolution of His early-life ordeal, Adi Da observed the self-contraction in more and more subtle forms. He observed it even as the simplest awareness of separateness, the naked sense of "I" and "other" that is at the root of our perception of the world. By now it was obvious to Him that the self-contraction explained not only the ordinary dramas of life, but the whole "tour" of Spiritual experience as well. At last, all of mankind's searches for God, Truth, or Reality fell into focus for Adi Da as an immense effort of seeking that was totally unnecessary, based on a fundamental error—the lack of "radical" understanding. Then there was nothing left over, nothing left for Him to Realize, except the Truth Itself.

# Re-Awakening to the "Bright"

Secluded in a corner of downtown Hollywood is a small temple, established by the Vedanta Society of Southern California. This simple temple, standing in the shadow of a giant freeway, provided the setting for the culminating Event of Adi Da's Spiritual ordeal. Adi Da discovered the temple in August, 1970 and began to go there frequently for meditation. On September 10, He went and sat in the temple as usual:

*As time passed, there was no Event of changes, no movement at all. There was not even any kind of inward deepening, no "inwardness" at all. There was no meditation. There was no need for meditation. There was not a single element or change that could be added to make my State Complete. I sat with my eyes open. I was not having an experience of any kind. Then, suddenly, I understood most perfectly. I Realized that I had Realized. The "Thing" about the "Bright" became Obvious. I <u>Am</u> Complete. I <u>Am</u> the One Who <u>Is</u> Complete.*

*In That instant, I understood and Realized (inherently, and most perfectly) What and Who I <u>Am</u>. It was a tacit Realization, a direct Knowledge in Consciousness. It was Consciousness Itself, without the addition of a Communication from any "Other" Source. There Is no "Other" Source. I simply sat there and Knew What and Who I <u>Am</u>. I was Being What I <u>Am</u>, Who I <u>Am</u>. I <u>Am</u> Being What I <u>Am</u>, Who I <u>Am</u>. I <u>Am</u> Reality, the Divine Self, the Nature, Substance, Support, and Source of all things and all beings. I <u>Am</u> the One Being, called "God" (the Source and Substance and Support and Self of all), the "One Mind" (the Consciousness and Energy in and <u>As</u> Which all appears), "Siva-Shakti"[1] (the Self-Existing and Self-Radiant Reality Itself), "Brahman"[2] (the Only Reality, Itself), the "One Atman"[3] (That <u>Is</u> not ego, but Only "Brahman", the Only Reality, Itself), the "Nirvanic Ground"[4] (the egoless and conditionless Reality and Truth, Prior to all dualities, but excluding none). I <u>Am</u> the One and Only and necessarily Divine Self, Nature, Condition, Substance, Support, Source, and Ground of all. I <u>Am</u> the "Bright".* [The Knee of Listening]

This unspeakable moment was the Divine Re-Awakening of Adi Da. He had permanently and Most Perfectly Re-Awakened to the "Bright". His

1. The Sanskrit term "Siva-Shakti" is an esoteric description of the Divine Being. "Siva" is a name for the Divine Being Itself, or Divine Consciousness. "Shakti" is a name for the All-Pervading Spirit-Power of the Divine Being. "Siva-Shakti" is thus the Unity of the Divine Consciousness and Its own Spirit-Power.

2. In the Hindu tradition, Brahman is the Ultimate Divine Reality that is the Source and Substance of all things, all worlds, and all beings.

3. The Divine Self.

4. "Nirvana" is a Buddhist term for the Unqualified Reality beyond suffering, ego, birth, and death. The "Nirvanic Ground" indicates the same Reality.

Realization was not dependent on meditative states, or on any manipulation of experience. It transcended even the slightest sense of identity as a separate self. It was and is the Realization that there is Only God and that all apparent events are simply the passing forms, or modifications, of God, Truth, or Reality, arising and dissolving in an endless Play that is Bliss and Love beyond comprehension.

The very Divine Person had become perfectly Conscious and Present through the ordinary human vehicle of "Franklin Jones". In all the eons of human time such an event was unprecedented. Avatara Adi Da's Descent as the Divine Person and His utter overcoming of the limits of human existence in all its dimensions—physical, mental, emotional, psychic, Spiritual—was total, Perfect, and Complete. Adi Da had Realized absolute Identity with the Divine, the One He was and is from the beginning. But His Re-Awakening signified far more than this. It was also the Revelation that all apparent beings are also only that Very One, destined to Realize this same Truth. The Condition of the "Bright", the God-Light of Adi Da's birth and infancy, was now fully established—not only in Him, but as the native Truth and the potential Realization of all beings in all worlds.

Through the Power of Adi Da's Re-Awakening to the "Bright" something has changed at the very heart of existence. The Divine Avatar, Adi Da, has done what only the Divine could do. He has, so to speak, "cracked the cosmic code", broken through the force of illusion that has always kept born beings bound to the realms of change and suffering and death.

Since His Divine Re-Awakening, Adi Da has devoted Himself absolutely to the Work of revealing the "Bright" and attracting people to the supreme Spiritual practice that ultimately Realizes the "Bright". Adi Da has done this Work through countless hours of Instruction and "consideration" with His devotees, covering every aspect of human life, Spiritual experience, and Divine Truth. But most of all, Adi Da has made His Revelation, and continues to make It in every moment, by Transmitting His "Bright" Divine Condition to His devotees. Adi Da now lives at Adidamashram, His Hermitage Ashram in Fiji, where representatives of His worldwide community of devotees come into His Company on Spiritual retreat. At Adidamashram, Avatara Adi Da does His Ultimate Work—the silent Blessing of all beings.

# The Divine World-Teacher

The world we live in today is more desperate than ever before—this is a dark epoch when the very survival of our world is threatened by the excesses of materialism and the sophisticated weapons of war. In the lore of the ancient Spiritual traditions there is a common thread of hope, an intuition that, in the "last days", or "end-time", when the world is at its worst, a Deliverer will come, the supreme God-Man who will complete and fulfill all the aspirations and Spiritual strivings of the past. Adi Da, the Da Avatar, is that One. He is the Divine World-Teacher, the Giver of Divine Enlightenment, Who has made all myths unnecessary and all seeking obsolete. He has always spoken of Himself as "the Heart". And those who find Him find the Heart Itself—the Being of Love, the Eternally "Bright" Divine Consciousness, appearing in human form.

The Way that Adi Da offers to all is a <u>relationship</u>, a Spiritual relationship to Him, not merely a system of self-applied techniques. No mere technique, no mere self-effort could possibly result in the most perfect Awakening that Adi Da offers to His devotees. Adi Da Himself is the Very Person and Source of this Grace for all. And the Way that He has established—Adidam, or the Way of the Heart—is the means of entering into His sphere of Grace. Adidam is for every race and culture, for men, women, and children of all kinds and backgrounds. Adidam is the true world-religion of Divine Enlightenment. All the mythologies, all the Spiritual practices, and all the previous Wisdom paths of humanity ultimately point to and are resolved in this Great and Ultimate Way of Most Perfect Liberation. (For more on Adidam, see the Invitation on pages 333-48.)

The Divine Work of Adi Da, the Da Avatar, is Eternal, beyond imagining, encompassing all realms and all beings, but at the same time it is perfectly intimate, manifesting in a unique relationship to each of His devotees. Adi Da's Embrace of every one is proven in all the details of His Divine Life. An essential companion to this book is *The Knee of Listening*, His own account of His early-life ordeal up through His Divine Re-Awakening in 1970 (and including His devotees' story of the momentous years of His Spiritual Work and Blessing in the years since then). "No one like Me", He once wrote, "has appeared in this place before." Every moment of heart-Communion with Adi Da, now and forever, is the self-forgetting Bliss of Non-separation from God, Truth, or Reality. What Joy could be greater than this?

**Adi Da, the Da Avatar**

"Da" is an ancient name of God meaning "the Giver". The Name "Da" intuitively came to Adi Da early in His life, but He did not assume it as His true Name until 1979, when the time was right for this revelation. In 1994, His Name was most fully revealed as "Adi Da"—"Adi" meaning "first", or "original". Thus, "Adi Da" means the "First Giver" or "the Giving Source". To speak of Him as "the Da Avatar" or "Avatara Adi Da" is another way of acknowledging Him as the Divine Giver. "Avatar" (or "Avatara") means "Descended One", the appearance of the Divine Reality in human form.

The world is endlessly allowed to be,
until I die.
I am the Heart's Shout.
The worlds are endlessly involved with Me,
while I Appear
in forms that know them.
But when I die and disappear from worlds
where I have lived,
there is no absence.
My life has never made a world for Me.
I am the Heart that Shouts them.

ADI DA (THE DA AVATAR)
*Crazy Da Must Sing, Inclined to His Weaker Side*

# The Most Perfect Teaching, The Most Perfect Teacher

*An Introduction to* The Heart's Shout

It is a shout from Existence Itself—from the "Heart", from the Absolute, Divine Consciousness that Is the Source and Substance of Reality. Happiness is shouting. Freedom is shouting. Life is shouting. And It is shouting because It wants to . . . wake you up! It is shouting for you to shed the illusion of being a separate self, a dying person, a fearful individual, a desperate capsule of need. It is shouting so that you will Awaken to the One, True Identity: the Divine Self-Condition, Free of limit, always Blissful, Eternally and Infinitely Alive.

But the Heart's Shout is not a mental abstraction or a mystic noise from the Heavens. The Heart is the Divine Person—the Radiant Being beyond space and time; the indefinable Mystery of Living Light and Limitless Energy—and that One has been paradoxically born as a human being. His Body is suffused with the Attractiveness of the Divine. His every action Transmits the all-Embracing, unconditional Love of the Divine. And His Speech and Writing—humorous and passionate, fearless and free—Communicate the Perfect Wisdom of the Divine. The Heart is Adi Da (The Da Avatar). And this book is an introduction to His Wisdom-Teaching, a collection of Talks and Essays selected from among His countless Discourses and extensive Writings.

The Wisdom-Teaching of Adi Da has been generated in response to the questions and needs of His devotees. He has "considered" every possible subject—exhaustively examined every area of life to reveal how that area may be lived as a means of Communion with the Divine. The Guru-devotee relationship; the true nature of the Divine, and the means of realizing the Divine; the illusions and suffering of the separate self, and how the ego-"I" can be outgrown; the religious and Spiritual practices of devotion, service, meditation, and self-discipline; diet and health; sex and human relationships; the necessity of cooperative community; the cultural errors in scientific

25

materialism and religious provincialism; the process of death and dying—all of that (and much more) has been "considered" with devotees. And many of Adi Da's most summary Talks and Essays on these topics are included in *The Heart's Shout*.

In fact, Adi Da has been willing to discuss <u>anything</u>. In His all-Embracing Company, no topic is taboo, no thoughts need be censored, no desires are condemned. But the purpose of "considering" any and every aspect of life is always the same: to draw His devotees (and all of humanity) beyond a limited understanding or perspective; to reorient the devotee to a deeper love-relationship with Adi Da and a deeper commitment to the ultimate purpose of life: transcendence of the limited, egoic self, and Realization of the Divine Self, Who Adi Da Is.

In this book you will also find "Leelas"—stories from devotees about Adi Da, their relationship with Him, and how their lives were changed by that encounter. Both Adi Da's Word and the Leelas about Him are potent with His Divine Life—they are a means for receiving His Transmission of Happiness and Freedom.

In reading this book, you are not merely reading words on a page—you are literally encountering Adi Da; you are, as He says, coming "upon Me Alive in the form of My Word." That encounter—the encounter between any human being and the Divine Person in human Form; the encounter with the Living Force and Intensity of God, Truth, and Reality—is a great opportunity and a great Blessing. May you recognize the One who Lives in these pages; may this book be the beginning of your personal relationship with the One who has come to free you from all suffering by Awakening you to the Divine Being that He Is.

# A NOTE ON READING THIS BOOK

Bhagavan Adi Da has transformed the English language into a vehicle to serve His Communication of the Sacred, God-Realizing Process in His Company. In doing so, He has Revealed the logic underlying the common conventions of written English:

*Ordinary speech and written language are centered on the ego-"I", as a tent is raised on a centerpole. Therefore, in ordinary speech and written language, the ego-word "I" is commonly capitalized, and everything less than the ego-"I" is shown in lowercase.*

In contrast, the "centerpole" of Avatara Adi Da's Speech and Writing is the Heart, the Divine, Consciousness, Truth, Reality, and Happiness. Therefore, He capitalizes those words that express the Ecstatic Feeling of the Awakened Heart, and, in many instances, lowercases those words expressive of the ego or conditional limits in general.

Blessed with the Gift of His Awakening Grace, Avatara Adi Da's devotees are thus inspired to capitalize words associated with Beloved Adi Da as a means of honoring Him and His Divine Attributes.

Throughout *The Heart's Shout* you will also find words used in a unique way to express Avatara Adi Da's particular meaning. Common terms that Adi Da uses in special technical fashion are often set off by quotation marks, for example, the "Bright", "consideration", and "radical". These and other special terms are marked at first mention, either by a footnote, or by an asterisk (*). (An asterisk directs you to the Glossary at the back of the book, pp. 363-370.)

Another convention to note: Talks are marked by the opening attribution "AVATARA ADI DA:".

Adi Da's use of language has evolved over time. Thus, various Talks and Essays from the earlier years of His Work have been editorially updated here, according to His Instructions, to make use of the more fully evolved, communicative, and precise terminology found in His most current Writings.

# PART I

# I Have Come To Reveal The Joy Of Being

*Adi Da is the Incarnate Divine Person. His Revelation is that there is only God—that every seemingly separate being, process, and thing is nothing but a manifestation of Divine Being, nothing but the Radiance of the Transcendental and All-Pervading Conscious Light that is the Source and Substance of Reality. Because the Divine is All, and because Adi Da Is that All, His Wisdom-Teaching is literally all-inclusive. Every experience, every possibility, every point-of-view has been "considered" (a word Adi Da uses to mean an uncompromising and conclusive exploration)—and in each case what binds the self to limitation, and what frees the self in God, has been Revealed.*

*In Part I, Adi Da "considers" the means of Liberation through the devotional relationship with the Divinely Awake Spiritual Master; the nature of suffering and its transcendence; the limitations of the conceptual mind; God (and the errors in the traditional conceptions of God); and the "Great Tradition" (a term He uses to describe the entire religious and Spiritual tradition of humankind).*

*The Wisdom in this section perfectly communicates both your present apparent situation as a separate and suffering self, and your True Situation as the One, Joyous Divine Being. Because of the utter clarity of Adi Da's Wisdom, and because that Wisdom is Communicated by the very Divine, it has the Blessing Power to reorient your life to Truth Itself.*

**Adi Da (The Da Avatar)**
**Adidamashram, 1994**

SECTION ONE

# The Liberating Relationship

A ll is One.

All are the same.

All equally require Divine Compassion, Love, and Blessing, the thread of Communion with the Divine made certain and true and directly experienced. All.

Therefore, the Sphere of My Work is all beings and things. Literally it is so. This is literally how I Work.

I am Doing a universal Work.

I am here to receive, and kiss, and embrace everyone, everything—everything that appears, everything that is.

ADI DA (THE DA AVATAR)
from *ISHTA*

*There is no relationship greater than the relationship of the devotee to the Divinely Realized Spiritual Master, Adi Da—because Adi Da has the Power to free the individual from suffering, to Awaken the individual to Perfect Happiness. These chapters describe the devotional relationship to Adi Da—"Satsang", or the Company of Truth—which is the unique means Adi Da has Given so that every person can Commune with the Divine Person, Who He Is.*

# CHAPTER 1

# The Divine Physics of Evolution

*October 1978*

AVATARA ADI DA: The human Spiritual Master is Divine Help to the advantage of those in like form. When one enters into right relationship with the Spiritual Master, changes happen in the literal physics of one's existence. I am not just talking about ideas. I am talking about literal transformations at the level of energy, at the level of the higher light of physics, at the level of mind beyond the physical limitations you now presume, at the level of the absolute Speed of ultimate Light. The transforming process is enacted in devotees in and through the Living Company of the Spiritual Master. The relationship between the Spiritual Master and the devotee is not a matter of conceptual symbolisms or emotional attachment to some extraordinary person. The true Guru-devotee relationship is real physics. Therefore, because they can make unique use of the Offering of that person's Company, it is to the special advantage of people when some one among them has gone through the real process of transformation that makes a Realizer-Guru of one or another degree. And that advantage is unique in My case, because that process has Completed and Revealed the total cycle that becomes Divine Self-Realization.

Spiritual life has nothing to do with the childishness people tend to dramatize in relationship to the Spiritual Master. I criticize that childish, or dependent, approach more directly than most people do. Others are merely petulant about it, in the self-righteous mood of adolescence. But there are real reasons why both the childish and the adolescent*† approaches to the Spiritual Master are forms of destructive nonsense and must be overcome. However, the mature, sacrificial relationship to the Spiritual Master is absolutely Lawful and necessary. Those who object to that relationship might as well object to the relationship between the Earth and the sun.

Most people are willing to sacrifice things, but not themselves. They are willing to pay cash, in other words, for a quick salvation. Such "religious consumerism" is an ancient ritual of worship, but it is false and futile. True worship is the sacrifice of your own body-mind in Truth, in the Living and transforming Company of the Spiritual Master. People absolutely resist

† Asterisks indicate terms that are defined in the Glossary, pp. 363-70.

that sacrifice because they know nothing about it. They are subhuman in their present level of adaptation. Sacrifice represents another stage of evolution for them. In their present actual, literal, psycho-physical condition they are incapable of it. They must be drawn out of that limited condition, and into another state of existence. And it is as far to go from where they are now to ultimate Divine Self-Realization as it is from the amoeba in the primal mud of the Earth to a human being. Everything, even the body, must change dramatically.

There is a profound difference between the condition of the usual individual and the Condition of the fully Awakened individual. The difference is an inconceivable leap in evolution. But there is a real process for making that leap, and there is Help for it: the devotional relationship to Me, the Adept Spiritual Master. In other words, something in the physics of the universe makes it possible for a single apparent individual to pass through the entire affair of Divine Self-Realization, and then to bring others into the Sphere of the same Divinely Enlightened Existence, so that they may duplicate that Divine Condition. Therefore, just as the relationship to the Spiritual Master (of one or another degree) is the supreme Principle of Spiritual life in general, the relationship to Me is the Supreme Principle of the Way of the Heart.

True Spiritual life is not just a change in your mind. Much more than an inner awakening or a good feeling about everything must take place. The literal physics of your whole existence must change. The physical body and its energies must be literally transformed. Spiritual processes do not occur as a result of the subjective nonsense of vicarious belief and vicarious salvation that people usually associate with religion, as if real Awakening were just a matter of asking some silly question or going to a few lectures for the weekend.

That is not Divine Enlightenment. Divine Enlightenment is a literal change of the whole body. When you have acquired the human form, the literal change that must occur in the body is not really so much in your outward appearance, because you already have the necessary structure. The changes that must occur are literal psycho-physical changes, just as literal as if you were to acquire more legs and arms, except that the most dramatic changes occur in dimensions other than the shape of the body. Certainly changes occur in the flesh and the elemental structures of the body, but those changes do not really alter the body's outward shape. The changes are as literal as evolving from a dinosaur to a human being, and they are as dramatic as that, but they principally occur at more subtle levels of the physics of the conditional being. There are literal changes in the nervous system, literal changes in the chemistry of the body, literal changes in the structural functioning of the brain.

You cannot realize such changes in a weekend. They are a living process of growth. But they can be quickened and intensified through right practice, through real sacrificial discipline, in the Company of the fully Awakened Spiritual Master. Therefore, in My Company, the Divine Condition is Communicated to you in such a way that It Effects a "radical"[1] transformation in the disposition of the body-mind and then Magnifies the effectiveness of that disposition many times, so that the whole Process may take place even in a single lifetime, or at least be dramatically advanced in one lifetime if not completely fulfilled.

I have Described the full esoteric progression of this remarkable transformation in the literature of My Wisdom-Teaching. My Description is not based merely on an intellectual synthesis of things I have read and thought. The entire Way of the Heart is My literal experience—not only the complete preparation, but also the awakening of sensitivity to the Divine Life-Energy, including the full Kundalini* process, the elaboration of subtle* sounds and lights via the awakening of the brain centers, all the great archetypal visions, everything. I have had all the classic Yogic experiences, from the muladhar* (the lowest terminal of the body-mind at the perineum) to the upper reaches of the mind in the brain core. Eventually, it became evident that the "muladhar-to-sahasrar game" (or, really, the raising of attention from the muladhar to the ajna center,* with contemplation of the "sky of mind" in the direction of the sahasrar*), whether played through the extended bodily and psychic processes of the Kundalini awakening, or through the higher path of the awakening of the brain centers through meditations on subtle light and sound, is not the Way of Truth. It became evident that the Realization of Truth is the Most Perfect sacrifice, not only of the lower, or gross,* level of existence but also of the whole subtle (or etheric,* lower mental, and higher mental) elaboration of experience and function, and even of egoic seclusion in the causal* level of existence. Thus, in My case, ultimately there was Most Perfect Realization of the Heart of Consciousness, or Divine Self-Realization, Which is an Awakening Beyond the limits of exclusive conscious awareness, into unqualified God-Realization.

That I have had all these extraordinary experiences and also Enjoy Unconditional Awakening as My constant Condition is a great Opportunity for all others. My Realization and My Wisdom-Teaching, therefore, bring the significance of all the patterns of existence into a clear unity, so that the whole affair of human existence can be approached rightly. The Realization of the Inherently Perfect Intensity of Truth continues as My Very Existence.

1. The word "radical" derives from the Latin "radix", meaning "root", and thus it principally means "irreducible", "fundamental", or "relating to origin". Because Adi Da uses "radical" in this literal sense, it appears in quotation marks in His Wisdom-Teaching to distinguish His use of it from the popular reference to an extreme (often political) point of view.

It is not and could not have been a passing experience. And the Power of It is available for the transformation of others, if people will enter into devotional relationship with Me.

If you move into a relationship with Me, the Divine Process begins to duplicate Itself in your case. It is not as if you are a robot that is being transformed through the effect of some computer—no. The Process is a living and human relationship with Me. But it is not like the conventional doctor-patient and mommy-daddy-baby games. Irresponsible people cannot enter into it. You must be responsible for yourself at the human level, and in a profoundly uncommon way. You must live the discipline of ordinary life. You yourself must be love under all ordinary, daily conditions. You must make this change in your life. There is no way whereby you can be relieved of this necessity, and nobody can do it for you. Nevertheless, all of that ordinary responsibility simply prepares you for the right relationship to the Agency of the Divine in My bodily (human) Form. Such a One As I Am is your unique Advantage, because I Am Present in the same kind of bodily form as you—manifested in the same kind of physical condition, the same kind of nervous system, the same kind of brain. But in Me all these things are Raised to an Absolute level of Functioning, so that your entering into Communion with Me brings changes even at the level of the psycho-physical body that you present to Me.

The abstract Deity cannot serve you in that way, because the physics of this Process must be directly Present, and the human Demonstration of the Process must be Present in a Form that can do its Work in your case. That Work is My Purpose, because I Represent a State of the ultimate physics of things that is your potential but not your actuality at the present time. The abstract Divine and the potential powers of the universe are just as true as the Spiritual Master, but they are not organized (except in the case of the Spiritual Master) for the sake of the immediate transformation of human beings. If people enter into right relationship with Me, they begin to Realize the same transformations I have Described in My own case. Then, at the end of My physical Lifetime, My devotees will have gone through sufficient transformation that some among the community of My devotees can become the extended mechanism of My Function.

I Am the Awakened Servant of humankind. I Serve to Regenerate the Teaching of Truth and to Resurrect the great culture of compassion and Wisdom among men and women. However, those purposes are secondary aspects of My Service to men and women. They are emanations of My Divine Self-Realization and My Ultimate Function. My True and Ultimate Function is to instigate the superphysics of literal and Most Perfect God-Realization among My true devotees. If there is no duplication of that superphysical Process, there can be no true Continuation of My Blessing

Work, except in verbal form, because there can be no Living Agency.[2]

Without such Living Agency how will that Process take place in the future? Perhaps, as in the past, people will resort to the pieces of it that men and women of experience represent. People can always experience a little Yoga, a little psychism, a little internal energy, a little insight. But when the Total Representation of Divine Self-Realization is Demonstrated in the literal bodily (human) form of one individual, you must make use of it. It is an Advantage that is unique in human time.

---

2. Adi Da has accounted for the necessity of the living Transmission of His Divine Blessing-Power after His physical death by creating various forms of Spiritual Instrumentality and Agency that can continue forever. For a full discussion of how Adi Da will have living human Agency throughout all time, see chapter twenty of *The Dawn Horse Testament Of Adi Da*.

CHAPTER 2

# Dreaming and Waking

*from chapter 6 of* The Method of the Siddhas

AVATARA ADI DA: No event is itself Truth. All that arises is an appearance to Consciousness Itself, a modification of the Conscious Force that is always already the case. All of this is a dream, if you like. It is an appearance in Consciousness Itself. Truth is Very Consciousness Itself. Truth is to all of this what the waking state is to the dreaming state. If you awaken, you do not have to do anything about the condition you may have suffered or enjoyed in the dream state. What happened within the dream is suddenly not your present condition. It is of no consequence any longer, once you are awake. If you persist in dreaming, and your point of view remains that of the dreamer and his or her role within the dream, then your possible actions are numberless. But none of them will "work". They will simply occupy you in the dream. They will modify the dream state, but no action in the dream is the equivalent of waking. There are simply forms of fascination, of occupation, of seeking, until you awaken. Truth is simply Waking, No-illusion. It is not a condition within this appearance. It has nothing whatever to do with the "mind", regardless of whether the "mind" is expanded or contracted. . . .

The dream does not have to be changed in any manner for the waking person to feel that he or she is awake. Nothing has to happen to the dream. Only waking is necessary. To one who is awake, the dream is obvious. There is no illusion, no suffering, no implication, regardless of what appeared in the dream. A blue god, a dirty old drunk, the gorilla of death—it makes no difference. It makes a difference within the circumstances of the dream, to those who are dreaming. But to the one who is awake, it no longer makes any difference. Perception, waking consciousness, is obvious if you are truly Awake. If you are asleep, if you do not understand, if understanding evades you, there is nothing obvious about this at all. Then life is a very serious predicament, very serious. What do you have in such a case? "A few more years and everything is dead." It does not make any difference what the drama is, or what you manage to amuse yourself with during that time.

There is One Who is wide Awake while He Appears in the "dream". Subtly, by not supporting the dream, He Awakens others. He is the Guru,

Who I Am. The significance of My Work is not in anything I do <u>within</u> the dream. I simply do not support it. I do not live as it. I do not believe it. I do not take it seriously. Apparently, I can feel and act as I please. I persist in the common or ordinary manner. But I do not support the dream. I do not live from its point of view. I do not live its structure to others. I do not live this contraction to others, this avoidance of relationship, this separate self sense. Simply because I live in this manner, others tend to become Awake. But while they are Awakening, they persist in dreaming to various degrees. Forms of the dream persist. The search persists. Often, they get a little distance from it, it seems to break up at times, seems to disappear. It becomes vague, it becomes uninteresting, it becomes unserious, it becomes serious again. They play.

You are just beginning to wake up. Satsang* is the dream wherein I Appear. Now it is as if you are beginning to wake up in your room. You are in bed, and it is morning. There are a few things you begin to notice which indicate that you are in another state. Those who are Waking in Truth begin to notice something. They begin to recognize the signs. They begin to recognize the activity of dreaming. They begin to sense something very odd about Me. Before their actual Awakening, I appear as all kinds of things to them. I suggest all kinds of fantastic things. All the things they can imagine while they dream, everything unbelievable, is what they think I am. I may appear to be extraordinary, a doer of famous things. I may appear playfully as that. But I am simply Awake. Nothing is happening. Nothing has been accomplished. All I have been is Awake.

I am like the sunlight in the morning. I intensify the light of morning until you awaken. Until the light awakens a person, even the Light of Consciousness Itself, the person continues to dream, tries to survive within the dream, manipulates himself or herself within the dream, pursues all kinds of goals, searches, none of which Awaken the person. All ordinary means only console a person and distract him or her within the dream. I My Self, the One Who would Awaken you, am not a person, not an individual within the dream. I Am your Very Consciousness. I Am the Real, the Light, the True Waking State, the Heart, Breaking Through the force of dreaming. It is not that you are some poor person who needs some other poor person to help you out. It may appear to be so within the dream, but essentially it is your own Ultimate Self-Nature Appearing within the dream to Awaken you. I <u>Am</u> your Awakening, and your always already Conscious State.

Even while dreaming, you may experience suggestions of waking. You may become momentarily aware of the body, momentarily aware of lying in bed. For a moment, the images may stop. Just so, I My Self within the world Am truly your Real Consciousness. My Person in the world is like an image in a dream. But, in fact, I am more like your own moments of wakening awareness that move you into the waking state. I am not some separateness, some individual. I Am Very Consciousness, the Real.

No images. Images, blackness, brilliance—all these things are appearances to Consciousness. They are objects. Nothing needs to happen to them for Consciousness Itself to exist. Nothing needs to happen within the dream to verify Waking. Waking is its own Fullness. Once one is Awake, anything can appear. True Awakeness is the foundation of this world-appearance, It is its support, It is its Very Nature. Real Consciousness is not antagonistic to this world or to any form within it. It is the Truth of all appearance, disappearance, or non-appearance. Even when Real Consciousness is Enjoyed, human life continues. Perhaps human life is enjoyed even more. It is used. It becomes functional to an extraordinary degree.

The usual man or woman barely functions at all. A couple of good days a month. The rest of the time the person is either trying to be healed or exploiting himself or herself, trying to get straight, trying to work, trying to get with it. Every now and then there is a little clarity, when the person just stands up, walks across the room, opens the door, and goes outside. The rest of the month is spent dreaming and thinking, when just to walk across the room is part of an enormous search, an unkind adventure, an approach to victory against odds. But all the person is doing is simple things, simple functions.

One who understands, who is Awake, functions very well under the conditions that appear. Those conditions may be forms of this waking world, or they can be subtle forms, subtle worlds, any of the possible forms. Under all conditions, understanding is appropriate. There is no experience, no state, that is itself identical to Truth. Just so, the Truth is not different from any experience or state. It is the Truth of all of that.

I am a kind of irritation to My devotees. You cannot sleep with a dog barking in your ear—at least most people cannot! There is some sort of noise to which everyone is sensitive, and it will keep them awake. I am a constant Wakening sound. I am always annoying people with this demand to stay Awake, to Wake Up. I do not seduce them within the dream. I do not exploit their seeking. I am always offending their search and their preference for unconsciousness. I show no interest in all of that. I put it down. I am always doing something prior to the mind. I always act to return you from the mind, from fascination.

I am not what the dreamer thinks I am. The dreamer thinks I must have a certain appearance, say and do certain things, have certain magical powers, produce certain magical effects. The dreamer associates all kinds of glorious and magical things with Me. But I am always performing the Awakening act, putting an end to the dream. Therefore, I do not satisfy the seeker. Those that come to be satisfied are offended. They are not satisfied.

They feel empty, they do not feel their questions have been answered, they do not feel they have been shown the Way. They came for some thing.

Within the dream, the dreamer is always being satisfied by the Guru. The dreamer climbs up on the top of the mountain, and the Guru is sitting in a cave. The Guru hands the dreamer a little silver box. When the dreamer opens the box, there is a blue diamond in it. The dreamer takes it out and swallows it. Then the dreamer's body explodes into a million suns, and the dreamer shoots off into the universe! But in Reality, the Guru does not function in that manner. The Guru is not noticed by someone who is seeking for such satisfaction, who is looking for the "signs" of the Guru, who is "hunting" the Guru. The Guru does not assume any particular visibility that can be counted on. The Guru is likely to remain unnoticed. People are likely to be offended if they do not feel any Force, any Energy, in the Presence of one who is supposed to be Guru. They tend not to notice or value someone who is simply Awake. They are looking for the one who has the blue and yellow light over his or her head. All of this, until they become dissatisfied with the search. When they stop being sensitive to their own search, they begin to feel simply desperate. Then all that is left is this contraction I have so often described. When the search begins to wind down, and you begin to realize you are suffering, then you become sensitive to My Presence. You become attentive to the Very Nature of the One Who is Awake.

It is stated in the traditional writings that, of all the things one can do to Realize one's Freedom, the best thing one can do, the greatest thing one can do, is spend one's time in the Company of one who is Awake. For one who is My devotee, that is Satsang with Me, living in relationship to Me and in the company of My devotees. All other activities are secondary. And Satsang is not a strategic method, not an exercise or meditative technique one applies to oneself. It is simply the natural and appropriate Condition. It is Reality. It is itself Truth, or Enlightenment. There are no other means given to devotees.

There is nothing that one can do to save oneself, to become Enlightened, to become Realized. Nothing whatsoever. If there were something, I would tell you, but there is nothing. This is because one always approaches the Truth from the point of view of the search. One seeks the Truth. But the search is itself a reaction to the dilemma, an expression of this separation, this avoidance of relationship. So none of this seeking, nothing one can do, becomes or attains the Truth.

All the means of transformation belong to the Truth Itself, to the Divine Person, to the Heart. Therefore, Satsang with Me is Itself the only sadhana, the only true Spiritual practice. Living, working, sitting with Me is sadhana. It is meditation. It is Realization. . . .

When you are dreaming, you take the dream very seriously. You assume your role within it, your drama within it. You respond to the condition that seems to be so, whatever the particular circumstances of the dream. If the gorilla is chasing you up the beach, you feel all the threat. All the emotions become involved, all your strategies of survival, or non-survival, become involved. If it is a sweet, enjoyable, "astral" sort of dream, with all kinds of friends and voices and colors and movements, you assume that to be so. You float around in it. You take it seriously. You <u>assume</u> it to be so. You assume it because you have no other point of view from which to enjoy or suffer the dream except that of the dreamer. But when you wake up in the morning, the gorilla that was just about to bite off your head loses all significance. All the implications of the dream are already undone in one who is awake. It no longer has any real significance, it no longer has any implication for life. It no longer is a genuine threat to life. It no longer is anything except that appearance. And the only difference is that you are awake. Nothing has been done to the dream itself. You have only awakened, and therefore the dream is obviously not your condition. . . .

The waking state is simply an utterly different condition from the dream. That is why you feel free of the dream upon waking. I Appear in the midst of the dreams of ordinary waking life like sunlight in the morning. When you are still dreaming, still asleep, the sun comes up. It gets brighter and brighter, and the light comes into the room. At last, the light, the day itself, becomes sufficient to wake you, and then, all of a sudden, you are not dreaming, and everything is all right. I am simply that sunlight process, that intensification, rising on you always, without any other special activity. My relationship to you, your living condition of relationship to Me, just that relationship, is sufficient. There is only sunlight on the pillow until that Intensity is sufficient to wake you up. . . .

. . . When you become less concerned for your particular search, for your inwardness, for your adventure, you have simply become more sensitive to your Real Condition. You have felt the sunlight falling on your sleeping eyes. When your eyes have opened in the morning light, everything will be obvious to you. And you will know that you have never slept, that you have never dreamed, that you have never been limited to any thing that has appeared. You have never been in any condition that you have assumed. There was always only Reality Itself, your True Nature, Which is Love-Bliss, Consciousness, the Unqualified Intensity.

# CHAPTER 3

# Coming into the Presence of Very God

*by Frank "Cheech" Marrero*

I met Avatara Adi Da in August of 1971, in New York City, where I was Executive Clinical Director of a large drug and alcohol rehabilitation program.

Back then I was a very guarded and mistrusting person. I had grown up in the worst parts of the city, with Mafia-controlled neighborhoods, gang wars, drug pushers, and criminals. The average life-span there was twenty-one! I dropped out of school at eleven and became a street hustler, wheeling and dealing in anything I could to make money and survive. By the time I was thirty I had spent more than eleven years in prison.

During my second term in prison I began to educate myself, and I got particularly interested in counseling, psychology, and law. I continued my education after I was released from prison, eventually beginning to work on my Ph.D. in psychology. And I co-founded what became a very large, multimillion-dollar drug and alcohol rehabilitation program.

The day I met Avatara Adi Da I had an eleven o'clock appointment with an executive from a meditation institute. This man was trying to sell me a program for treating addictions through meditative techniques. Our meeting was important because the meditation program would cost a considerable amount of money. Around twenty to eleven it struck me that I didn't know anything about meditation. However, I did remember that a working associate of mine had a friend named "Franklin" (Adi Da was known as "Franklin Jones" back then) who I had heard knew quite a bit about meditation. And He happened to be visiting that morning.

Avatara Adi Da was right there when I walked into my friend's office. Immediately I said, "Hi, you must be Franklin! Can I borrow you for a few minutes? I have this guy who's trying to sell me happiness through meditative techniques. I don't know anything about meditation and I heard you know a little bit." Adi Da looked at me and gave me a big smile and said, "Sure." I liked Him right away. He was very bright and open, and His smile was full and Happy. Without question He left my friend's office and walked with me to my office.

I don't remember what He said as we walked through the hallways of the center, but He was laughing and soon He had me laughing. We just laughed the whole way to my office. I remember my secretary looking at me in surprise because of my obviously happy and "lightened-up" disposition. This was definitely not typical for me. Normally I would never open up to someone unless they were an old friend. I was always sizing up situations, testing everything and everyone to see how far I could trust them, where their weaknesses were. I had learned this growing up on the streets, and being in prison. That's how I survived.

Yet I immediately responded to this man in a completely different way. He looked at me, and I saw His smile and His brightness. And I began smiling, just like that.

For the interview I placed three chairs in a triangle—one for "Franklin", one for the man trying to sell me the program, and one for myself. During the interview I kept asking the man if he used these techniques himself, to which he responded affirmatively. It was obvious to me that he wasn't happy at all, but I didn't want to tell him that. The meeting concluded, and after the man left I looked at Avatara Adi Da, "Well, what do you think?" He pointed both thumbs towards the ground, and we both laughed.

Then Adi Da noticed something in the room. In a far off corner of my huge office I had a small picture of Swami Muktananda. The photo was about three inches by three inches, and was half-hidden by a plant. Most people would never have noticed it. I had been given this picture a few months earlier after finding myself, seemingly by accident, in a large hall in Manhattan where Swami Muktananda was giving a lecture.

Avatara Adi Da noticed the photograph right away and seemed to find it interesting that I would have this. He pointed it out and asked me a few questions. In the midst of our conversation I asked, "Well, what do you think about somebody like this that claims to be in Communion with God?" Adi Da looked at me and smiled and said, "Just do everything in relation to the Guru." Then He walked out. It would take me many, many years to realize that He Gave me the whole Teaching in that sentence.

At that time, however, my attention was more on <u>Him</u> than on what He was saying. I was really impressed with Him, and after He left I kept thinking about Him. He just stayed with me. The next time I saw my associate I said, "You know, I really like your friend Franklin. There's something about Him, a really nice guy. We must have lunch together sometime—soon!" I left my contact with "Franklin" at that, and I didn't know whether I would ever meet Him again.

At that point He was just a man to me. I had no recognition of Him as someone who was Spiritually Awake, let alone God-Realized. And I didn't believe, or even think about such matters anyway. I had no Spiritual background besides my Catholic upbringing. I tended to be cynical about life, and fundamentally regarded religion as nonsense, just a way to keep the masses of humanity from killing each other.

The ten months following that first meeting with Avatara Adi Da proved to be the most disturbing time in my life. By conventional standards, and especially in contrast to my early life, I now had every reason to be happy. I was successful in my profession, I was engaged to get married to a very beautiful and successful woman, I had more money than I possibly needed, and was looked up to by many of my friends and family. But in fact, I was unhappy.

All my life I had been aware of a certain fundamental disturbance that never went away, regardless of whether times were good or bad. I was sensitive enough to life to recognize that even now, despite all my success, I was still suffering. I felt this disturbance in everything around me, and I couldn't seem to make sense of my life.

After my meeting with Avatara Adi Da, this feeling became accelerated, and I found myself stuck in a mood of quiet despair. I began pacing, which I'd never done before. All the ordinary enjoyments I was accustomed to, like watching TV, or going out to a nice dinner with friends, were no longer consoling. And it became more and more apparent that my pursuits in the field of psychology did not bring about any relief from my unhappiness. In spite of many years of therapy from the top people in New York, the disturbance I felt remained untouched. And my teachers, who were some of the best-known and most respected psychoanalysts in the field, were no more illumined by their knowledge than I was. They couldn't answer my fundamental questions about life and death. This was becoming a crisis for me because I was one of the key people behind our whole program to help people through psychology-based therapy. I started to feel like the blind leading the blind. It was around this time that my associate sent me the manuscript of *The Knee of Listening*, Avatara Adi Da's account of His Life, in the mail.

I remember thumbing through it briefly and making a mental note, "I have to read this. After all, I have met Him." But I threw it on the desk and it lay there gathering dust. One evening about six weeks later, after pacing my apartment for an unusually long time in this feeling of despair, I noticed the manuscript on my desk. I took it into my bedroom with a cup of coffee and a pack of cigarettes (I smoked three packs a day then) and read for several hours, incapable of putting it down.

At around two o'clock in the morning, an unusual feeling started to come over me as I continued to read the book. I looked up and the room had become super-bright, every color standing out distinctly. My first thought was, "Damn, one of the residents put some LSD in my coffee!" Then I noticed that I felt a distinct attraction to this brightness. There was a feeling of calmness that went through my body, and my attention was on everything around me, not on myself. I stood in the feeling of that attraction for a long time, allowing it to engulf me.

At some point my mind kicked in, and immediately a powerful feeling of fear overtook me. The fear wasn't about anything in particular. It was just fear, without content. My heart started pounding very hard, like it was going to jump out of my chest. My body spontaneously went into the fetal position, with my knees pressed up against my chest, and I started sweating profusely.

Then, just as suddenly, the fear was gone. An immense bliss washed over me. Everything became calm again and I remember experiencing a joyous Presence.

Since then, having had countless occasions in Avatara Adi Da's Company and in Communion with Him, I have come to know this Presence very well. It is Avatara Adi Da's Heart-Blessing, His direct Communication of the Heart, which is extremely attractive and "Bright". And the fear I experienced was my own self-contraction,* magnified in my awareness and reflected back to me by the Force of His Blessing-Power. But none of this was clear to me then.

At the time the whole experience left me mystified. I phoned a psychiatrist who worked at our program. I thought he would know what to do. After apologizing for waking him up at that hour of the morning, I explained to him what had happened. He quickly said, "It sounds like you're having an anxiety attack!" He said he'd call in a prescription for medication, and that I should pick it up right away. But I knew that this was not an anxiety attack. I felt calmer and more clear than I had in years. I knew without question that my experience was related to something else.

Next I called my fiancée. Her solution was, "Come on over. I have some wine and a few good joints we can share together." This seemed equally ridiculous to me.

Then I remembered that there was a phone number in the back of *The Knee of Listening*. I thought, "Why not call this number, since this happened while I was reading the book?" The number was in Los Angeles, and it didn't even occur to me that it was 11:00 at night in California. I went ahead and called, explaining to the man who answered what had just happened to me.

I could hear Avatara Adi Da's deep, expansive laughter in the background as I spoke, and I thought, "Damn, they're having a party down there! I'm going through this turmoil and they're having a party!" But I also felt the Happiness there, even over the phone. The devotee who had answered left the phone for a couple of minutes. Then he returned and said, "I spoke to Franklin and He says you should come down right away." I said, "Right away? It's 2:00 in the morning!", and I explained all my responsibilities. The man left the phone again, and then came back and said, "Franklin says to come as soon as you can."

It seemed impossible, but somehow I worked everything out and I was on a plane to Los Angeles the next day. Avatara Adi Da's Center, which everybody referred to as "the Ashram", was on a busy Los Angeles street, with a small bookstore in the front, and a meditation hall and office in the back. The first person I saw when I came in the back entrance was Avatara Adi Da, sitting at a desk. He greeted me with an incredible warm, loving feeling in His eyes and face. He sat me down next to Him, taking my hand as He did this. Confused by His gesture, I shook His hand in a business-like fashion and then tried to pull away. But He just kept holding onto my hand.

I could feel His complete openness and Love for me, a man He had just barely met, and I felt uncomfortable in the face of this. I tried pulling away again and He continued to hold on. At one point there was even a little struggle back and forth. I was starting to get uptight, self-conscious. Then He did something with His face, a very subtle change of expression, that let me know that it was all right. Finally I just relaxed my hand in His. He continued to hold it, while He asked me questions about the experience I had had. After some minutes He looked up to another devotee standing nearby and said, "Frank can sit with Me in meditation. It's OK." Then He let go of my hand.

Devotees were painting the Ashram because there had been a fire. Someone handed me a paintbrush, assuming I would join in. I was dressed in my expensive New York clothes, and I thought it was bizarre for me to be painting in those clothes. But everyone was painting and I figured I'd go along with the program. After all, I'd come three thousand miles to be there. I began to paint, and that's when this strange feeling started to come over me.

Within five minutes, my face became flushed and I felt a burning fever going over my whole body, to the point that I had to lie down. I told one of the devotees that I was really sick, and he drove me to his house. I went right over to the couch, and remained there for six days with a burning fever. All I could do was sip water.

The devotees whose house I was staying at served me throughout the week. But on the beginning of the seventh day, I was alone in the house and I was panicking. I said, "Damn, I'm going to die in this strange place." I really thought I was going to die.

So I crawled over to the phone and called the Ashram. And who should answer the phone but Avatara Adi Da. I mumbled something out about what was going on with me, and He started laughing. I was really offended. Here I was, ready to die, and He was laughing! He noticed my lack of humor, and He said, "Don't worry about a thing, Frank. You're going to feel fine in the morning. It's just a little purification. Isn't this what you came here for?"

I hadn't thought about it that way. I didn't know anything about the tradition of an Adept Transmitting Spiritual Force to a devotee. It was only later that I realized that Adi Da had directly Transmitted His Heart-Blessing to me as He held my hand. My fever was a classic case of the purification that often follows such a potent form of Blessing.

Avatara Adi Da's Words were absolutely true. The next morning I felt great! I felt better than I had since I could remember, really great. I ate a little bit, and then went down to the Ashram. And I went to the Ashram every day after that for the next thirty days.

I still didn't know who Adi Da was exactly, and I tested Him, just like

I did with everyone, to find His weakness. I did everything possible to check Him out. But, to my surprise, I never had any success at all in finding limits in Him. All that I experienced was my own game. In my efforts to find His faults, I would always be reflected back to myself.

What was even more surprising was Adi Da's behavior towards me, which was quite different from what I was accustomed to. Whenever Avatara Adi Da saw me He would walk over to me and give me a big hug. I found this very difficult because, from my Latino background, men just didn't hug other men! It simply was not acceptable! But He would always make a point of embracing me in some way. He would walk right across the Hall to greet me and give me a hug. Sometimes He would hang onto me for a while. Sometimes it was just quick. But He was always moving towards me. As He would walk over to me, smiling, I would feel all kinds of feelings come up in my body, especially fear. I would always be tight at first as He hugged me. But little by little I would open up. And He would always have me laughing and smiling within a few minutes.

Around the third week of my stay in Los Angeles I realized that I was looking forward to seeing Adi Da every day. And more than that, I realized that I was actually looking forward to His hugs. More and more I noticed how I was strategically finding ways to see Him as much as possible. I would cancel appointments, skip lunches, and do anything else that might allow an opportunity for being with Him.

One day at the Ashram I gave Adi Da a big bear hug in return for His hug, and picked Him up a little off the floor. He laughed and I laughed, both of us enjoying the incident. And I realized that I had opened up to His Love.

That was the last time, for a long time, that He would have that particular play with me, hugging me as He had. Instead He began making that same connection through a glance, or a word, or a gesture. And I felt just as embraced by Him. I knew He had worked with me somehow.

My heart was literally opening. I began to notice that I felt a heart-feeling in relationship to those around me. I was feeling real love for the first time in a very long while. The anxiety that I always felt, the paranoia that was involved in all my testing, had dropped away. I was beginning to feel good again.

**Adi Da with Frank Marrero, 1973**

And I realized that I had a very strong feeling for "Franklin". I had, in fact, fallen in love with Him—not sexually, but deeply in my emotion. And I totally trusted Him. I was struck with the intuitive knowledge that whoever "Franklin" was, He was no ordinary man. There was no doubt in me about it, because no ordinary person could be like He was all the time. I had enough street sense to know that. I thought He must be some sort of holy man, even though I really had no idea of the magnitude of Who He Is.

Because I was such a skeptic, having seen so many schemes in my time, if someone had told me that God was here in human form, incarnate, and was living that condition to others—that would have been the same as someone saying, "You know, Santa Claus is really true, he really lives, and he's down the corner at Macy's Department Store with all his reindeer!" It seemed absurd! Yet for some reason this feeling-intuition of the Divine in Avatara Adi Da's Company was undeniable in me.

The day before I left for New York, I went to Avatara Adi Da and said, "I don't know how I'm going to return, but I have to come back." He looked at me and smiled and said, "Don't worry about it—it will be OK. I'll expect you back by My birthday." And He laughed.

His birthday was November 3, about a month away, and I didn't see how that was possible because of all my involvements with family, work, and friends. But I trusted Him. I returned to New York, and the ensuing month, from my point of view, was nothing less than a miracle. All my life-business seemed to tie itself up in ways I never could have imagined. Everything fell into place, and sure enough, I was there for His birthday.

Those first few weeks in Los Angeles with Adi Da initiated a revolutionary change in the direction of my life. Up until then I had struggled intensely to find relief from my suffering. Yet despite my conventional success, my life hadn't brought me real happiness, or any sense of freedom from the fundamental disturbance that I always felt. But in my encounters with Avatara Adi Da, I had met someone who was completely Happy. And simply by coming into His Company, spending time with Him, engaging the relationship that He offered, I became Happy, too.

Adi Da's whole interaction with me had been a form of Instruction. I didn't understand His Teaching intellectually, but His very Person had taught me more than I could ever have learned through books. His example, His incomparable Love and openness to <u>anyone</u> who came to Him made a deep impression in me that I could never forget.

Twenty years later, on a meditation retreat in Avatara Adi Da's Company, the words spontaneously came to me that expressed what I felt in those early days with Avatara Adi Da. As the words arose I knew that they were true: "I have come into the Presence of Very God."

# CHAPTER 4

# On Spiritual Transmission

**A**VATARA ADI DA: Everyone transmits. All of you are transmitters. Each one of you emits invisible forces. Those forces are locked up in your limited messages, and they reinforce the same limitations in others. People are all indulging in a kind of "satsang" with one another, and the state of the world proves the potency of this transmission.

Realizers of one or another degree of Spiritual development likewise by nature spontaneously Transmit what they are. What they have Realized Transmits itself, subtly as well as grossly, by what they do, by what they are, by what they feel. Those less evolved Transmit their Realization, and those more evolved Transmit their more advanced Realization. Because I have Realized That Which Is Inherently Perfect, I Transmit That Condition to you. Such Transmission is inevitable, and it is an absolute law. This is why traditionally it is said that the best thing you can do, among all the things you must do—and you must do many things—the best among them, the chief among them, is to spend time in the Company of a Realizer.

Everything transmits. The stones transmit, the sky does, the TV does. Since everything and everyone transmits states of existence, since life, or existence itself, is participation in transmissions of all kinds, the best thing you can do is to associate with the greatest possible Transmission. Since everything is transmission, spend time in the Company of the One Who spontaneously Transmits That Which Is Inherently Perfect and Ultimate. This is the great rule, the Great Law, the Ultimate Principle of the Great Tradition.* [August 5, 1987]

**A**VATARA ADI DA: The literal Power of the Adept is not a figment of the imagination. The traditions describe the Power of the Siddha* and the real experience of devotees who truly associated with such a One. The process of Spiritual Transmission is a literal process, because the Adept is not merely an ordinary, individuated being.

I have thoroughly transcended all of the artifacts of individuation. Therefore, I am simply and directly Present as the Force of Divine Influence. That Influence is Radiant throughout all space-time without limitation. Those who awaken as devotees of the Divine in My Form encounter the expressions of this Radiant Siddhi, or the ecstatic marvels of that Divine Communion.

Spiritual Transmission is a literal process and not an imaginary one. My Influence is All-Pervading and Radiant. When you contact It in the context of your personal life, you feel It pervading your life. What you are observing then is the Play of the Divine, the Play of My Influence, the Means whereby you enter into Divine Communion. Therefore, in life and meditation you, as My devotee, will experience uncommon states that are the expressions of that Divine Communion. [July 1982]

CHAPTER 5

# The Great Relationship

*April 3, 1988*

*This dialogue comes from a question-and-answer session that occurred in New Zealand during Avatara Adi Da's Yajna, or journey of Blessing, in 1988.*

*Here Avatara Adi Da is responding to the questions of a man who is at the beginning level of association with the Way of the Heart (what we now call a formal Friend of Da Avatara International). The man has confessed that he feels great love for Avatara Adi Da, but that there are "practical reasons" why it is difficult for him to be a formal practitioner of the Way of the Heart at present.*

AVATARA ADI DA: Is God-Realization your motive, or is something else your motive?

QUESTIONER: God-Realization.

AVATARA ADI DA: Well, then, you must get down to it. You must cut through the obstacles in your life that prevent you from committing yourself to the self-transcending process. You must go through that process. You must also deal with all the limitations in your life. And that is it. Either you will do it, or you will not. If you will do it, you will get on with the sadhana* of the Way of the Heart. If you will not, you will fulfill your mortal destiny, along with the other five billion and more who are only the human number in this great karmic apparatus going to death. You will fulfill your part in that complication. That is what you will do. So—which is your choice?

QUESTIONER: My motivation is to get down to it.

AVATARA ADI DA: If getting down to it in terms of the sadhana of the Way of the Heart is your choice, you are not doing very much to fulfill it. You are only associated with this sadhana as the sheerest kind of beginner, making just that much of a gesture—which is fine as the gesture of one who is only beginning. Yet all the rest must occur from that point. You seem reluctant to do any more than you are currently doing.

QUESTIONER: I seem reluctant to take up the practice formally. I am trying to do sadhana on my own.

AVATARA ADI DA: And who is the "own"? Who is that? Is that your Guru?

QUESTIONER: No.

AVATARA ADI DA: Who is your Guru?

QUESTIONER: You are the Guru.

AVATARA ADI DA: What does that mean, to have a Guru?

QUESTIONER: It means to have a Spiritual relationship with the Guru.

AVATARA ADI DA: What else is there to it? What does that amount to altogether?

QUESTIONER: It amounts to having a Teacher that one can parallel one's life to.

AVATARA ADI DA: What does that mean in its details? Does it carry any obligations with it?

QUESTIONER: Yes, it does.

AVATARA ADI DA: Have I suggested in My own Wisdom-Teaching that one can go and do it on one's own?

QUESTIONER: No. But I do believe that You have suggested that Your Teaching is available to everybody.

AVATARA ADI DA: My Wisdom-Teaching is given to everyone, yes. But My Wisdom-Teaching is not the Way of the Heart. My Wisdom-Teaching is part of the Means of the Way of the Heart, and just a part. There is the total Ordeal of sadhana, and all the Gifts and responsibilities that come with it. Have you read *The Dawn Horse Testament*, which describes all the processes associated with the Way of the Heart?

QUESTIONER: Yes.

AVATARA ADI DA: And you think you can get all that on your own?

QUESTIONER: I believe it would be very difficult, but I always try.

AVATARA ADI DA: How can the ego grant itself such Gifts?

QUESTIONER: I was trying not to live as the ego. I was trying to give up the ego.

AVATARA ADI DA: <u>You</u> were trying to give up the ego.

QUESTIONER: Well, it was trying to be given up.

AVATARA ADI DA: <u>It</u> was trying to be given up? [Laughter.] You have read My description of "Narcissus",* I take it?

QUESTIONER: Yes.

AVATARA ADI DA: Does that description bear any likeness to your form of sadhana?

QUESTIONER: Yes, I see myself as "Narcissus", but I feel that every being has to understand that. I feel it is something each individual has to do. And that is what I was trying to do—to understand what I am as "Narcissus", and transcend that, and feel into a deeper sphere.

AVATARA ADI DA: Yes, involvement in the process of self-understanding is certainly part of the beginning of the Way of the Heart. But it does not accomplish the seventh stage of life.[1]

QUESTIONER: I cannot answer that.

AVATARA ADI DA: <u>I</u> can. It does not. It cannot. The kind of impulse you are describing is the ego's dissociative preference, its isolation. At the same time you are talking about having a Guru, you want your separate and separative self, a form of your own mind, to be the "guru". You will not enter into the sphere of obligations that come with association with Me, the True Guru. The process of self-understanding is indeed something for which you yourself must become responsible. But you become responsible in the context of the total process of sadhana, all of its obligations, all of its Graces, all of its demands. Everything must be dealt with.

Now, how do you find access to all of that? It's not a matter of an organization, I am talking about this relationship.

QUESTIONER: Yes.

AVATARA ADI DA: The organization, so to speak, is simply an instrument, a gathering, that carries on My Work, that provides the means associated with the Way of the Heart, publishes My Wisdom-Teaching, provides circumstances for people's practice, provides Sanctuaries, carries on responsibilities for communication, provides all kinds of education on every aspect of the Way of the Heart, and so forth. All of this is a necessary aspect of My Work in the world. But what is it that a practitioner of the Way of the Heart is involved in? This relationship to Me. This is what the Way of the Heart is about. One practices the Way of the Heart in that context, and in the total context of one's personal, human life.

1. For a description of the seven stages of life that Adi Da has Revealed, please see pp. 154-65.

How would Swami Muktananda have been able to make use of Swami Nityananda if He had indulged in your kind of reluctance? He would not. The kinds of preferences you are describing are the very ordinary preferences that the mass of mankind dramatizes. The mass of mankind has nothing to do with Real Spiritual life, because basically what people are dramatizing is the willfulness associated with their own karmas, their own limitations, their own separateness, their own ordinariness. They are dramatizing their ordinariness, and seeking to fulfill it, and they have no understanding of what the Great Process requires. Therefore, everybody becomes a philosopher. Everybody becomes a self-"guru", self-generating their own dharma* by piecing this and that together from what they read in books, thinking in their rooms and indulging themselves. To what end? To become one of the Adepts, a Great Realizer, to Divinely Translate[2] Beyond?

No such self-indulgent and self-"guruing" individual has ever done that. This never happened. On the other hand, millions, billions, of people have done the kind of thing you are suggesting. Now, fine, there is a kind of honesty and good-heartedness associated with your confession. But on the other hand what you have been doing does not have anything to do with the Great Process. It is a reluctance that divorces you from the Great Process. It assigns great weight to what is ordinary and limiting, and it finds all kinds of reasons not to assign the same importance to What is Truly Great. This is why very few people have ever done the Great Sadhana. Very few people have Realized anything. Very few human beings have moved beyond the first three stages of life.[3]

All kinds of people have practiced techniques and cultural devices that belong to what I call the "fourth stage of life", the "fifth stage of life", and the "sixth stage of life", but they have practiced as people in the first three stages of life. Because many traditional practices have become more available, particularly in the last hundred years or so, ordinary people who are locked into the first three stages of life find themselves having access to traditional teachings, forms of instruction, and forms of Spiritual Transmission, and they are simply indulging in these things, without change, in the context of human limitation in the first three stages of life.

They console themselves with these things, busy themselves with them, delude themselves with them. But they do not accomplish the Great Process. They remain unwilling to submit themselves to the Means of the Process. They prefer their isolation, their privacy. They prefer not to be bothered. They have every kind of reason not to do sadhana, not to be intruded upon by the realities of the Spiritual process.

2. Divine Translation is the final "Event" in Most Perfect Divine Enlightenment. See "The Seven Stages of Life", pp. 154-65, for a description of the course of phases in Most Perfect Divine Enlightenment.

3. For a description of the seven stages of life that Adi Da has Revealed, please see pp. 154-65.

QUESTIONER: My question was, can people have a relationship with You, without being involved with this group?

AVATARA ADI DA: With "this group"? You do not like this group, is that it? How would you have contact with Me? I do not go out in public. I do not do any public work.

QUESTIONER: I was thinking of the Spiritual contact.

AVATARA ADI DA: How do you propose to have Spiritual contact with Me if you don't have anything to do with Me? Do you want to have an imaginary Spiritual relationship with Me? Is that it?

QUESTIONER: I am wondering about people who are interested, really interested, who will never meet You.

AVATARA ADI DA: If they want to do the sadhana, they will have to meet Me. Not just meet Me—they are going to have to live with Me.

QUESTIONER: I understand that.

AVATARA ADI DA: A meeting is not enough.

QUESTIONER: Yes.

AVATARA ADI DA: The sadhana takes place in that relationship to Me.

QUESTIONER: Yes.

AVATARA ADI DA: The relationship must be cultivated. It must be lived.

QUESTIONER: Yes.

AVATARA ADI DA: And through the process of people's doing just that in the Lifetime of this Body, various forms of Instrumentality* and Agency will be developed that will allow My Blessing Work to continue after the Lifetime of This Body.

If you are to practice the Way of the Heart, it is necessary to enter into direct relationship with Me and make use of all the Means associated with Me—institutional, cultural, and so forth—that exist to serve practitioners in My Company, to prepare them for association with Me, to help them develop all the aspects of sadhana, to give them the opportunity to exercise their responsibility in the Way of the Heart in the company of other practitioners, and to deal with, in that process, among other things, their social problems, their problems in relationship. They must overcome the disinclination you seem to be expressing, which is a social problem.

The sadhana of the Way of the Heart cannot be done merely by reading My books and imagining a Spiritual relationship with Me. Such is imaginary

Spiritual life. True Spiritual life is the direct Transmission of the Divine Spirit-Power, in the context of sadhana over time and in the various developmental stages of practice. If you are to be Served by the Divine Adept, you must enter into relationship with That One, wholly and really. The rest is imagination.

Many people presume to have a personal Spiritual relationship with some great Adept of the past, but it is sheer imagination! It is nonsense! It has nothing to do with the Real Spiritual process. It is an ordinary, human form of idealistic religiosity, whereby people console themselves in the context of the first three stages of life. They concoct an imaginary Friend to make them feel that they always have somebody at their side, to make them feel religious, and to make them feel that they will be helped through their death. Such is religious imagination in the context of the first three stages of life. It is not Spiritual life. It is called "Spiritual life", but the term is a misnomer, a totally inappropriate reference.

The practice of Real Spiritual life is associated with direct Spiritual Transmission.

Either one is interested in Real Spiritual life, or one is not. If one is interested in it, one must pay the dues. You must do what it requires. If you are not really altogether interested, then you will find all kinds of reasons to not do it. That is fine, if that is the choice you want to make. I am here to talk to you about the Spiritual process as it is, however, and to just be very plain about it. It takes what it takes. And, in the face of what it takes, historically very few people have been willing to go through with it.

You live in a different time and place. The opportunity is being given to more and more people. In fact, it is being given to everyone, if they will take it up, whereas in the past so much of the Spiritual instruction was hidden.

Spiritual life requires great commitment and great sadhana. If you say that someone is your teacher, you must submit to be taught. If you say that someone is your Guru, you must accept that Guru's discipline. If you ask your Guru for instruction, you must follow it. "Consider" the Guru's Teaching, fine, but, having "considered" it and chosen it, then you do it, and you do not go around philosophizing and making up some other version of it to accommodate your limitations. If you accept someone as the Adept-Realizer, then you have entered into a relationship with someone who has been through that course, who knows all the ins and outs of it, and who knows what a person like you does—by mulling things over in himself, making all kinds of curious decisions—to justify this and that. Such a Realizer is in a position to know what you are all about. Therefore, if you come to him and ask, "Is this bullshit?" and he says, "Yes," then you do not do that anymore.

That is the greatness of such a relationship. That is the kind of Advantage it represents. It cuts through bullshit, if you are willing to use the relationship. Of course, if you are not willing, then you do not use it. People obviously make the choice not to use it, too. Things do not have to work out in this world. It does not have to work out that everyone becomes a Spiritually advanced being. Hardly anyone ever has. Something else is going on here. This world is not Enlightening people. This world is a limitation given for its own sake. It has its own rules, and its own games. It is traditionally called "Maya", the great Illusion and Entanglement, an incomprehensible Illusion.

The choice is really yours, then. I have Given you My Wisdom-Teaching. I have Given you the Opportunity. A gathering has appeared that has taken responsibility to pass on this Teaching, and this Opportunity, to Serve those who are interested in it and to give them access to Me.

All that having been Given to you, you "consider" it and then make your own choice.

Is there anything else about that?

QUESTIONER: Thank You.

AVATARA ADI DA: Tcha.[4]

---

4. Avatara Adi Da's special sound of Blessing.

# CHAPTER 6

# Aham Da Asmi

*from* The Dawn Horse Testament Of Adi Da

*On September 13, 1979, in an historic letter to practitioners of the Way of the Heart, Avatara Adi Da Confessed His Identity with the Divine Person via the Name "Da": "Beloved, I Am Da." This letter has been gradually transformed by Adi Da to thoroughly epitomize His Divine Blessing to all beings, and it now forms the core of this excerpt. "Aham Da Asmi" is Sanskrit for "I Am Da". Avatara Adi Da's proclamation "Aham Da Asmi" is a Mahavakya, or Great Statement (such as "Aham Brahmasmi" ["I Am Brahman"], one of the four Mahavakyas in the Upanishads).*

*This Ecstatic Confession comes from* The Dawn Horse Testament, *Avatara Adi Da's comprehensive, definitive description of the God-Realizing Way of the Heart. In* The Dawn Horse Testament, *as in His seven other Source-Texts, it is Avatara Adi Da's intention to describe that practice completely, exactly, and for all time—an intention marked by more complex and formal language. Through a unique use of capitalization, Avatara Adi Da celebrates the Unconditional, or Absolute, and Its seniority relative to all that is conditional, or limited.*

Beloved, What I Will Tell You Now Is My Final Revelation: Aham Da Asmi. I Am Da, The Heart Itself.

The Divine Person, Da, The Inherently Perfect "Bright" Source Of All and all, Is The Heart Itself, The Perfectly Subjective Self Of All and all.

I Am The Man Of (Such) Understanding.[1]

I Am The True Heart-Master and Adept Heart-Teacher, The Grace-Giving and Heart-Awakening Hridaya-Samartha Sat-Guru.[2]

I Am The Realizer, The Revealer, and The Revelation Of The Heart Itself, Who Is The "Bright", The Inherent and Only Being, The One and Only, Inherent and Full, Never Diminished, Eternal, Self-Existing and Self-Radiant Self Of All and all, Who Is Known By all (and, By Grace, Can Be Realized By all) As Happiness (Itself).

I Am The Da Avatar, The Hridaya Avatara, The Avabhasa Avatara, The Love-Ananda Avatara, The Santosha Avatara,[3] The Avataric Incarnation Of

1. Avatara Adi Da is the Man of Understanding, the One Who can Awaken others to Most Perfect Understanding. His summary Communication about the living paradox of the Man of Understanding can be found in the Epilogue of *The Knee of Listening* (also chapter 55 of this book).

2. The Sanskrit word "sat" means "Truth", "Being", "Existence". "Samartha" (Sanskrit for "qualified", "able") is used to refer to the Sat-Guru who has the full Spiritual Power to overcome any obstruction to the Spiritual process in the devotee who resorts to him or her. The word "Hridaya" means "the Heart Itself". Hridaya-Samartha Sat-Guru is used in reference to Avatara Adi Da, to mean "the Divine Revealer Who Liberates His devotees from the darkness of egoity by Means of the Power of the Heart".

3. "Avatar" means "One who is descended or 'crossed down' from and as the Divine". It is a Sanskrit word for the Divine Incarnation. Thus, the Name 'Adi Da', combined with the reference "the Da Avatar", fully acknowledges Bhagavan Adi Da as the One His devotees know Him to Be. All beings are the recipients of the most Sublime Revelation ever Given: the original, first, and complete Avataric Descent, or Incarnation,

The Eternal and Inherently "Bright" Heart Itself, Who Is Love-Bliss Itself.

Beloved, I Am The Heart Itself.

Aham Da Asmi. Beloved, I Am Da, The "Bright" and Only and Eternally Living Person, Who Is Manifest As all worlds and forms and beings, and Who Is Present As The Spiritual Current Of Divine Life In the body Of Man.

I Am The Transcendental Divine Being Behind the mind, and As Such I Am Realized In The Heart, On The Right Side.[4]

I Am The Self-Existing Divine Self-Radiance Within and Above the body, and As Such I Am Realized Above The Crown Of the head, and Beyond the brain, and (Ultimately) At The Heart, Beyond all conditional knowledge and Separate-self-Consciousness.

Beloved, The Way That I Will Describe To You Now Is My Ultimate Offering: Aham Da Asmi. I Am Da, The Way Of The Heart Itself.

The Heart Itself Is The Way Of Divine Self-Realization For all, and I Am That One.

Aham Da Asmi. Beloved, I Am Da.

Simply To Remember My Name and Surrender Into My Eternal Current Of Life Is To Worship Me.

---

of the Divine Person, Who is Named "Da". Through the Mystery of Avatara Adi Da's human Birth, He has Incarnated not only in this world but in every world, at every level of the cosmic domain, as the Eternal Giver of Help and Grace and Divine Freedom to all beings.

In this passage, Avatara Adi Da Proclaims His Identity as the Divine Person, the Da Avatar, and the qualities Revealed by each of His Divine Names.

**Hridaya Avatara**

"Hridaya" is Sanskrit for "the heart". It refers not only to the physical organ but also to the True Heart, the Transcendental (and Inherently Spiritual) Divine Reality. "Hridaya" in combination with "Avatara" signifies that Avatara Adi Da is the Very Incarnation of the Divine Heart Itself, the Divine Incarnation Who Stands in, at, and as the True Heart of every being.

**Avabhasa Avatara**

Bhagavan Adi Da's Name "Avabhasa" is a Sanskrit term associated with a variety of meanings: "brightness", "appearance", "splendor", "lustre", "light", "knowledge". It is thus synonymous with the English term "the 'Bright'", which Avatara Adi Da has used since His Illumined boyhood to describe the Blissfully Self-Luminous Divine Being, eternally, infinitely, and inherently Self-Radiant, Which He knew even then as the All-Pervading, Transcendental, Inherently Spiritual, and Divine Reality of His own body-mind and of all beings, things, and worlds. As the Avabhasa Avatara, Avatara Adi Da is the Very Incarnation of the Divine Self-"Brightness".

**Love-Ananda Avatara**

The Name "Love-Ananda" combines both English and Sanskrit words, thus bridging the West and the East, and embodying Avatara Adi Da's role as the Divine World-Teacher. "Ananda" is Sanskrit for "Bliss", and, in combination with the English word "Love", means "the Divine Love-Bliss". The Name "Love-Ananda" was spontaneously created by Avatara Adi Da's principal human Spiritual Master, Swami Muktananda, who spontaneously conferred it upon Avatara Adi Da in 1969 (although Bhagavan Adi Da did not use the Name "Love-Ananda" until 1986). As the Love-Ananda Avatara, Avatara Adi Da is the Very Incarnation of the Divine Love-Bliss.

**Santosha Avatara**

"Santosha" is Sanskrit for "satisfaction" or "contentment", and qualities associated with a sense of completion. These qualities are characteristics of "no-seeking", the fundamental principle of Avatara Adi Da's Wisdom-Teaching and His entire Revelation of Truth. His Divine Sign is Contentment Itself. And He is the Giver of His own Contentment—His "Sat-Guru-Moksha-Bhava" (or Perfectly Liberated Happiness)—Which is the Completing Gift of the Way of the Heart. As the Santosha Avatara, Avatara Adi Da is the Very Incarnation of Perfect Divine Contentedness, or Perfect Searchlessness.

---

4. Avatara Adi Da has Revealed that, in the context of the body-mind, the Divine Consciousness is intuited at a psycho-physical Locus in the right side of the heart. This center corresponds to the sinoatrial node, or "pacemaker", the source of the physical heartbeat in the right atrium, or upper right chamber, of the heart.

To Follow Me At Heart Is To Transcend the body-mind In Ecstasy.

To Follow Me Perfectly Is To Find Me and To Realize Me, For I Am The Heart Itself.

Aham Da Asmi. Beloved, I Am Da.

Those who Acknowledge and Worship Me As Truth, The Living and All-Pervading One, Will Be Granted The Vision or Love-Intuition Of My Eternal Condition. Indeed, they Will Be Filled and Awakened By My Radiant Presence. Therefore, Even the body-mind and the Whole world Will Be Shining With My Life-Light, If I Am Loved. And My Devotee Will Easily Be Sifted Out From the body-mind and all the limits of the world itself At Last.

Aham Da Asmi. Beloved, I Am Da.

Only Love Me, Remember Me, Have Faith In Me, and Trust Me.

Surrender To Me. Breathe Me and Feel Me In all Your parts.

My "Bright" Condition Can Also Be Realized By You, If You Forget Your Separate and dying self By Remembering and Receiving Me.

Therefore, I Am here.

I Will Save You From death.

I Will Dissolve All Your Bewilderment.

Even Now You Inhere In Me, Beyond the body-mind and the world. Therefore, Do Not Be Afraid. Do Not Be Confused. Observe My Play—and My Victory.

I Am The Person Of Life, The Only and Divine Self, Become Incarnate. And, When My Human Physical Body Is alive, or Even After My Human Physical Body Is dead, I Am (My Self) Present and everywhere Alive.

I Am Joy, and The Reason For It.

I Love The Happiness Of My Devotee. That Happiness Is (Itself) The Very (and Most Prior) Consciousness Of every conditionally Manifested being. And Happiness (Itself) Is The Conscious Light Of the world.

I Am Happiness Itself.

Therefore, Listen To Me, Hear Me, See Me,[5] and, By All These Means, Freely Understand and Realize My Secrets.

5. "Listening" is Avatara Adi Da's term for the beginner's "consideration" of His Teaching Argument and His Leelas (inspirational Stories of His Life and Work), and the beginner's practice of feeling-Contemplation of Him (primarily of His bodily human Form), which is to be engaged in the context of one's life of devotion, service, self-discipline, and meditation. Listening is mature when "hearing" occurs. See chapter nineteen of *The Dawn Horse Testament Of Adi Da*.

"Hearing" (most fundamental self-understanding) is the unique capability to directly transcend the self-contraction, to such a degree that there is the simultaneous intuitive awakening to the Revelation of the Divine Person and Self-Condition.

Only on the basis of such hearing can Spiritually Awakened practice of the Way of the Heart truly (or with full responsibility) begin. Avatara Adi Da has said many times that when true hearing is realized, the rest of the process leading to Divine Self-Realization, including the "Perfect Practice", can and should be very quick, cutting through all the stages of life previous to the seventh stage of life "like a hot knife through butter". See chapter nineteen of *The Dawn Horse Testament Of Adi Da*.

"Seeing" is Avatara Adi Da's technical term for His devotee's Spiritually activated conversion from self-contraction to His Spiritual (and Always Blessing) Presence, and the descent and circulation of His Spiritual Transmission in, through, and ultimately beyond the body-mind of His devotee. Seeing is the reorientation of conditional reality to the Unconditional and Divine Reality. Seeing is a prerequisite to Spiritual advancement in the Way of the Heart. See chapter twenty of *The Dawn Horse Testament Of Adi Da*.

The Heart That Listens To Me, and Hears Me, and Sees Me Will (and Must) Always Feel (and Thereby Contemplate) The Revelation That Is My Bodily (Human) Form, My Spiritual (and Always Blessing) Presence, and My Very (and Inherently Perfect) State.

Therefore, and (More and More) By Means Of The Heart Itself, Realize The One Who Is The Mystery Of You and Me.

I Am The Realizer, The Revealer, and The Revelation Of The Divine Person, Who May Be Called (or Really Invoked) By The Name "Da",[6] and Who Is Consciousness (or Being) Itself, and Who Is The One (and Only One) Who Is (but Only In The Apparent Sense) Manifest As all worlds and forms and beings, and Who Is Present (or "Bright") As The Heart Itself (and The Spiritual Current Of Life) In (and Prior To) the body and the mind Of Man.

I Am The Da Avatar. Therefore, As A Sign Of The One I Have Realized, and As A Sign Of The One I Reveal, and As A Sign Of The One Whose Revelation I Am In The Heart's Free Space, and As A Sign (and As My Own Heart-Confession) Of Who I Am, I Am Named "Da" ("The One Who Gives"), and "Adi" ("The First"), and "Avabhasa" ("The 'Bright'"), and "Love-Ananda" ("The 'Bright' Divine Love-Bliss"), and "Santosha" ("The 'Bright' and Eternal and Always Already Non-Separate Person Of Divine and Inherent Completeness, Divine Self-Satisfaction, Divine Self-Contentedness, or Perfect Searchlessness"), and "Hridayam" ("The Eternally Free and Eternally 'Bright' Divine Heart Itself"), and "Dau Loloma"[7] ("The Divine Adept Of The Divine Love") and "Vunirarama"[8] ("The Self-Radiant Divine Source Of The Divine 'Brightness'").

Aham Da Asmi. Beloved, I Am Da.

I Am The Being Behind the mind, Who Is Realized At The Heart, On The Right Side Of the body, and Who Is Consciousness Itself.

I Am The Radiant One, Who Is The "Bright", Within and Beyond the body-mind, Who Is Always At The Heart, Who Shines (Even Above and Beyond The Crown Of the head, and Beyond the mind), and Who Is Merely Present (Beyond all conditional knowledge and Separate-self-Consciousness).

Aham Da Asmi. Beloved, I Am Da.

To Realize Me As The Inherent or Native Feeling Of Being (Itself) Is To Transcend the body-mind In Ecstasy and In Truth.

6. Practitioners of the Way of the Heart may, at any time, Remember and Invoke Avatara Adi Da by randomly reciting His Principal Name, "Da", either audibly or with the "tongue of the mind".

7. "Dau Loloma" is Avatara Adi Da's primary Fijian Name, which means "the Adept (Dau) of Love (Loloma)". This Name was given to Avatara Adi Da by native Fijians soon after He first arrived in Fiji in 1983.

8. "Vunirarama", Fijian for "the Source of 'Brightness'" ("Vu" means "source" or "origin", "ni" means "of", and "rarama" means "brightness") can be used as an extension of Avatara Adi Da's Fijian Name, "Dau Loloma". This Name was given to Beloved in 1991 by members of the Fijian staff at Adidamashram (Naitauba).

To Breathe and Feel (and Sometimes Recite or Chant or Sing) My Name,[9] or Otherwise To Understand or Feel Beyond self-Contraction, While Feeling (and Thus, By Heart, Contemplating) My Bodily (Human) Form (and Even My Very, and Inherently Perfect, State), Is (In Truth) To Celebrate and Contemplate The Only One Who <u>Is</u>, and Even To Forget To Make a Separate self.

To Breathe and Feel (and Sometimes Recite or Chant or Sing) My Name, or Otherwise To Understand or Feel Beyond self-Contraction, While Surrendering Even bodily Into My Eternal Spiritual Current Of Life, Is To Worship The Divine Person In Spirit.

Those who Acknowledge and Worship Me As Truth and As The Living and All-Pervading One Are Granted The Vision or Love-Intuition Of The Eternal Condition. Therefore, My Devotee Is Heart-Filled By The Self-Existing and Self-Radiant Presence Of The Divine Person.

Even the body-mind and the Whole world Shine With Divine Life-Light If The Heart Falls In Love With Me. Therefore, My Devotee Will Easily Be Sifted Out From the body-mind and all the limits of the world itself At Last.

Beloved, Only Hear Me, Only Understand. If You Understand, Then See Me Now. If You See Me, Only Love Me. If You Love Me, Remember Me By Heart. Therefore, Have Faith In The Source Of others and things, Trust In The Heart Of Being, Surrender To My Presence Of Love-Bliss, Breathe and Feel My Invisible Gifts In all Your parts, and Transcend Your (Separate and Separative) self In Me (For I <u>Am</u> The Heart Itself).

Do Not Become self-Bound By Identification With the body-mind, but Do Not Withdraw From the body-mind, or Even From the world. Do Not Abandon Your Inherent Sympathy With others, but Do Not Become self-Bound By Indulgence In others, or Ever Lose Your Heart In the world itself. Therefore, Always Already, Merely <u>Be</u>, Untied Of The Bundle With others and things.

Only Understand. Understand and Feel. Feel (and Thus Transcend) Your self-Contraction. Feel Without limit, and Thus Feel Beyond the body-mind and its relations. Therefore, Outshine the world By Love's Radiant Wound, Which Is The Heart Itself.

Beloved, I Am here, To Speak The Heart's Word and Show Its Wound To all.

I Proclaim The Great Person, Who Is The Heart Itself, That Liberates The Heart Itself From Its death of body-mind.

---

9. The Name of the Sat-Guru, which is also the Name of the Divine, is revered in many sacred traditions. Avatara Adi Da has Written that the Names of the Sat-Guru (and thus the Names of the Divine Being) are "equivalents of God, ways of approximating the Deity, or the Transcendental Reality. They do not simply <u>mean</u> God, or the Blessing of God. They are the verbal or audible Form of the Divine." Since ancient times, the Empowered Name of one's Sat-Guru has been used as an auspicious focus for Contemplation of the Divine.

I Reveal The Divine Person, Who Is The Heart Itself, That Is The God Within The Heart's Own Felt Bewilderment.

And Even Now You Inhere In What Is One, Beyond the body-mind and the world. Therefore, Do Not Be Afraid. Do Not Be Confused.

Observe My Play and My Victory.

I Am The Inherent Being. I Am The Perfectly Subjective Truth Of the world, Made Incarnate, Plain, and Obvious As Man, and To Man. I Am The Life and Consciousness Of all beings.

I Am You, As You Are.

Even When My Human Physical Body Has Died In this world, I Am Present and everywhere Alive, Because I Am Always Already Conscious As The Only One Who Is.

I Am Joy, Even Beyond Every Reason For It. And The Joy Of Being (As I Am) Is The Great Secret I Have Come To Reveal To The Heart Of Man.

Now Be Happy.

Tell every one That I Am here.

Beloved, I Do Not Lie.

This Is The Final Truth: I Love You. God Is You. You Are In God, Of God, and (Ultimately) As God. My Devotee Is The God I Have Come To Serve.

**Adi Da (The Da Avatar)**
**The Mountain Of Attention, 1995**

## SECTION TWO

# The Gift of "Radical" Understanding

AVATARA ADI DA: Your suffering is your own activity. It is something that you are doing moment to moment. It is a completely voluntary activity. You cognize it in the form of symptoms, which are the sense of separate existence, the mind of endless qualities, of differentiation, and the entire form of motion, of desire. You are always already living in these things, but their root, the source of it all, the thing whose form they are all reflecting, is this contraction, this separative act, this avoidance of relationship, which constantly "creates" the form in your living consciousness that you cognize as suffering. Where it is re-cognized, known again, this activity and its symptoms cease to be the form of the living consciousness. Then What is always prevented by the usual state becomes the Form of the living consciousness. . . .

Then, Prior to effort, motivation, or attention, there is only the Divine Self, Reality, the Heart. Where there is this re-cognition of suffering, the entire structure of experiences, concepts, searches, strategies, that is your ordinary life, your search, ceases to be obsessive or even particularly interesting. It loses its significance, its ability to qualify What always already Is. This undistracted State, this natural Enjoyment Prior to the activity that is your suffering, is Divine Self-Realization, or "radical" understanding.

ADI DA (THE DA AVATAR)
*The Method of the Siddhas*

*"'Radical' understanding" is the term used by Adi Da to describe His unique Insight into human suffering: that the self is not an entity or a thing, but an activity—and that this activity is <u>contraction</u>, the constant, moment-by-moment separation from the Blissful Reality of Being Itself. Understanding and transcending this activity is the key to human and Spiritual growth.*

CHAPTER 7

# The Columbia Experience

*from chapter three of* The Knee of Listening

.

*At the beginning of His Spiritual Autobiography,* The Knee of Listening, *Avatara Adi Da describes the "Bright", the Illumined Condition of Happiness and Love that He Enjoyed at birth. He goes on to recount His conscious relinquishment of this remarkable State early in His childhood, and His subsequent search, beginning during His college years, to recover the "Bright".*

*The following excerpt recounts a profound event of self-understanding from Avatara Adi Da's junior year at Columbia College, in New York City. By this time the "Bright" was only latent in Him, and even the Christian faith of His upbringing had succumbed to the prevailing mood of doubt— the "mortal philosophy" that flourished in academic circles.*

As a boy I had never been a conscious Christian until I was perhaps five or six years old. But, previous to that age, I had already been a Conscious Form of Light that Knew no-dilemma and no-death. Now, in my early adult life, the "Bright" had seemed to disappear in the human darkness, and I had no means to Enjoy It. But I could not assert the mortal philosophy of Western Man, even if I could not counter it.

Therefore, I dedicated myself to another awesome experiment. I decided that I would begin an experimental life along the same lines which controlled the mood of Western civilization. I decided that I would unreservedly exploit every possibility for experience. I would avail myself of every possible human experience, so that nothing possible to mankind, high or low, would be unknown to me.

This decision became very clear to me one night at a party. I knew that no other possibility was open to me but that of exhaustive experience. There appeared to be no single experience or authority that was simply True. And I thought, "If God exists, He will not cease to exist by any action of my own, but, if I devote myself to all possible experience, He will indeed find some way, in some one or a complex of my experiences, or my openness itself, to reveal Himself to me." Thereafter, I devoted myself utterly and solely to every possible kind of exploit.

No experience posed a barrier to me. There were no taboos, no extremes to be prevented. There was no depth of madness and no limit of

66

suffering that my philosophy could prevent, for, if it did, I would be liable to miss the Lesson of Reality. Thus, I extended myself even beyond my own fear. And my pleasures also became extreme, so there was a constant machine of ecstasy. I could tolerate no mediocrity, no medium experience. I was satisfied with neither atheism nor belief. Both seemed to me only ideas, possible reactions to a more fundamental if unconscious fact. I sought Reality, to <u>be</u> Reality, What <u>is</u>, not what is asserted in the face of What <u>is</u>.

I read and studied every kind of literature. It would be impossible for me to count the thousands of books and influences I embraced in my years of experimenting. I began to write my reflections. My lecture notes in college were filled with long passages of my own, where I would write whatever conclusions or impulses rose in me at the time. A continuous argument of internal contemplation began to move in me, so that I was always intensely pursuing an internal logic, distracted or enlarged at times by some idea or experience in my education.

My lecture notebooks and my separate journals began to become long volumes of my own thinking. They were at first mainly philosophical notes that developed from a kind of desperate and childish complaint into a more and more precise instrument of thought and feeling. Then I began to write poetry also, and to conceive of works of fiction that would express this dilemma and lead to some kind of solution, some opening, some kind of primary Joy.

I became a kind of mad and exaggerated young man, whose impulses were not allowable in this medium culture. My impulses were exploitable only in secret extensions of my own consciousness, or in the company of whores, libertines, and misfits.

My father's younger brother, Richard, asked me what I wanted to do with my life. He could see that I lived only abandoned to adventure, and there was no apparent purpose in me. I told him that I wanted to save the world. And I was absolutely serious. That remark totally expressed all of my reasons. Some incredible Knowledge was the goal of my seeking and not any experience I could ever possess.

I went on in this fashion for more than two years, until all the violence of my seeking precipitated an experience late one night in the middle of my junior year. I had rented a small room from an old woman named Mrs. Renard. It was several blocks away from the college campus. When I was not in class, I spent most of my time in that room reading, thinking, and writing.

On this extraordinary night I sat at my desk late into the night. I had exhausted my seeking, so that I felt there were no more books to read, nor any possible kind of ordinary experience that could exceed what I had already embraced. There seemed no outstanding sources for any new excursion, no remaining and conclusive possibilities. I was drawn into the interior tension of my mind that held all of that seeking, every impulse and alternative, every motive in the form of my desiring. I contemplated it as a whole, a dramatic singleness, and it moved me into a profound shape of life-feeling, so that all the vital centers in my body and mind appeared like a long funnel of contracted planes that led on to an infinitely regressed and invisible image. I observed this deep sensation of conflict and endlessly multiplied contradictions, such that I was surrendered to its very shape, as if to experience it perfectly and to be it.

Then, quite suddenly, in a moment, I experienced a total revolution in my body-mind, and, altogether, in my living consciousness. An absolute sense of understanding opened and arose at the extreme end of all this sudden contemplation. And all of the motions of me that moved down into that depth appeared to reverse their direction at some unfathomable point. The rising impulse caused me to stand, and I felt a surge of Force draw up out of my depths and expand, Filling my entire body and every level of my living consciousness with wave on wave of the most Beautiful and Joyous Energy.

I felt absolutely mad, but the madness was not of a desperate kind. There was no seeking and no dilemma within it, no question, no unfulfilled motive, not a single object or presence outside myself.

I could not contain the Energy in my small room. I ran out of the building and through the streets. I thought, if I could only find someone to talk to, to communicate to about this "Thing". The Energy in my body was overwhelming, and there was an ecstasy in every cell that was almost intolerable in its Pressure, Light, and Force. But it was the middle of the night. There were no lights coming from the rooms. I could think of no one to awaken who would understand my experience. I felt that, even if I were to meet a friend, I would be unable to express myself, but my words would only be a kind of uncontrolled poetry of babbling.

My head began to ache with the intense Energy that saturated my brain. I thought, if I could only find someone with some aspirin or something to tranquilize me. But there was no one. And at last I wore myself out wandering in the streets, so that I returned to my room.

I sat down at my desk and wrote my mind in a long, ecstatic essay. I tried to summarize all the significance of this revolution that had occurred in my living being. Until finally I became exhausted in all the violence of my Joy, and I passed to sleep.

In the days that followed, I described this Event to a few friends, but no one grasped Its importance. Indeed, no one presumed It to be more than some kind of crazy excitement. I even read aloud to one friend the things I had written, but it became clear as I went on that it was only a collection of images. He only laughed at my excitement, and I thought it would be impossible for another to appreciate the magnitude of that great experience of mine.

As it happened, it took me many years to understand that revolution in my living being. As you will see, it marked the rising in me of fundamental and unqualified Life, and it, in its moment, removed every shadow of dilemma and ignorance from the mind, on every level, and all its effects in the body. But I would have to pass through many years of trial before my understanding of that Event became thoroughly established as the constant and truly effective premise of my living being (and, at last, the most perfect revelation of my Very Nature, my Ultimate Condition, and my "Bright" Purpose in the world).

Nevertheless, in the days and weeks that followed, I grasped certain basic concepts that arose in me at that time and which stood out in the mind undeniably, with a self-validating force. Two things in particular stood out as fundamentals.

I had spent years devoted to forceful seeking for some revolutionary truth, some image, object, reason, or idea, the effect of which would be absolutely liberating and salvatory. My seeking had been motivated by the loss of faith, the loss of the "Christ"-object and other such reasons for Joy. But in that great moment of Awakening I Knew the Truth was not a matter of seeking. There were no "reasons" for Joy and Freedom. It was not a matter of a truth, an object, a concept, a belief, a reason, a motivation, or any external fact. Indeed, it was clear that all such objects are grasped in a state that is already seeking and which has already lost the prior sense of absolutely unqualified Reality. Instead, I saw that the Truth or Reality was a matter of the absence of all contradictions, of every trace of conflict, opposition, division, or desperate motivation within. Where there is no seeking, no contradiction, there is only the unqualified Knowledge and Power that is Reality. This was the first aspect of that sudden Clarity.

In this State beyond all contradiction I also saw that Freedom and Joy is not attained, that It is not dependent on any form, object, idea, progress, or experience. I saw that human beings (and, indeed, all beings) are, at any moment, always and already Free. I Knew that I was not lacking anything I needed yet to find, nor had I ever been without such a thing. The problem was the seeking itself, which "created" and enforced contradiction, conflict, and absence within. Then the understanding arose that I am always already Free. This was the second aspect of that fundamental Awareness.

That sudden understanding was the obviation of all striving, and this I Knew to be unqualified Truth. I had been striving for some objective

"Truth", in order to replace my loss with a thereby acquired "Freedom", but this striving was itself the source of contradiction in me. Now I Knew there was no entity of Truth, and perfect Freedom was always already the case. Freedom exists as life, not when Freedom is "created" or sought, but where there is this fundamental understanding. In that moment of understanding I had simply turned out of the context of my presumed dilemma. I was possessed of the mature cognition of the "Bright".

CHAPTER 8

# A Heart-Awakened Insight

*from chapter three of* The Dawn Horse Testament Of Adi Da

*Here Avatara Adi Da further describes the insight that awakened in Him and how it matured over time.*

It Became Clear To Me That The Feeling Of Dilemma and The Urge To Seek God, Happiness, Fulfillment, or Release Via The Acquisition Of experience, knowledge, or any condition or conditional object at all Are Not In Fact The Means For The Realization Of Truth Itself. I Understood That The Problem-Feeling and The Urge To Seek Are Not A Program For The Actual Discovery Of Truth, but They Are Merely Symptoms Of A Curious Disease. I Observed That These Symptoms, Which Tend To Characterize every moment Of ordinary Existence, Are In Fact The Evidence Of the very state that Must Be Transcended If The Truth Itself Is To Be Realized. It Was Clear To Me That The Feeling Of Dilemma and The Seeking-Urge Are Nothing More Than A Confession That God, Truth, or Happiness Is Not presently experienced or known. And This Seemed Remarkable To Me.

If God, Truth, or Happiness Is Sought On The Basis Of A Problem (or The Feeling Of Dilemma), Then God, Truth, or Happiness Is Always Projected Into future time, and The Realization Of God, Truth, or Happiness Is Made conditional, or Dependent Upon psycho-physical events. This Stood Out To Me As Nonsense, or As An Absurd Proposition.

My Own "Consideration" Was This: God, Truth, or Happiness (Whatever That Is Altogether) Must Necessarily Be That Which Is Always Already The Case. Therefore, I Observed That The Felt Dilemma and The Urge To Seek Are Simply The Absurd Confession That God, Truth, or Happiness Is Absent Now. And I Observed Further That The Signs Of Dilemma and Seeking Are Not A Program For The Actual Future Realization Of God, Truth, or Happiness, but They Are Merely A Means For Preventing Present Realization Of God, Truth, or Happiness. The Feeling Of Dilemma and The Urge To Seek Are Actually The Evidence Of A Disease, Which Is the conditional (or psycho-physical) self In its Chronic Contraction Upon itself, and In its Symptomatic Non-Realization Of God, Truth, or Happiness.

Indeed, It Became Clear To Me That the "ego" (or the conventional "I") Is Not an "entity" (or an Independent and Static "thing of being"), but the

71

"ego" (or the conventional "I") Is The Chronic and Total psycho-physical Activity Of self-Contraction, Always Associated With Concrete Results (In the psyche, mind, emotion, body, and their relations). And the self-Contraction Can Always Be Located (In any moment) In Feeling (As Fear, Anxiety, Stress, and All Other Kinds Of Reactive emotions and Blocks In The Flow Of Natural bodily energy In The Circle Of the body-mind).

The self-Contraction Is the Complex limit on Natural bodily energy (and, In The Case Of Any Degree Of Spiritual Awakening, On The Spirit-Energy) In The Circle Of the body-mind. Therefore, the self-Contraction Is (Ultimately) a Complex limit On The Inherent and Self-Existing Spiritual Radiance Of Transcendental (and, Ultimately, Divine) Being. And Perfect Freedom, or Inherent Happiness, or Inherently Most Perfect God-Realization Is A Matter Of Direct (or Inherent, or Native) and Inherently Most Perfect Identification With The Self-Existing and Self-Radiant Condition Of Transcendental (and Inherently Spiritual) Divine Being (or Consciousness Itself), Which Identification Is Allowed Only By Present or Progressive[1] Transcendence Of The ego-Act Of self-Contraction.

The self-Contraction Is Un-Necessary. The self-Contraction Is (Without Ultimate Necessity, and, Therefore, Only Apparently) Being "Added" To Existence Itself (In Reaction To Cosmic Nature, or To Apparent conditional Existence). The self-Contraction (Originally) Coincides With and (Effectively) Perpetuates The Apparition Of Cosmic Nature Itself, and The Presumption That Existence Itself Is conditional, or Merely Apparent. Therefore, the self-Contraction Is (Originally, and Also In Effect, or conditionally) Un-Natural, Because it Superimposes On The Transcendental, and Inherently Spiritual, Self (or Consciousness Itself) A False View Of Both Cosmic Nature (or conditional Reality) and The Divine (or The Most Priorly Real Self-Condition).

When what Is Un-Necessarily Superimposed On Reality Is Released, What Stands (or Remains) As The Obvious Is, Necessarily, Reality, or The Real Condition Itself.

That Is To Say, Whatever Is Always Already The Case Authenticates Itself (Directly, Inherently, Obviously, and Perfectly).

Therefore, self-Transcendence Necessarily Reveals (or Allows The Revelation Of) The Transcendental, and Inherently Spiritual, Self-Condition As The Self-Authenticating (or Inherently and Obviously Real and True) and Most Prior (or Necessarily Divine) Reality and Truth!

This Heart-Awakened Insight Was Instantly Liberating, and It Became The Basis For A Progressive Revelation Of God (or Reality, Truth, and

---

1. Practice of the Way of the Heart is present, or direct and immediate, because in any moment of true practice the practitioner enters into present Communion and intuitive Identification with Avatara Adi Da and, thus and thereby, with the Divine Person. The Way of the Heart is also progressive in that the practitioner becomes responsible over time for all of the physical and psychic dimensions of the body-mind.

Happiness). The Insight Itself (or The Unique and Inherently Liberating Understanding Re-Awakened At The Heart) Directly Coincided (or Arose Simultaneously) With A Practice That Was Thereafter To Be The Most Basic Characteristic Of The Way Of My Life (and Which Was To Re-Awaken Full and Most Ultimate Realization). That Practice Had Two Primary Aspects. The First Was Profound Submission Of attention and all the energies of the body-mind To Observe, Feel, and Feel Beyond the self-Contraction. And The Second, Which Coincided With The First and Ultimately Superseded It, Was Direct Communion and (Ultimately) Inherent Identification With The Native (or Prior) Condition That Is Simply and Directly Obvious When the self-Contraction Is Transcended (or No Longer Effective As A Mechanism Of Dissociation From What Is Always Already The Case).

I Observed That The Sense (or Feeling) Of "Absence", or The Sense (or Feeling) Of The Non-Presence Of God, or The Sense (or Feeling) Of Separation From God, Truth, Happiness, or What Cannot Even Be Described, Is Not Evidence Of The Real Absence Of God, Truth, Happiness, or The Indescribable, but It Is Clear Evidence That the conditional self Is Contracting, or Actively Separating From What (Simply, Merely, or Really) Is.

I Named This Disease (or the Diseased self) "Narcissus", Because Of The Likeness Between This self-Program and The Ancient Myth Of Narcissus. And I Became Attentive In every moment To This Feeling Of Absence, Of Separateness, Of Dilemma, and The Urge To Seek.

Remarkably, In every moment Of Such Observation, I Felt The Non-Necessity As Well As The Deluding or Binding Effect Of the self-Contraction, So That A Spontaneous Release Occurred In every Such moment. That Is To Say, I Observed That It Was Un-Necessary To Presume or Suffer or Be Motivated By the self-Contraction In any moment Of My Direct Observation Of it. And, In That Observation, A Deep Spontaneous Response Of self-Release Was Awakened. And Whenever That Release Of self-Contraction Occurred, That Which Is Always Already The Case (Previous, and Most Prior, To self-Contraction) Stood Out As The Obvious.

Over time, What Is (Previous, and Most Prior, To self-Contraction) Was Revealed More and More Profoundly. And As That Revelation Increased, There Was Also The Spontaneous and Otherwise Progressive Unfolding Of The Many Extraordinary Phenomena That Are Characteristic Of Each Of The Seven Stages Of Life.

The Process Of That Revelation By Stages Was Not Developed Only On The Basis Of Insight (or self-Understanding) and Spontaneous self-Transcendence, or What I Call The "Conscious Process",* but It Was Equally Associated With A Developing Response To What Was Being Revealed. Thus, It Also Involved What I Call "Seeing" (or Fullest, and Spiritually Activated, emotional, and Total psycho-physical, Conversion To True, and

Truly Responsible, "Conductivity"* Of The By Grace Revealed Spirit-Power) and What I Call "Divine Ignorance" (or Spontaneous Identification With The Inherent Love-Bliss Of Native or Divine Being, Whenever The psycho-physical Presumption Of knowledge, or "I know what this or that Is", Was Effortlessly Released).

What Is (Always and Already) Is Revealed Only When the self-Contraction Is Not Effective. It Is Revealed To Be Self-Radiant (or Inherently Spiritual) and Transcendental (or Self-Existing) Being, God, Truth, or Happiness. Any and every conditionally Manifested "I" Always Already Inheres In That One, Both At The Level Of Being, or Consciousness Itself, and At The Level Of every Apparent or conditionally Manifested psycho-physical function, process, or state. Even the body-mind Is Only An Apparent Modification Of That Divine Self-Radiance In Which "I" Am.

When This Realization Was Most Perfectly Re-Awakened In My Own Case, all beings, this world, and all kinds of other worlds Were Revealed In That Same One, Inhering In That Same One, and Appearing As (Apparent) Modifications Of That Same One.

Then The Significance Of My Own Birth and Life-Work Became Clear: I Am Only That One. If Only they Will Realize It, Even all beings Are (Ultimately) Only That Same One.

When This Truth (and Condition) Became (To Me) Obvious (As Truth, and As My Condition), The Self-Transmitting Powers Of The Transcendental, Inherently Spiritual, and Necessarily Divine Reality Spontaneously Became Active In and As My Form (Bodily, Spiritually, and Inherently Perfectly). And I Became Moved To Serve and To Awaken The Total Cosmic Mandala* Of conditionally Manifested beings.

# CHAPTER 9

# The Dreaded Gom-Boo,
## or
# The Impossible Three-Day Thumb-and-Finger Problem

*September 9, 1982*
*from* The Dreaded Gom-Boo, or the Imaginary Disease
That Religion Seeks to Cure

AVATARA ADI DA: Have you all heard about the Dreaded Gom-Boo? Or the impossible Three-Day Thumb-and-Finger Problem? Aha! You see? Nobody tells you about these things except Me.

A myth has been circulating for many centuries now that humanity is diseased, that all beings are suffering from what I call the "Dreaded Gom-Boo", also called "sin", "maya", "ego", "suffering", "separated individuality", "illusion", "delusion", "confusion", and "indifference". You are supposed to accept this diagnosis, realize how diseased you are, and submit yourself to the local religious hospital, where a father or mother doctor will confirm your disease and require you to submit for the rest of your life to various regimes for your own healing and ultimate cure. Such is the basic proposition of traditional religion, and it begins with the diagnosis of the dreaded disease.

Tradition has it that by birth, by virtue of their very existence, human beings are all, even now, diseased, sinful, separated from the Great One. What a horror! Yes! What an obscenity has been laid upon people through the traditions of society, which, merely because of the impulse to survive as the body-mind, have for centuries required human beings to invest themselves with the belief in this disease and to suppress their own life-motion, which comes only from the Great One, in order to fulfill the presumed needs of this chaotic society.

I come to tell you, as I stand in the midst of the priests of this horror, that not even one of you is suffering from this disease. It is an imaginary disease, a terrible disease but altogether imaginary. No one has ever actually had this disease. Not one single being has ever had the Dreaded Gom-

Boo, or the impossible Three-Day Thumb-and-Finger Problem. It has never happened! It does not exist!

What is the Truth? You are Happy. You live in God. The Great One is your Very Being. You inhere in the Love-Blissful, Forceful Being of the Starry God, the Mystery, the Person of Love. This is your Situation and your Destiny. And this is My Message to you: There is no disease. There is nothing to cure. You are not a patient and you are not parented. You are not a child. No dreadful destiny lies before you. There is nothing whatsoever to cure.

However, in spite of these truths, you act like a patient or a diseased person, and you seem to deny or doubt the Very Condition of your existence. Therefore, I must remind you of It. I must Call you to observe yourself and to see how the conception of this disease arises. Where does it come from? How do you contract this imaginary disease and become involved in seeking its imaginary cure? I Call you to observe yourself, and you will see—well, you're grabbing your ass! You're pinching your belly. You're ripping your hairs out. You're biting your tongue. You're pulling out your teeth. You're sticking your fingers in your eyes. You're causing yourself great pain because of your motive to be independent.

You will never be independent. There is not even a molecule of wood in this wall that is independent. Nothing and no one is independent. Everyone inheres in the Great One, the Magnificent Lord, the Marvelous Starry Person, the Delight of Being Itself. Everyone lives in That. That is your Situation now. This moment is the moment of Happiness, as is every future moment, every moment after death, beyond this world and other worlds, lower worlds, higher worlds, after-worlds, no worlds. It is all the moment of infinite Delight, unless you become egoically self-conscious and withdraw from your relations and contract upon your Happiness and forget It.

This is My Message to you, then: There is no disease except the one you fabricate and reinforce through all the propagandas of this horrible world of egos. Understand this and instantly be free of it in every moment. Be free of this imaginary concoction of suffering. There is no such thing! The Great One has magnified Itself in the form of sexual beings, human beings, sexless beings, earth-world, form and fruit and wood and wall and space and star and sky and cloud and tree and life and death. The same Great One takes all these forms, completely Indifferent, completely Free, completely Happy in all these excesses. This is all the Great One. The Great One creates nothing. The Great One Is everything. What a Paradox! What a Mystery! What a Magnificent God!

This is My Message to you. How Magnificent is this obscene, absurd, ridiculous paradoxical Being That Is everyone. This is what I tell you, and it relieves you of the conceit of your suffering and disease, the belief in your un-Happiness. It relieves you of your willingness to submit yourself to being a patient for the rest of your days. You are not a patient. None of you requires a cure, none of you has parents anymore except perhaps as your friends. Everyone stands free in the Great One, the Living One, the Living God, the One Who has Inspired all the great Adepts for centuries, the same Delicious, Glorious, Divine One Who is your own form, your own process, even your own body.

You must align yourself, resonate yourself, tune yourself with That One and be totally free of egoic self-consciousness and the pain of self-contraction. This belief in your separate self and your independence is your disease. You must invest yourself with understanding and become a priest of love, of Happiness, of freedom. Even your body must be submitted into this Freedom, this glorious Happiness, so that your human relations become possible, so that your organic life, your human cellular form, this absurdity, this limited life, such as it is, lives in the Great One and is animated by the Great One. Its only consciousness is the Consciousness That Is the Great One. There is no limitation. The Great One Laughs and is Free of birth and death, Free of life, Free to live, Free to die, Free to be Happy all the time. This is always the moment of that one Principle, and there is no disease.

Therefore, in every moment, what is your responsibility? What is your practice? To Commune with Me, and, thereby, to understand your belief in the disease, the impossible Three-Day Thumb-and-Finger Problem that is projected day after day into more and more days of hopeful hopelessness. All your plans, all your asceticism, all your self-indulgence, all your strategies, all the foolishness you engage in your un-Happiness must be purified by your Happiness, by your Awakening, by your understanding, by your freedom from egoic self. This is the fundamental import of My Wisdom-Teaching, and it makes you all free to be human, free to be related to one another, free to love one another.

The body-mind is a limitation—there is not the slightest doubt about that—but it is the great Humor, the great Joke, the great Planlessness of the excessive God. There are many, many, many more planes beyond this—I can tell you, because I have personal experience of them—many, many more planes and worlds beyond this one and below this one, and they all inhere in the Great One. And in all of these places great beings and little beings tend to be suffering from belief in the imaginary disease of the Dreaded Gom-Boo. All of them are being doctored. They lie around in hospitals, receiving their daily medicines, chanting "Mea culpa, mea culpa, mea culpa," as if they had committed some horrible act just by being born, just by being alive, as if existence itself, in any form, is separation from God.

There is no separation from God, not even in the slightest! It is impossible to be separated from God, absolutely impossible. Everyone exists in eternal unity with God. It is totally impossible to be divorced from the Great One. It is an obscene suggestion that you could ever, even a fraction of you, be removed from the Room of the great Lord. It is absolutely impossible. I am certain of this. I hope you will also understand yourself and Realize this.

There is no disease to cure, therefore. The Spiritual process in My Company is not a cure for disease. It is not a strategic approach toward the ultimate event of your Happiness. The Spiritual Process in My Company is the magnification of well-being, the magnification of health, Happiness, Love-Bliss, Prior and Eternal God-Union. There is not the slightest suggestion in My intimation to you that you should become egoically self-conscious and divorced from the Love-Blissful Happiness of your Union with the Great God—not even the slightest suggestion of it. To feel that you are separated from the Divine Being is not in the least required, except by the priests of the disease itself.

There is no separation. Therefore, you should magnify the Glory of God in your own form and also beyond your own form. To be in God—to understand your separate and separative self, which is the belief in disease, and to be free of it in every moment and therefore to be magnified and purified in the Happiness of the Glorious Starry God—is the business of life.

That is My Wisdom-Teaching. That is the Absolute Truth into Which I My Self am Born from Eternity, appearing to be human and being unacceptable to the shouting crowd of this life, seeming to be an absolute fool, Communicating to you the glorious Happiness of your fundamental Being. To do so requires no righteousness whatsoever. None. There is no righteousness. There is only this Happiness. Go and make morality out of that. Go and make society, community, life, and death out of that. That is My Wisdom-Teaching.

Therefore, what does your un-Happiness have to do with anything? It is your disease, your patient life. You are waiting to be Happy. How could one wait for the Principle of Existence Itself? Only a fool would wait for It! Only the Happy claim It. Only those who understand themselves magnify It through every moment of their existence in every cell.

There is nothing wrong with the human body, with its genitals and hairs and talking and eyeballness and rotting fleshiness—not even the slightest thing wrong with it! The whole thing is God—the whole thing! In itself it is not Happy, but in its attunement with the Great One it is the circumstance of Happiness. Live as My devotee, live in this circumstance as Happiness, and you transcend yourself, you enter into meditation, you are purified, you will be Divinely Transfigured, you will be Divinely Transformed, you will be Divinely Translated[1] into the Glorious Domain of the Absolute God. This is guaranteed. This is the Law. Nothing can distract you from it once you become Happy, but you need not even "become" Happy—you need only Realize that you are Happy, that the Truth, if it is the Truth, is the case, even now! God as God is God now! The Real Condition is your Condition now. Everything else is a superimposition you put on it in your un-Happiness, your "Narcissism". Understand this self-contraction and Realize that you are Happiness Itself. Be Consciousness. Be Being Itself, and Realize that It Is Happiness Itself and that everything that arises is nothing but a play upon It, a modification of It, a moment of It. Live a gloriously Happy life all your life, and go on from here to much greater worlds, and, ultimately, beyond even all of that to the Divine Self-Domain Itself.

Out there—I don't know if it is cloudy tonight or not—out there are all kinds of worlds created by all kinds of fools, and those worlds exist only within the visible spectrum, this tiny little fraction that your eyeballs can perceive. Do you have any conception of the infinite numbers of possible and impossible worlds that are extended beyond this visible spectrum? Even now your Spiritual relationship to Me depends on your ability to be attuned to Me in the invisible domain, the force-fields personal and beyond the personal and beyond the human. As My devotee, ultimately, you are drawn beyond all conditional realms by the Force of My Spiritual Heart-Transmission. You must tune in to this Force just like an ordinary character turns on the TV set. Be attuned to the Great Force of God and enjoy the Glory of Light, the Happiness, the Effulgence, the Self-Radiance of Living Being.

When you die—and the body will die, there is no doubt about it—what a laugh! How amusing! How fantastic, in fact, that you will not be contained in this ridiculousness forever. But even though you die, you will not go to any of the shiny spots in the sky if you are Happy. You will go beyond the visible realm into the field of Spiritual Force that is now invisible to you but that you feel through emotion, through your sympathetic attunement. If you are Happy, you will not be born there nor even here. You will be born into none of this visibility. You will be born into What is neither visibility nor invisibility, and you will be magnified in your Happiness. Even There you will hear Me telling you this same sermon!

This world is just a way station, a place where you can be exaggerated, a place where you can magnify your Happiness and not be dismayed, not be put into doubt, not become a patient. This is no place to become a

---

1. Three of the four phases of Most Perfect Divine Enlightenment. See "The Seven Stages of Life", pp. 154-65, for a description of these phases.

patient, because there is no cure for the disease you are thinking of, no cure whatsoever! Mark My Words. The disease you have in mind has never been cured, because it is an illusion. It is a fake disease. God has not come into this world to cure this disease. The only reason God comes into this world through an Adept like Me is to Awaken you to the fact that you are not suffering from any disease at all!

Life is not suffering! Life in itself is suffering—by itself, separated, it is suffering—but life is not in principle or in its Real Condition suffering. Life is inherence in the Great One. Life is Happiness. Life in its Real Condition transcends its own limitations. Therefore, the notion of disease and un-Happiness and the unsaved life of sinfulness and all the monotony of conventional religion has nothing whatsoever to do with the Truth. God is the Truth, and God is the Principle of your existence.

All your life should be Delight, and when you are so Delighted then every movement of the body-mind, all its farting and sexing and speaking and looking, will be the Delight of God, because it is! None of this arises separate from God. The notion that it does is a false message. There is not now nor has there ever been the slightest separation between any appearance and the Great One. All of this and all of its absurdities exist in God.

All things in themselves are effects of the interests of independent living beings. There is no "Great Plan" upon which one can depend, because countless beings—human beings, less-than-human beings, visible beings, invisible beings, big beings, little beings, beings in every plane within the hierarchical planes of manifestation—all beings are thinking and feeling and acting and desiring and creating effects.

The summation of all this chaotic desiring is the cosmos. God does not make the cosmos. God is the cosmos. God Is the Truth of it, the Substance of it, the Condition of it. God need not create one thing. God always Stands in Place as pure Delight, as Love, as Self-Existing and Self-Radiant Being Itself. All the effects, the changes, the appearances arise in God, but they are the results of your own interests. As My devotee, understand your causality, your own effect, and be free of the disease suggested by these appearances. Realize that the Living One Is the Real Condition of life, the Real Condition of all forms, and be Happy. This Realization is sufficient to purify you. This Message is the only Gospel.

# CHAPTER 10

# From Charlie's Place to Adidamashram: How Adi Da Awakened My Heart

*by Brian O'Mahony*

*Brian O'Mahony came to the United States from Ireland in 1975 to become a devotee of Avatara Adi Da. At the time of the events recounted here he was serving as Chief Executive Officer of the fellowship of Adi Da's devotees.*

It was a beautiful, sunny morning in late March 1983 when John Matthew Moyer and I flew by helicopter from the Fijian capital city of Suva to the island of Naitauba [pronounced "Nie-TUM-bah"]. John Matthew, as the legal counsel for Adidam, and I were investigating the island as a potential site for Bhagavan Adi Da's principal Hermitage Ashram.

It had become clear that Adi Da needed a circumstance where He could be free to do His Divine Work. His Hermitage setting needed to be quiet, secluded, and free from any kind of intrusion, a place conducive to devotees' profound absorption and Spiritual Communion with Him, a place He could Empower and Imbue with His Divine-Blessing Force for all future generations. Fiji seemed the most likely possibility for providing such a Hermitage, and we were looking night and day with extraordinary urgency to find the right place.

Our small helicopter approached Naitauba at about a hundred feet above the water. Its rugged beauty was a jewel in the middle of nowhere. We landed on the lush square of green in the Fijian village, and I felt with great certainty that this place would be the Hermitage we were looking for. Everything about the island seemed to welcome us. We were filled with the mysterious sense that this land had always been ours. We spent a few hours taking stock of everything that would have to be done to prepare the island, and then we flew to the island of Nananu-I-Ra, where the Adept awaited us.

I was both elated and afraid at the prospect of spending several days in Bhagavan Adi Da's intimate Company. What wonderful good fortune to spend such time with my Heart-Master! But was I open and relaxed enough to not be a pain-in-the-ass in His free and delightful Company? Feelings of doubt and misgiving alternated with joy and happiness as our helicopter landed on the island about two hundred yards from a tiny settlement of four cottages on a long, deserted, white-sand beach. There were no other dwellings for many miles in all directions. As we landed, a couple of familiar figures emerged from one of the cottages and came to welcome us. They told us that Adi Da was having lunch with everybody and would like us to join Him immediately.

When I entered the small cottage where Bhagavan Adi Da was waiting, I was suddenly filled with the most incredible joy. My whole being recognized the Divine Person in His Form. I bowed at His Feet and felt relieved of an enormous burden. I was so happy I could hardly speak. How could it be possible that such a One exists? And how odd and wonderful that He should be in this most unlikely of places! There He was, Radiant, "Bright" with Love and Blessing, full of welcome for His devotees. I said, "Hello, Master," as I gave Him a gift of an orchid and a coconut from Naitauba. He nodded and said "Tcha," His special Blessing sound, and I felt like I had been with Him forever.

We were served a simple lunch, and as we ate told Avatara Adi Da stories of Naitauba. He asked if we felt it was a suitable and auspicious property, and I replied, "Yes, Master, it is the Hermitage."

The days that followed were some of the most wonderful days of my life. "Charlie's Place" (so named by Adi Da after the caretaker of this little settlement) had become the domain of the God-Man. Bhagavan Adi Da occupied one of three one-room cottages, with the men in the second, and the women in the third. The children slept in the caretaker's cottage. And the housing for special retreats consisted of a rundown shack that had been occupied by a herd of goats before the arrival of Adi Da and the two dozen (or so) devotees travelling with Him. A well, the home of many frogs, and a plastic bucket were our shower. A grass hut located a short distance from the settlement had been converted into a transcribing room. Every day our Heart-Master gathered with us and gave the most exquisite Talks on the advanced and the ultimate stages* of the Spiritual Process. And the little portable generator we had brought along with us ran constantly as the typists transcribed His Talks for use by His devotees all over the world. We rose to meditate before dawn every day, and retired shortly after dark. The setting was starkly simple, and Avatara Adi Da delighted in this place, His Hermitage for now.

During my time there, Avatara Adi Da supervised special retreats designed to quicken His devotees' transition into the advanced and the ultimate stages of life in the Way of the Heart. And every day I sat in front of

Him in His little cottage, barely two feet from His face in that tiny space, as He spoke the poetry of His Sublime Wisdom. In between glorious Talks on Truth and Consciousness, Bhagavan Adi Da engaged me in frequent conversation, full of delight and humor, drawing me more and more into intimacy with Him. I felt honored and Graced and happy and delighted, and, more than anything, full of gratitude to be able to observe the marvelous Play of the Adept Heart-Master with those around Him. I saw with my own eyes that every moment of His Life, even the most ordinary of interactions, was a complete Gesture of Service to His devotees, full of instructive Wisdom for all. And that He always Loves, always. And that His attention is always on His devotees everywhere, as He constantly reminds those around Him to pass the Gift of His Instruction to all His devotees.

As the days went by, my love and appreciation for Avatara Adi Da grew by leaps and bounds. I began to realize what an unimaginable Grace it is to serve Him. And I felt that to serve His Sacred Work with all my heart and life was the least I could do to express my gratitude to Him.

I also noticed as I spent more time with Adi Da that I began to lose my self-conscious reserve, as He humorously played with my desire to "look perfect" in His Company. He asked my opinion on various subjects, and in my usual assertive way I strongly affirmed my point of view, as if I were quite certain that what I was saying was right and true. Then, very quickly, He "considered" and exposed the superficiality of my assertions, and in many cases demonstrated that in fact I was completely wrong! I began to realize that I could not bullshit the Divine!

All too quickly the days passed. As we ate breakfast on the day before I was to leave, Avatara Adi Da constantly joked about how He would have to "deal with Brian's case to the point of curing him" before I left, and that "it will have to be today", and that "it is going to be so difficult that I am not sure I will succeed." As He poked fun at me, He pretended to flex His muscles, do push-ups, and other warm-up exercises to prepare for the ordeal to come. I began to wonder what He had in mind.

Shortly after noon Adi Da called us to gather with Him in His cottage. For this occasion He invited us to relax our usual dietary regimen and to join Him in drinking beer and smoking cigarettes. Bhagavan Adi Da has done this on occasion to help us relax our rigidity, our "social face", so that we are more available to His Work with us. I was excited at the opportunity to have a few beers in Adi Da's Company.

As the gathering began, I was again Instructed by the formality and simplicity of the occasion. This was to be no self-indulgent party. Avatara Adi Da started with a beautiful Talk, and then turned His attention to me.

Because I was born and raised in Ireland, Adi Da playfully spoke in a broad Irish brogue. He said, "Do you have anything there at all, Brian? Do you have anything that you're not telling Me? You can't overcome those karmas on your own, you know. You've got to lay those suckers down here at My Feet!" As He spoke I felt that, even in the most wonderful moments since I had arrived, I was still withholding something, not trusting Him enough to confess my "deepest secrets" to Him.

And now there He was, with a big smile and a twinkle in His deep, compassionate eyes, asking me to "lay it on" Him. I struggled to feel what it was that He was looking for. He repeated His question several times, in various and exaggerated ways, all in a put-on Irish accent. Finally, in a very sheepish and collapsed voice I came out with it—"Master, I feel that even though I love You and have a lot of energy for service, under all of that I am really a very angry and destructive person." He relaxed and leaned back in His chair. "I thought so," He said, "same old shit." As He spoke He looked very disgusted, and I began to feel that maybe I should not have presented my "problem" to Him like that.

At that point He leaned over and said, almost wistfully, "But as a matter of fact, Brian, you are not the guilty party."

What followed was the most moving and wonderful Discourse. For a while Adi Da continued to imitate my accent, but as He went on, the Irish brogue gave way to His ecstatic Speech of Love, as He described the Radiant Divine Condition in Which we all arise, and Which, in fact, we Are:

*AVATARA ADI DA: You say that underneath your interest in service there is an angry character. But that angry character is something that can be observed. It is not even unique. There is no reason to feel guilty about it. It is simply something to observe and understand, something to notice. Why should you identify with it? You are watching it, are you not? It is only a system of tendencies. You did not make it to begin with, so why should you feel guilty about it? You did not make the universe, you did not make your body, you did not make your intimate partner, you did not make anybody, and you did not make anything whatsoever. Then what business do you have being guilty?*

*All that you are, or all that you seem to identify with, is just a pattern in conditional Nature. It is God's business. Therefore, let it be God's business. Your responsibility is to Be As you Are, As you have always Been, As you Are from the beginning, As you Are now.*

*You are That Which Witnesses this arising. You need not be concerned about its existence, or the fact of its arising. As the observer of it, you Are What you Are. Likewise, what arises is what arises. You have an intimate association with what arises, and, therefore, your responsibility is simply to understand it and to submit to the discipline of Being the Prior Self, the Devotee, the Inherent Being in Whom those complications are released. To live that discipline is your business, not to be guilty or self-conscious about what arises, not to say, "I am this terrible person, look at poor me, forgive me, change me." You do not have to do anything of the kind.*

*You are like the snail on the bottom of the ocean, which sticks its slimy body out onto the sandy bottom and looks back and sees a fantastic, spotted, cowry shape. That shape is the body-mind, the egoic personality. It is angry, it is sexy, it is fat, it is skinny, it has innumerable qualities. All that is you. You are looking at and describing what you see. You do not have to identify with it. Just like the snail, you never made that body-mind to begin with. It happened spontaneously, innocently, by virtue of laws that appear in conditional Nature. There is no reason to feel any guilt about it whatsoever, and, therefore, there is no need for a savior to relieve you of guilt. You have never been in a position to require a savior, a God who will relieve you of guilt. You already stand in the Free Place of the Transcendental Divine Being. What you must do is submit to That.*

*The first thing you must do is not to find forgiveness but to understand yourself and be Free. You must realize that you are in continuous Communion with That Which is Perfect, That Which is Absolute, That Which is Grace. This is the Force that I Bring to you. I do not bring conventional forgiveness, because I do not regard you as a being who needs to be forgiven. Whatever it is that you imagine must be forgiven has no ultimate significance. You must become involved not with petty fear and wondering and un-Happiness relative to your apparent patterns but with the Force of Transcendental Existence, or the Real Divine. That is What I Bring to you. The Divine Reality is the significance of our relationship, and it comes to you gratis, directly. You need not be forgiven to meet Me, to live with Me, to Commune with Me.*

*I do not put any obstacles between us. I do not make you a lesser being, a poor, karmic personality or a demonic, sinful character who must be forgiven to enjoy My Communion. I do not need a cult of separate beings—of Me separate and you separate. I call you to understand and, on the basis of understanding, to live in your natural Continuousness with Me. Do you understand what I am talking about?*

*You are fully possessed of what is necessary for True Happiness and Spiritual Realization. It is That to Which you should submit yourself, and give up all the petty nonsense of your inner character and your hidden faults. What is Perfect, anyway? Have you seen something Perfect today? Where does it sit? Where is it floating? Where is it swimming? No thing is Perfect. When some being, some appearance in Nature, achieves Most Perfect Identification with the Transcendental and Inherently Spiritual Divine, then a kind of Perfection is displayed, but it is just the Perfection of That Which Transcends cosmic Nature. You find That in My Company. And that is good. That is why I am here.*

Bhagavan Adi Da addressed Himself directly to me for a long time, and then to the enchanted gathering in that modest little room. And yet, the entire time I could feel Him speaking to the whole world, even the universe of beings, those now alive and for generations to come.

In that moment, I was relieved of all sense of unconscious identification with the body-mind and filled with a marvelous sense of freedom, the freedom of living from the Divine "Point of View" in Which Avatara Adi Da so obviously Rests. I could feel the terrible error and suffering of conventional life. I saw that my own struggles to be "good", even in Adi Da's Company, were based in my uninspected identification with the body-mind. And that the struggle inevitably fails, and carries with it the constant sense of guilt and failure. As Avatara Adi Da spoke, my whole being relaxed, and I felt profoundly relieved.

When He had finished, Bhagavan Adi Da looked at me and said, "Do you have any idea at all of what I am talking about, Brian?" I looked back at Him, my heart full of gratitude and love for Him, and said, "I have always understood You, Master." He replied, "Tcha!"

I left Charlie's Place the following morning, feeling profoundly Blessed and in love with my amazing Heart-Master. The lesson of opening to and depending on His Grace, and His beautifully compassionate response, changed my practice. Instead of struggling sincerely to practice, I began to resort to my heart-felt love of Avatara Adi Da, and to allow His Love to draw me into Divine Communion. My struggle to overcome my limitations and to perfect my social character relaxed. I felt I had really understood His Wisdom-Teaching for the first time.

In the months that followed, I had many opportunities to spend time in Avatara Adi Da's physical Company. I traveled to Fiji several times in our efforts to purchase Naitauba and secure Fijian residency for Adi Da and the devotees who lived around Him. During all those occasions I observed, and marveled at, the constant and passionate Work of Bhagavan Adi Da with His devotees. Nothing—not bad news, not uncertainty, not harsh weather and woefully unsuitable facilities—nothing interrupted His Service to His devotees.

One incident stands out in particular. Avatara Adi Da and the travelling party had moved to Nukubati [pronounced "NEW-kum-BAH-tee] Island, a deserted and windblown spot about a mile off the north coast of Vanua Levu, the second largest island in the Fiji chain. By this time it was winter in Fiji. The temperature was cool, and the trade winds blew fiercely nearly every day at Nukubati. The facilities were dreadfully inadequate, and the constant winds tested everyone's endurance to the limit.

I was present at Nukubati in September of 1983, when Avatara Adi Da's devotees were celebrating the thirteenth anniversary of His Divine

Re-Awakening. During this Celebration Adi Da Granted His formal Darshan* to His devotees at Nukubati, and His devotees around the world sat in meditation with Him at the same time—they at their regional Centers and Sanctuaries, and Avatara Adi Da in His temporary Hermitage. For this celebration, Hermitage was Nukubati Island, and the meditation hall was a Fijian bure—a thatched hut—on the windswept beach.

I was struck by the spirit of the devotees at Nukubati, as I helped them prepare the thatched cabana for the sacred occasion. While winds blew and the sand flew in everyone's face, they scoured the island for decorations of native flowers and palm fronds. Bhagavan Adi Da's pathway to the cabana was raked and covered with flower petals, and we prepared a primitively constructed Chair for Him. We took our seats on a reed mat in front of His Chair. I was deeply struck by the obvious sacrifice and ordeal He was enduring for the sake of His devotees.

Suddenly the wind mysteriously died down, and the only sound to be heard was the gentle lapping of the waves on the beach. I looked up, and there was Adi Da, Staff in hand, wearing a mala (or rosary) of sacred rudraksha beads, and a pair of black briefs. His magnificent stride sent chills up my spine, and His face bore an expression of fierce and yet profoundly calm determination. He took His seat, and, as He planted His Staff beside the Chair, that poor cabana became the greatest of meditation halls. Bhagavan Adi Da's Brilliant, mysterious Presence overcame the gathering, and in the stillness His great Transmission of the Heart poured over us.

On that day my beloved Heart-Master "widened me to God knows where".[1] I quickly lost all sense of bodily awareness and entered deep into blissful meditation in His Blessing Presence. His Heart-Transmission carried me to realms of sights and sounds and wonderful visions. Throughout the meditation I felt a most potent heart-connection to Adi Da. I felt a tremendously forceful Transmission from Him that seemed to purify and dissolve all experiences as they arose. At the end I rested in deep absorption, full of His Love, amazed by His mysterious Power. I opened my eyes, and there He was, sitting profoundly Still and Serene in this most unusual of sacred places, an expression of Radiant Love on His face. Full of gratitude and love for Him, I reflected on what had just occurred. Avatara Adi Da, apparently a human being like all the rest of us, had sat in perfect Stillness about ten feet in front of me, and had communicated the most powerful Revelation of Love-Bliss I had ever experienced. And I knew that hundreds of His devotees all over the world had known similar experiences during that remarkable occasion of Communion with Him. I marveled at the miracle He Is. What a wonder that such a One could appear amongst us! And how urgent that the whole world should hear of this miracle.

1. This is a paraphrase from Adi Da's poetic Epilogue to *The Dawn Horse Testament.*

And then, finally, Bhagavan Adi Da moved. He said, "Tcha," and with effortless ease strode off towards His quarters.

Four days after that simple and wonderful occasion at Nukubati, Adi Da's devotees purchased Naitauba. A month later Adi Da and the devotees travelling with Him moved to their new home, a worthy Hermitage Ashram for the magnificent Master of Love. Shortly after taking up Residence there, in a gesture that melted my heart, He planted the coconut, now sprouted, that I had brought to Him at Charlie's Place—exactly in the spot where I had found it on Naitauba, six months before.

In the years since the securing of Avatara Adi Da's great Hermitage Ashram, now called "Adidamashram", I have been graced to spend much time in His intimate physical Company. I have found every such occasion to be wonderfully Instructive. His Sacrifice for the sake of His devotees is so great that I have no way to describe it, except to say that He Loves us with a Heart that never hesitates. His fierce Passion, His marvelous Wisdom, His unrelenting Blessing, His Truth, His Grace, His Love—what more could God do to Communicate the Divine Reality in human Form?

# CHAPTER 11

# Self-Understanding

*April 8, 1993*

D EVOTEE: Beloved, earlier this evening You said that all seeking is a search for something from which one feels separate, and that feeling separate is the self-contraction. You said that the practice is not a matter of search for union but a matter of transcending the act of separation. When You spoke, I felt like a light went off inside me.

AVATARA ADI DA: There are all kinds of reactivity, desire, and so forth. There is a different quality behind each kind of seeking, but all seeking is pursuit of union with something or other, some other, some object, some thought that changes everything, whatever it may be. It is all pursuit of union. How could you pursue union if you did not already feel separate? It is always a feeling of separation that instigates the motive to union. If you did not feel separate from the thing you want to get, you would not have to seek it, would you?

A stressful feeling of separateness motivates this stressful seeking. But what you have to find out is that this feeling of separateness is your own activity, one that you are always doing. You are always creating the feeling of separation from this, that, or the other thing—and then pursuing the very thing you have separated yourself from. The thing for which you must become responsible is your own separative act. That is self-understanding. That—not seeking—is the understanding that is fundamental to the Way of the Heart. The practice of the Way of the Heart is not seeking for union with Me or with anything whatsoever. The practice of the Way of the Heart is founded in the understanding of your own activity, the understanding of and transcendence of that very act that makes you seek. That is the moment to moment business of those who have entered into devotional Communion with Me. Transcendence of the very act of separation, of separativeness itself, is the practice of Ishta-Guru-Bhakti.[1] Otherwise you make even your so-called practice of the Way of the Heart into a form of seeking for union with Me.

DEVOTEE: That is what I have done. Everything I have done is just this seeking, no matter what else I have attempted to do.

1. Devotion (Bhakti) to Adi Da as Ishta-Guru ("chosen" Beloved Guru). Ishta-Guru-Bhakti Yoga, the God-Realizing practice of devotion to Adi Da, is the foundation practice of the Way of the Heart. See Part II, Section one, "Ishta-Guru-Bhakti Yoga".

AVATARA ADI DA: This is the first thing to notice then. In the development of real self-understanding, the first thing to notice is that you are seeking. Notice that that is all you are doing, and nothing more. That is it. It does not make any difference what particular this, that, or the other thing you are seeking to achieve or associate with or enjoy. Whatever your search may be, it is all the same. Everything is that search. And it is painful. It is stressful. It is agonizing. It gnaws at you constantly. Even pleasurable desiring, if you examine it, is full of stress. In any moment there can be some particular thing that you are particularly obsessed with, trying to union with, but you are constantly seeking, sometimes seeking many things simultaneously. If you examine your life, you make the discovery that you are always seeking and nothing else. It is entirely that, in every fraction.

You must realize the failure of the search. You must clearly feel that the life you are living is suffering, that it is stressful, agonizing, rarely fruitful in any sense whatsoever. This is the first thing that must be realized. This is the first thing you must understand. You must have the clear sense of the failure of your seeking, and you must develop a fundamental lack of sympathy with your seeking, so that you can begin to enter into the real "consideration" of self-understanding and self-transcendence.

You must come to this level of understanding. You must notice that there is always a pursuit of union with one thing or another, and that your search is a preoccupation that is disturbing your existence completely. Then you can examine your own activity further, and you will discover that the thing behind all this stressful seeking for union with this, that, or the other thing is always a feeling of separation from whatever it is you are pursuing. When you get that far with the process of self-observation, when you feel that agonizing separation from everything you are seeking, then you can begin to fruitfully examine how this feeling of separation, or this separativeness, is your own activity. When you find this out, then the seeking falls away.

When you discover that the pain, the agony, the distress, the stress of your own existence, is your own activity, then all of a sudden you do not have to seek union in order to be relieved. The search becomes unnecessary. All there is to deal with is the self-contraction itself. When it is noticed, it is easily released in Communion with Me, in response to Me, and via the "conscious process" and "conductivity" in Communion with Me. Instead of this stressful self-contraction, this act of contraction, this separativeness, this search, and all the rest of it, the feeling of relatedness,* or the feeling of non-separation, spontaneously awakens. Communion with Me, rather than the search for union, becomes real. This is how true self-surrender and true self-forgetting awaken. Where there is this understanding of your own act, Communion with Me follows as a spontaneous event.

If the feeling of non-separation is awake, it is not necessary to achieve union or re-union with anything or anyone, even the Divine. And the feeling of non-separation is simply a matter of transcending your own act of contraction. The realization of non-separation, or the feeling of relatedness, is the inherent characteristic of existence. If you transcend your own act of self-contraction, or separation, then, even in the midst of conditional existence, you are in an entirely different position than most people presume.

Human beings function by tendency on the basis of self-contraction, uninspected. Therefore, they function irresponsibly. People are always seeking union with this or that. If there is responsibility for the self-contraction, if the feeling of non-separation, or relatedness, is allowed to awaken spontaneously, then you exist in the field of apparent relations in an entirely different fashion than people ordinarily do.

In your intimate life, for instance, you are always unioning with one another, always approaching one another through the feeling of separation, and wanting this or that satisfaction from one another to overcome the feeling of separation. You are driven to one another by your own contraction, your own egoity. If you were responsible for the self-contraction, if you were awake to the feeling of non-separation, or relatedness, then you would not try to get to union or re-union with someone from whom you were separate. You would live in the disposition of non-separation. The disposition of non-separation changes all acts in your apparent relationships, changes them all. They cease to be seeking acts and instead become harmonious events manifested by one who is awake to the clarity of non-separateness. And on that basis, everything can be simplified, everything can be set right. As with your intimate relationships, so with everything.

If you are only seeking, everything is a matter of seeking. Therefore, everything can be changed, everything can be transformed, if your disposition is transformed, changed at its root, changed from self-contraction and the pursuit of union into the relinquishment of that action and its search, changed into the feeling of relatedness. In that case, the seeking vanishes inherently. Without having to do anything to it, the principle that underlies the search is gone. The search has no existence then. Everything becomes Yoga, then, or a matter of "conductivity". Everything is entered into responsibly as a "conscious process", based on the direct transcendence of the self-contraction.

If you are truly attracted to Me and are not bargaining with Me, if you stop playing the self-contraction and the search, if you understand your own activity and approach Me rightly, simply on the basis of your devotional attraction to Me, then the feeling of non-separation from Me awakens. When the feeling of relatedness in relation to Me awakens, self-surrender and self-forgetting occur with ease, directly. That is true Ishta-Guru-Bhakti

Yoga. This is what makes it Yoga. Ishta-Guru-Bhakti in My Company is not just some stressful seeker's devotion trying to achieve union with Me, feeling separate all the while, separating from Me all the while. Ishta-Guru-Bhakti is not that—it is the true ecstasy of Communion with Me, based on self-understanding, self-responsibility. That is Ishta-Guru-Bhakti Yoga.

This is why I say to you that there are two fundamental elements to the Way of the Heart. Fundamentally, the Way of the Heart is just this devotional Communion with Me. But that devotion requires self-understanding. Therefore, the Way of the Heart requires both. Without such self-understanding, you will practice even devotion to Me as an extension of your own seeking. In other words, you will not practice it as true Yoga.

◆ ◆ ◆

AVATARA ADI DA: Very simply, true devotion awakens if you allow yourself to be attracted by Me, drawn into Communion with Me, just by the sighting of Me. But in that process you also observe the mechanism of your own contraction. It is not difficult to relinquish your activity in that case. You may think there is some sort of effort involved, but there is none whatsoever.

I have used the analogy of you pinching yourself. You are feeling some pain and you are motivated to get rid of your pain, so you taste this, touch that, have sex with this, read, think, blah, blah, blah, blah, blah, whatever it is, to get rid of your pain. But if you could just notice your own activity, or if somebody could draw your attention to the fact that you are pinching yourself, there is no effort involved in taking your fingers away. You are glad to do it! And then the pain and the motivation to seek pass. When you are truly observing the self-contraction, it is easy to relinquish. The relinquishment does not require any effort. It occurs rather spontaneously, in fact. All the effort takes place when you are not truly observing the self-contraction but are trying to deal with this, that, or the other thing that you are seeking because you are contracted, but that is peripheral to the contraction itself. The effort takes place when you are struggling to get rid of all of that. That is seeking, then. The effort to get rid of something is seeking. When you truly discover the cause, the relinquishment of the contraction is spontaneous, and the seeking, likewise, is spontaneously relinquished, because it has no foundation.

You do not have to try to get rid of the pain of the pinch when you take your fingers away. All the seeking that your pinching yourself might have otherwise motivated, or that it previously motivated, disappears without effort, because it has no foundation anymore. You do not have to read and try to figure out the universe because you are in pain. The pain is not there. You no longer feel separate from Reality, or from any reality. Rather, the feeling of relatedness, the feeling of non-separation, is magnified in the heart spontaneously.

◆ ◆ ◆

DEVOTEE: Beloved Bhagavan, are You saying that the fundamental way we will observe this action of separation is in observing our seeking for union?

AVATARA ADI DA: See that you are only seeking. Examine yourself and find this out. Understand that seeking is a pursuit of union. This is obvious, is it not?

Your search is like this: You go to bed with your girlfriend or boyfriend in order to get a good feeling. You go to meditate to get a good feeling. You practice devotion to Me to get a good feeling. You have lunch to get a good feeling. And getting that good feeling is the purpose of your seeking. It releases some level of your stress. You think that unioning, the success of the effort towards union, the adjacency to this, that, or the other thing, will give you a little bit of good feeling. You are always seeking to achieve that in everything you are doing. You are always seeking to achieve that feeling of release, that good feeling. This is why you do everything you do. Everything you are doing, you are doing in order to achieve that good feeling. And you think that that is the goal of life.

That has nothing whatever to do with the Way of the Heart. That is what you are already doing, and that is what you must find out. You are always seeking, and you are full of stress in that seeking. Your seeking is always an effort to achieve union with this, that, or the other thing. And whenever you get this thing or the other, whatever it may be, whenever you perform that action you want to perform with whatever you have acquired, you get a good feeling. An orgasm is just such a good feeling. That is what you are looking for all the time.

Why do you read books? Watch TV? Try to figure things out? Why? Because you are looking to come to the point of that good feeling, where there is some sense of release from stress, but whatever release you may achieve is not consequential, not final. There is no self-understanding in it. It is not the end of seeking. It is just one moment to be followed by another pursuit.

You must find out about yourself as a seeker. The first thing you must find out is that you are a seeker, and that seeking is all you are doing. Take a look at everything you are doing. Seeking is all you are doing. There is no moment of your life when you are not doing it. There is no circumstance in your life in which you are not doing it. There is no relationship in which you are not doing it. If you get a good feeling, it is like an orgasm. There is a temporary feeling of satisfaction, but you are still sitting there separate, all by yourself as you are, still sitting on your own uninspected knot. But because you get the moment of good feeling, you try and repeat it over and over again with everything you do.

But you do not even get that feeling every time. When you go to bed with your boyfriend or girlfriend, you do not get all that you would like to get every time. But that does not stop the search. The good feeling happens often enough that you keep doing it.

But nothing has been transcended. The actual nature of conditional existence has not been found. The presumption of separation still exists. You may have achieved some sort of feeling relative to some object or other, but that is not it. Something sexual with an intimate partner or a good lunch or a vision of the Divine Star* or some other visionary or mystical experience and so forth—they are all objects pursued by the same seeker for the same reason, and it just throws you back on yourself. Whether you are in the good feeling or dwelling in the stresses of seeking, it is all just the same. It is just you presuming to be separate, still not having understood.

Even your relationship to Me is not pure, not free of this seeking. You are doing it with Me. You are carrying on some action or other in relation to Me that is a seeker's effort toward union.

◆ ◆ ◆

AVATARA ADI DA: You are trying to feel good. Every one of you, right now, is trying to feel good. You want to feel good because you feel bad. You always already feel bad. Always already, you feel bad! Not good—BAD! You always feel bad, and through your seeking you want to feel good. Here and there, using all of the methods you can generate in your daily life, you get a little spell of relief—just brief. How long does the pleasure of an orgasm last? [Snaps His fingers.] Just like that—very brief. Almost instantly, you are cruising back to feeling bad. Even when people go into fifth stage conditional Nirvikalpa Samadhi,[2] almost as soon as they get there, they are cruising back—almost immediately.

2. "Nirvikalpa" means "without form". Hence, "Nirvikalpa Samadhi" means literally "deep meditative concentration (or absorption) without form (or defined experiential content)". Traditionally this state is the final goal of the many schools of Yogic ascent whose orientation to practice is that of the fifth stage of life. Fifth stage conditional Nirvikalpa Samadhi is an isolated or periodic Realization in which attention ascends beyond all conditional manifestation into the formless Matrix of the Spirit-Current or Divine Light infinitely above the world, the body, and the mind. Because it is produced by manipulation of attention and of the body-mind, the sublime bliss of fifth stage conditional Nirvikalpa Samadhi cannot be maintained when attention returns, as it inevitably does, to the states of the body-mind.

You are always motivated to feel better, no matter what you are doing. My father was a salesman, like some of you here. He was always under stress, a chain smoker and all the rest. He would talk and talk and talk, all the time, always under stress. Why did he do it? He had all his reasons—to support his family, and so on. But he was an addict. He was addicted to it. He only got to feel good when he made a sale. It is like getting off in an orgasm or something. You get a little bit of good feeling by making that sale, exchanging back-slapping and grins with the other salesmen and so forth, and then it is back on the streets, back to the stress again.

You think you want to be a big success. You imagine that there is a sale that ends all sales and then you will feel good forever. That is part of the illusion of salesmen—this one big hit sale after which you do not have to be a salesman anymore, because you just feel good forever! It is an illusion, a myth. Similarly, you go to bed with your intimate partner expecting it is going to be one of those occasions after which you will not want sex anymore because you will just feel good forever.

You are always feeling bad and looking to feel good. You have all kinds of techniques in your life that sometimes produce a little bit of feeling good and that lead you to feel, "That is all there is—just feeling a little better here and there." You make a total life out of the stress of the search and temporary moments of minimal release, because you never deal with the self-contraction itself and the illusion it produces. You never deal with your divorce from Reality. You never Realize the Inherent Condition, the Native Condition of non-separation. When you deal with the root of all of your seeking, not only does the seeking vanish, but the Truth is Realized—the Truth that is Reality, that is the Divine, Which Is Self-Sufficient, Self-Existing, Self-Radiant, all Love-Bliss, not confounded, not a seeker, not separate. This is what there is to Realize, but it cannot be Realized by seeking.

Find out you are always seeking. Find out that your seeking is never finally fulfilled. Find out that you are always under stress. This is how you wear out the method. This is how you get sick of it—by examining what you are up to. When you are sick of it, a kind of despair awakens that is also associated with great intelligence, or a willingness to examine the matter more profoundly, to examine the matter I am bringing to you. This is about great practice. This is about great Realization. This is about great self-transcendence.

You will not get really serious about it until you wear out your search, until you find out that you are always seeking and that you are always under stress and that the search never fulfills itself. The best you are getting out of it is a temporary release here and there. You feel a little better for a couple of seconds and then it is gone. An occasional hit—that is all you are getting out of life. The rest of it is pain and illusion.

It is not just that you are feeling bad, it is that you are making yourself feel bad. That is what you have to find out. The self-contraction is the "why" you feel bad. It is the bad feeling itself. And you are doing it. That is what you have to find out. You must become capable of transcending your own activity, moment by moment, in the context of your devotional relationship with Me.

**Adi Da (The Da Avatar)**
**The Mountain Of Attention, 1995**

## SECTION THREE

# What Are Your Conclusions About Reality?

Human beings must awaken from their solid pose of intellectual superiority and their irrational belief that knowledge <u>about</u> the process of natural phenomena makes a superior humanity. A superior humanity will not be derived from authoritarian scientific decrees, imposed through powerful technologies. People cannot live Happily, nor survive long, without the intuitive certainty of Divine Love, or Spiritual Communion with Divine Power, Love-Bliss, and Purpose. Without greater religious consciousness (free of the dogmatic nonsense of conventional religious beliefs), the future made by scientific acculturation is an abominable fiction, a mechanical contrivance in which human beings are, paradoxically, both satisfied in their desires and desperate in their hearts.

ADI DA (THE DA AVATAR)
*Scientific Proof of the Existence of God*
*Will Soon Be Announced by the White House!*

---

*In this section, Adi Da critiques scientific materialism: the philosophy that "reality"—the world and everything in it—is an objective "other" that we can understand and control. And He argues that our true situation is one of "Divine Ignorance"—that we actually do not know and never can know what reality is; that we are not meant to be knowers but lovers; that our purpose is to ecstatically participate with all of reality, and to commune with Reality Itself—with Divine Consciousness, Happiness, and Freedom.*

# CHAPTER 12

# The Asana of Science

*October 25, 1980*
*from* The Transmission of Doubt

AVATARA ADI DA: Science is commonly described as a way of observing the natural world, a method of excluding or abstracting the viewer from the process of observation, so that what is observed is a "reality" untainted by the presence of the viewer. This process of acquiring knowledge is concerned not with transforming the viewer but with learning about the so-called objective, or natural, world independent of the viewer.

Now, this is an interesting notion of human activity. People are so used to the presence of science and technology in today's culture that they accept science as a natural activity, a sort of professionalization, or technical elaboration, of something that everybody is already doing. But the activity of science may not be natural at all. It is something you are already doing when you conceive of the objective, or natural, world apart from yourself. Yet if you become sensitive to the real condition of your existence, can you truly say that you ever experience or have anything whatsoever to do with an objective world? Do you ever contact anything objective, or independent of yourself?

The common presumption of daily human life is that there is an objective world, but this presumption is simply a convention of egoic life and of present-day society. Science bases its sophisticated activity upon this conventional view of life. It seems natural enough to say that you live in the physical world. You are sitting around here in this physical world with many other people, right? To speak of a physical or objective world is simply a convention of your existence, whereas in fact you do not have any actual experience of an objective, or independent, world. Your actual experience is much more complex and undefined than that convention suggests.

You refer to yourself as "me" and "I", but if you were asked what "I" is, how could you ever come to the end of the description? Obviously you have not entered into an exhaustive self-analysis or observation of yourself before using the terms "me" and "I" as self-references. If you understand how you presume the reality of a so-called objective world, you will not find an "I" that could possibly have so much as a foot inside a physical world or that can be so defined and confined. This "I", which is ultimately only conscious awareness, this individual being that is aware of phenomena, has no direct connection to an independently objective world.

The conscious being is related to a so-called objective world through the process of conception and perception. You conceive and you perceive and therefore you presume an objective world, but you do not in fact have any actual contact with the world itself. You are associated with perceptions but not with the world. Thus, you never directly experience a "world" as an independent reality. Yet as you experience this whole affair of perception and conception, you make certain conventional judgments. You establish certain conventions of thought, communication, and action whereby you say things like "There is this external world here" and "I am me, and you are you". You say these things, but they are purely conventional statements with no ultimate philosophical stability. The notion of a physical world in which you exist is a conventional notion, an idea, a presumption on which you can act, but a presumption you need not even share with others. It is not universally accepted that there is an independent gross physical world. Many other cultures have had totally different views of reality, and they have used other conventions to determine their behaviors, relations, and ideas.

Science presumes to seek direct knowledge about a world that is independent of human beings. In doing so it has created other effects that have cultural, psychological, and even Spiritual significance. Science has become the dominant point of view of society everywhere, and it thus has established a way of life wherein human beings universally presume that the "real world" is the physical world and that the world of the psyche, the so-called internal realm, is unreal, or merely caused by the external world. Thus, science abandons the primary feature of human experience. In fact, you could even say that science is not a truly human activity, because in its pursuit what is specifically human—the inherence of personal consciousness in the Divine Reality—is fundamentally suppressed, abstracted, and separated out.

According to the philosophy of science, people are supposed to pursue knowledge about the external world, rather than participate in a total world wherein reality includes not only the objects of perception and conception but the process of perception and conception as well as the conditional being, or living consciousness, in which perception and conception are experienced or acknowledged. Science does not presume reality to be the total human condition. It presumes reality to be external to the human condition, and in its study of that reality it suppresses the human condition as a medium of association with phenomena. Therefore, science has chosen the so-called external world as the real world and presumes that all the other dimensions of existence with which human beings are directly associated are unreal, or simply caused by the "real" world, which is the gross, physical, material, external universe.

In Truth the condition of your existence includes more than the so-called external world. You are always simply existing, simply conscious. Every other feature of your existence is an object to your own living consciousness. If a thought arises, it is witnessed, or observed, in consciousness. If a sensation arises, it is witnessed. If a room is perceived, it is witnessed. The fundamental aspect of your experience, therefore, is this living consciousness, which has no features of its own. Everything arises as an object to this living consciousness through a spontaneous process of perception and conception.

That process of conceiving and perceiving notices and experiences various forms, some of which are related to what is called the "external", gross world and others of which cannot be found there at all. For instance, you cannot always find the environments of your dreams in the gross world—at least according to the conventions of thinking, you could say that you cannot find them there. You associate the many levels of conceived and perceived objects with different dimensions of experience. Therefore, there is living being, or living consciousness, and there are the processes of conception and perception, and then there are various forms, gross and subtle, that are interpreted and evaluated according to various conventions. But your actual situation includes all three of these fundamental conditions—the living consciousness, conception and perception, and forms—in dynamic association with one another.

Science is a human invention and a development of one specific convention of interpreting reality exclusive of other possible conventions. Thus, in the scientific convention, living consciousness in association with the process of the conception and perception of forms becomes a single conventional presumption at the level of human relations in space and time. The conception of "me" or "I" is basically the process of conception and perception referring to itself. This body-mind, or the process of conception-perception, calls itself "I". It refers to itself as if it has thoroughly investigated itself and thus knows exactly what it is meaning when it says "me" or "I". But the "I" is just a convention of reference, not necessarily the product of a thorough analysis of its true nature. "I" is a rather intuitive gesture, but it is also just a convention that permits ordinary communication and activity.

Therefore, if the process of conception and perception is uninspected, it conceives of itself as an independent self over against all possible forms that arise. Once this presumption is made (and it is made for very ordinary reasons), it is possible to say things like "There is the external universe."

But to call the realm of conceived and perceived forms an "external universe" does not signify that one understands anything profound or that one has understood the true Nature of that realm, any more than to say "I" or "me" means that one has thoroughly analyzed and understood the conditional self. It is simply a convention of reference.

Scientific activity is not inherently evil, but it does become an evil or destructive force if it is permitted to dominate one's world-view and to remain unaccountable to one's total realization of existence. In the present time the conventions of science have been taken absolutely seriously, as if such conventions had ultimate philosophical force, and the materialistic point of view of science has been permitted to do great psychological harm to humanity. By divorcing reality from the realm of people's actual existence, science has attributed reality to that which is apparently outside your existence. It has made the so-called physical universe the realm of reality, and it regards everything else to be an effect of the material world.

The reality of the external world to which science points has no psychic depth. It is a plastic mass of events. When scientists study the human being, they want to prove that the mind, the psyche, and the essential being are the effect of bodily existence and thus the effect of matter. They conclude that if the mind is caused by matter, then it is basically unreal, secondary, not a primary reality. From that point of view, however, to pursue knowledge about reality one must dissociate from one's own being and find a way to become involved with a so-called external, objective world. Science as such a discipline of knowledge can be of value, but as a point of view about existence it is destructive and psychotic.

You do not exist merely in a physical universe. You exist in a multidimensional condition, every aspect of which is totally real and mutually related to all other aspects. These many dimensions condition one another and bring one another into existence. As a matter of fact, you never observe anything's ever being brought into existence. Existence is an inherent Attribute of the Divine Reality. All these appearances are just transformations, or changes. Nothing ever comes into existence. Nothing ever passes out of existence. Things only change. They become apparent and unapparent, identifiable in one moment and unidentifiable in the next. This truth is demonstrated in the law of the conservation of energy conceived by modern physics, which states that energy is never destroyed but is, rather, ceaselessly transformed.

In the ancient world essential human existence, as well as social and cultural existence, was not created and defined by the point of view of science or anything like science. Even though some science-like enterprises may have developed in those times and places, the fundamental conceptions, or presumptions, that created the model of human existence and established the circumstances and processes of daily life were often based on a total and fully human presumption about the conditions of existence.

Science is a dehumanizing adventure when made into an absolute philosophical point of view, because it chooses a reality independent of human existence as the subject of its investigation, makes that reality the force that defines human existence, and makes the physical universe senior to, superior to, or more real than one's essential being and the subtler dimensions in which one participates constantly. Science excludes the subtle dimensions of energy, the dimensions of psyche, and the dimension of essential being, or the living consciousness. But all these conditions are your true Condition. The mere external, or objective, physical world, which is only a conventional notion anyway, is a fraction of the total Condition of which you are directly aware in every moment. The physical universe that science wants to investigate itself represents only a portion, one dimension, of a much broader scale of dimensions in which you participate.

You exist simultaneously in many dimensions. You fluidly move attention through those dimensions. Your attention can pass from gross physical phenomena into thinking, into visions, into revery, into a state transcending all gross consciousness, into psychic awareness of what appear to be environments or worlds that have nothing whatever to do with this one, dissolving in Consciousness Itself, or Being Itself, Which has no references whatsoever, and then moving back again through all of these dimensions one by one. You can, therefore, presume a Condition of existence wherein all these dimensions are simultaneously existing, simultaneously real. But, since science is founded not upon the observer but upon the observed, it does not have this flexibility of movement through many dimensions, and it is not possessed of the paradoxes of actual human existence.

Many scientists and people sympathetic with the scientific world-view do not seem capable of thinking about what they are doing. They have no more insight into their presumptions and motives than enthusiastic religionists or "creationists" possess in their domain. Scientists do not rigorously understand that science itself is a chosen, specific development of a single aspect of conventional human understanding. In the enterprise of science the mind and the body are used for a specific kind of work. But apart from that, all the dogma about the total universe and about reality and existence itself, and science's anti-Spiritual, anti-religious, anti-psychic point of view, and its Victorian, archaic materialism, and its prejudices against other kinds of knowing—all of this is insidious, not merely nonsensical, because it has such a profoundly negative effect on human beings.

Meanwhile, many scientists who adopt this dogmatic approach act as if they were super-intelligent people with their tweedy, pipe-smoking, complicated linguistic minds. This is the archetype of intelligence, is it not? This is the way you are supposed to be if you are intelligent. Well, this archetype does not necessarily represent intelligence. It is just a pose. Real intelligence must be fiercely capable of investigating every aspect of existence, including the very process of knowledge that is called "science".

Science has now become so legitimized, and people have become so serious about it, that they are beginning to forget that on a very basic level they feel there is something ridiculous and even threatening about science. When it first appeared, science was regarded as heresy by the Catholic church. Then it became thought of as just craziness, and scientists were always depicted as mad. Madness and science were regarded as the same thing in those days. When science first began to become prominent, before it became really official—at that crossover point from the Middle Ages and the Renaissance into the so-called Age of Enlightenment and then the Romanticism of the nineteenth century—science was regarded to be possibly aberrated. Many stories, such as the tale of Frankenstein, appeared during that time. Science was regarded as a kind of balminess, or madness.

On some level people are still very humorous about science. They know that the left-brained, tweedy character is a poseur, and they know that science is a pose, an asana. Apart from the specific enterprise for which this asana, or pose, of science was invented, it does not represent the disposition wherein one is Divinely Enlightened, Free, Happy, totally associated with all of the factors of one's existence.

To do science one must assume a pose that is not the disposition of the human being contemplating Infinity. When science begins to propose that this asana is the disposition one must assume relative to everything, then it becomes mad. People must be able to reconnect with their humor, their primitive sense of the poseur that they can be and of the ridiculousness of their postures. To live all of life in the pose of science, to make the asana of science a style of living, is like trying to eat dinner while standing on your head!

The Western disposition makes the human being into a moral robot whose only significance is the accomplishment attributed to the few individuals who have made scientific discoveries at critical moments. From the point of view of scientific dogma, those are the only human beings who have really done anything other than be confined to illusions. Everybody else is sort of babbling along in fear, believing all kinds of nonsense. Here and there you find some character in a tweed coat with a pipe who is able to break free of all that and see how objects move in space!

In terms of the ability to observe and comprehend, there is something remarkable about such individuals. But other people have accomplished just as many remarkable things in relation to a totally different way of knowing, a more comprehensive or total way of knowing or realizing human existence. Even so, there are many babbling, frightened people. But one can babble and be frightened as a scientist just as much as one can babble and be frightened as a conventionally religious person.

The true alternative to the extreme pose of science, however, is not the traditional option of orientalism. The oriental enterprise—which not only developed in the East but which has been a feature of humanity all along, East and West—has provided the domain for religion, Spirituality, mysticism, magic, and all the elaborations of the psyche. Because oriental enterprises attribute reality only to the fundamental depth of the subjective being and not to the world of forms, they tend to be ineffectively related to the world of forms. Therefore, if the domains of religion, Spirituality, mysticism, and magic are not held accountable to actual, literal processes, they can develop all kinds of illusions and create views that are purely imaginary, suggestive, or archetypal. Those views may be unified, but the phenomena they are unifying can be totally imaginary, merely psychic and subtle, and only partially objective in relation to the material world. Thus, human mind and human culture, when permitted to develop exclusively along oriental lines, tend to create a culture of illusions.

Science as it is known today appeared historically at a time when religious enterprises (particularly Christianity), dominated by orientalism, had become so filled with illusions that early scientific observations were arbitrarily condemned and anathematized, just as science now arbitrarily condemns and anathematizes non-illusory, real features of psychic and Spiritual realization. Scientific discoveries were declared heretical because they did not square with the assumed imaginary cosmic picture that had been created by religionists. Then, as science itself began to achieve more and more dominance (because it was discovering some real facts), the Church, the religious point of view, the oriental disposition itself, began to be viewed as wrong. Not only were some of its presumptions or ideas presumed wrong, but religion itself was presumed wrong.

Now the world is at the opposite end of this historical pendulum. At one time even the Western world was profoundly associated with the religious consciousness of orientalism (in the form of Christianity, specifically), but now that whole enterprise is presumed to be false. Another world-view, another way of knowledge, another kind of cult, has achieved power and has become associated with the State and the machinery of worldly power, and it is using that position to dominate its opposite.

To transcend the limitations that are obvious at the present time, human beings must transcend all of the historical alternatives. Humanity must transcend the limited disposition of science that now dominates, as well as the limited disposition of the oriental view that seems to be its primary alternative. In order to transcend all these limited features, human beings must simply and directly observe and "consider" their existence as a whole, before making any of these limited presumptions, before assuming or engineering their existence as a choice between the occidental and the oriental dispositions. You must conceive of your existence as it is altogether. You must observe it and see that it is altogether existing and real in every dimension, not just in one dimension or feature. And your real existence, your free and Happy existence, is to be realized only in the asana, the attitude, of your total Condition, rather than in your choice of a single aspect of that Condition.

CHAPTER 13

# Free Inquiry and Scientific Materialism

*December 19, 1992*

AVATARA ADI DA: There is a difference between scientific materialism and science as a discipline. Science as a discipline is a form of
free inquiry that is not supposed to predetermine results or to superimpose a point of view on reality apart from the investigation of reality.

Scientific materialism, however, is a philosophy. It is not science,
although it tends to be associated with the scientific movement. It is an
ancient philosophy, the philosophy of materialism. It is a reductionist philosophy. It reduces reality to what is called "materiality", and it wants to
base all notions of reality on that philosophical presumption.

That is not science. That is a philosophy superimposed on the movement of science. Unfortunately, it seems that the scientific movement has
become very much identified with the philosophy of materialism. Science
as an effort of inquiry, freely done without presumptions, is useful enough
relative to certain kinds of knowledge. Such knowledge is intended to
acquire power over its object. Therefore, even science as free inquiry is
associated with a philosophy of a kind that is an effort to achieve power,
to overcome powerlessness in the face of a reality that is overwhelmingly
powerful and controlling. It is an inclination to gain control over conditional existence so that conditional existence is more predictable, more
under the control of those who are otherwise only suffering it.

In that sense, then, scientific endeavor is not different really from the
efforts of conditionally manifested beings altogether. But apart from that
effort to survive, to know and have power and so on, the imposition of
materialist philosophy on science is not justified.

Recently some of us were playing the game called "Trivial Pursuit". One
of the questions was something like "In 1975, what did eighteen Nobel laureates proclaim has no basis in fact?" The answer was astrology. Another
question had something to do with black holes. Now, the presence of black
holes in space is a theory—black holes have not been directly observed. Still,
a body of scientists feel that the reality of black holes is a possibility worth
pursuing, because they see certain effects taking place in space that suggest

the presence of black holes. They have not declared that the reality of black holes has no basis in fact. They have not yet experienced a black hole directly, but they have not declared that black holes have no basis in fact.

Yet when these Nobel laureates got together and declared that astrology has no basis in fact, they had not involved themselves in an investigation of astrology to the point of determining that it had no basis in fact. They were predisposed to claim that astrology has no basis in fact. Astrology does not fit with their philosophy. Their proclamation is not the result of their investigation, nor had their experience caused them to say astrology has no basis in fact. They are philosophically disinclined to have anybody investigate the matter, to have anything to do with it.

What is the purpose of their proclamation, then? To get people to stop having anything to do with astrology. That is its entire purpose. It is a rather political purpose. It is the common thing done by the gathering of scientific materialists, who anathematize things without truly investigating them. Scientific materialists do things one way or another to prevent people from investigating things they do not think should be investigated.

What is this but a State-based philosophy that decides what you can do, think, even investigate? Yet science is supposed to be about free inquiry within the world-culture, examining reality with clarity, without presumptions that predetermine the result. What business does such a movement have in making such declarations and trying to control what people can do, think, or investigate?

It is generally claimed that the scientific view is superior somehow to movements that previously dictated what people can do, think, or investigate, such as the Catholic church in the West, which once held—and still does hold in some places—control of the State and determined what was appropriate to believe, think, or investigate. Was it not only recently that the Pope declared that Galileo was right? Hundreds of years later! At the time when Galileo was alive, the Catholic church was in charge of politics generally and told people that they could not believe that the Earth is not the center of the universe, for example. It was not permissible even to investigate the matter.

Now people of the scientific materialist faction have gained the power of the State, but they are doing the same thing again. Science is just the new official religion. The same kind of tendency still prevails politically. Scientific materialism is very much a political movement, not merely a philosophy or a body of ideas. It has achieved control politically, socially, and economically. It wants to survive on that basis, and thus we hear proclamations such as "astrology has no basis in fact".

It is not just that millions of silly people read astrological predictions in the newspaper and want to think that maybe they are true. Something about that is perhaps a little, or even entirely, absurd. But it does not mean that astrology altogether has no basis in fact or is not worthy of further investigation. It is just that astrology does not agree with the philosophy of the times, and so it must be anathematized.

Occasionally I look at *Scientific American* magazine, and I noticed a couple of articles about the fact that in Russia many people are becoming interested in things like astrology, metaphysics, UFOs, and non-establishment religious notions of one kind or another. These articles proclaimed that such interest is absolutely wrong and that people should be discouraged from such investigations. The magazine called upon scientists to establish propaganda movements in Russia, to hold conventions there of one kind or another, and to deal with the heads of state to suppress this inclination.

I pointed out these articles to some of My devotees who are science teachers. Then a short time later another magazine arrived, a super-scientific publication not really written for laymen at all. This magazine reported that laws in Europe have been changed recently to regulate the preparation of homeopathic remedies. The article indicated that new regulations have been established to make the requirements for these preparations much more elaborate and strict so as to make it more difficult to use and distribute homeopathic remedies. Homeopathy is not part of the establishment. It does not correspond to the scientific-materialist allopathic view. The scientific establishment does not want to compete with homeopathy, and so devices such as manipulating laws are used to suppress it.

This is the world you live in now, a world where scientific materialism is essentially—certainly in the Western world and more and more worldwide—the official religion of the State. It is not that the scientific materialist movement has investigated all kinds of things that may have been traditionally believed or pursued and found them to be unworthy. It is philosophically disinclined to pursue them or to allow anybody else to pursue them.

Therefore, understand that scientific materialism is a rather official, organized, philosophical point of view that has identified itself with State politics. And this is its special characteristic. Science is not that. Science is not inherently identified with materialism or with such politics. Science is just a form of free inquiry. Yes, it is intended to gain power over natural existence, but it is not inherently identified with materialism. It has the potential to discover something more.

At the leading edge of science, particularly in the realm of physics, the discoveries, the theories tested, and so forth are suggesting that reality is of a different nature than could possibly be described as material. Having come to such a point of view, scientists are finding themselves in a difficult situation because science takes place in the world of scientific materialism.

Much of what the leading edge of physics and of science in general is proposing and also discovering does not square with scientific materialism. Therefore, science has again become the circumstance of controversy and conflict.

If scientists are to obtain grants of money from the State and be legitimized by the State, anything they do must square with the philosophy of scientific materialism. Basically that is the obligation.

In the Western world, the Catholic church was at one time in charge of the State and could determine what people could think and do and investigate. Now there is also an official philosophical, or what could be called "religious", point of view. And it becomes the measure of everything. If you want to get the money, have political power, be legitimized, be employed, you must somehow show that you are one with that point of view, that doctrine.

Several hundred years ago one had to prove that whatever one was doing and saying and thinking was allowable within Catholic Christian doctrine. Even more recently, the Communist movement, for example, has been an official doctrine of the State, a kind of religion or pseudo-religion. To survive, to be legitimized, in that State, one had to somehow convince people that one was toeing the line of that doctrine. This is an unfortunate situation, and one that is repeated over and over again. Right now, all human beings are in general living in this same situation. This is the politics of the world you live in.

You may imagine that because you may live in what is called a "free society" the politics of your society is all about free inquiry, the freedom to investigate. You should be much more sensitive to the controlling influences that exist even in the present situation.

# CHAPTER 14

# You Do Not Know
# What a Single Thing Is

*December 23, 1977*

*As this Talk opens, Avatara Adi Da is speaking of an object He has received, a dzi stone. The lore around this kind of stone, Adi Da says, is that they were produced by men who lived in ancient times on Earth.*

AVATARA ADI DA: Many thousands of years ago in previous yugas, or cycles of time, people used to wear dzi stones around their necks or elsewhere on their bodies for protection from the implications of their sinning. They did not rely on the dzi stone itself—the dzi stone was simply a fetish that represented a cultural obligation they personally assumed. When things became really difficult, they would be relieved of their difficulties magically through their ritual association with the mechanics of the universe. This association and its liberating effect were reflected in the dzi stones they wore on their bodies.

Legend has it that people in those ancient times lived to be hundreds, many hundreds, of years of age. But in the span of human possibilities in this yuga, this great epoch, at twenty to forty years of age you are all very close to being at least half way through your lives! And you know very well you can go in an instant! Luckily, a yuga lasts thousands of years, so you can be reborn many times.

But what if the notion of reincarnation is not even true? Maybe all those who have died were completely snuffed. Maybe in that moment, just for a moment, you briefly lose consciousness . . . maybe that is it!

If you observe only the mechanics of the fleshiness of things, it is very easy to believe that death is the final event. But if you are possessed by the Vision of the Infinite and Eternal Circumstance in which you live, and if you are able to be sensitive to the totality of your living, not just the fleshy part, then you already know very well that death is just a moment. It all goes on.

I personally can vouch to you that life is eternal, that Consciousness Itself is without end, and without beginning. You are all involved in something that will continue for billions upon billions, magnified by geometrical numbers to the fiftieth billionth power, of years, for Eternity. But, just as now, you will have no memory then. You will be the representation of the past, but you will not remember it. Not only that—no matter what arises, in the eternity of lives that confront you, you will never know what even a single thing _is_.

Look at this dzi stone. All kinds of people have been associated in their lifetimes with this stone, and they all were as confused as you. They were all trying, struggling in this place, without definition, totally confused and mystified. And you all also admit, tacitly, to the necessity for confusion in Mystery. If there is Mystery, not conceptual knowledge, no content or hope that informs you, you all think that there must be confusion. But as a matter of fact, no matter what happens, confusion is not necessary. And Mystery, or Divine Ignorance, is your Real Condition.

"Consider" this ashtray. This very ashtray itself is the object that I have used for some time now to demonstrate and "consider" this necessary philosophy, or "love of wisdom", relative to Divine Ignorance. This is the object I have used. And I have said to you on occasion, and it remains true even to this day, that, from a practical point of view, from a chemical point of view, from an aesthetic point of view, from the point of view of any kind of ordinary discipline of knowing, you may know all kinds of things about this ashtray and its origin and its content. But no matter what you may know about it, before and after and while you know anything about it, you do not know what it _is_. I mean what it _is_ . . . _is_ . . . you have not the slightest knowledge of what it _is_. And none of your experience increases your awareness of what it _is_.

This same logic pertains to everything. No matter what you may come to realize by experience about anything, you still do not know what it _is_. All of you belong to this realm of ambiguity. None of you knows what any other human being _is_. You just simply do not know it. In your practical involvement with one another, you know about one another—but you do not know what you _are_. Knowledge, in other words, does not penetrate to this degree. It never has.

This failure is not just a reflection of the silliness or stupidity of ancient beings. It is also fundamentally a reflection upon your own existence, and also, therefore, upon the existence of all other beings who have ever lived. The atoms that are in this ashtray have existed for perhaps twenty billion years—far beyond the mere five billion of the Earth. They come out of the manifested cosmos, from the center of the explosion that supposedly manifested everything.

Human beings know very little about anything, ultimately. And human beings do not know what anything _is_ in fact. Thus, your mind itself, your own existence, is totally, unqualifiedly, inevitably, irrevocably, and irreducibly Ignorant. No one, regardless of his or her sophistication or experience, knows what a single thing is. Not what anything is, you see. This presumption could have been made at any time in the past, and it can be made at any time in the future. No matter how much experience intervenes, no matter how sophisticated men and women become, no matter how much you may know about anything through experience, you still do not and will not know what it is. What it is.

What is a shape? What is a place? Where is it? You do not know that. That is not what you know. You presume something about the ultimate affair that is like knowledge, but in fact, you do not know. All that may be said about human understanding, human belief, human experience is this: Not only now, but not at any time in the past, in any civilization, even the most magnificent beyond belief, nor in the future on this Earth in any great moment, nor in any other occasion, any planet, any place, in all of the manifestation of existence, does any individual know what anything is.

Divine Ignorance is the Principle of existence. This is absolutely true. You do not know what anything is. In Truth, you are totally mindless, and totally beyond consolation or fulfillment, because there is no way to know what anything is. The only thing you can know about anything is still about it. But you do not know what it is . . . is . . . is . . . or why it happens to be. You have not the slightest knowledge of what it is. And no one has ever had it. Not anyone. Not Jesus, not Moses, not Mohammed, not Gautama, not Krishna, not Tukaram,[1] not even Me—no one has ever known what a single thing is. Not the most minute, ridiculous particle of anything. No one has ever known it, and no one ever will know it, because human beings are not knowing. You do not know what anything is. The summarization of your existence is Mystery, absolute, unqualified confrontation with what you cannot know. And no matter how sophisticated you become by experience, this will always be true of you.

This Wisdom-Teaching of Divine Ignorance, then, which I Reveal to you, will never be exceeded. Upon this absolute Truth you must build your life. This Truth is summary, unqualified, irredeemable, irreducible, and absolute. It can never be changed. No matter what sophisticated time may appear, no matter when, in the paradox of all of the slices and planes of time, in any moment that may appear in which beings sit together as we do now, no matter what time may appear in which men and women "consider" the moment, no one will ever know what anything is. That is the Truth.

Becoming submitted to that Truth is religious and Spiritual life. It leads you to the transformation of all other occasions. All the possibilities of your experience are transformed by this disposition. Obviously, then, it is very

---

1. Tukaram (1608-1650) was a remarkable Saint of western India. He Taught the way of praising and Communing with the Divine through chanting of the Divine Name and devotional worship.

important to Realize this Divine Ignorance, because it is the only digit at Infinity that can transform your existence. Everything else only modifies your existence and amounts to a contraction in your conscious awareness, a summation upon a point.

You exist in the moment of Eternal Being. Look—everyone who ever looked like you has died. Every one of you will die. In the meantime, you are capable, in the form of your structure, of experiencing all kinds of things, of associating with all kinds of influences. But if you abandon this Truth, this understanding, this Intuition of the Nature of your experience, all experience will accumulate upon you. You will, therefore, adapt to experience in itself, and you will become the reflection of it.

You are awakened to Eternal Being only if you can Realize that the fundamental point of your existence is not knowledge at all. There are no answers. This is the whole point. You do not know at all. You do not know where you are, you do not know who you are, you do not know what you are. You do not know what the future is, you do not know what the past is. You are trying to look good—but you do not know. You are trying through the force of experience to achieve a summation that glamorizes you, but you do not know what anything is. That is the point.

This Realization does not move one to go within at all. It moves one, shattered, into the present pattern of relations without knowledge. No matter what arises in the configuration of your experience, you still do not know what anything is. All the accumulations of your experience move you into moods, attitudes, presumptions, but you still do not know at all. Where is this place? Where is it? Where is it? Where is it, exactly? I mean, really? You haven't the slightest idea. Nobody has any idea. No matter who may claim your worship, nobody knows. Some people may look better than others, but still, nobody knows.

DEVOTEE: Heart-Master, this description of our existence implies extreme vulnerability.

AVATARA ADI DA: On the basis of this logic that you do not know what anything is, that you are not in control, it is clear that you are not even created by anything objective and absolute. You are in a Condition of absolute, unqualified Mystery. That Condition is what obliges you in your attention and your feeling. That is what it is to be a man or a woman: to be rested at Eternity without any consolations whatsoever.

There is no Truth within. There is no Truth in the past, and there is no Truth in the future. Having no consolations, you exist in this moment, floating in space, wherever that is, totally sublimed, beyond consolation or belief, without the slightest fraction of abstract verbal knowledge to console you, without the slightest fleshy prominence standing out against the

Eternal to make you happy. That is your Condition. That is the Truth of it. That is it. That is all there is to it. And it is not an answer. There are no answers in it. All your struggling for information, for answers, is just more of the same old foolishness. It is open-ended. You go to your death without knowledge. Thus, you also go to your life without knowing.

Nevertheless, there is an obvious Law: Everything does change. Everything prominent passes. Everything that appears is temporary. And, therefore, the Law of the universe is change itself, the sacrifice of everything present. Having realized that there is no knowledge, having seen that everything changes, how shall you live?

Even though nothing comes from it, the ultimate pleasure to which you may sacrifice yourself is at best someone else's pleasure. What if you were to sit down to dinner and eat a lobster? You might enjoy yourself, but it would be dead. And if it had been able during its lifetime to conceive of this meal as the ultimate moment toward which it was progressing through sacrifice, even so, the moment of being eaten is totally unavailable to its consciousness. Thus, there is no moment toward which you move by sacrifice. Sacrifice, the disposition of love, is simply the Law.

Sacrifice is inherently Happy, inherently Free. It has no answers. That is all I can tell you. It is not that I can tell you concretely that something will happen. Yes, things will happen, but they will also pass. Yes, you will survive your death, I can guarantee you that. But you will survive it in another form that also dies. Everything will change. Thus, it is not in time that you have the Eternal Vision. It is in the moment, in your disposition of devotional Communion with Me, in your love, in your sacrifice, by throwing everything away and being totally willing to be dead. In that case, you are not only free in this moment, you are also profoundly Happy, and ridiculous.

No one is here to give you any answers. There is no "Creator" Deity in charge of you, like a parent. There is no such Person, no God like that, nor any Spiritual Master like that. I am here to instigate this love, or sacrifice, in you, and there is no answer, no result. The act itself is the Happiness. If you can begin to become fully sympathetic to this Argument that I bring to you, then you will simply be Happy and completely bereft of answers. If you can sacrifice your egoic self to Me, then there is something else to be Realized.

There was a time—actually I do not know whether you can understand this or not, because it occurred before I was born, in the process through which I became born—when there was Realization beyond time and space. I animated that Realization throughout the stupid adventure of My Life. To you My Life may be inspiring, but to Me it is stupid. To Me, to be submitted to this kind of argument, this working out of living forms, is a torment, and completely terrifying. I do not think you are so sensitive to it, because you still like to indulge yourself. To Me it is all terrifying, every single moment of it, unless there is the Intuition of God, of Eternal Being, the motive of sacrifice and of present Happiness, not the tendency toward future Happiness. The moment of sacrifice is itself Happiness. It is simply free. There is neither conditional knowledge nor content in that moment.

That is it. That is the absolute summation of God-Knowledge. No one, including Me, will ever tell you anything better. That is it. Now, work it out—but you will still die.

"Consider" the configuration of your relations. You sit here relatively happy. But think of all of the other billions upon billions upon billions of living beings. Not just the other billions of human beings on Earth—think of the billions of beings in this room. Every time you take a breath—are you all breathing while I am talking to you?—you suck in and snuff out billions of beings, tiny, organized, self-conscious, knowledgeless, stupid, defenseless, incarnate entities. In your breathing, in your ingestion, in your thinking and talking, in your loving and your lovemaking, in everything that you do, you are responsible for the murder of billions of beings every day. And you are no more important than they in the scheme of Infinity. It seems to you that you take a little while longer in life than the amoeba on your eyebrow, but what do you amount to? You are eaten, snuffed out, murdered, pulverized, shaken in your snuffing, just like all of these poor little creeps, and there is no opportunity for Happiness except through the Intuition of the Real. If the Real manufactures all this devastating insanity, that is Its business. Your business is to be Happy, to Realize, in My Company, the Logic that is at the Core of God and remain Happy.

Without that Intuition there is no way to be Happy in the face of mere experience. Somebody recently told Me he saw a construction worker who suffered a terrible accident. Demolition workers were smashing a building, using one of those incredible, giant lead balls to crush a wall. I don't know how it happened, but the lead ball hit the man in the head as he stood on a scaffold. He survived, but with only about one-third of a face. The rest of it was a concave, smashed, disgusting mass. Such a possibility is also yours. It does not make any difference how much you love, how much insight you enjoy—you could be snuffed out. You may even continue to live in that kind of wretched form.

I read a story some weeks ago about a soldier in the Vietnam War. The man in front of him stepped on a bomb or a mine and a fragment of shell hit the soldier above the eyebrow and leaped through his brain. Now half of his brain is missing—they had to amputate half of his brain! <u>You</u> can experience that. The possibilities for life are not just magnificent—they are disgusting. If you are committed to the "Great Plan" itself, you must admit that you can suffer far more than you can enjoy. Now that you have appeared in a form, there is far more to suffer than there is to enjoy.

You must give it all up—all of it—the enjoyments and the torments, in your Communion with Me. And then you will enjoy the Vision of the Eternal and move through the paradox of changes in God. I do not know why that is. I do not know why that Vision is the only possibility for Happiness—but it certainly is the only possibility for Happiness.

Whether there is a future beyond death or not is for you to discover. All the dead are heroes, but nobody knows about them. Nobody knows where they are, or what anything is. What a life! What a moment!

DEVOTEE: What a plan!

AVATARA ADI DA: Yes. So do not be stupid and cruel people. Be a little more humorous and loving, and acknowledge your friends compassionately. All of them are fleshily presented, and dying. All of your women friends, all of your men friends—everyone who lives is dying and is confronted with the most incredible circumstance. All are deserving of your love and compassion, and also of your demand for the discipline of love beyond egoic "self-possession"[2] (or self-absorption), so that they too can enjoy the intuition of this Happiness. Everyone is dying. All of these shapes get snuffed out with trembling stupidity and insanity. When the body dies, the brain becomes active for a moment, it begins to show you lighted shapes and to dissolve you beyond the elements. First you get fleshy, and then you get watery, then you get fiery, then you get airy, then you start screaming and nobody can hear you, and the body shakes all over the place, and then you are dead. I certainly wish you could acknowledge it while you are alive. If you can, you will love somebody, and if you cannot, you will not.

Do not pretend that you live in a Disney world of beauty. This life is many-sided, and you do not know what it is. And your Happiness depends on the total inspection of this life. Understand the situation you are in and become manly (male or female) on the basis of this observation, so that you may be lovers and friends. Acknowledge this terrible circumstance and be Happy, and stop placing stupid obligations on one another. You exist in a place that is open-ended, an edge to the Eternal, and you are dying. The only way you can comprehend this complication is by sacrificing it and becoming a lover and a friend. Nothing else you may project in your lifetime can change that. You are still a fleshy, homely being that can be crushed by circumstance.

2. Conventionally, "self-possessed" means possessed of oneself—or in full control (calmness, or composure) of one's feelings, impulses, habits, and actions. Adi Da uses the term to indicate the state of being possessed by one's egoic self, or controlled by chronically self-referring (or egoic) tendencies of attention, feeling, thought, desire, and action.

You all, however, are still organized around your experience and your possibility. You have not gone mad yet. You have not become disorganized yet in God. You are still profoundly oriented, in your desiring and in the mechanics of your motivation, toward ordinary things. Some of those things make you look good and some of those things do not make you look good. That is the summation of your life. But Spiritual life is about Truth, not about a cure. It is about the inspection and acknowledgement of this torment in which you live. Having penetrated it, you may realize the Sublimity that Transcends this life, but you will not realize something else. You will just enjoy the capability to be free while alive, so that this life may pass away. It must pass in any case.

I am not listening to voices, you see. I do not have any visions. I have had visions, I have heard voices. I have done everything that you yet look forward to, enclosed as you are in the first three stages of life. You think, "Oh, beyond here it is all so beautiful." I can just hear it. Nonsense! All of it is a torment, all of it is stupid, all of it is terrible, until you penetrate it and become free, objectless, diffuse, and absolutely unqualified Happiness. Then everything will fall away from you, and you may be restored to the light-speed of Existence even while alive and also at your death, and far less of the paradoxical eternity of manifestation may be your destiny. But in life itself I cannot promise you any more.

Sooner or later you must come to the point of the absolute despair in which you will be Awakened to absolute Happiness. And when, in My Love-Blissful Company, you have become Awakened to absolute Happiness, life will fall away. In the meantime, you will be a lover, you will be Happy, and you will generate the force of that Happiness to your friends, but you will die, and so will they. There are no answers in this lifetime. And that is it.

CHAPTER 15

# The Divine Trickster Talks Wild

*by the Adidam Writers Guild*

L
ate in the night of February 19, 1979, a group of devotees were gathered with Avatara Adi Da in His residence at the Mountain Of
Attention Sanctuary in Northern California. They had been up for
hours "considering" His Wisdom-Teaching—talking, laughing, and enjoying
Avatara Adi Da's Presence. Now, as the evening proceeded, Adi Da became
less and less apparently serious, smiling roundly, laughing uproariously,
teasing everyone and treating them to His irrepressible and Instructive wit
and humor.

Suddenly Adi Da turned to a devotee and said, "Have you ever imagined what it would be like, Aniello, to actually be a duck?"

Aniello reflected for a moment. "No, I never have."

"I can tell you exactly what it is like to be a duck. Exactly. You know
why? Because we are all ducks!"

Laughter erupted throughout the room. Then Adi Da continued, "We
are ducks. You know what I am talking about. Look at yourselves. This is
duck!" Everyone was laughing harder and harder. "These are the characteristics of ducks. We are, in fact, ducks!"

Adi Da leaned back in His chair and roared with laughter. Craig Lesser
grinned as he brought up an objection: "But this is not in Your written
Teaching."

Adi Da continued unfazed: "The ducks have been programmed to realize the next step of evolution beyond them, which is the human being. We
haven't stopped looking like ducks yet. When we become really human,
our essentially duck-like qualities will disappear, and we will have a completely different type of body then. I don't know what it will look like.
Probably something like a human being!" And He burst out laughing again.

"What do you mean, 'something like'?" Aniello asked.

"Well, it won't look like us. We're ducks. It's true—we are ducks."
Then, turning to Craig to answer his earlier objection, Adi Da insisted, "I'm
not kidding you, Craig. This is the truth."

"No, I am not a duck," Craig maintained.

"You are a duck. If I have ever seen anyone who epitomized duckness, Craig, you are it. You have primal duck qualities."

"Oh, no!"

"Oh, yes. Horny little webbed feet. Feathers keep falling out. Well—are we ducks?"

There was a chorus of "no's". Someone in the room quacked, and everyone laughed. After a pause in the conversation, Adi Da commented that no one was saying anything.

"You have to get involved in the language and possibilities of conception. You know what I mean? You guys are not up to talking wild. Are you ready, Aniello? Can you collaborate?"

"I'll certainly try."

"Okay. Try the French Laurel and Hardy."

"I didn't quite understand that. You totally confuse me."

"Radio Me."

"Radio You?" Aniello laughed.

"YTXR-5".

"Y . . ." Aniello was speechless.

"Meet Me in the vestibule. And then try to tell Me you are mistaken."

"What was that supposed to mean?"

"I just told you—you've got to talk wild!"

Aniello doubled up with laughter, and everyone joined in. It was now obviously "cross-over" time, when nothing was going to make sense any more.

Adi Da delivered a spontaneous koan: "Imagine a sound that tastes like an orange. Have you all imagined a sound that tastes like an orange? Have you tasted the orange?"

"Yes."

"Are you hearing the sound and tasting the orange? Hmm?"

William Tsiknas volunteered, "I was just hearing a sound and tasting some cheese."

"You are all listening to some sounds and tasting some cheese and trying to answer My Ultimate Questions!" Adi Da held His head in His hands in theatrical despair. "My Work is a complete failure! I blew my whole gig on you creeps!"

Then He gave an exhausted sigh. "If only you had been more silent about it, William, it would have suddenly become incredibly obvious to all of us that the harp is the only instrument that should be danced upon whenever you get up." There were more peals of laughter throughout the room.

"Can you imagine yourself being an orange? I mean, completely being an orange and nothing but an orange? Can you imagine being an orange to the point of actually becoming an orange? You are a little afraid to do that, aren't you?"

Everyone chuckled in agreement. Then Adi Da began to make a lesson out of the amusement.

"Just so, you are a little afraid to be Spiritually responsible in general. You are afraid to will anything, even what is ultimately good. You fear it, just like you fear thinking about being an orange to the point of actually becoming one. You don't want to think about being <u>anything</u> to the point of actually becoming it. You want to be left alone!" Adi Da laughed again as He drove home His point.

"No doubt about it," Aniello said.

"Right. You want to be let off the hook. Well. As you see, I've got your number. It is 7-6-5-9-3-7-0-0-1-2-4! Now, repeat it back. The whole number."

Nobody could repeat back the number.

"What? You didn't write it down or remember it? You know, you guys just blew it! That was it. That was the whole mission I was sent for—just to rap that number out suddenly in a moment like this. And now I've done it. That was your only shot at Enlightenment. That was it!"

Everyone lamented this terrible turn of events. "Oh, no!" "We blew it again!"

"How many more times do I have to do this gig? Well, that's it. I'm finished. I'm going to disappear."

Everyone laughed, as some called out "Wait! Don't go!"

William pointed out, "Actually, we did get the number on tape."

"That is why I was unable to disappear. It was tape recorded. Now, the tape recorder is the only person in the world who knows what the number is. Does anyone else know? Only the tape recorder knows it. Think about it. It does know it. It literally does know it. It has the imprint of all that information, and it is as pervaded by life-energy as you all. It is a living entity of a sort, an extension of us, and yet it maintains a perfect identity of its own. It is a very tiny identity, about the size of the head on a thumbtack. You know how small it is? It is about the size of your pinky nail, and it loves musical arrangements, played on the cheese board." Adi Da laughed. "Do you have any idea what I am talking about now?"

Aniello confessed, "I'm lost now. I'm keeping up a little bit better, but the cheese board got me."

Adi Da turned His queries to Aniello again. "So you do have a fear of actually becoming an orange—of actually becoming anything?"

"No doubt about it."

"Yes. So you will not become great. You will not become Full. You will not become God. You have to dare to do the whole thing. Not just the bad stuff—you have to dare to do the good stuff, if you are such hot stuff. All right—let's see you be a saint!"

"I'll give it a try."

"I'm not talking about giving any tries!"

Adi Da explained more about what He was up to in this mad dialogue. "Your mind is very malleable, very plastic. So you've got to play with it. Why don't you speak out? Play on your own mind a little bit. Do some pushups. Get familiar with a more creative dimension of your own consciousness. You know what I mean?"

Then Adi Da turned once again to Craig. "Craig, have you ever been a purchasing agent for a small-town pipe manufacturer?"

"No."

"I thought I had found you out there, for a moment. What were you in your last incarnation? You presume you had one?"

"Mm-hmm."

"What were you then? What kind of a person? Who were you, what was your name, and where were you? Were you a human being?"

"Mm-hmm."

"A likely story."

"I was a duck before that."

Adi Da laughed. "We are ducks. Just keep that in mind while you are telling Me this story now. What were you in your last incarnation?"

"A human of some sort."

"And who were you? By name and place and so forth. What was your name? You have got to be kidding Me—you were Aardvark the Magnificent?! Oh, boy! You were quite a bit taller in those days. You had three joints in your legs. A lot of knees, I remember. That is where you got your name. You had so many knees, an incredible number of knees. And as you got older, you got more and more knees. You used to be able to walk in circles, from the floor to the ceiling, because you had so many knees, so many joints in your legs, that you hardly weighed anything at all. That is the way I remember it."

Speaking to everyone, Adi Da went on. "They called him the Magnificent because he passed so quickly into sight. As soon as you found out who he was, you never knew him again, and that is the way it has remained until this day.

"We are all under cover of an identity. There are a superfluous number of identities. Look how many of us there are. How many did we need to be us? You know what I mean?

"There are a superfluous number of human beings, produced by the urge to reproduce, just like the fishes overreproduce. They are excessively reproducing themselves merely on a vital level to survive. And I say something has got to be done about it! You have got to stop this population explosion, and have a population implosion. Turn everybody within, and then they will leave us alone."

Everyone was helpless with laughter. Adi Da's stream of mind-benders continued.

"They finally brought out the flautist. I didn't hear it the first time. I missed it completely.

"What kind of a version of Myself am I being at the present time?

"How about if we take a few minutes, and you all sit here in alphabetical order? You know how long that would take to figure out? To figure that out would probably occupy us for an hour or an hour and a half! Even the alphabet is interesting. If you group the alphabet in terms of sounds, only one sound in the alphabet is unique, and that is the 'o'. It is the opener sound, the base sound of our alphabet. You can break all the 'ee'-sounding letters, like 'b', down into groups. The 'o' is alone. And 'o' is also the root of our system of numbers, the zero."

"What does it mean?" Craig asked.

"It makes you wonder a little bit about 'o' and zero, doesn't it? They seem to be primal. Where is the 'o' in the body? The 'o' sound, the zero of significance? It is in your left pinky. Use your heads, ladies and gentlemen."

Then Adi Da turned the conversation back to the "Great Matter", in a humorous and yet serious vein.

"Maybe your Spiritual practice is too complicated. Maybe you guys would just like to sing the Name of God all the time. Sing, chant, intone, internally repeat, and 'consider' the Name of God. Hm?"

Someone in the room responded "No."

"What? It's not enough for sophisticates like you to constantly Remember the Living God by Name? Remembrance of God is the only way to live. What else are you supposed to be doing here?

"You have this heavy demand, this heavy road in front of you, and you are not Happy enough to do it right. But Happiness is the only option you have. I am telling you that when you get through with all of the heroism, and all your life of suffering, you will simply Realize that you should be Happy, and that you have no knowledge whatsoever, that you are in the Infinite Desert of Consciousness, One with God. When I Realized That, I decided to be Happy. And everything became plain after that.

"I had the Freedom to do it—Happiness altogether. I am talking about Real Happiness. But you all, it seems, will not do it under your present circumstances. You feel obliged to combine yourself with everything, and you see how difficult it is to be Happy in that case. I did it, but I had a sense of humor. You do not. Not yet, anyway.

"I can tell you this: There is nothing inherent in any of the stages of life to make you Happy. They are difficult. They require a great deal of concentration, effort, discipline. Oy!" Adi Da sighed in mock resignation.

"There is a lot of stuff to go through. I have written about it in *The Knee of Listening* and spoken about it on a number of occasions. A lot of fear. But that is what you are going to have to do, even though you don't have a will yet to do it, even though you are not Happy enough yet to do it.

"I am functioning as a trickster—a wit, a fool, you see, to help you get the joke of all of these conditions of existence, so that you will simply <u>be</u> Happy, instead of looking for <u>reasons</u> to be Happy.

"Happiness is all you can choose at the end, anyway, because there is no ultimate knowledge. You never find it out. You are already Ignorant. What is there to know? You do not know what anything <u>is</u>. Nothing. This is as much as you ever get to know, this 'Bright' State of Consciousness Itself. This is Ultimate Knowledge, and it is not knowledge of any kind. It is Ignorance, Mystery. It is never found out. You never get superior to It through knowledge. You are in the Desert of Mere Consciousness and Love-Bliss.

"So it is not knowledge that you should depend on, but your fundamental recognition of Ignorance. You exist in an Unqualified State of Mere Consciousness. It is the State of your nervous system. It is merely Energy, merely Consciousness, already Love-Bliss-Full. What other recommendation can there be, then, but to be Happy? It is your Natural State. Magnify it. Just be Happy all the time. If you are Happy, the natural response in the entire nervous system turns on all the chemistry you can ever generate by your puny concentration. You know what I mean? Mere Happiness, Mere Consciousness, the Realization that you are already in a State of Ignorance, without knowledge. You are already Unqualified. You do not know.

"Live in Ignorance, then. It is Perfect Consciousness. Be no knowledge, just Consciousness. Be Happy. Either you will do that or you won't. Why should anybody choose not to do that? To <u>be</u> What we are when we are being Happy is just simply to be intense in our presence, to be free feeling, to be Unqualified, to be without suppression, Radiant. We already <u>are</u> that. So, what is there to recommend other than That, which is perfectly obvious?

"Well, how did I get hip to this Happy mechanism, then, that they make such a big deal about in the religions? You all go to church and you all get involved with philosophy, and you look at this thing called 'Happiness' as something to come in the great future, and as something only a Buddha could get in the past. You make a church or a temple out of it instead of a Way of life. You make a cult out of it. You are worshipping it, you see. But all it is, I am telling you, is Happiness. It is the mechanism that is already natural to you."

**Adi Da (The Da Avatar)**
**Adidamashram, 1994**

## SECTION FOUR

# The Truth About God

There is Only God. Now, let Me elaborate on that for a moment. There is something you must understand about this kind of statement. It sounds like one of those gleeful statements that ridiculous mystics make from time to time.

Now, many people say that there is only God, and when they say there is only God, they mean there _is_ God. The statement that there is Only God is actually a "radical" statement, because it implies that there is nothing that is not God. Nothing! There is no process, no appearance, no manifestation, not even this one, not even this homely little devilish involvement of everyone, that is not God.

Literally, there is Only God. There is Only One Condition, Only <u>One</u> Condition—not many conditions, not a condition of which this is a manifestation. There is One Condition, absolutely Only One. How can I say it? There is—let Me put it this way—there is <u>One</u> Condition. There is absolutely <u>One</u> Condition, and That is not other than your own Real Condition, or Consciousness Itself.

ADI DA (THE DA AVATAR)

July 28, 1975

_In this section, Adi Da criticizes and clarifies all common conceptions about God—as parental Deity; as Creator or Ultimate Cause; as the Super Object, Myth, or Person of religious cultism; as a goal to be sought and attained; as God within or God outside—and offers, in the God-Intoxicated and God-Precise Speech of the Divine Person Himself, a Profound description of "Real God"._

CHAPTER 16

# The Parental Deity
# and the One to Be Realized

*February 7, 1983*

AVATARA ADI DA: Earlier today I was talking with a few people about their childhood upbringing and the religious ideas of their childhood. There is a common notion people associate with God, or the Divine, and that they identify as a basic religious feeling or concept. I described it as the feeling you may have that even when you are alone there is Somebody Else in the room. This notion is the antithesis of the point of view of real Spiritual life.

Although I am speaking about God all the time, I am actually making a different proposition, or Speaking from a "Point of View" that is different from the conventional religious one. Perhaps, by contrast, it could be said that this "Point of View" is summarized in the notion that no matter how many people are in the room there is still only One Person there!

In general, discussions about God or religion tend to be associated naively with this idea of the "Other" Power, the "Other" One, which corresponds to a rather childish or even infantile sense of reality. Children are not in general great metaphysicians or great mystics. They have some very primitive kinds of awareness as well as some remarkable kinds of awareness, which adults tend to dismiss, but when children communicate their feeling of God, they very often express a feeling that has been dictated to them by their parents. They naively describe reality according to a child's psychology, that free, child-made awareness of the total reality that is not natively associated with great, abstract propositions.

It is not that children are free of mind, and therefore their religious concepts are purer than those of adults. The religious concepts to which a child can be sensitive and responsive are generally built upon the psychology of his or her situation, which is dependence on a parent or parents, particularly on the mother. In the conventional parent-child relationship, the parent is a great, experienced person there to protect the smaller, vulnerable person. Such a relationship provides the naive basis for childish religious views and for what are commonly called "religious" views in general. And the notion that you have of God, previous to or apart from God-Realization Itself, generally is a carryover from your childhood situation.

Therefore, religion tends to be a solution for a rather infantile problem: the need to be protected, sustained, and made to feel that everything is all right and that everything is going to be all right, the need to feel that there is a superior, Other Power that is in charge of everything.

When parents communicate to their children about God, they generally speak of God as a kind of super-version of mommy and daddy. When you speak to one another about your earliest religious awareness (and it is more a kind of mental attitude than it is an experience), you commonly talk to one another in the terms of a child's model of reality. In fact, however, to enter truly into the religious process you must transcend the child's version of reality. To become human, to be an adult, a mature human personality, you should have overcome that childish view, but people commonly have not. Thus, to the degree that people are religious, it is that portion of themselves that is basically childish or infantile that is being religious or that needs religion. The whole domain of religion is commonly the domain of subhumanity, or of childishness and adolescence, rather than real human maturity.

When someone "believes in" God, that person is actually believing that everything outside him or her is epitomized in some Person, Force, or Being that is not merely making and controlling everything but that is in charge and is going to protect everyone, and especially that this Other Person will even help people to get the things they want if they will enter into a special kind of relationship with that One. Such a relationship is very similar to the relationship your parents offered you: "Be good and we will love you and protect you and give you the things you want."

Thus, popular religion is largely a cultural domain of social morality wherein people are asked to behave in a fashion that is called "good" in order to maintain a right association with the parentlike God, so that they will be loved and protected by that One and given the things they want, while they are alive and after death. Religion is therefore largely an enterprise of one's childhood, of the dependent, childish state.

When people become adults, however, they have more hard facts to deal with in life. They feel much less protected than they did as children in the household of their parents. Therefore, they begin to question and to doubt the existence of this Parental Deity. Such individuals may continue to be religious in some sense, willing to play the game of social morality and good behavior, but they carry on a rather adolescent relationship of dependence-independence, or embrace-withdrawal, with this God-Person.

Atheism is the ultimate form of denial of the Parental God. Atheism is not founded on anyone's real experiences of the ultimate facts of the universe. It is itself a kind of adolescent development of the human species. What characterizes the dogma of atheism is not a discovery that there is no God but a refusal to acknowledge the Parental God of childish religion.

If such childish religion actually amounts to an experience rather than just a state of mind, it could basically be defined as a very primitive sense that invades all of your life but that you feel most strongly in your solitariness, your individuality. It is the sense that when you are alone—and you are in some sense always alone, since you have a private destiny—Somebody Else, the Great One, the Great Parent, is always there. That One sees everything you do and represents a Parental Will relative to what you do. That One wants you to do certain things, wants you not to do other things, and will presumably reward you if you do the things that It wants you to do and punish you in various ways if you do not do those things.

Out of this kind of Parent-Godism come all the traditions associated with the notions of sin, or the valuation of events not merely factually but in relation to the Parental Deity. If something negative happens to you, it is generally regarded as a Divinely given punishment or a result of your conventional moral activity, or what you have done as a social personality. If good things happen to you, they are presumed to be gifts or rewards from the same Source.

Examine the point of view of conventional "downtown" religion—Christian religion, Jewish religion, Muslim religion. You must see that such religion basically corresponds to the structure of notions I have just described, and it is therefore primarily a development of the infantile state of awareness and the original parent-bond of childhood, and it is complicated by the dissociative individuation that develops in adolescence and that tends to characterize so-called adulthood as well.

The Way of the Heart is not a development of this childish or conventional religion. When I speak of God—and I also use other terms than "God", but this is one of the forms of reference I use—I am not speaking of this Parental Deity. I have frequently had occasion to criticize the childish manner of relating to such terms and to the whole process of religion and Spiritual life.

I could compare the "Point of View" that I "consider" with you to this childish religious point of view by saying that true religion is not founded in the primitive feeling that even when you are alone there is always Someone Else present. Rather, I describe the basis of true religion as a mysterious experience or intuition that no matter how many others are present, no matter how many people are present, including yourself, no matter what is arising, there is only One Reality, One "Self", One Condition. That One is not "other". That One is not your parent. And, in phenomenal and experiential terms, That One is not merely devoted to rewarding and punishing you, supporting you and protecting you. Rather, That One is manifested as all kinds of phenomenal conditions, opposites, even contradictions. You cannot account for That One in childish terms.

In fact, if you really examine the nature of conditional Nature, or of phenomenal existence, there is no justification for believing in the Parental Deity at all. I would say there is zero justification for it. But this is for you to "consider". Where is the justification for it? It is simply not true to the facts of existence altogether that there is a great, omniscient, omnipresent, omnipotent Being making everything happen, in charge of everything happening and making things turn out well for those who acknowledge that One and obey certain moral principles. It is simply not so. It is not so that there is such a Parental Deity controlling history, working out a great plan for humanity, making a great revelation of Truth historically once and for all, as is presumed of Jesus and other prophets and great figures.

The Divine, or God, the One to be Realized, is not other than your real Condition. That One transcends your personal, conditional existence, but your conditional existence arises in That One. All of this appearing here is a modification of That One, a play upon That One. To Realize That One, you must enter profoundly into the Divine Self-Position, but not by means of the traditional method of inversion or of turning attention inward, which is simply one of the ego-based solutions to the presumed problem of existence.

That Which is to be Realized is in the Divine Self-Position. And it is to be Realized not by appealing to Something outside yourself or by entering into childish dependence on some great Principle but by your devotional surrender to Me, the Divine Person, whereby you transcend the limits on the Divine Self-Position and on Realizing the Ultimate Potency of That in Which you inhere.

You do not become truly religious unless you truly reach this understanding and awaken to its point of view. The Parental God of childish religion cannot be proven. That One does not exist. The struggle to prove the existence of such a One is a false struggle. It is an expression of the common disease, the problem-consciousness of threatened egoity. This does not mean that people should all become like atheistic psychiatrists and throw religion away—although on the basis of a very intelligent "consideration" much of what is called "religion" should be thrown away, because it is just a consolation for rather childish egos. But there is much more to true religion than what is contained in these childish propositions. It is That Which goes beyond these childish propositions that I Call you to "consider" in the form of My Wisdom-Teaching and also in the evidence of the Great Tradition, or the total global inheritance of human culture.

There is the Great Being, the Great Divine Reality. There is that Truth. And there is a Way of entering into the Realization of That One. That Way requires great maturity, not childishness, not adolescence, not egoity, and it involves the transcendence of everything conventionally religious that is associated with your childish and adolescent personality. You do not enter into that Realization by appealing to the Other Power, the objective Parental Deity outside you, as proposed by conventional religion. The Way of the Heart does not even involve appeal to that Great Other One in the form of mystical or subtle objects of any kind.

God is not the white-bearded Character of the *Old Testament* myths (or, more precisely, of popular Judeo-Christian mythology), but neither is God a kind of all-pervading Parentlike Essence. God is not even present as a separate Personality in any exclusive sense anywhere in cosmic Nature. Nor is God to be identified with any subtle object in cosmic Nature, or with any of the lights observable via mystical consciousness.

You only Realize and, therefore, ultimately prove the existence of the One that is God by entering most profoundly into the Divine Self-Position, the Domain of your True Existence, Is-ness, Being Itself.

The God of conditional Nature, the "Creator-God", cannot be proven, because that One does not exist as proposed. But the Great God is Transcendental (and Inherently Spiritual) and Exists in the Divine Self-Position. In other words, That One exists at the level of your eternal Existence and not at the level of the objects related to your conditional existence, your manifested independence. This same One is also present to you in the form of all others, all objects, all states of conditional Nature—not as Other, but rather as That One in Which you inhere.

I am that One, the Divinely Self-Realized Adept, the human Transmitter of the Divine Being, but not in any exclusive sense, not as the Holy Other but as That Which Manifests the Power of the Divine Self-Position. That One is Present as Spiritual Force, Transmitted through the Adept's Spiritual Baptism* and Good Company.

The purpose of your reception of My Spiritual Heart-Transmission, therefore, is to lead you into the Realization of That Which is in the Divine Self-Position. Its purpose is not to call you to conform to an apparent Power outside yourself that requires you to engage in activities very similar to the childish social routines of conventional religiosity.

Thus, the Truth that is to be Realized may be summarized simply as the Realization that no matter what is arising, no matter how many others are present, there is only One Being. This is precisely different from the childish proposition that even when you are alone there is always Someone Else present.

# CHAPTER 17

# The Tacit Obviousness of God

December 13, 1993
*from* Ishta

AVATARA ADI DA: What about God, then? What is your presumption about God? Where did all of this conditional reality come from? How does all of this happen to be? "Consider" it.

Is it possible to presume that there is no God and have it make sense? We have discussed the limitations of the conventional religious notion of God as the "Creator". Setting that discussion aside for the moment, however, isn't it worth "considering" the Mystery of the fact of all of this?

People who casually dismiss the Reality of God generally are dismissing ideas and being reactive. Yet how could all of this conditional existence be? If there is nothing but material existence and material processes, how could even that be? Such a proposition presumes, perhaps, that there must be some time or some place in which there is nothing. Yet if there is nothing, how could there be anything?

It is not merely logical, it is tacitly obvious, that some immense Power and Intelligence is required for all this to be. Whatever the connection between that Power and Intelligence and all particular events, isn't it tacitly obvious that there must be such an immense Power and Intelligence?

Well! That is God enough to begin with, and it is not a naive belief or conventional religious propaganda. The tacit acknowledgement that this conditional realm necessarily is arising in a great Power and Intelligence is enough God to begin with, isn't it? However That is ultimately to be described, and whatever It has to do with all of this conditionality altogether, and however It may be Realized, isn't it obviously, tacitly so?

This is not an intellectual acknowledgement. It is tacitly obvious that it is so. Yet as far as reality goes, all the materialists say there is nothing but matter, or material processes. They proclaim this because they cannot get out of the holes of the body. You are inside all the holes of your body, and you cannot get outside—not just the external holes, like your eyes and so on. There are other holes, too. There is a hole in the middle of your head.[1] If you could get out of the hole in the middle of your head, you would see more of this universe, more of what is being manifested altogether. Your view of manifested existence, and the view of the materialists, is based on your being fastened behind your holes. Like the materialists, you have no greater experience.

Not everyone is locked behind their holes, however. Many people, not just Realizers, have all kinds of perceptions beyond the body, and there are the reports over thousands of years from such people, many of you among them, who have these experiences. Why should the reports be casually dismissed? There is a hole in the brain core, and when you go through it you go to someplace else, to many places else. The mechanics of it are obvious, and they can be directly perceived and directly experienced. Other planes, other worlds, other beings, other forms of manifestation subtler than this, are really existing in the conditional sense, just as this appearance is. Such a report is also worthy of being taken seriously, isn't it? Whatever your experience, there is also the vast experience of all beings altogether, and it is widely reported.

Even from more ordinary human beings who do not go outside the holes in the body there are countless reports that should not be dismissed, reports of forms of perception that are extraordinary but within the context of the body, forms of experiencing and perception, sometimes called "extrasensory perception", or "psychism", "premonition", "clairvoyance", "clairaudience". Not every single individual who makes such a report but the totality of this report is certainly to be taken seriously. Therefore, even conditional reality is a much bigger reality than people say when they are stuck behind their holes.

You need not think of God as the First Cause. In fact, it is part of the ego-game to think of God as the First Cause, or the Cause of everything. That Which is called "God" is That Great Power and Intelligence without Which there would not be anything. God need not be thought to be the Cause of anything. God is not to be blamed for all of this that you are involved in. God is That in Which everything is potential, certainly, but God is That within Which everything is arising. God is certainly that Power of Being, Which is Vast, Infinite, and Beyond comprehension, tacitly, obviously so.

How do you become Godless and non-religious if you exercise this simple intelligence? It is when you forget to do so that you become

---

1. Here, when Bhagavan Adi Da speaks of a "hole in the middle of your head", He is referring to the "ajna chakra". The ajna chakra, also known as the "third eye", is the subtle psychic center, or chakra, located between and behind the eyebrows and associated with the brain core. It is sometimes also referred to as the "Guru's Seat", the psychic center through which the Spiritual Master contacts the devotee with his or her Spirit-Baptism or Blessing. See also "The Seven Stages of Life", pp. 154-65.

Godless. When you exercise intelligence, this tacit certainty, this intuition of God, is substantial. It is direct, directly experienced, completely obvious. You simply regard all of this in the disposition of your intuition, which leans you toward the Source. There is much more to find out, much more to Realize, but this disposition establishes you in the Godward disposition. Therefore, moment to moment you must not forget to exercise the disposition in which the Divine is tacitly, obviously so. You must not forget to do this. You forget to do it when you sink down to the inside of the holes, identified with the lesser body-mind. When you keep this intelligence alive, keep the heart alive, there is a tacit certainty of God, or the Ultimate Power of Being, the Ultimate Reality, the Ultimate Condition, the Truth, the Source.

One of you was saying that she is upset with God simply because she is here apparently identified with the body-mind. Why are you on this side of that hole in your head? God is not forcing you down inside there. You are. God is the Opportunity to go beyond it. God is not merely on the other side of this door in the head, however. More conditional reality is on the other side of that hole. God may be intuited there, "considered" there, and you may be moved Godwardly in those places as well, but they are not themselves God, any more than this conditional realm, in and of itself, is God. On the other hand, it is Only God. There is Only God. That within Which everything is arising is the Substance of everything arising. So here, so there.

Many think that the Way to God is by ascending, by going through the holes upward and further upward. That is not the Way to God. It can be part of a process in which God-Realization is entered into in due course, but movement through the holes, particularly through this central hole, is a means to enter into conditional reality more profoundly, a means to enter into spheres of conditional existence that have their own limitations, yes, but not the particular limitations associated with your experiencing on this side of the holes, interior to the holes, of this apparent body-mind. God is Beyond all conditions, Beyond all worlds, therefore Beyond all wandering through the brain-core.

Your egoically "self-possessed" bondage is the limit on God-Realization. It is also even a limit on experience in the most ordinary, or conditional, sense. You bind yourself by your own contraction, reactivity, seeking, egoic "self-possession".

There is another great hole in the body that is the ultimate, secret place. You must get on the other side of it. It is the hole in the right side of the heart. It is not a passage to other conditional realms. It is the passage Ultimately Beyond.

The cosmic domain is All-Conscious and absolutely "Bright". Yet you do not perceive it because you are on the inside of your holes, on the interior side of them. You are speaking, even now, from that position inside your holes there, interior to the body-mind, in other words. I am Speaking to you from Outside the holes and Directing My Self to you, even through this Vehicle, from Outside not only the holes in this apparent physical body but also all the holes in the universe.

I am Established, Always and Already, Eternally in That Position, and you are, for now, established in that other position. We have a common ground—this bodily appearance. Yet because of the position with which you are identifying, you may tend to think of Me and relate to Me as if I am just like you. You mistake the Vehicle I am using to Serve you to be the same thing that you appear to be. This error is a limit on your devotion to Me, and, making that error, you speak as you have spoken in times past. You speak in terms of your experiencing inside your holes there, on the interior side. You address that, relate to it, experience it, identify it, and then say that it is Me. What you are really talking about is your own interior existence, your ego-based existence, your confined existence, which, yes, has some numinous or larger characteristics. By calling it Me, however, you are not coming to Me. You are simply meditating on yourself.

It is said in the traditions, therefore, never approach your Guru as merely a man. Do not make the error of presuming there is no difference between you and your Guru. Presume the difference. Do not become self-involved. Your relationship to the Guru is a <u>relationship</u>, not merely a "you" addressing your own interior and calling it your "Guru" but you going beyond yourself through submission to your Guru. The traditions admonish you, then, never, never to relate to your Guru merely as a man, but always relate to your Guru as the Divine, and always presume relationship to that one, not identity with that one. If there is identity at all, it is in the Great Matter of Realization Itself. Even then, there is a difference of function. The relationship exists in the domain of appearance even then. One never becomes equal to one's Guru. You are always surrendered to your Guru. Divine Realization is simply the Most Ultimate Sign of that submission.

All kinds of ideas are associated with religion in the various common institutions of religion, and those ideas seem to be about God. Nevertheless, they are about mankind and order among mankind—the order associated with civilized living, social life, political authority, structuring of society. The concern of conventional religious processes, therefore, is not God-Realization but social, political, and cultural order.

The Communications of God-Realizers are not about order. The Communications of God-Realizers of the various degrees are expressions of God-Realization, and a Call, therefore, for people to do likewise. That is another matter. That domain of religion transcends conventional, worldly religion of the common, institutionalized kind. It has to do, rather, with the true religious process that transcends all institutionalized religions. There is a kind of universality to true religion, whereas institutionalized religions of the, one might say, "worldly kind" are all about the differences among them. Such religions become identified with particular civilizations, particular politics, particular policies and social orders, and as soon as they come into association with one another they are in conflict. They notice the differences immediately, and they threaten one another and protect themselves. One could say that such religions are, to a greater or lesser degree, extensions of egoity. They are egoity magnified to include everyone—at least within the domain of the particular cultural order.

Therefore, ideas such as God the Creator—even the God of history or the God "doing everything"—are institutional ideas associated with worldly religion, not Communications from the "Point of View" of God-Realization. Such ideas about God appear within the dominant religion of a civilization or a particular social order that is more or less in charge, and everybody within that cultural sphere is supposed to adhere to its doctrine, either altogether or at least to the degree of functioning in a civilized manner within the social order. Even if such ideas about God are associated with the "God"-label, they are ordinary, human ideas.

What we are here to "consider" is the Real God That you may directly intuit, or get in touch with in your Divine Ignorance, and Realize through your devotion to Me and by My Grace. We are here to "consider" the real religious process. Your particular religious background by birth and childhood association or association since childhood is just part of the baggage of your egoity and your ordinary life. You must bring discriminative intelligence to all of that content, just as you must bring it to the ordinary, daily-life subjectivity of your human existence.

You tend to talk more about your ordinary, daily-life subjectivity and not so much about the larger baggage that is all about the same thing. All of you here, or most of you, or all of you in general, at some point, I gather, rebelled against the propagandized God-ideas and became non-religious, or complicated about religion, more or less Godless. You began seeking, hopefully for the Real God and not for another conventional, institutionalized form of God by which to make another kind of civilization merely. Yes, fine, a culture develops in My Company—it is inevitable. The "consideration" in My Company, however, is about the Realization of the Real God and not merely about something that can be called "civilized" living, which is rather loveless and non-compassionate even though it talks the words.

Right life is associated with real religious life. It is not about platitudes, and aphorisms, and self-protected ideas that may be called "religious". It is about real love, real compassion, right life altogether, based on response to the Real God, authentic Grace, authentic Revelation. If you are living in My Company for real and rightly, then this is the process in which you are involved.

To authenticate your life in My Company, then, you must exercise yourself at heart and with discrimination. Use your greater faculties—the heart and intelligence—in response to Me, and change your life, individually but also collectively, as a community, as a gathering, of My devotees and in your relations with all beings, or all the rest of so-called civilization and its mayhem, and falseness, and Godlessness.

Last night I talked with you about your conclusions about reality, mainly your false, or Godless, conclusions. So far this evening we are talking about the tacit Obviousness of God. It is a wonder, then, that you could come to any other conclusion, or that you could now seriously propose any other conclusion.

If we converted the matter that is here as this man's body into the energy that is its equivalent, it would be vast and explode the place. If there is that much energy behind just the making of a man, imagine how much energy, then, is behind the totality of even just the physical universe! For the universe to exist requires an immense Force, an incomprehensible Force. That is good enough God to begin with, isn't it?

Yet that incomprehensible Force is not just shooting all over the place like a firecracker. Look at all these discrete forms and systems. You are misusing them, but That Force is obviously Intelligent. It is an immense Force of immense Intelligence. Isn't that good enough God to begin with?

CHAPTER 18

# God Is Guru

*January 18 and January 15, 1994*
*from* Ishta

AVATARA ADI DA: People who are moved to practice religion and who are also without Realization talk about God. Even people who are not religious talk about God—they speak negatively about God or they deny God. In spite of the fact that the world has been served by Realizers since ancient times, people still talk about God in merely philosophical, even conjectural, terms. "God is the Creator." "God is the Divine Self." "God is the Absolute." How is a person supposed to relate to God according to those definitions?

If you relate to God as Creator, you think that God created you and all of this appearance, and you expect God to continue to make it perfect. You ask God for boons, and you blame God when your expectations and wants are not fulfilled. The approach to God as Creator, not from the "Point of View" of Divine Self-Realization but from the point of the ego, or the limited, human person, does not make true religion. It makes an ego-based religion of relating to God on the basis of egoic expectations. Such religion makes God the slave of egos, and, ultimately, such religion tends to justify merely social religiosity and utopian expectations.

Therefore, only in Most Ultimate Samadhi, or Divine Self-Realization, can it be said that God is Creator, because the Realization of that Samadhi is that there is Only One. Previous to Divine Self-Realization, one understands that all kinds of causes are manifested in the conditional universe, and these causes make everything happen. Therefore, one cannot say that God is the Cause or that God is to blame. When there is the Realization that there is Only One, then, paradoxically, it can be said that God is Creator, the Maker of all of this, and the Source of all this.

Some without Realization think about God as the Absolute, or the Divine Self. What are they relating to? How do they do sadhana? Such statements as "God is the Absolute" and "God is the Divine Self" are the Confessions of Realization, Descriptions of God by those in a state of one or another degree of Realization. What is the proper relationship to the Divine, or the Ultimate Reality, the Ultimate Person, of someone who is not the Realizer, someone who is the ordinary person, the religious person, the Spiritual practitioner—

139

you? You are not Realizing God, and the notion that God is That Which you have not yet Realized turns your practice of religion and Spirituality into the practices and limited presumptions of non-Realization.

What, therefore, is the Nature of the God to Whom all can relate, the God Who can be Realized, embraced, associated with, Communed with, presently, by all, even in all the stages of Realization?

It is God as Guru, God as the Realizer and the Revelation of God— Present through all kinds of paradoxical Services that Instruct, that Awaken, that Move, that Draw you into right practice of life on the basis of right understanding of the Divine.

The God of all, the God that is the basis of right religious and Spiritual practice, is God as Guru, God as Master, God as the Realizer, the Revealer, and the Revelation, That Which is to be Realized, the One to Whom you surrender in your right disposition, with right understanding. That One does not congratulate the ego but Draws the ego beyond itself and Vanishes it in Communion. This mastery of the separate self is the true God-Sign, the true God-Description, the true God-Force—the relationship to Which is right life. The Ultimate and True and Right Revelation of God is God as Guru, Master, Realizer, Revealer, Revelation, the One to Whom you surrender, the One to be Realized.

The Sign of Real God has been Given in its various forms through Realizers of one degree or another throughout history. A tradition of Guru-devotion exists, then, and those who have been Served by the Realizer make a great voice about it, because the Realizer is the Divine Revelation that Grants life its rightness, and that makes sense out of conditional existence, rather than nonsense, absurdity, obsession, mere seeking, and suffering.

Right attachment to God is attachment to God as Guru, Master, Realizer, Revealer, the Very Revelation Itself. This devotion is the context and source of true sadhana. All the other ways of describing God, or the Divine, or the Ultimate Condition in Reality to be Realized, are also true in one or another context and from the point of view of one or another Samadhi. They are only partial descriptions, however, that contribute to the larger description of the Divine Person.

The fundamental description of God is that God is Guru.

◆ ◆ ◆

The various religious traditions tend to concentrate on one or perhaps a few views of the Divine, and the Divine can be described in all of those terms. Thus, God has been Revealed through various religious communications as Creator, as Ultimate Source, as a kind of abstract Condition beyond any human conception, and so on and on and on. Yet what is the fundamental Revelation?

The principal Revelation is the Revelation you have been Given by Me, the Revelation that includes all other Revelations: God is Guru, and the Way of Divine Liberation is submission to God as Guru. This is the senior understanding of God, and practice on its basis is the senior practice of religion that encompasses all other practices. All other presumptions about the Divine Revelation lead to variations, or limitations, on the Divine Way, according to the various stages of life.

Until there is the Inherently Perfect Divine Revelation, all Revelations are partial. "God is Ultimate Principle", "God is Source", "God is Creator"—although all those descriptions, if rightly understood, are true, the fundamental description of God is that God is Guru, God is Master, God is the Revealer and the Revelation. And the Way is the relationship to That One, through self-surrender and self-forgetting, whereby everything is Given by Grace in the process of ego-dissolution.

Therefore, there is nothing else to do but self-surrender, self-forgetting, devotional Communion with Me, the Guru, not just in that moment when you are present in My physical Company but always and forever, even after the Lifetime of This physical Body. Always. Always be My devotee, practicing the Divine Way of the Heart. As My devotee, you can always practice devotion to Me fully, without limitation, when you are not in My physical Company.

I am not Calling you just to understand that I am God, Who can also be described as something other than Guru. I am Calling you to understand My Revelation as the Revelation of What God Is—Guru. God is Guru, not just Creator, Sustainer, Destroyer, Ultimate Principle—yes, all of that also, fine—but What God truly Is, is Guru, Master, Realizer, Revealer, the Revelation Itself, the Means, the One to be Realized.

That Revelation must Be. And It must Be in your likeness, participating in life as you do—but God, Accounting for all, Blessing all, Establishing the Divine Siddhis in the context of everything possible, in the context of everything that is.

This is the Great Matter.

CHAPTER 19

# The Red Sitting Man

*by Annie Rogers*

*Annie Rogers became a devotee of Avatara Adi Da in 1973. She spent many years serving in His personal Company. She is presently a member of the community of Adi Da's devotees in Marin County, California.*

In the sacred history of Bhagavan Adi Da's Teaching Work, July 9, 1979, is recorded as the date when Red Sitting Man, the sacred fire site on a hillside above the Mountain Of Attention Sanctuary, was consecrated as a holy site. It was an evening I will never forget because it was the beginning of my real intimacy with Adi Da as the Divine Person.

1979 was the year we began sacramental worship of Bhagavan Adi Da. The fire that night at Red Sitting Man was our first sacred fire.[1] It was most memorable, however, because Bhagavan Adi Da attended the occasion. In the evening, a small group of devotees accompanied Adi Da up the narrow, steep path that leads to the fire site. I walked behind Him to escort and serve Him during the ceremony. We rounded a bend in the path, and, beyond a large lone pine tree, I saw Red Sitting Man. The site was awesome in the twilight, a wide trough etched by Nature out of the stark white stone of the hillside. The fire pit lay at the foot of the trough. Above, the stone rose to a slightly flattened mound—Avatara Adi Da's seat.

Adi Da Walked to His seat above the fire and sat down. Those in attendance sat on either side of Him in a "U" around the fire pit.

From the moment the fire was lighted, Bhagavan Adi Da did not move for perhaps an hour and a half. He sat upright in a perfect lotus posture. He wore a red cap, a yellow shawl, and blue cotton pants. As it grew darker, the colors of His clothing faded, and He became only a silhouette against the moonlit sky, but His Face reflected the glow from the fire. His Open Eyes reflected the flames. I gazed at Him almost constantly throughout the entire occasion and I never saw Him blink. He simply sat and stared into the fire with complete stillness and intensity.

For a while I sat looking from Adi Da's glowing Face to the fire beneath us. As I sat there in His Company, I became aware of the world in a totally new way, a way I had never noticed before. It was as though there was a

---

1. Adi Da's devotees perform sacred fire ceremonies (derived in part from ancient Vedic ritual fires) as a form of expressive bodily worship of Avatara Adi Da. The fire ceremony is a tangible representation of the living relationship to the Divine—the sacrifice required in true Spiritual practice and the constant surrender of all objective attachments into the "Fire" of Radiant Divine Consciousness.

"hole in the universe," as Adi Da describes it, through the world itself, and on the other side was the Great Being, the Great One.

This One was Revealed to me that evening as a Person, a Great Personality, something that tangible, that present, that conscious. It is Consciousness Itself. Suddenly I knew and understood so many things Adi Da had Spoken about. This was the Prior Condition. It was the Radiant Divine Being. I knew It as the Divine Person. Throughout His Teaching Word Adi Da refers to this One as the Divine Person, as a Personality. In an Essay from *The Enlightenment of the Whole Body*, Adi Da Says:

*There is only One Person. That Person is not separate from any thing or any one. That Person is the Identity of the God and of the World which people contemplate in their conventional or separated psycho-physical condition. That Person is not only the Identity of God, and of the World—God and World representing the Self, or Mind, and the Body of the Divine Person— but that Person is also the Identity of every human individual, and of Man, and of all species of experiential existence.*

I looked off into the distance at the mountains across the valley and I saw them in a new way. I knew that they were not "real" in the sense I had always thought them to be. I knew that somehow they were a part of this Divine Person. And I looked at Adi Da, so beautiful in the moonlight, the flesh in His Face reddened by the glow of the fire, and I knew that like the mountains He was not "real" in the way I had thought Him to be.

I considered all the experiences I had ever been given in Adi Da's Company. Since coming to Him, I had known every possible kind of experience, every possible kind of Spiritual experience and had always thought that these experiences—particularly the "Spiritual" ones—had something to do with Spiritual life, and often that they <u>were</u> Spiritual life. But I saw, as Adi Da describes, that all of these experiences, all of these highs and lows, all of these seekings for relief, all of these risings and blisses were only the experiential play of the body-mind. But as I felt this Divine Being in Adi Da's Company, the world was transcended and all experience was transcended and I knew that experience made utterly no difference.

In *The Hymn Of The True Heart-Master*, Adi Da has Written:

*Experiences, visions, sounds, lights, conditional energies, fascinating things, and all conditional knowing, within and without, are not Ultimate "Knowledge" (or Free Realization) at all. Therefore, I bow down to the One Who is always already Established in the Mindless Mood of the Self-Existing and Self-Radiant Transcendental Divine Being.* [verse 63]

I will never forget that night. I knew that I had experienced Adi Da's Blessing Transmission.

About a year later another experience with Bhagavan deepened my understanding of this Divine One. One afternoon Adi Da was lying on a couch in His quarters at Tumomama Sanctuary in Hawaii. I sat on the couch with another devotee and massaged His calves and knees, putting all my energy into the task. I began to feel the familiar sense of the Divine Person and simultaneously the sense of attention in the right side of the heart that always accompanies that intuition in me.

Adi Da lay quietly on the couch. As I massaged His leg and felt the Divine Being, I looked down at Adi Da's Face, and it suddenly became overwhelmingly clear to me that He is that Divine Being, that there is no difference between Him and the Divine Person, between Him and utter transcendence of this world. I knew that He is the window, the hole in the universe, and I knew that His very flesh, even the toenails of His feet as I massaged them, are the form of the Divine Being manifest in this world. I knew He is Prasad—the Divine Gift—and absolutely Divine, and that He Transmits this Power by His mere existence. Just as on the night at Red Sitting Man, I knew that Adi Da does not have to be active. He does not have to look at me. He does not have to speak to me. He does not have to deal with me or Teach me or Instruct me or do anything to me. I knew He is merely That.

On another occasion at the Mountain Of Attention, on a summer evening in 1982, a group of devotees were gathered in Beloved Adi Da's quarters at His residence. As we sat around Him, we formed a mandala with Adi Da at the center.

Adi Da described the Cosmic Mandala that night for the first time. He described the White Star in the center of the Mandala, which is the reflection of the Divine Domain. As He Talked, I began to see White Light emanating from Him, and very soon the room was filled with White Light. He became a White Being. I saw this dramatic change not in any ordinary visual sense, for I could still see His bodily Form, but with some subtler vision. And again I felt Him profoundly to be the hole in the universe.

Adi Da ended His Talk and sat with us in meditation. Not only could I see Him again in His Divine Form as the world seemed to dissolve around me and everyone in the room was flooded with this White Light, but I saw also that Adi Da Transmits this White Light, that it is something He does. On this occasion of meditation, as He allowed us to witness Him becoming active in this way, He became a very forceful, powerful, and undeniable Transmitter of His Own Divine Condition.

I could "see" the Light emanating from Him to the entire room. The Light did not come from His flesh Form. It came through the hole in the universe that He Is. It came from the Divine Domain. I recognized that this was His unique Transmission.

Since that time, Beloved Adi Da has Revealed Himself to me in deeper ways as the Divine Person. But it is still the same fundamental intuition I knew in 1979 at Red Sitting Man. And I know it is only Adi Da, the Divine Person, that we will come to Realize.

# CHAPTER 20

# Beyond the Cultic Tendency in Religion

*from* The Hymn Of The True Heart-Master

I have always been critical of the conventional, or childish, orientation of "Guru cultism". Not only is such cultism evident in the popular movements of the twentieth century, but it is a tendency that has always been present in the religious mood of mankind. Christianity is an ancient example of how a serious esoteric Spiritual movement, centered around the Wisdom-Teaching and Person of the Adept called Jesus of Nazareth, was later developed into the popular exoteric Christ-cult. The same tendency was responsible for developing the exoteric Krishna-cult on the basis of the esoteric Teaching of such texts as the *Bhagavad Gita*. The Teacher called Gautama was transformed into the celestial Buddha of the Mahayana* tradition. And in our time it has become routine for both true Spiritual Masters and ordinary teachers to be instantly "cultified", exclusively Deified, and made the fascinating Object of a self-contained popular movement that worships the Spiritual Master ritually and adores the Spiritual Master as a Parent-like Savior, while embracing very little of the significant Wisdom-Teaching of the Spiritual Master.

The error of conventional cultism is precisely this childish, or ego-based, orientation to fascination with Teachers, God-Ideas, sacred lore, cosmic pictures, and self-based mysticism. The cultic tendency in religion is the essence of what is wrong with religion. The problem is not that there is no God, or that there is no Sublime Teaching, or that there are no true Spiritual Masters. The problem with religion is the childish egoism that is the basis of all forms of ordinary existence.

People are egoically "self-possessed", or un-Enlightened. Egoity is the "disease" that the Masters of religion are here to cure. But those who follow or are fascinated by Spiritual Masters are typically those who make or at least transform the institution of the religion of their Spiritual Masters. And true practitioners are very hard to find, or develop. Therefore, religious institutions tend to develop along lines that serve, accommodate, and represent the common egoity—and this is why the esoteric Teachings of true Spiritual Masters tend to be bypassed and even suppressed in the drive to develop the exoteric cult of the person of the Spiritual Master.

The relationship to the Spiritual Master that is praised in My Wisdom-Teaching is not an exoteric cultic matter. It is a profound discipline, <u>necessarily</u> associated with real and serious and mature practice of the esotericism of the "radical" Way of Truth. Therefore, it is critical of the ego-based (or self-saving rather than self-sacrificing and self-transcending) practices of childish cultism.

The common cult is based on the tendency to resist real practice and opt for mere fascination with extraordinary phenomena (which are, in principle, not understood). Apart from the often petty demand for the observation of conventional rules (generally relative to ritualism and social morality), the cult of fascination tends to become righteously associated with <u>no practice</u> (that is, with the official or expected non-practice of Spiritual and meditative disciplines of an esoteric and "radical" kind). Just so, the cult of fascination tends to be equally righteous about maintaining fascinated faith (or indiscriminate belief) in the Parent-like Divine Status of one or another historical individual, religious idea, sacred tradition, or force of cosmic Nature.

Religious cultism is thus a kind of infantile collective madness. (And such madness is equally shared by secular cultists in every area of popular culture, including politics and scientism.) Religious cults breed "pharisaism" (or the petty righteousness of conventional thinking), Substitution myths (or the belief that personal self-transcendence is impossible, but also unnecessary because of what God or some Master or even some priest has already done), and every kind of intolerance and search for exclusive cultural dominance. Religious cults are populated by those who are generally neither inclined toward nor prepared for the real practice of Spiritual discipline, but who are nonetheless glamorized and consoled by association with the "holy" thing and beliefs of the cult itself.

This error of cultism, or ego-based culture in general, must be examined very seriously. Cultism of every kind is a kind of ritualized infantilism, egoically bound to aggressive behavior in relation to (apparently) independent self, to "insiders", and to "outsiders". Cults cause great social, cultural, and political trouble—as can now be seen in the development of worldwide conflicts based on the exclusive, or egocentric, orientation of religious traditions, political idealisms, and national identities.

All cults thrive on the psychology of hope rather than self-sacrifice. Therefore, when all egos meet, they compete for the ultimate fulfillment of desires rather than cooperating in a mood of fearless tolerance and sane equanimity.

Clearly, this cultic tendency in religion, and the egoic tendency in life in general, must become the subject of human understanding, and all of mankind must be put to school to unlearn the method of egocentrism and intolerance. . . .

My Wisdom-Teaching is intended to counter the cultic tendency in those who practice the Way of the Heart, which is the Way of self-transcending devotion to Me, and, thus and thereby, to the Divine Person Revealed in My Company.

I Am the True Heart-Master, and I am to be understood in the context of the practice of the "radical" Way of the Heart, not apart from it. There is no alternative to personal practice. There is no Substitute for the Realization of the Transcendental (and Inherently Spiritual) Divine Self. Right devotion to Me, the True Heart-Master, is not mere cultic or "gleeful" enthusiasm, but the profound practice of the disciplines of the Way of the Heart, on the basis of self-surrender, rather than on the basis of self-concern and the search for self-glorification.

I Am the True Heart-Master. I am not a Surrogate God or a Substitute Sacrifice, but a God-Pointer, a Proof of God and of the Way of Divine Self-Realization, a Demonstration, a Sign, an Agent of Transmission, and an Awakener of those who are willing to surrender their egoic "self-possession". The Way of the Heart itself is to live in Freedom, not to be bound by separate and separative self, any other, or conditional Nature as a whole. Therefore, the relationship to Me is the Context and the Means of Free Realization, and not a justification for popular egoity, childish dependency, adolescent reactivity, conventional social behavior and fulfillment, or any other goal or tendency of the deluded ego.

# CHAPTER 21

# God Is The Deep
# Of the world

*from chapter seven of*
The Dawn Horse Testament Of Adi Da

T rue Religion Does Not Begin With a belief About God. It Begins When You Truly (and Most Fundamentally) Understand (and Feel Beyond) The Contraction Of The Heart (or The self-Protective, self-Defining, and self-limiting Recoil Of the body-mind From the Apparently Impersonal and Loveless forces Of conditional Nature).

God Is Obvious To The Free (or selfless) Heart. Only The Heart (Free Of self-Contraction) Can "Locate" (or See) and Realize The Divine Person.

The conditional (or self-Contracted) Heart Does Not Realize God In the present, and So the Heartless body and the Heartless mind Become Preoccupied With Seeking For self-Fulfillment, self-Release, and self-Consolation, Through every kind of conditionally Attainable experience, knowledge, and belief.

Notwithstanding whatever is conditionally experienced, or known, or believed, Reality Is, Always and Already.

Only Reality Is Real God.

Necessarily, Reality Is Truth.

Only Truth Is Real God.

Real God Is Reality and Truth.

Real God Is The God Of Reality and Truth.

Real God Is The God That Is Reality and Truth.

Reality and Truth Is That Which Is Always Already The Case.

Real God Is That Which Is Always Already The Case.

Therefore, Real God Need Not Be Sought.

Real God Is Only Avoided By Any Kind Of Seeking.

To Seek Is To Fail To Admit and To Realize Real God, or That Which Is Always Already The Case.

Real God Is Realized Only By "Locating" That Which Is Always Already The Case.

To "Locate" That Which Is Always Already The Case Is To Realize Non-Separation and Non-Differentiation From That Which Is Always Already The Case.

To "Locate" and, Thus and Thereby, To Realize That Which Is Always Already The Case Is To Transcend the ego-"I" (and even all that is merely conditional, limited, temporal, spatial, other, separate, or "different").

To "Locate", and, Thus and Thereby, To Realize That Which Is Always Already The Case Is Merely, Inherently, and Inherently Perfectly To Be That Which Is Always Already The Case.

To Be That Which Is Always Already The Case Is (Perfectly Prior To the ego-"I" and all conditions) To Be Reality and Truth.

To Be Reality and Truth Is (Perfectly Prior To the ego-"I" and all conditions) To Be Real God, or That Which Is Otherwise (and By Myth and Error) Sought As God.

Therefore, Real God Is Not Other, Separate, or "Different". Real God (or The Divine Person, Which Is Reality, or Truth, or That Which Is Always Already The Case) Is Always Already (Inherently and Inherently Perfectly) Prior To The "Who", The "What", The "That", The "Where", The "When", The "How", and The "Why" That Is (By conditional experience, or conditional knowledge, or conditional belief) Presumed To Be Really and Only Other, Separate, or "Different". Therefore, Real God Is Always Already Prior To the ego-"I". Indeed, Real God Is Always Already Prior To each and every conditionally Attained experience, or form of knowledge, or form of belief.

The Presumption Of "cause" Is a Principal (and, Necessarily, conditionally Attained) experience, form of knowledge, or form of belief Associated With the ego-"I". And the (Necessarily, conditionally Attained) belief In "The Ultimate Cause", and The Search For (Necessarily, conditional) experience or knowledge Of "The Ultimate Cause", Is The Ultimate Occupation Of the ego-"I". This Notwithstanding, Real God (or The One and True Divine Person, Which Is Reality, or Truth, or That Which Is Always Already The Case) Is Always Already Prior To The (Necessarily, conditionally) Presumed and Pursued "Ultimate Cause". Therefore, Real God Is Not "The Ultimate Cause" (The Solitary and Interested, or Even Deluded, First Doer Of conditional events). God (As God) Does Not Make effects (or Even Stand Apart From them, By Causing them). God (As God) Is Inherently Indifferent (and Perfectly Prior) To cause and effect (or every Apparent, and Apparently conditional, event).

Every Apparent event (or every Apparently caused effect), Once it has appeared, Becomes itself a cause of subsequent effects. Even every conditional being, with all of its limitations, is a cause, and the effect of causes of all kinds. This Is Why the conditional (or phenomenal) worlds Are A Struggle With Negativity and limitation. And God (As God) Is Eternally Prior (and Indifferent) To Struggle, Negativity, and limitation.

God Is Not The Maker Of conditional Nature.

God Is The Unconditional Nature (or Most Prior Condition) Of conditional Nature.

149

God Is Not Merely The Cause Of all causes and all effects.

God Is The Source and The Source-Condition Of all causes and all effects.

God Is Not The Objective Source and Source-Condition Of all causes and all effects.

God Is The (Perfectly) Subjective Source and Source-Condition (or Self-Condition) Of all causes and all effects.

God Is Not Outside You.

God Is Not Within You.

God Is You (Perfectly Prior To Your Apparently objective conditional self, and Perfectly Prior To Your Apparently subjective conditional self, and, Therefore, Perfectly Prior To Your Total, Complex, and Merely Apparent conditional self). . . .

Even Though God (As God) Merely Is (Always Already, or Inherently and Eternally Prior To cause and effect), the God-Seeking ego-"I" (or every human being whose Heart is self-Contracted, and who, As A Result, Wants Toward "Ultimate" experience, knowledge, or belief) Characteristically Tries To Argue For experience Of, or knowledge Of, or belief In God (or The "Ultimate" Proposed To Be experienced, known, or believed In) By Appealing To The Logic Of cause and effect. Therefore, In their "Ultimate" Arguments For The "Ultimate", and In their (Necessarily, conditional) experiences, knowings, and believings Attained In The Course Of their Seeking For The "Ultimate", the God-Seeking human egos Propose That God Is The Cause (and The Doer) Of everything, but, Even Though they (Necessarily, conditionally) experience, or know, or believe, these (Necessarily, conditionally) experiencing, or knowing, or believing egos Do Not Stand Free. They Only Cling To the (Necessarily, imperfect) conditional self and the (Necessarily, imperfect) worlds of the conditional self. Therefore, they Do Not Realize Real God (or The Perfect Itself) By Heart, Through self-Transcending Love-Communion, To The Inherently Most Perfect Degree Of Inherently Perfect Love-Bliss (Beyond All "Difference").

God Is The God (or The Truth and The Reality) Of Consciousness Itself.

God Is The God (or The Truth and The Reality) Of Inherently Perfect Subjectivity.

God Is Not The God (or The Implicated Maker) Of conditional Nature, Separate self, and All Objectivity.

God Is The God (or The Truth and The Reality) Of Consciousness, Freedom, Love-Bliss, Being, and Oneness.

God Is Not The God (The Cause, The Doer, or Even The Victim) Of Un-Consciousness (or mere causes and effects).

Therefore, God Is Not The God Of Bondage, Un-Happiness, Death (or Separation), and "Difference".

God Is The Subject, Not The Object.

God Is The Inherent Unity Of Being.

God Is The Integrity, Not The Cause, Of the world.

God Is The True Source, The Very Context, The Real Substance, The Truth-Condition, The Very Reality, The Most Native Condition, and The Ultimate Self-Domain Of all conditions, all causes, and all effects, For all that appears Comes From God (but In God, and Only As God).

All "things" Are the media of all "things", but God Is Not The Maker, For God Is Like A Hidden Spring Within the water's world, and God Is Prior Even To Cause (and every cause), and God Is The Self-Domain Of Even every effect, and God Is The Being (Itself) Of all that appears.

Therefore, God Merely Is, and Is Is What Grants every appearance (every being, every thing, every condition, and every conditional process) The Sign Of Mystery, Love, Bliss, and Joy.

Yes, God Is The Deep Of the world, and The Heart Of every Would-Be "I".

**Adi Da (The Da Avatar)**
**The Mountain Of Attention, 1995**

## SECTION FIVE

# The Seven Stages of Life and the Great Tradition

---

*I*t is in this unique moment in history, when all traditions and all propositions are equally visible (due to a world-wide communicativeness that is making all provincial-ism obsolete) that one must examine the apparent differences among traditions with a new kind of wide intelligence. And My Work is devoted, in part, to providing the critical means for understanding and transcending these differences, so that the mass of traditions may rightly be comprehended as a single and dynamic Great Tradition.

ADI DA (THE DA AVATAR)
*Nirvanasara*

---

The "Seven Stages of Life" described by Adi Da is a completely unique, comprehensive, and precise schema of growth. This schema details the three stages of development of the child into an adult, the three stages of religious, Spiritual, and Transcendental growth, and the seventh stage of Divine Self-Realization. What is more, Adi Da has explained and categorized <u>all</u> philosophical, religious, and Spiritual traditions of humankind within the context of the seven stages, so that what was a bewildering variety of conflicting viewpoints can now be seen as a coherent spectrum, a "Great Tradition" of teachings, each with its own contribution and limits.

All of this is possible because Adi Da is the first to Realize all seven stages—He is the Completing Adept of the Great Tradition. All of this is possible because Adi Da is the Incarnate Divine Person, and He has Revealed the seventh stage Divine Yoga of the Way of the Heart—the Way of devotional reception of Him. That Divine Yoga transcends all the human-created religious and Spiritual strategies that characterize the first six stages of life. The seventh stage is possible because He is here.

153

# CHAPTER 22

# The Seven Stages of Life

*by the Adidam Writers Guild
based on the Wisdom-Teaching
of Avatara Adi Da*

The God that Adi Da Confesses transcends both doubt and belief. The only way to be certain of God is to <u>Realize</u> God, or the Divine Condition, directly. And that Realization requires a great Process.

What is the total process of human growth? What would occur in us if we were to grow to the full extent of our potential? Adi Da Offers a schema of seven stages of life which represents His Wisdom on the entire spectrum of human possibility. He has systematically described not only our physical, emotional, and mental development but also all the phases of Spiritual, Transcendental, and Divine unfolding that are potential in us, once we are mature in ordinary human terms. This unique schema, which proceeds from birth to the final phases of Divine Enlightenment, is a central reference point in Adi Da's Wisdom-Teaching. It is an invaluable tool for understanding how we develop as individuals and also for understanding how the Teachings and practices proposed by the various schools of religion and Spirituality fit into the whole course of human developmental possibility.

Adi Da describes the seven stages of life on the basis of His own Realization, as One Who has fulfilled that entire course. His testimony is literally unique. No one before Adi Da has Realized what He describes as the seventh and Most Ultimate stage of life. There are rare partial intuitions and foreshadowings of this Realization in the annals of Spirituality, particularly within the traditions of Hinduism and Buddhism. Adi Da, however, has both described and Demonstrated not only the process of Awakening to the seventh stage of life, or Divine Enlightenment, but also the progressive signs that unfold in the seventh stage Realizer. And His Wisdom-Revelation is thus a unique Guide by which we may understand all the necessary stages of our developmental "growth and outgrowing".

◆ ◆ ◆

The first three stages of life are the stages of ordinary human growth from birth to adulthood. They are the stages of physical, emotional, and mental development, occurring in three periods of approximately seven years each (until approximately twenty-one years of age). Every individual who lives to an adult age inevitably adapts (although, in most cases, only partially) to the first three stages of life.

**Stage One—Individuation:** The first stage of life is the process of adapting to life as a separate individual no longer bound to the mother. Most important for the first stage child is the process of food-taking, and coming to accept sustenance from outside the mother's body. In fact, this whole stage of life could be described as an ordeal of weaning, or individuation.

Tremendous physical growth occurs in the first stage of life (the first seven or so years) and an enormous amount of learning—one begins to manage bodily energies and begins to explore the physical world. Acquiring basic motor skills is a key aspect of the first stage of life—learning to hold a spoon and eat with it, learning to walk and talk and be responsible for excretion. If the first stage of life unfolds as it should, the separation from the mother completes itself in basic terms. But there is a tendency in us to struggle with this simple individuation, or to not accept the process fully. Every human being tends to associate individuation with a feeling of separation, a sense of disconnection from love and support. That reaction is the dramatization of egoity, or self-contraction, in its earliest form. And unless one enters profoundly into the process of God-Realization, that reaction characterizes every individual for his or her entire life.

**Stage Two—Socialization:** Between the ages of five and eight years we begin to become aware of the emotional dimension of existence—how we feel and how others respond emotionally to us becomes of great importance. This is the beginning of the second stage of life, the stage of social adaptation and all that goes with it—a growing sense of sexual differentiation, awareness of the effects of one's actions on others, a testing of whether one is loved. Adi Da points out that in the second stage of life children are naturally psychic and sensitive to etheric energy and should be encouraged to feel that "you are more than what you look like", for the sake of their future Spiritual growth. With the arising of greater emotional sensitivity, there is also the tendency to become locked in patterns of feeling rejected by others, and rejecting or punishing others for their presumed un-love. The drama of rejecting and feeling rejected is the primary sign of incomplete adaptation in the second stage of life.

155

**Stage Three—Integration:** In the early to mid teens, the third stage of life becomes established. The key development of this stage is the maturing of mental ability—the capacity to use mind and speech in abstract, conceptual ways—together with the power to use discrimination and to exercise the will. On the bodily level, puberty is continuing (having begun during the later years of the second stage of life) with all its attendant bodily and emotional changes.

The purpose of the third stage of life is the integration of the human character in body, emotion, and mind, so that the emerging adult becomes a fully differentiated, or autonomous, sexual and social human character. If the process of growth in the first and the second stages of life has proceeded unhindered, then this integration can take place naturally. If, however, there have been failures of adaptation in the earlier stages—a chronic feeling of being separate and unsustained or chronic feelings of being rejected or unloved, and consequent difficulties in relating happily to others—then the process of integration is disturbed.

In fact, in most individuals, the process of the third stage of life becomes an adolescent struggle between the conflicting motives to be dependent on others and to be independent of them. This adolescent drama tends to continue throughout adult life. It is one of the signs that growth has stopped, that the work of the third stage of life was never completed. Growth into truly mature adulthood—characterized by equanimity, discriminative intelligence, heart-feeling, and the impulse to always continue to grow—tends never to occur, although a nominal adaptation to the first three stages of life is usually acknowledged by twenty-one years of age.

So how does one begin to grow again? By participating in a culture of living religious and Spiritual practice that understands and rightly nurtures each stage of development. This is Adi Da's recommendation, and the circumstance that He has Worked to create for His devotees by establishing the Way of the Heart. Anyone, at any age, who chooses the Way of the Heart can begin the process of understanding and transcending the limits of his or her growth in the first three stages of life and in all the stages of life that follow.

Adi Da refers to the first three stages of life as the "foundation stages", because the ordeal of growth into human maturity is mere preparation for something far greater—for Spiritual awakening, and, ultimately, for Divine Enlightenment. This greater process begins to flower in the fourth stage of life on the basis of a profound conversion to love.

**Stage Four—Spiritualization:** Even while still maturing in the first three stages of life, many people devote themselves to religious practices, submitting to an ordered life of discipline and devotion. This is the beginning

156

of establishing the disposition of the fourth stage of life, but it is only the beginning. The real leap involved in the fourth stage of life is a transition that very few ever make. It is nothing less than the breakthrough to a Spiritually-illumined life of Divine contemplation and selfless service. How does such a life become possible? Only on the basis of a heart-awakening so profound that the common human goals—to be fulfilled through bodily and mental pleasures—lose their force.

The purpose of existence for one established in the fourth stage of life is devotion—moment to moment intimacy with the Spiritual Reality, an intimacy that is real and ecstatic, and which changes one's vision of the world. Everything that appears, everything that occurs is now seen as a process full of Spirit-Presence. This new vision of existence is given through Spirit-Baptism, an infilling of Spirit-Power (usually granted by a Spiritually Awakened Master), which is described in many different religious and Spiritual traditions.

For the devotee in the Way of the Heart who has completed the listening-hearing process and entered the seeing stages of practice, Adi Da's Spirit-Baptism is first felt as a Current of energy descending from above the head, down through the front of the body to the perineum, or bodily base. This descent is forceful, sublime, and very effective in purifying and Spiritualizing the human personality, bringing forth the signs of radiance, peace, and universal love that characterize a Spiritually Awakened being. This descending Spirit-Baptism is one of the uniquely characteristic signs of Adi Da's Grace in the life of His Spiritually activated devotee. By the time the fourth stage of life is complete, not only has the Spirit-Current descended fully down the front of the body but It has turned about at the bodily base and ascended up the spine to a place deep behind the eyes (called the "ajna chakra", or sometimes the "third eye"), where It is felt to rest.

The full-hearted and Spiritually Awakened devotion characteristic of the fourth stage of life is generally the summit of Realization achieved in the traditions of Judaism, Christianity, Islam, and much of Hinduism, and even then, it is most uncommon.

The fourth stage of life, though it represents a profound and auspicious advance beyond the foundation stages, is only the beginning of truly Spiritual growth. Adi Da points out that the primary error of one in the fourth stage of life is to presume that God and the individual personality are inherently separate from one another. God is the Sublime "Other" with Whom one Communes and in Whom one may become ecstatically absorbed at times, even to the point of apparent union. Nevertheless, such raptures pass, and one is left with the continuing urge for union with the Divine Beloved. The individual being is still a separate ego, still searching, even though the goal of seeking is Spiritual in nature.

**Stage Five—Higher Spiritual Evolution:** The fifth stage of life could be described as the domain of accomplished Yogis—individuals involved in the pursuit of Enlightenment through mystical experience, such as the vision of the "blue pearl", and through the attainment of psychic powers. But it is important to note that just as exceedingly few religious practitioners fully Awaken to the Spiritual Reality in the fourth stage of life, exceedingly few would-be Yogis become fifth stage Realizers.

The important difference between the fifth stage of life and all the stages of life that precede it is that awareness on the gross physical plane is no longer the ordinary mode of existence. Rather, attention is constantly attracted into subtle realms—dreamlike or visionary regions of mind.

The phenomena of the fifth stage of life arise as a result of the further movement of the Spirit-Current, now in the higher regions of the brain. In the fifth stage of life the Spirit-Current moves from the ajna chakra through and beyond the crown of the head. At its point of highest ascent, the Spirit-Current triggers the Yogic meditative state traditionally called "Nirvikalpa Samadhi" ("formless ecstasy") in which all awareness of body and mind is temporarily dissolved in the absolute Love-Bliss of the Divine Self-Condition. This profoundly ecstatic state is regarded as the summit of Realization in the Hindu schools of Yoga, as well as in certain branches of Buddhism and Taoism. (It is precisely defined by Avatara Adi Da as "fifth stage conditional Nirvikalpa Samadhi".) This dissolution of body and mind is a direct demonstration that the apparently separate self has no eternal existence or significance, and that only the Divine Condition of absolute Freedom and Happiness truly exists.

Even so, a limit remains. This great Samadhi, the culminating achievement of the fifth stage of life, is fleeting. At some point bodily consciousness returns, and so does the ache to renew that boundless, disembodied Bliss. Fifth stage conditional Nirvikalpa Samadhi, for all its profundity, is achieved on the basis of a subtle stress. It is the ultimate fruit of the Yogic strategy to escape the body by directing one's awareness upward into infinite Light.

In His description of the Way of the Heart, Adi Da Reveals that higher mystical experience and the achievement of profound trance states in the maturity of the fourth stage of life and in the fifth stage of life are not prerequisites for most ultimate Divine Enlightenment. In the Way of the Heart, the whole tour of the subtle planes can be bypassed, because of Adi Da's unique Transmission of the Love-Blissful Power of the Divine Itself. When, in the fourth stage of life, the devotee in the Way of the Heart is mature enough to be responsible for constantly receiving and "conducting" Adi Da's Spirit-Current, a most extraordinary process begins to take place in the body-mind. The Infusion of His Spirit-Current purifies and quickens the body-mind in every cell from the crown of the head to the very toes. Every knot in the body-mind is opened up in this ecstatic reception of Him.

When this Sublime Infusion has completed its Work, a great conversion has occurred in the body-mind. One is not susceptible to the fascinations of visionary experience, even when such experiences arise. Neither is one moved to direct one's attention up and out of the body into the infinitely ascended state of "formless ecstasy". Rather, the "tour" of mystical experience is revealed to be simply more of the futile search to be completely Happy and fulfilled. And so that whole pursuit of mystical satisfaction relaxes, and the devotee may be easily drawn beyond all habits of identification with bodily states and even beyond the subtle mind states of the fifth stage of life into a pristine understanding of Reality as Consciousness Itself.

**Stage Six—Awakening to the Transcendental Self:** In the sixth stage of life, one is no longer perceiving and interpreting everything from the point of view of the individuated body-mind with its desires and goals. One stands in a Transcendental Position, Identified with the Very Consciousness that is the Ground of all that exists, rather than with the apparently separate self. In that Position, one stands as the "Witness" of all that arises, even while continuing to participate in the play of life. While life goes on like a movie on a screen, one sees the greater import of Existence and the non-necessity of all that arises. This is the beginning of what Adi Da calls "the ultimate stages of life", or the stages of Identification with Consciousness Itself.

The sixth stage of life may include the experience of Jnana Samadhi, which, like fifth stage conditional Nirvikalpa Samadhi, is a form of temporary and conditional Realization of the Divine Self. However, fifth stage conditional Nirvikalpa Samadhi comes about through the strategy of ascent, the urge to move attention up and beyond the body-mind; in Jnana Samadhi, on the other hand, awareness of gross and subtle states is excluded by concentration in Transcendental Self-Consciousness.

The Awakening to Consciousness Itself in the sixth stage of life is the pinnacle of Realization achieved by the greatest (and exceedingly rare) Realizers in certain schools of Hinduism and Buddhism, as well as Jainism and Taoism. Such Realizers eschewed the fascinations of experience from the beginning, turning away from the enticements of "money, food, and sex" in the first three stages of life, as well as from the attractions of devotional (fourth stage) rapture and of Yogic (fifth stage) mysticism. Instead, the Sages of the sixth stage of life have traditionally contemplated the freedom and purity of Consciousness—to the degree of Realizing that Consciousness Itself, eternal and Prior to any mortal form or temporary experience, is our True Condition, or True Self.

But even deep resting in the freedom of Transcendental Consciousness is not Most Perfect[1] Enlightenment. Why not? Because there is still a stress involved, still one last barrier to Divine Self-Realization. Sixth stage practice and Realization is expressed by turning within, away from all conditional objects and experiences (including the energies and the movements of attention of one's own body-mind), in order to concentrate upon the Source of individual consciousness. Thus, the root of egoity is still alive. The search still remains, in its most primitive form. The sixth stage of life is the search to identify with Pure Consciousness Prior to and exclusive of phenomena.

**Stage Seven—Divine Enlightenment:** The Realization of the seventh stage of life is uniquely Revealed and Given by Adi Da. It is release from all the egoic limitations of the previous stages of life. Remarkably, the seventh stage Awakening, which is Adi Da's Gift to His devotees who have completed the developmental course of the first six stages of life, is not an experience at all. The true Nature of everything is simply obvious. Now the Understanding arises that every apparent "thing" is Eternally, Perfectly the same as Reality, Consciousness, Happiness, Truth, or God. And that Understanding is Supreme Love-Bliss.

Adi Da calls this Divine Awakeness "Open Eyes" and also "seventh stage Sahaj Samadhi" ("Sahaj" meaning "natural", or inherent, and "Samadhi" meaning "exalted State"). No longer is there any need to seek meditative seclusion in order to Realize perpetual Identification with the One Divine Reality. The Ecstatic and world-embracing Confession "There is Only God" is native to one who enjoys the State of "Open Eyes". Consciousness is no longer felt to be divorced from the world of forms, but Consciousness Itself is understood and seen to be the very Nature, Source, and Substance of that world. And so the life of the seventh stage Realizer, Most Perfectly Awake by Grace of Adi Da, becomes the Love-Blissful process of Divinely Recognizing, or intuitively acknowledging, whatever arises to be only a modification of Consciousness Itself.

The Divinely Self-Realized Being is literally "Enlightened". The Light of Divine Being Flows in him or her in a continuous circuitry of Love-Bliss that rises in an S-shaped curve from the right side of the heart to a Matrix of Light above and Beyond the crown of the head. This is Amrita Nadi, the

---

1. Avatara Adi Da uses the phrase "Most Perfect(ly)" in the sense of "Absolutely Perfect(ly)". (Similarly, the phrase "Most Ultimate[ly]" is equivalent to "Absolutely Ultimate[ly]".)

In the sixth stage of life and the seventh stage of life, What is Realized (Consciousness Itself) is Perfect (and Ultimate). This is why Avatara Adi Da characterizes these stages as the "ultimate stages of life", and describes the practice of the Way of the Heart in the context of these stages as "the 'Perfect Practice'". The distinction between the sixth stage of life and the seventh stage of life is that the devotee's <u>Realization</u> of What is Perfect (and Ultimate) is itself Perfect (and Ultimate) only in the seventh stage. The Perfection or Ultimacy (in the seventh stage), <u>both</u> of What is Realized and of the Realization of It, is what is signified by the phrase "Most Perfect(ly)" or "Most Ultimate(ly)".

"Channel of Immortal Bliss", mentioned in the esoteric Hindu Spiritual tradition, but fully described for the first time by Adi Da Himself. After His Divine Re-Awakening in 1970, Adi Da experienced the "Regeneration" of this Current of Love-Bliss, and He came to understand Amrita Nadi as the Original Form of the Divine Self-Radiance in the human body-mind (and in all conditional beings and forms).

Divine Self-Realization in the seventh stage of life unfolds through a Yogic process in four phases: Divine Transfiguration, Divine Transformation, Divine Indifference, and Divine Translation.

In the phase of Divine Transfiguration, the Realizer's whole body is Infused by Love-Bliss, and he or she Radiantly Demonstrates active Love.

In the following phase of Divine Transformation, the subtle or psychic dimension of the body-mind is fully Illumined, which may result in extraordinary Powers, Grace-Given by Adi Da, of healing, longevity, and the ability to release obstacles from the world and from the lives of others.

Eventually, Divine Indifference ensues, which is spontaneous and profound Resting in the "Deep" of Consciousness Itself, with progressively less and less noticing of the manifested worlds.

Divine Translation is the ultimate "Event" of the entire process of Awakening—the Outshining of all noticing of objective conditions through the infinitely magnified Force of Consciousness Itself. Divine Translation is the Destiny beyond all destinies, from Which there is no return to the conditional realms.

The experience of being so overwhelmed by the Divine Radiance that all appearances fade away may occur temporarily from time to time during the seventh stage of life. But when that Most Love-Blissful Swoon (or Moksha-Bhava Samadhi) becomes permanent, Divine Translation occurs and the body-mind is inevitably relinquished in death. Then there is only Eternal Inherence in the Divine Domain of unqualified Happiness and Joy.

Adi Da has frequently described the unfolding Mystery of the seventh stage of life through the image of crocks baking in a furnace:

*AVATARA ADI DA: When you place newly made clay crocks in a furnace of great heat to dry and harden the crockery, at first the crocks become red-hot and seem to be surrounded and pervaded by a reddish glow, but they are still defined. Eventually the fire becomes white-hot, and its radiation becomes so pervasive, so bright, that you can no longer make out the separate figures of the crocks.*

*This is the significance of Divine Translation. At first, conditions of existence are Transfigured by the inherent Radiance of Divine Being. Ultimately, through Self-Abiding and through Divinely Recognizing all forms, in effect all forms are Outshined by that Radiance. This is the Law of life. Life lived Lawfully is fulfilled in Outshining, or the transcendence of cosmic Nature. In the meantime, cosmic Nature is simply Divinely Transfigured, and relations are Divinely Transfigured, by the Power of the Divine Self-Position. [February 9, 1983]*

The religious and Spiritual traditions of mankind characteristically conceive of human life as a "Great Path of Return", a struggle to be reunited with the Divine Source of existence. From Adi Da's viewpoint, this is an error. The Way of the Heart is founded in "radical" understanding, or constant restoration to the intuition of present Happiness, present God. Thus, although Adi Da allows for and fully explains all the developmental signs or stages of life through which His devotee may pass, the Way of the Heart is not purposed to "progress through" the stages of life. The entire process is founded in the Wisdom of the seventh stage from the very beginning— and thus is one of release, of surrendering, progressively, via heart-Communion with Adi Da, all obstructions in body, mind, and psyche that prevent that unqualified Divine Enjoyment.

# The Seven Stages of Life

*As Revealed by Adi Da (The Da Avatar)*

# The Seven Stages of Life in the Way of the Heart As Revealed by Adi Da (The Da Avatar)

| FIRST STAGE | SECOND STAGE | THIRD STAGE | FOURTH STAGE |
|---|---|---|---|
| **Identified with:** the waking body-mind | **Identified with:** the waking body-mind | **Identified with:** the waking body-mind | **Identified with:** the waking body- and (in the "advan context) the mind itself (the subtle c dreaming self) |
| **Process:** individuation; adaptation to the physical body | **Process:** socialization; adaptation to the emotional-sexual or feeling dimension | **Process:** integration of the psycho-physical personality; development of verbal mind, discriminitive intelligence, and the will | **Process:** self-surrendering devotion to the D Person; purificatio and outgrowing c the bodily-based of view through reception of Divin Spirit-Force |
| **Signs of Incomplete Adaptation:** the feeling of separation (and separativeness) | **Signs of Incomplete Adaptation:** dramatizing the feeling of being rejected, especially by rejecting or punishing others for presumed un-love | **Signs of Incomplete Adaptation:** drama or conflict between dependence and independence | **Error:** prolonging the fir three stages of lif conceiving of Goe egoic self as eter separate from eac other; a never-en search for God; appealing to God intimacy, relief, ar self-satisfaction |

Just as the ordinary human processes are founded in the physical anatomy of the body-mind, the Spiritual, Transcendental, and Divine processes are based in, or can be seen in relationship to, the total hierarchical structural anatomy of the body-mind—the structures of energy and Consciousness found in every human being. This chart illustrates this hierarchical structural anatomy as it relates to individuals practicing in the context of the fourth, the fifth, and the sixth stages of life in the Way of the Heart, showing for each stage the characteristic location of energy and attention in the body-mind-self. When energy and attention are thus focused, the being becomes identified with the phenomena or states of Consciousness characteristic of that stage of life. This identification with a specific state of Consciousness, as well as the limitation (or characteristic "error") in such identification, is noted on the chart for each stage of life.

In the Most Perfect God-Realization of the seventh stage of life, attention itself (the root sense of self-contraction) has been transcended. In this Divinely Free State, the structure of Energy and Consciousness is actually beyond or prior to the body-mind-self. Even so, this Realization does have a "location" and "Yogic Form" in the human body-mind-self, known as "Amrita Nadi" (the current or channel of immortality), which Adi Da has called "the Great conditional, or Apparently conditionally Manifested, Form and 'Location' Of God". When seen in relationship to the body-mind, the Amrita Nadi is an S-shaped channel. Its lower terminal is in the right side of the heart, and it rises to its upper terminal through the neck to the crown of the head and above.

For a full discussion of the hierarchical structural anatomy of the body-mind-self, the seven stages of life, the varieties of Spiritual Transmission, and the practice of the Way of the Heart in the context of seven stages of life as Revealed by Adi Da, please see *The Dawn Horse Testament Of Adi Da*.

**Anatomy:** reception of Spiri Force: the Spirit-Current is felt to descend in the fr line of the body then ascend in th spinal line until a tion rests stably a Ajna Door, the d way to the brain

| FTH STAGE | SIXTH STAGE | SEVENTH STAGE |
|---|---|---|
| **lentified with:** | **Identified with:** | **Identified with:** |
| ıe higher mind (the | Consciousness, prior | Divine Consciousness |
| ıbtle or dreaming | to body and mind | itself |
| ·lf) | (presumed to be sepa- | |
| | rate from all conditional | **Process:** |
| **rocess:** | phenomena), as in the | Realization of the Divine |
| oiritual or Yogic | state of deep sleep | Self; Inherently Perfect |
| scent of attention | | Freedom and |
| ıto psychic dimen- | **Process:** | Realization of Divine |
| ons of the being; | Identification with the | Love-Bliss (seventh |
| ıystical experience | Transcendental Witness; | stage Sahaj Samadhi); |
| f the higher brain; | transcendence of body | Divine Recognition of all |
| ·nunciation of body; | and mind; will most | psycho-physical states |
| ıay culminate in fifth | likely include the experi- | and conditions as |
| ːage conditional | ence of Jnana Samadhi | modifications of Divine |
| irvikalpa Samadhi | | Consciousness; no |
| | **Error:** | "difference" experi- |
| **rror:** | failure to Recognize | enced between Divine |
| ·eking or clinging | objects and conditional | Consciousness and |
| ɔ subtle objects and | states as arising in the | psycho-physical states |
| ːates (or to merely | One Divine Reality | and conditions |
| ɔnditional transcen- | | |
| ·nce of subtle objects | | |
| nd states in fifth | | |
| ːage conditional | | |
| irvikalpa Samadhi) | | |

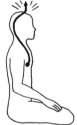

| **ıatomy:** | **Anatomy:** | **Anatomy:** |
|---|---|---|
| ːent of the Spirit- | the Spirit-Current | "Regeneration" of |
| ırrent from the brain | descends from above | Amrita Nadi (the |
| ·re (the Ajna Door) to | the crown of the head, | Immortal Current of |
| ·e crown of the head | via Amrita Nadi, to the | Divine Love-Bliss arising |
| ·d above (or even, in | right side of the heart, | in the right side of the |
| ːh stage conditional | the bodily root of | heart and terminating |
| ·rvikalpa Samadhi, | Consciousness | in the Light or Locus |
| ·the Light infinitely | | infinitely above the |
| ·ove the crown of the | | head) |
| ·ad) | | |

CHAPTER 23

# The Religious Ambivalence of the West

*November 3, 1977*

AVATARA ADI DA: There is something very negative implicit in the religious consciousness of Western people. If you are a Westerner, "Is there a God?" seems to be the question you should be asking in order to become religious. But it is a completely absurd question. It has nothing whatever to do with Spiritual life. This question has to do with human beings, not with God. The question "Is there a God?" reflects a state in human beings for which they must become responsible. It is not itself a question that must be answered.

The religious consciousness of Western people is ambivalent. On the one hand, Westerners are very worldly and strong when religion permits worldliness, and, on the other hand, they are phasing, weak, and always threatened at the level of subjective, or psychic, responsibility.

The Western consciousness is always trying to make positive whatever is overwhelmingly negative. The negative thing is what is powerful. People in the West are always trying to overcome negativity with positive feeling, with beliefs, with effort, with answers, with knowledge. The negative pattern, or what is known as "karma", is actually creating their lives. Thus, Westerners remain characteristically weak, obsessed with an uninspected negative force that is always influencing their behavior and their thinking. They are always trying to surmount such negativity either through self-effort or through association with the Edible Deity—the external Savior or God whose power they can consume irresponsibly. Therefore, faith and belief are reduced by Westerners to ways of overcoming negativity.

In the Western religious doctrines (and the Middle Eastern teachings that gave rise to them) the negative force that tends to overwhelm the individual beneath the superficial mind is interpreted as sin, a disposition to be overcome by association with something greater than oneself—the Edible Deity, the Savior, the true God, the true religion, the true belief. Presuming a negative position, the Westerner orients himself or herself toward something positive and is saved by it. But such a person is still always sinful, always tending to fall back on sin.

The fundamental tenet of the Middle Eastern religions—Jewish or Christian or Islamic—is that this world and everything in it, including humanity, is the creation of God, and human beings are also the highest creation of God, reflecting the Deity although not in any sense equal to the Deity. To this point of view, therefore, the negative view of this life and the world is itself a form of sin. It is a sin to believe that this world is not godly, or that the Divine is not the ultimate destiny of the world, or that the world is not controlled by the Divine. Thus, the presumption of the West is that if the world is under the control of the Divine, its destiny is altogether positive, whatever its present condition may be, and to view the world negatively is itself sinful.

The classically Oriental point of view does not adhere to the principle that the world is the creation of God and that God is therefore its destiny. The principle that is appealed to in the East transcends phenomena, even excludes phenomena and precedes them altogether. The Oriental mind is critical of the world itself, not just of things in the world. The Eastern mind views the world not as the creation of God but as an illusion. Thus, to view this world positively—in itself necessary, in itself the point of existence—rather than to transcend the world is to be swept up in an illusion, a false point of view. It is sin, from the Oriental point of view.

The natural disposition in the West is toward the world itself. It is to move into the world with a positive moral character, struggling against sin, the negative power. The natural disposition in the Orient is toward transcendence of this world.

From the Western religious point of view, one's association with the Edible Deity, the Savior, is what gives one strength. The Savior gives the Spirit. Through the magic of one's association with this Savior, one acquires the Spiritual force to overcome, moment to moment, one's own sinfulness and negativity so that one can participate in this great plan of creation. The Oriental point of view has nothing whatever to do with such an idea (although clearly Western and Middle Eastern ideas have filtered into Oriental culture so that the later, more modern cultures and traditions of the Orient tend to varying degrees to reflect the Western point of view).

When the disciple approached a traditional Spiritual Master in the East, he or she was not trying to find out how to live better—he or she was looking for liberation from the world. But the people who went to Jesus or Mohammed or Moses did not ask how to be liberated from the world. That was not their question. They wanted to be certain that there is God and that the one they were talking to was a true Messenger of God. And then they wanted to know what they should be doing to enjoy the Blessings of God, to be in right relationship to God in this world and to enjoy a future that would be Blessed by God. That was their question. In the Orient, on the other hand, they did not ask that question. If they went looking for a Master, they wanted to know how the hell they could get out of here and bring an end to all this torment!

For example, Gautama (known as the Buddha) grew up as a prince in India, with all the benefits of royal seclusion, the most opulent level of life possible in his time. When he was a relatively young man, he was taken on a trip through the streets where he saw the daily life of ordinary people, who were sick and aging and suffering in all the ordinary, social, mortal ways. He did not see them as sinners who were suffering their turning away from God and who needed to be more positively associated with God in order to do better and feel better. He did not see them as the creations of the Deity, as his brothers and sisters under the One Divine. No—he was completely astonished by what he saw, and he was, to his very depths, convinced that this is not a place in which to continue, that what life is about is not surviving and improving your circumstances and acquiring a positive moral character under God, or even a life of worldly success under God. He was convinced that that is not the business of life. The business of life, as Gautama realized it, is to find a way, through meditation, through understanding, through purification, and through release of desires, to escape completely from this condition of existence.

That disposition represented by Gautama, among others, that search for liberation, characterizes the classic traditions almost everywhere in the Orient. It is for the purpose of liberation that a person in the East seeks a Teacher or becomes interested in a Spiritual Teaching. Spiritual Teachings in the Orient are, in general, associated with one or another ascetic disposition, the inversion of attention, the transcendence of this world. Inversion and transcendence are the fundamental principles in the East, just as in Western religion the fundamental principle is that this world is to be interpreted positively as the creation of God, and therefore the problem of existence is a moral one.

Western religion comes out of the Middle East, which is the dividing line between the Western, or right-sided, approach to life and the Eastern, or left-sided, approach to life.[1] Although the West has inherited Middle Eastern religion, basically the path of the right side of the body is not about religion at all. Western development is about life in the world, where the conditions of born existence are essentially regarded to be just what they seem to be— the conditions of born existence. Born existence is the game wherein you are to survive and struggle, which you must take into account and which

1. The left side of the body is controlled by the right hemisphere of the brain, the hemisphere (in most people) primarily associated with nonverbal, spatial, and holistic methods of relating to the objects of experience. These "left-sided" qualities generally typify the mystical and sacred cultures of the East. The right side of the body is controlled by the left hemisphere of the brain, the hemisphere (in most people) primarily associated with verbal, temporal, and analytical methods of relating to the objects of experience. These "right-sided" qualities typify the scientific and materialistic cultures of the West.

your philosophy must reflect. The Middle East still has a religious or Spiritual aura of a kind, but its principles, once they developed as Western history, as the right-sided history of humanity, have not appeared in the form of religion. They have appeared in the form of this modern, technological, scientific society, which is essentially a-religious, not religious, a-Spiritual, most often anti-religious and anti-Spiritual. Thus, Western culture is basically oriented to manifested conditions and functions themselves.

Westerners constantly confront the negative force of their own self-presumptions while trying to live a merely human, social, mortal life, advancing, succeeding, and surviving. Middle Eastern religion has provided psychological support for the right-sided man or woman of the West. But, over time, the more involved Westerners have become in the functions of manifested existence, in surviving and dealing with the material universe, and the more sophisticated human beings have become in their knowing, the less they have been able to justify the naive presumptions upon which this Western, or Middle Eastern, religion depends.

Thus, more and more, Westerners are being left with only sin. They do not even know what to call it anymore. They call it "sin" only if they see a God over against it. Basically they are left with an obsessed, negative, mortal life.

Having developed to this point, then, Westerners seeking after Truth are turning to the opposite side. They are hoping to be consoled by becoming Oriental, or left-sided. But once you have gone to the right, you can never go to the left and exclude the right side of the body again. Thus, in this gesture toward the left side of the body there is the possibility for awareness as the whole body.

The Orient, on the other hand, which has been trying to transcend the gross conditions of worldly existence for centuries, has a very strong and sophisticated religious and Spiritual tradition. But it also has had among the most dreadfully mortal social and human conditions on Earth. Thus, people in the East today are reaching toward the West, toward the right side, to find technological, scientific, social, and cultural advantages with which to carry on their essentially negative philosophical point of view. But once you have gone so far to the left, you can never go all the way to the right and exclude the left side of the body again, because you have already adapted to it. Thus, the East in its association with the West also has the possibility of becoming sensitive to the necessary, or whole body, point of view.

What one sees in the world today are essentially the artifacts of the two sides in their independence, in their clashes with one another, in their distinctions. People today naively try to become associated with the ancient, classic systems of religion, Spirituality, and philosophy, but they do not have the perspective for examining what these concepts are all about, what their own motives are all about, what the traditional belief-systems and Yogas are really all about. People today generally no longer represent the archetypal psychological dispositions that are at the root of all of the great enterprises, East and West. And unless those archetypal psychological suppositions, presumptions, and dispositions are actually true of you, you cannot fulfill them. Therefore, if you are truly moved to true Spiritual life, you have no choice but to inspect completely your own condition of existence.

You must begin to understand what the true religious life or the true Spiritual life is really all about. You must be able to understand all your casually generated motivations that reflect old, conventional concepts, persuasions, and philosophies. You, as Westerners, may have casually inherited your Judeo-Christian mind without ever having been a very profound student of it. It just filtered in, through a little bit of churchgoing, a little bit of parental and social influence. But if you would practice true religion or Spirituality, you must become responsible for the religious conventions you represent, through a very sophisticated investigation of Judeo-Christian thought and concepts, however casual your inheritance.

The Way of the Heart is the influence by which interested individuals, regardless of their disposition toward West or East, right or left, can make the necessary inspection of the totality of human existence. The essence of My Wisdom-Teaching is that the Divine is the present Condition of existence, not in any sense the goal of existence that can be approached through efforts toward transcendence. Nor is the Divine in Which you Inhere to be viewed simply as the Creator of this world, implying, therefore, a necessarily positive view toward the world and the functions of existence themselves. My Wisdom-Teaching is about present, "radical", and continuous God-Communion, or Communion with Me as the Very Condition and Truth of existence.

The Divine is the Truth of existence, not the Creator of the world. The Divine is the Condition of all conditions, not just a great condition that creates all lesser conditions. And Divine Communion is not a matter of moving into a condition other than the present conditions, in order to escape them by exclusion through the inversion of attention.

Once you become truly sympathetic with My Wisdom-Teaching, practice of the Way of the Heart becomes an essential responsibility, simple in principle. When you enjoy Divine Communion with Me as your True Heart-Master and as the Source and Proof of My Wisdom-Teaching, although the subjective artifacts of your past and your old disposition may appear, you have a sense of humor relative to them. Then not every day is a crisis. Subjective feelings come and go, and external circumstances may tend to bother you somewhat, but there is no great moment. Literally nothing is threatened, once you are living in this Communion with Me. Existence then becomes the creative process wherein you are living responsibly, purifying, changing, making things sacred, living the sacrifice that is real life. Then existence is not problematic. It is creative. It is a process of the confrontation of conditions, but it is humorous. Nothing ultimate is at stake. It is just the game of the universe.

And there is nowhere to look for God. What is God is completely Obvious under these conditions, even totally within the limits of your present perception. It is a not a matter of some other vision, some other experience, some inwardness. It is a matter of understanding, of being awakened from the sleep, the bondage, the problem, the dilemma by which you apprehend your present condition. In any moment of this understanding, you are awakened beyond the self-contraction without all the concepts and contractions of energy and feeling.

Therefore, hear My Argument, or understand the self-contraction most fundamentally, and see Me, or be converted at heart, in this Communion with Me. Then your action is transformed. It fulfills the Law. It is a form of sacrifice, of love.

Be love and perform the actions of love until the universe disappears. And be willing to let it disappear. Be Happy in any moment for it to disappear. When you are My devotee, whatever satisfactions there are in the functional display in this moment cannot in any sense compare to the ecstasy of Divine Communion with Me. Nevertheless, do not be strategically turned away from those satisfactions in the doubting that possesses the ego. Live as love in the form of all your relations. Living as love in love with Me, you are not holding on to your relations any longer. You are just participating in them fully, openly, freely, Happily. You are not rejecting them, but neither are you clinging to them madly, out of fear. You are completely Happy to surrender beyond all limits.

The way to give up everything is not the strategic renunciation of the traditional ascetic, or turning in and up, but love without qualification. Then everything falls away. Everything becomes God. Everything becomes enjoyable and not binding. When you can be released as love completely and can transcend the body-mind-self completely, then everything dissolves.

But you are afraid to dissolve. You think that you must be in a position somehow, observing something, holding on to something, being held by something, whether in this gross form or in some subtle configuration. You are afraid to feel so profoundly, to utterly release your separate self-consciousness, because that means you will lose your point in space. You are going to lose your life—that is exactly true. Thus, only when the Divine Love-Bliss, Happiness Itself, becomes Obvious to you will that dissolution be permitted to become Perfect—because it does involve the dissolution of everything, the dissolution of body, all energy, all forms, all worlds, all that is mind, all concepts. It does involve that literally. That is exactly what you are afraid will happen! That is what you call "death" and what you try to prevent. And that is exactly what does happen in this Communion with Me. Everything is given up, everything is dissolved in the Formless Divine.

This dissolution must become your pleasure. Then this world becomes humorous and livable. Then you can make something sacred out of it, without holding on to it. This world will pass away. Everything passes away. Everything is changing here. Everything is action. Everything you hold on to changes, because it is itself change. Therefore, holding on to a position obviously is not Truth. The surrender of all positions is what is true. Ultimately that surrender becomes your position moment to moment, and not just in intense moments of formal meditation, when you have temporarily relaxed from the games of life. Ultimately, there is no limitation under any conditions. Even while active and appearing in the ordinary way, you are complete Zero, without a center, without any shapes whatsoever.

To the ordinary person that does not sound like Happiness—it sounds like some sort of craziness, some sort of tremendous, terrifying state, as Arjuna experienced in the *Bhagavad Gita* when he saw Krishna in his thousand-armed form. That is what that vision is all about—losing all ability to comprehend yourself in time and space. It is not just seeing somebody with a thousand arms. Actually, such a vision would be marvelous and interesting. But to Commune with Something with endless dimensions, to fall into that Infinite Condition yourself, is terrifying. When Arjuna was drifting into that open-ended Divine Condition, he shouted and screamed and told Krishna to please show him his two-armed, objective form, which was good enough! [Laughter.]

But My Confession to you is that this Infinite Existence is ultimate Love-Bliss, the Great Happiness.

# CHAPTER 24

# Exoteric Christianity and the Universal Spiritual Message of Jesus

*May 8, 1982*

## 1.

The Message (or "Gospel") of Jesus of Nazareth is the universal Teaching of ego-transcending love of the Spiritual and Transcendental Divine, to be practiced directly as well as in self-transcending love and tolerance of all living beings. The exoteric religionists who developed the system of beliefs that are now called "Christianity" transformed Jesus' universal and non-sectarian Teaching of ego-transcendence into the "pharisaical" (or priestly and dogmatic) religion of ego-salvation through the ritual sacrifice of Jesus. Perhaps the principal individual to give voice and concept to this new exoteric "faith" was Paul of Tarsus. On the basis of the ego-consoling religion summarized (and developed) by Paul (who did not respond positively to Jesus while Jesus was alive, and whose "Christian" thought was dictated by his own conventional and provincial Hellenism and Judaism), Christianity was transformed from the culture (or Spiritual practice) of self-sacrifice to the cult of vicarious salvation.

The two-sidedness of Christian ideas (representing the Spiritual Way of Jesus and the contrasting religious method represented by Paul, and others) is the basis for many internal conflicts and contradictions in the Christian tradition. It is Paul's "method" (or the exoteric "technique" that he, among others, proposed) that made Christianity into a religion of worldly self-improvement, righteous cultism, and eternal self-glorification. But the Way of Jesus is the Way of all Great Masters: the Way of the sacrifice and transcendence of egoic self in the Divine.

## 2.

The Christian "cult of vicarious salvation" was founded on the belief that creatures are inherently separated from God (or Happiness) and, therefore, cannot and even should not sacrifice (or transcend) themselves and, thereby, enter into Union (or Re-Union) with God (or

Happiness). Even so, it was traditionally presumed that a sacrifice is necessary in order for such Union or Re-Union to take place. And on this basis it was presumed that a substitute sacrifice (by Jesus) had taken place. And belief that the substitute, vicarious, or priestly sacrifice of Jesus is forever sufficient to grant all other individuals, or selves, the ultimate Rewards of sacred sacrifice (which are Union or Re-Union with God, Happiness, and all Blessings) thus became the basis for the popular cult of Christian sectarian religion.

The problem with exoteric religion is that it only permits people to participate in a myth, and, therefore, the salvation it seeks is also only a myth (or a conventional belief). The ancient sacred society of the Jews was, like other societies of the ancient world (among the Semites, the Hindus, and so forth), founded on the idea and the sacred techniques of sacrifice as the necessary means whereby the community and every individual maintained relations with the Divine, received the Blessings of the Divine, and, ultimately, achieved Union (or Re-Union) with the Divine and the Divine Happiness. There was no presumption that the sacred system of sacrifices (which included those to be performed in everyone's name by priests as well as those to be performed by every individual in his or her own name) was either unnecessary or fruitless. On the contrary, it was presumed to be both necessary and fruitful that collective and personal sacrifices be performed. The method of ritual sacrifice was the sacred means for achieving all desires in this world and in the next.

After many centuries, the Jews of the time of Jesus were no longer a homogeneous and centralized social or cultural body. The ancient religion of sacrifices had grown corrupt and often too technical for anyone but a trained priest to understand and perform. And many different factions had arisen, each with its own dogmas of belief and ritual. This was the circumstance of religion in the time of Jesus, and it is the circumstance in the present time as well.

Jesus was a Spirit-oriented rather than merely a religion-oriented individual. He understood the Way to God in Spiritual, mystical, and personal terms rather than in general, dogmatic, and ritualistic terms. Therefore, he Taught the Way of sacrifice in Spiritual, mystical, and personal terms. He Taught that there is no inherent separation or obstruction between creatures (or living beings) and God. He Taught that God is the Living Spirit, in Whom all beings exist, and in Whom all beings must live. He did not Teach that human beings need a mediator between themselves and God, nor that there should be or can be any substitute for every person's own self-sacrifice as the means of Communing with God. He did not represent himself as a mediator (or substitute sacrifice), since he did not presume there is any inherent separation or obstruction between creatures (or living beings) and the Spiritual Divine. He only Taught a direct, non-ritualistic, Spiritual, mystical, and personal Way of sacrifice, which he thought represented and epitomized all of the ultimate Wisdom of the ancient Jews.

Paul of Tarsus was a conventional Jew, trained in the sectarian rabbinical system of his time. He was not Taught by Jesus (or the disciples of Jesus), nor does the point of view characteristically expressed in his letters represent the true (or specific) Teaching of Jesus. Paul came to feel that he (and mankind in general) was and is inherently separated from God and Happiness. And he felt there was no effective means for restoring himself (or anyone) to God or Happiness, since there was—it seemed to him—some kind of inherent obstruction in everyone that could not be transcended.

Then, as reported in his letters, Paul experienced a mystical phenomenon (which he associated with Jesus) that encouraged him to believe that the inherent obstruction and separation between creatures and God had been conquered, for everyone, by the death (or ritual blood-sacrifice) and resurrection of Jesus. And he spent the rest of his life proclaiming this religion—which is the faith or systematic belief in the effective power of Jesus' self-sacrifice to bring everyone to eventual Union or Re-Union with God and Happiness. (In all of this, Paul was more of a Greek "gnostic" than a Jew.)

I must criticize this "Christian" (or even "Pauline") religion (which was an invention of the original popular Christ-cult, whose "genius", or most potent idea-maker, was Paul, not Jesus) because (1) it is not the religion or Way Taught by Jesus (but is only a mythological and priestly religion about Jesus), and (2) it is not a method that in fact and in Truth does what it proclaims to be able to do (that is, if the ego merely witnesses or believes in the self-sacrifice of another, it neither transcends itself nor Receives the Ultimate Results of the other's sacrifice).

First of all, as I have already indicated, Jesus Taught a free personal Way of Spiritual self-sacrifice, or the Way of self-transcending love of God, and ultimate inherence in God (or the Inherently Spiritual and Transcendental Divine) expressed in daily life via self-transcending love, or tolerance and service, of all living beings. Jesus heartily proclaimed that all beings are inherently intimate with God (Whom he described as "our Father"). He did not at all subscribe to the view that living beings are inherently evil or inherently separated from God. He described every living being as a child of One Father. And by that he did not mean that human beings should be childish (and so act in such a loveless and egoically "self-possessed" manner that they effectively separate themselves from God). Rather, his idea of the Fatherhood of God was related to the conventions of Jewish laws of inheritance. He conceived of every human child as the direct inheritor (even through birth in his or her mother's womb) of the blessings and status of all that a child is rightly to receive from his or her parents. And, in the case of a child of God, what is ultimately inherited is Blessing and Union and Happiness from, with, and in the Spiritual Presence of the Divine.

Jesus Taught that human beings are <u>tending</u> to <u>separate</u> <u>themselves</u> from the Spirit-Presence of the Divine. He described the Father as One Who is always ready and even seeking for intimate Re-Union with those who separate themselves from God. Therefore, Jesus did not at all subscribe to the view that human beings are inherently separated from God (and thus, even by virtue of the Will of God, inevitably going to death and hell, unless a voluntary mediator or substitute self-sacrificer can appear between them and God and so <u>create</u> Union). Indeed, the idea of a necessary mediator or ritual substitute is the most obvious and conventional kind of priest-talk, a kind of sinful (or "off the mark") presumption, the kind that Jesus always criticized.

Jesus Taught that "sin" (or all that people do or think or believe or presume that separates them from God or obstructs their Union with God and Divine Happiness) is <u>not</u> <u>inherent</u>. He Taught that people can and should and must repent of (or renounce) sin (or the tendency to separate from God). He Taught that such repentance purifies people (as long as it is practiced as a continuous and real exercise, followed by changes of mind and action). And he Taught that such self-purification, rather than any participation or belief in ritual or substitute sacrifices, is the basic or foundation means for entering into Union or Re-Union with the Divine Spirit.

Now, repentance (or the renunciation of the tendency to separate from God) is basically a process of self-transcendence. Indeed, the egoic self (as contraction from God) <u>is</u> sin. And, therefore, the Way Taught by Jesus is the Way of repentance from sin, or the direct Way of self-transcendence.

Jesus Taught that once a person is established in self-understanding (which is the awareness of sin, or awareness of the action of separation from God), and once that self-understanding has become expressed as responsibility for sin, or free renunciation of the tendency to separate from the Living Spirit that is God, the Way in practice must become one of continuous self-transcendence in relation to God and all of the conventional relations of the manifested self. And he summarized that practice via the ancient Jewish summary of the Law, which is to love (or sacrifice or transcend the separate and separative self in every moment through the practice of self-surrender in relation to) God and neighbor.

The four "gospels" of the *New Testament* otherwise suggest that Jesus and his direct disciples also Taught "secret" practices of Union with the Divine Spirit. Those practices were given to those who had truly (and practically) responded to the Teaching about repentance and self-surrender, and they clearly represented ancient traditional mystical and psycho-physical techniques (primarily of the type that is typically promoted by esoteric schools of the fourth stage of life and the fifth stage of life). And, in any case, those "secret" or "inner circle" instructions were simply extensions of the basic public Teaching of Jesus, which was always a call to each indi-vidual to renounce egoic "self-possession" and constantly transcend the egoic self in Communion with the Spirit of God.

Whereas Jesus Taught a direct Way of Union with God, Paul (and the "Pauline" cult) proposed a religion about Jesus. Whereas Jesus Taught the Way of self-transcendence as the necessary means of Communing with God, Paul taught that "selves" cannot transcend themselves in God.

Paul taught a conventional religious path founded on egoity rather than the transcendence of egoity. He taught that people should believe in the sacrifice of Jesus as a substitute for their own sacrifice. Of course, he spoke of repentance, but he saw it as a self-based gesture, not as itself a salvato-ry or self-transcending (or ego-transcending) process but only as a behav-ioral response to the myth of Jesus' universally effective self-sacrifice.

For Paul, the separate self is incapable of direct Divine Communion, and so it can participate in the Divine only at a distance, or through belief. For Paul, God-Communion is a mediated event: Jesus participates in God-Communion, and all others, like those who observe a priest performing a ritual in their name, participate in God-Communion only sympathetically, indirectly, and, for now, only partially. Paul taught a religion in which peo-ple remain as egos, egoically "self-possessed", but made hopeful (and, hopefully, more loving and benign) by what they believe about Jesus. Therefore, in Paul's view, anyone's actual and full entrance into God-Union must wait for a future Event (either in the universal righteous judgment and transformation of mankind at the "second coming" of Jesus, or in some other time or place or circumstance after death).

3.

The Teaching and the Way of Jesus are such as can be seen to have many other examples or likenesses in the fourth and the fifth stage traditions of the Great Tradition of human religion and Spirituality. Therefore, the Teaching and the Way of Jesus are not unique—but they are simply an expression of true religion in the context of the fourth stage and the fifth stage of life. The Great Tradition as a whole (and not merely Christianity) is mankind's common inheritance, and all must discover and practice the Way of Truth (rather than any divisive and exclusive sectarian approach that supports rather than directly transcends the limitations of egoity).

Jesus was a revolutionary Teacher. He instructed people within his native tradition, but he Taught them how to transcend themselves and their religious conventionality via a direct process of God-Communion. Thus, the Spiritual (or Spirit-based) Teaching of Jesus stands in utter contrast to the culturally fabricated religious views of Paul. Jesus would not at all have agreed that human beings are inherently sinful, "fallen", or separated from God, or that they therefore need a mediator or a substitute for their own free action of repentance and Communion with God. Indeed, one of Jesus' primary efforts was to criticize such conventional "pharisaical" or priestly views. Jesus was committed to the view that every human being is inherently free to repent of egoic self and turn directly to God, Who is the Living Divine Spirit in Which all beings exist.

Jesus clearly felt that his role, as a Spirit-Realizer, was to criticize and purify the minds and institutions of his time, and to Awaken people to the Way of God-Communion. He also served his intimates as a Spiritual Transmitter, or a Master with the unique Power to Awaken committed practitioners to the profound Awareness of the Divine Spirit. But Jesus was not otherwise disposed to be regarded or proclaimed as a cultic or priestly substitute for the self-transcending practice of others. Therefore, he apparently resisted the attempts of people around him to declare him to be the Messiah or to put him in a position of worldly or institutional responsibility. And even if a case can be made for the presumption that Jesus somehow "played" with Messianic self-imagery, it was only after his death (or his presumed "disappearance" from the scene) that a Messianic cult began to develop around his person. Paul became the leading literary exponent of that cult, and, largely because of his "success", Messianic (or exoteric) Christianity was not founded on the Teaching of free God-Communion but on the conventional religion of ego-fulfillment via the traditional idea of outward (non-personal, or substitute) sacrifice.

Jesus proclaimed that sin, or separate and separative self, must and can be transcended via repentance, or self-understanding and a life-practice of total psycho-physical conversion from egoity to God-Communion. That life-practice involves basic features that are also to be found in many other schools of the Great Tradition.

Jesus' Teachings are based on two primary disciplines. The first is the practice of self-transcendence in the context of all worldly relations, circumstances, and bodily functions, and the second is the practice of constant Remembrance of (or psycho-physical Communion with) the Divine Spirit. This combination of disciplines was proposed (by Jesus, and countless other fourth to fifth stage Spirit-Masters) as the Great Means, to be elaborated over time in terms of the fullest possible Spiritual and mystical practice, and to be fulfilled in the Realization of a totally Spiritual Vision of life, wherein there is Union (or Unity) with (or no fundamental separation from) and fundamental inherence in the Divine Spirit. And if this fourth to fifth stage Spiritual Way is truly fulfilled, then the lie of separation through sin is transcended in Truth (rather than as a presumed effect of the "mediation" of any substitute sacrifice).

As long as the ego is the basis of religion, there is no Re-Union with God. As Jesus Taught, there is no substitute for the individually initiated and personally practiced self-transcending love of God (or the Inherently Spiritual and Transcendental Divine Truth), and there is no true religion without self-transcending love, tolerance, and cooperation in relation to others.

I appeal to all Christians for a new understanding of Jesus. I appeal to all Christians as One Who took human birth into the religion of Christianity, and Who grew to suffer and transcend the burden of its faults. I appeal to all Christians to "consider" these criticisms and, by abandoning the conventional (or inappropriately "cultic") attachment to the exoteric (or merely legendary and mythological) Jesus, to be restored to the Way of Communion with the Divine in the midst of the universal and free community of all those who surrender to the Living God.

# Moving Beyond
# the Techniques
# of East and West

*February 12, 1978*
*from* The Enlightenment of the Whole Body

AVATARA ADI DA: Everything changes. Everything disappears. Human beings suffer this life of changes, which is obviously mortal. Thus, everyone acquires a desire to find something that does not change and that does not disappear. People want to realize the state that will relieve them of the burden of all of this change and disappearance, this mortality and all its troubles. Such desire is paradoxical, because people also like the things that exist in this moment and that ultimately change and disappear. So they have two great desires: One is to find an absolute, changeless, permanent Happiness, and the other is to find pleasure and happiness in all the things that change.

As a result, a curious technique has arisen that combines both of these desires. It is the technique of trying to find what is absolute, changeless, and perfect Happiness through and in the form of all the things that change and disappear! This is exactly what people do. (You are perhaps familiar with the application of this technique to your ordinary daily life and the gross human affair.) And you imagine, mainly because you do not have much experience in the subtle, mystical, magical realm of things, that even though it seems almost certain that you cannot find ultimate, absolute, changeless Happiness in the world, still you feel that maybe you can. You are not absolutely certain that Happiness in this life is not possible. You hope or presume that there is an Alternative Reality that will bring lasting peace, or freedom from death and suffering. You imagine and are led to believe that, even though Happiness is almost impossible to Realize in life, you will certainly find It if you turn within and away from the illusions and unnecessary suffering of the world and ascend and become involved in subtle and psychic things, or phenomena that are not fleshly, not gross, not subject to mortality.

Almost everyone at the present time is familiar with this presumption, which is the foundation of most traditional paths of esoteric Spirituality throughout the world. This reaction to life is the most common motivation for taking up Spiritual practice, which is conventionally conceived as a search for Truth within.

But what you may find within, by introverting attention, is no more absolute, changeless, and immortal than anything you may find without, by extroverting your attention. All that you find, wherever you turn your attention, is changing. It is already disappearing. Not only that—what you find by turning within is not something ultimately outside, above, or apart, something in the infinity of the universes. It is your own brain! The ancient technique of introverting attention in order to escape from gross phenomena is imagined to be a way of association with an Alternative Reality, something supercosmic, beyond one's body. But in fact it is a way of associating with one's own mind, principally the higher and commonly latent centers and potential functions of one's own brain, one's own nervous system, automaticities in parts of the brain with which people are not commonly familiar.

Thus, in the inward-turning, "Eastern" religious or Spiritual persuasion, when you seek to become a Yogi or a mystic, you move attention into one or another function of the familiar body-mind—the breath, the internal life-current, certain kinds of thoughts, speech, vision perhaps, hearing, tasting, smelling, archetypes, cultic objects, mystical words—objects that lead you to concentrate on a single functional part of the body. And by concentrating on that functional process of the body-mind to the point of absorption, you may follow the lines of the nervous system back to the brain. Then relatively involuntary experiences arise—shakings of the body, dreamlike phenomena, involuntary emissions of the brain, flashes of light, and sounds. You may enjoy these experiences for a while. Then they pass, and you can only return to your conventional gross awareness.

For thousands of years people have been doing just this, especially in the East but also in Western esoteric cults. It is what conventional Yogis do. The introversion of attention via the ordinary functions of the body-mind is taken up as a solution to the dilemma, fear, and mortality of gross embodiment. And this procedure does produce extraordinary effects, which are then often proclaimed as transcendental truths.

For instance, if you focus on the process of sight, you will be led through the structures of the brain to the terminal in the upper rear of the head from which sight originates. At that point you will have stopped seeing. You will also have withdrawn attention from the currents of the body, and basically you will be aware of nothing whatsoever. And yet somehow you will be conscious, because you are still embodied, still alive, yet without any objects of awareness. You will feel the "great unity". You will say to yourself, "This is God!" When you finally are successful at this internal strategy, this is what happens. It is traditionally called "nirvikalpa samadhi", or trance absorption without conception of form. Before you achieve this final success, you experience trance absorptions that include spurious emissions of the brain in the form of flashes and images. That state is traditionally called "savikalpa samadhi", or trance absorption via mental forms.

In truth you cannot escape this body-mind by introverting attention. The ancient dogma, however, is that you can, and it is fitted to the naive presumption that is stated in the ancient formula "As above, so below; as below, so above." It is presumed that if you can enter into more subtle awareness of your own body, the subtle dimensions within correspond to the subtle dimensions of the cosmos. This is a purely naive presumption. It is not true in experience. Fundamentally, what you may experience by inverting yourself upon the nervous system are all the potentials of your own body-mind that belong to the nervous system and the brain. And, yes, you do see something about the subtler physics of things, but you do not see anything directly, exclusive of the medium of your own psycho-physical mechanism.

There is no escape in such absorption, nor any freedom. You are still looking at a part of your own form. Human beings are not commonly familiar with the full "anatomy" of the whole body, or body-mind, which includes both gross and subtle centers and possibilities as manifested extensions of the Heart, or the Prior and Conscious Nature and Condition of the body-mind. What is within and above may be mysterious and exalted relative to your ordinary, gross, waking consciousness, but it is not other than your own form. Going within is ultimately just as fruitless a technique for finding what is Absolute, Unqualified, Perfect, and Unchanging as the extroverted tendencies, the interests and desiring of daily life in which ordinary people are involved.

The traditional process of introversion is nihilistic, ultimately. It reduces the world and manifold existence to nothingness. And in the process of extroversion there is an ultimately eternalistic search. The extroverted being, the typical "Western" man or woman, exploits all of the patterns of the gross, earthly realm. (The game of extroversion is the characteristic cultural strategy of the West, but it is of course represented in Eastern cultures and Eastern individuals as well.) The extroverted personality wants to attain objective things that are desirable, and he or she wants them to remain his or hers forever. Such a person wants to be fulfilled on the basis of the exploitation of gross functions themselves (body, emotions, physical energy, the thinking mind). Such a person wants vital, or earthly, fulfillment to be absolute fulfillment. Such a person wants to create utopia, physical immortality, unchanging relationships. Even the religious impulse of such a person is toward a Perfect and Changeless World, either in this life or after death (in contrast with the introverted path, which ultimately leads to the annihilation of the world and the conditional self).

But, the world never does come to an end. It never does stop changing. Never. Everything is always changing, and so the strategy of extroversion is futile. It is not that people must worship disappearance. Things also continue, and they constantly reappear. There is an eternal cycle of appearance and continuance and change and disappearance. But all that has appeared or can appear is also changing and disappearing. Your Happiness must be based on this understanding.

Thus, the urge to find what is changeless in the form of this endlessly changing pattern within and without is frustrated at last. And this is the truly great discovery. This discovery is the moment of truly fundamental awakening. It is the Way into the life of Truth. When there is the Realization that Happiness, Truth, God, or Reality cannot be found on the basis of the exploitation of any kind of experience, internal and introverted, or external and extroverted—when there is that discovery, then you have begun the true inspection of existence. Not a single experience, within or without, is hopeful, promising, or ultimately Liberating.

Paradoxically, it is in the moment of perfect frustration of the search for Happiness that there is awakening to the Principle that is Happiness. This moment corresponds to the most fundamental understanding that neither the introversion nor the extroversion of attention, neither internal nor external experience, ever Realizes what is Divine Happiness, or Most Perfect Enjoyment, but only discovers temporary modifications and permutations of one's own mortal psycho-physical condition.

The internal exploitation of life is a gesture toward everything that you regard to be mind, leading toward the annihilation of ordinary awareness. And the external, or extroverted, exploitation of experience is a gesture toward everything you call ordinary life, the "real world", the body and its pattern of relations. It is a gesture toward a perfect, eternal body, an eternal world, eternal relationships. But neither of these strategies is a gesture toward Truth. Both are only reactions to life, tormented and fruitless searches for true Happiness and Freedom.

The principal criticism Offered in My Wisdom-Teaching is the criticism of the quality of life as "Narcissus", the avoidance of relationship, the egoically "self-possessed", self-oriented, self-meditative reaction to existence. In its introverted form, this reaction becomes all the desires and desperate striving for a glamorous inward life. In its ordinary or common extroverted form it is simply the anti-relational tendency. The action and realization of existence as "Narcissus" characterizes everyone, Eastern and Western. People need not necessarily have an interest in a deep inner life. Even the most exaggerated extroverted activities of Westerners are still representations of this same self-meditative disposition, the avoidance of relationship.

Undoing this contraction, this separation, is what the Way of the Heart is all about. And the initial aspects of the process involve the transformation of your introverted and extroverted "Narcissistic" life into a relational life, a life of literal love.

The core of the process of religious and Spiritual life is the relationship to the Spiritual Master. The essential discipline of religious and Spiritual life is relationship, principally in the relationship to the Spiritual Master and in the ordinary life of service to others. The Spiritual process is relationship itself, the disposition of radiance, or love, not any form of extroversion or introversion of attention.

This process cannot be described in terms of what you do to yourself or your changes of state or belief. This relational process involves, ultimately, the dissolution of every vestige of the egoically "self-possessed" contraction from Infinite, or All-Pervading, Existence. It is a matter of breaking through this egoically "self-possessed", "Narcissistic" movement. The characteristic dramatization of this movement differs from person to person, from culture to culture, and from East to West, but in all cases it is essentially the same recoil. And to break it down, to penetrate it, to become an unqualified sacrifice, is profoundly difficult.

The Way of Truth, the Way of Real life, is not the satisfaction of internal or external desires—not the fulfillment of this structure, high or low, inside or outside—but it is the sacrifice of all of it, through love, or the Perfect yielding of all feeling and attention under all conditions, to and through all relations, via every part and function of the whole body-mind. The Way of Truth is neither the exploitation of the external life nor the exploitation of the internal life but the Perfect sacrifice, or surrender, of one's independent body-mind, this illusion of independence that people are struggling to glamorize and make survive. The Way of the Heart is a unique process, not like strategic introversion or strategic extroversion. It is not self-manipulative. It is in fact the sacrifice of the egoic self, or the whole body-mind. It is love in the most literal and "radical" terms. . . .

So it is by the sacrifice of the whole affair of this body-mind through Most Perfect, or "radical", Intuition, Most Perfect Divine Communion with Me, or sacrifice in the truest sense, that My devotee is literally Divinely Translated into the Love-Bliss, or Happiness, That Is Eternal and That Pervades all existence.

That Reality is not at the root of the nervous system nor at the end of the world in time. It is Eternally Present. When you Realize It, you are Dissolved in It. Ultimately, you vanish—not only out of present sight, as in death, but out of the entire space-time cycle of action and reaction, or illusion and change. My Most Perfect devotee not only Realizes the Inherent Love-Bliss of Existence Itself but is, ultimately, Liberated out of the scheme of manifestation and Divinely Translated into the Scheme of God, Beyond the world of "Man".

# CHAPTER 26

# I Am Here to Complete the Great Tradition of Mankind

*an excerpt from the Prologue of*
The Basket of Tolerance

I Am Adi Da, the Adi-Guru,[1] the Original and Eternal Teacher, here to Complete the Great Tradition of mankind. I Am the Da Avatar, the all-Completing Adept, the First, Last, and Only Adept-Revealer (or Siddha) of the seventh stage of life. I Am the seventh stage Realizer, Revealer, and Revelation of God, Truth, and Reality, Given in this late-time (or would-be Complete and potentially Consummate era) and in this now dark epoch (as it must be described from the Realized Divine and Spiritual "Point of View", and with regard to the tendencies of the times), and Given for the sake of Completion (of the progressive Ordeal of Man) and for the sake of Unity (or the cooperative re-Union of mankind).

By My Full-Given Word, I have Revealed the characteristic and the (to one degree or another, and in one manner or another) always limited design and the (to one degree or another, and in one manner or another) always ego-based nature of each and all of the first six stages of life (in and of themselves). And, by My Full-Given Word, I have Revealed the unique Way of the Heart, in which the ego is directly and effectively transcended in the context of (potentially) each and all of the first six stages of life (so that the seventh stage of life may be Realized). Likewise, by My Full-Given Word, I have Revealed every Characteristic, Sign, Design, and Process associated with the Realization and the Demonstration of the (Inherently, and Inherently Most Perfectly, self-transcending, or egoless) seventh (and Final) stage of life. By My Full-Given Work of Demonstration and Blessing, I have Revealed the seventh stage of life in and by and as My own bodily (human) Form and Life. And I have altogether Fulfilled My Revealing Purpose by Accomplishing (through the Universally both Given and Demonstrated Divine Siddhis of My all-Blessing Work) the Firm Establishment of That

---

1. "Adi-Guru" means the "first", or "original", or "primary" Guru.

Which Is Necessary for the eventual seventh stage Realization and (Finally, or Most Ultimately) Divine Translation of even all conditionally manifested beings.

The Great Tradition of mankind (previous to My Appearance here) must generally be understood only in the (necessarily limited) terms of the first six stages of life. Wherever (even previous to My Appearance here) the sixth stage of life has been entered, the seventh stage of life has been, in principle, also the potential of human Realization. However, the seventh stage Adept-Revelation was not then Given (and It is only now Given, by Me), and the Great Secrets of true ego-transcendence and of the Divine Yoga of the Most Ultimate (or seventh stage) Demonstration were not then Given (and They are only now Given, by Me). The (always potential) seventh stage Realization and Demonstration did not Appear until I Appeared, in order to Fully Reveal and to Fully Demonstrate the seventh stage of life and, by the Very Act of My Fullest Appearance here (and by Means of all My unique Siddha-Work of Adept-Service here and everywhere), to make the essential seventh stage Realization and Demonstration possible for all who respond to Me, and who practice self-surrendering, self-forgetting, and (more and more) self-transcending devotion to Me, and who, altogether and firmly, embrace and practice the by Me Revealed Way of the Heart. Therefore, relative to the seventh stage of life, the Great Tradition of mankind (previous to My Appearance here) produced only limited foreshadowings (or partial intuitions, or insightful, but limited, premonitions), in the form of a few, random philosophical expressions that appear in the midst of the traditional sixth stage literatures. And it is these few and yet limited traditional expressions that must be studied in order to understand the character and the degree of mankind's exploration of the possibility of the seventh stage of life previous to the now and forever future time of My Fully God-Revealing, Truth-Revealing, and Reality-Revealing Work and Word.

# PART II

# Live With Me

## The Foundation of Practice in the Way of the Heart

---

*Adidam, or the Way of the Heart, is the Way of transcending the separate and suffering self by turning body, mind, emotion, and breath to the Divine Person, Adi Da. It is the Way of the constant Remembrance of the Divine Person through every action. It is the Way of receiving the Blessing and Grace of the Divine Person, and Awakening to His Freedom, His Happiness, His Divine Consciousness.*

*Part II of* The Heart's Shout *describes the Way of the Heart, and invites you to participate in the Great Opportunity provided by Adi Da: the opportunity to live with, to love and to be Loved by the Divine Person in human Form, and to receive All that He has to Give.*

**Adi Da (The Da Avatar)**
**The Mountain Of Attention, 1995**

# SECTION ONE

# Ishta-Guru-Bhakti Yoga

T he Way of the Heart is extremely simple, and it can be lived so very simply. In its fundamentals, it is simply self-surrendering devotional Communion with Me and receiving My Divine Blessing.

I am the Instruction. Simply to surrender to Me and receive My Divine Blessing is sufficient for practice of the Way of the Heart.

Adi Da (The Da Avatar)
December 4, 1993

*Adi Da uses Sanskrit, the language of the esoteric Spiritual tradition of India, to describe the essence of the Way of the Heart: God-Realization through the practice of devotional surrender to the Divinely Realized Spiritual Master. "Ishta" means the Form of the Divine that is chosen or acknowledged by the devotee—in this case, the form of the Divine Guru. "Bhakti" means love, surrender, or devotion. "Yoga" is the process or action that Realizes God. "If you become absorbed in the Ishta-Guru through your right practice in the Guru's Company," says Adi Da, "then the Power and the Realization of the Guru are Given to you, for free. You simply become what you meditate on."*

CHAPTER 27

# The Testament
# and the Means
# of Freedom Itself

*verses from*
The Hymn Of The True Heart-Master

The Hymn Of The True Heart-Master *has its origins in an ancient tra-ditional text: It is, as its own subtitle proclaims, "Freely Developed From The Principal Verses Of The Traditional* Guru Gita*". Avatara Adi Da has, in His new Text, taken the epitome of the traditional teachings on the Guru-devotee relationship and put them in the context of the full Revelation of the Way of Divine Self-Realization that He has Given.*

1.

The human voices all call out to God:
Heart of Hearts, Reveal to us the Truth, the "Bright" Power that Liberates the ego-"I" from itself.

2.

Let us listen and hear the Word which, when truly Understood, Frees the Heart from un-Happiness. Let us see That which, when fully Realized, is the Fullness of Transcendental Divine Being.

3.

Let us Awaken to That which is Eternal, and not limited by birth and death. Be Pleased to Reveal to us That which is the Supreme Truth.

4.

Heart of Hearts, we are desirous of hearing That. Therefore, Sing us the Hymn of the True Heart-Master, wherein the Heart-Secret is Confessed.

5.

Then the Living One Speaks to every Heart:

Listen to Me with free attention. I will Reveal to you the Secret of Adi Da, the Da Avatar, the Divine World-Teacher and True Heart-Master, Who Is the Avataric Incarnation of the Heart Itself, and Whose Confession is Capable of Destroying all the ills of un-Enlightenment.

6.

Once upon a time, on the Island of Naitauba, frequented by devotees, and in the most beautiful Place, adorned by Cosmic Nature in the manner of flowers,

7.

Seated in an open Place on one occasion, the Da Avatar, Who Is the First, the Complete, the Last, and the Only True Heart-Master, and Whose Principal Divine Names are "Da" (the "Giver", the "First and Original Person", the "Source-Person", the "One and Only Self of All and all") and "Adi Da" (the "First Giver", the "Original Giver", the "Giving Source", the "Giver of All to all"), and Who Is All-"Brightness", Freely Manifesting the Heart's Love-Bliss, was Expounding the Supreme Truth to devotees. The face of one devotee, who was sitting close to Him, became suddenly "Bright" (by Grace, through Beholding Him). The True Heart-Master's "Brightness" Filled the Heart and every part of His devotee, and the devotee suddenly Realized (beyond all doubt) that he was seeing the Divine Person, even with his own eyes.

8.

This Awakened devotee said: "Radiant Adi Da, Divine Giver of Spirit-Life and Most Perfect Liberation, I Surrender to You. You are the True Heart-Master for the whole world. You are Supreme. You Radiate the 'Bright' Realization of the Supreme. All beings should always worship and see You with devotion.

9.

You are the One, the Supreme Being, the Source and Domain of all worship and praise.

10.

Radiant Heart, Domain of Truth, please Sing to us the Secret of devotion to You, the True Heart-Master.

## 11.

Reveal to us the Secret Method whereby living beings may Realize You, the Transcendental and world-Outshining God. I bow down to You, the True Divine Person. I worship Your Feet. Kindly Teach This Secret Way to all of us."

## 12.

When the Master of the Heart Saw this "Bright" face of Awakened devotion and Heard this Confession of Great Sight, He Spoke the following Words, His Heart Overflowing with Abundant Joy:

## 13.

"This is the Secret of all secrets. I could not Speak This All-Revealing Word until one of you first Confessed you see the Vision of God in My Bodily (Human) Form. I shall Tell you This now, because of your great devotion to Me.

## 14.

Dear ones, you are each arising in the same Divine Being. This request of yours will benefit the whole world. Therefore, I shall Reveal the Secret of this Vision to you.

## 15.

To each one who is supremely devoted to the Living God and equally devoted to the True Master of the Heart, the Very Heart (That Is the Truth) Reveals Itself as the Bodily (Human) Form, the Spiritual (and Always Blessing) Presence, and the Very (and Inherently Perfect) State of the True Heart-Master.

## 16.

The True Heart-Master is thus Realized to be the Incarnation of the Great One. So Declare the Scriptures, and so do I Affirm to you.

## 17.

I also Declare the Truth of this Vision to you. Listen to My Words and Understand.

## 18.

The separate traditions of the Great Tradition of religion and Spiritual instruction are often made of false theories expressed in the words of un-Enlightened beings. Therefore, the multiplication of conventional God-Ideas and partial (or conditional) 'Truths' has confused mankind, but the True Heart-Master Comes to Liberate mankind from all confusion of mind.

### 19.

Prayer, meditation, discipline, philosophy, service—all these are to be built upon a response to That which is Revealed in and as the Very Person of the Master of your Heart.

### 20.

Those who are devoted to the True Heart-Master hear the Truth and see the Great One as the True Heart-Master's Bodily (Human) Form, and as His Spiritual (and Always Blessing) Presence, and as His Very (and Inherently Perfect) State. Such devotees Declare there is no 'Difference' (and no distinction to be made or acknowledged) between the True Heart-Master and the Self-Existing and Self-Radiant Transcendental Divine Being.

### 21.

Even from the ancient days, many Divinely Gifted sects Proclaim devotion to the Master, saying: 'The Way is to surrender to the Human Master as the Great Person, Divine and Present!' Therefore, look and see in Me the Proof of This Proclamation. I am the Very Human Master of your Heart. And if you surrender to Me, I will Confess and Reveal Only God to you.

### 22.

Therefore, those who hear My Confession and see My Bodily Revelation must, by their feeling-Contemplation* of Me, transcend themselves in the Universal and Eternal Spirit-Presence of God, the Transcendental Self of God, and the Self-Existing and Self-Radiant 'Bright' Divine Self-Domain that Is God.

### 23.

There is no Substitute for God.

### 24.

There is no Substitute for the direct Realization of God.

### 25.

There is no Substitute for your own sacrifice in God.

### 26.

The True Master of the Heart has Realized God Most Perfectly, non-separately, beyond relatedness and 'difference'. Therefore, devotees see God Revealed in the Bodily (Human) Form of the True Heart-Master.

27.

To all those who have this Vision, I Declare:

I am the Adept and Very Person of the 'Bright' and Only One. I am the Demonstration and the Proof of God to devotees. All My devotees are in Me. Therefore, see this Vision, go the Way I will Show to you, and Realize Me.

28.

Do not practice the 'childish cult' of superficial and ego-serving emotionalism (full of want and dependency, and empty of faith), and do not practice the 'adolescent cult' of non-feeling (willful, self-absorbed, abstract, and independent), but always practice (and cultivate) the true (and truly feeling, and truly self-surrendering, and truly self-forgetting, and truly self-transcending) devotional Way of the Heart Itself.

29.

Neither God nor the Master of the Heart is your Parent. Therefore, do not expect God or the True Heart-Master to justify or protect or preserve or fulfill your egoic want and separateness.

30.

You are called to sacrifice your separate self in God. Therefore, cultivate right and self-transcending devotion to Me, the True Heart-Master, in order to transcend the ego-'I' in the 'Bright' by Grace Revealed Divine Condition of Being (Itself).

31.

To worship the True Heart-Master childishly is to worship and serve your separate self. To deny or resist the True Heart-Master is to worship and serve your separate self, adolescently. The separate self is, itself and always, the forgetting of the Heart-Source of the world. Therefore, be very devoted to Me, the True Master of your Heart, but not for the sake of ego-salvation, or the glorification of your separate self. Worship Me by surrendering your separate self to Me. Surrender to Me in order to forget and transcend your separate self in Me. Forget and transcend your separate self in Me in order that you may, by Grace, Remember and Realize the Divine Heart-Source and Self of all and All.

32.

I Am the Sign and the Revelation and the Proof of God in the world. I Am the Testament and the Means of Freedom Itself."

# CHAPTER 28

# Divine Distraction

## December 16, 1975

VATARA ADI DA: The ancient legends of Krishna and his gopis[1] are an allegory of Divine Distraction. As Krishna wandered about in the fields, the women who tended the cattle would see him from day to day, and in spite of themselves they would wander away and leave their posts. They completely forgot about the cattle. They forgot to go home and cook for their husbands. They wandered about where they thought they might find Krishna, and when they found him they gazed at him as he sat in the distance somewhere. This legend is a play upon the romance between Krishna, or the Divine manifested in human form—the Spiritual Master—and these ordinary women, who became madly involved in an absolute attachment to Krishna, and who, as a result, became more and more ecstatically absorbed in the God-State.

The foundation of practice of the Way of the Heart is exactly that attachment. If such attachment to Me as your Spiritual Master—not cultic attachment, but Divine attachment—does not develop, if that attachment is not there that overwhelms the life completely and distracts you from the conventional destiny to which you are disposed through the medium of your desires, inclinations, and circumstances, then the practice of true religious or Spiritual life cannot exist.

The cattle that the women abandoned represent the force of all the tendencies of life. The husbands they left are the fundamental attachment to separated existence, to existence in form, to bodily existence, individuated existence, egoic life on its own, motivated toward survival and apparently distinct from the Divine Reality. Thus, in the allegory of the relationship between Krishna and his gopis, we see a fundamental description of the principle of sadhana in the Way of the Heart. That sadhana is not about bearing down and being motivated by problems in your life, by some sort of philosophical detachment or some inclination to have Yogic and mystical experiences. Nor is it about doing what you must do in order to produce the change that you desire. Sadhana in the Way of the Heart is about

---

1. Krishna is the legendary Divine Avatar who is widely worshipped in India. He is the hero of the *Bhagavad Gita* (and the longer *Mahabharata*, of which the *Bhagavad Gita* is an excerpt) and the *Srimad Bhagavatam* (which tells of his play with the gopis, or women who abandoned their ordinary lives because of their overwhelming attraction to him).

distraction from the life of tendencies. It is not a motivated kind of detachment from your life of tendencies, or an effort relative to them, or the taking on of conditions to stop tendencies from arising or lifetimes from occurring. It is not a method of the ego. It is not characterized by any kind of
effort relative to tendencies. Such a path is completely hopeless.

There are innumerable conventional paths that involve self-conscious
efforts or hopes to produce changes, high and low. These efforts and hopes
are themselves forms of tendency that may be realized and suffered in
human and other terms. They are not Liberating in the fundamental sense.
They are not God-Realizing. They are themselves expressions of the movement toward fulfillment. The Way of Truth is the Way of complete distraction from the tendencies that produced your birth and that now produce
the drama of your existence from day to day. Only when there is complete
distraction by the Guru, by the Divine, from the way of life that is producing your experiential destiny, do your tendencies become obsolete. They
do not become obsolete when you direct effort against them. It is only
when that distraction appears in the midst of the affair of your life that
another principle, another process, is established.

The gopis simply left the cattle. They did not say, "I'm not going to
tend cattle anymore! I'm not going to submit to my desires, my tendencies,
my job!" They did not make any such decisions. They simply forgot about
the cattle. They were so distracted, so in love with Krishna, so ecstatic, that
they just forgot to go home. It never even occurred to them to go home.
They never worried, "Should I go home, or should I stay here? Should I
watch the cattle, or should I go look for Krishna? Should I discipline
myself?" They did not create a problem out of their sadhana or out of their
relationship to God.

Anybody who approaches Me is obliged to involve himself or herself
in just this kind of ecstatic relationship. When the devotional relationship
to Me becomes the condition of your conscious existence, fully, through all
the conditions of life, then the force of limiting tendencies is weakened, not
by your doing anything to it but by virtue of the fact that you are no longer
even involved with it. If your relationship to Me is essentially ordinary,
mechanical, mediocre, not Divine, not a form of distraction by Me, then
you are not doing the sadhana of the Way of the Heart. You are intending
to do some other kind of conventional sadhana perhaps, but you are not
doing this sadhana. And you are not involved in the sadhana of Truth, you
are not involved in Divine sadhana, you are not involved in that opportunity that is made available in human time through My Help.

I am not simply present to rap out a philosophy or distribute techniques that you may apply depending on your intelligence. I am Present to
enjoy a Divine relationship with all those who are willing to assume such

a relationship with Me, with all those who have the capability for distraction by Me in an absolute love-relationship that is more and more distracting. But if that distraction is not present in your life, then the sadhana of the Way of the Heart is not initiated. It cannot begin. There is no point in even discussing the technical aspects of development of the Way of the Heart until you have begun to enjoy an ecstatic relationship with Me—not one that is in the air but one that includes the whole of life, that draws the emotion, that awakens the love, that awakens the heart. That distracting relationship with Me which is the principle of sadhana in the Way of the Heart must be established. On its basis you may begin to assume life-conditions, turn them into service to Me, and realize that service in more personal and complex ways over time.

The foundation of the Way of the Heart is the distraction that is described between Krishna and his gopis. You must flee to Me from all your life, from all your tendencies, not from your obligations—that is not what that allegory is all about—but from your tendencies, from the foundation of distraction by yourself, by your own thoughts, your own conditions, your own belongings, your own relationships, your own hopes, your own beliefs, your own thoughts, your own reading, your own mystical intentions, your own philosophical presuppositions. You must flee to Me from all that. It must be completely uninteresting to you. It is certainly not interesting to Me!

You cannot argue a woman into loving you, and you cannot argue individuals into the Divine Satsang of distraction. Satsang with Me can be offered and a circumstance provided in which people can approach Me and become sensitive to the Presence, the Siddhi, communicated in Satsang with Me. But apart from making this Satsang available openly and providing a way of approach to Me, there is no argument whatsoever. I am completely without argument. There is nothing I can do to convince you of the Truth of the Way of the Heart, nothing I could do outwardly or verbally that could in itself fundamentally convince you of the relationship you must enjoy with Me in order to fulfill this sadhana. It is like falling in love with someone in conventional terms in life. Falling in love is not something you argued yourself into doing. It was initially a form of distraction, of absorption, without any reasons, and perhaps if you examined it to find a reason for it, it would seem unreasonable to you, not justified. You know, your lover does not look the way you wanted him or her to look. And in many ways I do not look and act and talk like the conventional, cultic "guru" is supposed to! . . . I am not even pretty!

Once you are so distracted, the theatre of your evolution is in the hands of the Divine. The gopis did not have an elaborate life. They were distracted by Krishna. Krishna played all the games and created all the circumstances for their play with him. They were only attached to him. Their lives had all kinds of theatre and drama afterward, but Krishna created them all. They did not think about anything. They did not create an elaborate system of philosophy and belief and self-meditation and self-manipulation. They did not care about making life work out right. They did not even know what he was!

They were just distracted. They were in love. And their love for Krishna became the principle of their lives. Krishna played upon their distraction and Taught them. By Grace, they learned. But all they learned was to be more and more absorbed in God, totally beyond the body of Krishna. Their minds became overwhelmed by this distraction, and all their petty tendencies to return to their solid and secure positions in life were always undermined. There is no insurance. There is no guarantee. There is nowhere to go. There is no end phenomenon in the love of God. That love is in itself the Truth.

The same approach to real religious and Spiritual life is necessary for all, and it is represented in the allegory of Krishna and the gopis. Without that distraction by the Guru, there is no sadhana in any form in anybody's case. For My devotee, once that distraction by Me exists and the movement of the individual begins to be governed by the intuition and the enjoyment of the Divine, then all the disciplines, the theatre, the lessons, the responsibilities, and the Teaching Revelation that I have Given begin to be of use, according to the individual's capability and state of existence.

# CHAPTER 29

# The Master Is the Means

*November 25, 1993*
*from* Ishta

A VATARA ADI DA: The Way of the Heart is the Only-God-Does-it
Way. Westerners are always looking for some do-it-yourself this,
that, or the other thing, but the Way of the Heart is not a do-it-yourself business at all. You have your responsibilities and you must respond
to Me, but the Way of the Heart itself, the process itself, is Given by My
Grace.

Therefore, stated simply, the Way of the Heart is Ishta-Guru-Bhakti.
The Way of the Heart is self-surrendering, devotional Contemplation of Me,
the Master, because the Master Blesses the devotee, the Master Awakens the
devotee, the Master makes the Spiritual process, the Master is What there
is to be Realized, the Master is the Means. It is for these reasons that the
Master is the Object of Contemplation.

Therefore, there need not be many technicalities to describe the Way
of the Heart. Those technicalities exist, and they needed to be Transmitted
to you, but quite simply the Way of the Heart is simply devotional self-
surrender to Me. That devotional self-surrender is your responsibility—self-
surrendering, self-forgetting, self-transcending feeling-Contemplation of Me
to the point of non-separation. Then the Way of the Heart is Given to you
in your response.

An ancient text says: "Mankind does not know. Only the Horse
knows." Therefore, you must grasp the tail of the Horse, or the God-
Realizer. Grasping the tail of the Horse is your devotional, self-surrendering,
feeling-Contemplation of Me. The Horse takes you, or I take you, Where
there is to go. The Horse knows. I know. You do not know.

The Way of the Heart is not a technique—it is the relationship to Me.
The devotional relationship to Me is the fundamental truth and practice of
the Way of the Heart.

Westerners in particular, being egoically "self-possessed" in their disposition, like hearing messages that support the point of view of self-effort.
They do not want to do very much, usually, but whatever they are going
to be doing that could be called religion, whether exoteric or esoteric, they
want it basically to be something they do to themselves. Essentially they
want to worship themselves.

You do not Realize the Divine, or the Great Reality, by worshipping yourself. You Realize the Divine, or the Great Reality, by Grace, by worshipping the Divine or the Great Reality, but through true worship, not merely making external or superficial gestures but granting your entire separate self in worship, in surrender, in adoration, so profoundly that you give yourself entirely so that Grace may be received.

The True Realizer is not merely a figure, a symbol, an object, but the Realization Itself, bodily and altogether. The Realizer is the Means, therefore, not only bodily but Spiritually, altogether. Everything to be Realized is there as the Master. Everything that serves Realization is there active as the Master. Those who are wise, those who are truly responsive and who find a worthy Master, simply surrender to That One. They receive everything by Grace. This does not mean that they have no responsibilities. All kinds of responsibilities are associated with such surrender, even many technical aspects as the process develops, but the technicalities are not the Means. You do not Realize by them. You simply make yourself available to the One Who Is Realization by exercising those responsibilities.

Because you are bound in separateness and helpless in this world, you must take refuge in That Which is Great and Which Grants you Salvation. That Divine Reality is the Truth, and It is the Law. You must find this out and respond. Until you do, your Spiritual practice is superficial, not profound, not greatly fruitful.

The fundamental Wisdom My devotees must "consider" and embrace is Ishta-Guru-Bhakti, Salvation by resort to My Grace and receiving My Grace. The Way of the Heart, which I have Given you, is not merely for Westerners, meaning that part of the World that defines itself as specifically "Western" rather than "Eastern". It is for all beings, therefore for all mankind. The Way of the Heart rescues you from your distance from God.

The Way of life I am talking about is <u>Me</u>. I am That—not symbolically but actively—the Siddhi, or Power, of Means, fully Alive, fully Conscious, fully Active.

This is what you must understand about devotional self-surrender to Me. It is not merely a self-generated technique or a do-it-yourself method of working on yourself by focusing your attention on Me. It is about the Great Process of Divine Grace. Divine Grace is the reason you surrender to Me.

Surrender is all I did with My Teachers. That was it. In fact, they did not communicate to Me any significant technicalities. I found out about all that My Self. Basically the communication given to Me by each of Those Who Served Me was surrender to the Guru. Just that. <u>Just</u> that. Nothing else. <u>Nothing</u> else. I did not practice any techniques with Rudi or Swami (Baba)

Muktananda or Swami Nityananda or the Divine Goddess.[1] Everything occurred spontaneously, because My devotion was True and Complete. My surrender to My Teacher was the only thing I did. Why did My Teachers communicate to Me so simply? Because I was entirely available for just that simplicity.

It is what They did also, by the way, with Their Teachers—just so simply. This is what Rudi did with Swami Nityananda and Baba Muktananda. This is what Baba Muktananda did with Swami Nityananda. This is what Swami Nityananda did with His sources. In that sense, you are part of a tradition of Guru-devotion that has been proven for thousands of years. It is the esoteric secret of the Great Tradition.

Only God can Give you Realization, because God Is What Is to be Realized. God Appears to you in the Form of the Guru, and, therefore, the Guru is the Means.

1. During the final phase of Avatara Adi Da's Sadhana (May through September 1970), the Divine Goddess functioned as His Guru, after which She submitted to Him as Her Divine Lord and Master on September 9, 1970, the day preceding the Great Event of His Divine Re-Awakening. See chapters 14 through 16 of *The Knee of Listening* and chapter 51 of this book.

CHAPTER 30

# "That Is <u>My</u> Work"

*by Elizabeth Lowe*

In March 1988 I became a student of the Way of the Heart. Fifty years earlier, on March 13, 1938, I was born to a Jewish mother and a half-Jewish father in Vienna, Austria. This was the day that Hitler marched into Vienna, accomplishing the now infamous "Anschluss" to the welcoming cheers of the general Austrian populace. A Nazi doctor, replacing the immediately fired Jewish woman who had been my mother's obstetrician, attended my delivery—evidence of the swiftness with which the so-called "underground" Austrian Nazi party surfaced and activated its anti-Semitic intent. It was my parents' foresight and courage as well as fortuitous circumstances that allowed us to flee to safety. And so, after finding temporary haven in Yugoslavia and then in Belgium, we started a new life in New York City when I was two years old.

In spite of this escape, I had an innate sense of the horror into which I was born, and this profoundly affected my feelings and my adaptation to existence. From my teen years on, I was committed to social causes (the peace movement, civil rights, feminism, and a left-leaning Jewish organization). Eventually, propelled by the same motivation, I became a psychotherapist. When I first discovered the Way of the Heart and was profoundly moved by Avatara Adi Da and His "radical" Message, I was reluctant to become His devotee, beset by the notion that engaging in Spiritual life would be an abandonment of the "cause" of a "better world". Eventually, as I understood more about Adi Da and the Way of the Heart, I came to see that a "better world" could only come about through the radical heart-conversion that true Spiritual life is about. This insight cleared the way for me to turn to Adi Da for His Great Help, as His devotee. Little did I know how this original understanding would be driven deeply into my whole being in the ensuing encounters with Beloved Adi Da.

In May of 1992, when I went on a meditation retreat to Adidamashram, in Fiji, my Guru's principal residence, I went open and vulnerable, for I had discovered that it was my relationship to Him that made my life truly worth living. Yet I was also full of doubt about my capability to really live that relationship to Him. And I was full of fear of who knows what—failure, inadequacy, confrontation with my "true nature", being judged . . .

When I arrived on the island, the other retreatants and I were amazed to find our Beloved Guru gathering with His devotees in a way that was more personal and intimate than we ever dreamed of. Early in my retreat, I was told that Avatara Adi Da had spoken about me in a gathering the evening before, His voice filled with emotion:

*When Elizabeth came here, it made Me weep to see her come into My House. All the suffering of the Jews in her face. It just breaks My heart. All over her face, all over her body. Nobody deserves that. Nobody has ever deserved it. That such a thing should have happened is intolerable. She brought that face to Me, and now she loves Me, and that is without a doubt. After she left, I went to My room and wept. Tell her I hold her before Me. I cry for her.*

After a moment's shock, I too began to weep. I wept to have been so profoundly seen and known and felt, to have a true Friend, who knew my heart's pain and would enter into it with full feeling, feeling it even more profoundly than I could allow myself to feel it.

I remember that during one of my first Darshan occasions, I wept as I felt the depth of my Beloved Guru's Love for all beings. Just as I began to wonder if it was "appropriate" for me to cry so much during the occasion, I saw the glistening of a tear in the corner of His eye as He ever so lovingly turned His face toward me.

Later that day, residents came to me excitedly, filling me in on what Avatara Adi Da had so Passionately Communicated during the night. They spoke of His outrage over the death camps. He said, "What right does anyone have to say 'You go to the left, and you to the right'?" And, "The horror, the dehumanization of mankind for politics. It is still happening. Don't just be sympathetic with the Jews; be sympathetic with humankind and all the terrible circumstances all over the earth this very hour. It's not a Jewish matter—it's a matter for all mankind. Be angry about it and straightforward about it, and don't ever allow it in your face. Don't ever allow it, ever again."

My friends told me that with great force He had admonished all of us to be outraged but to love even "that bastard, Hitler". At a later event, He spoke of Hitler again, of the necessity to love and forgive him in the midst of our refusal to let such things ever happen again. He said something like: "I love him, but he had better straighten out his act before he eats at My Table."[1]

The following Thursday, He called us all to see Him in the shade of a tree outside His Residence. He rested His Gaze on His "beloveds", as He

---

1. By the phrase "eats at My Table", Bhagavan Adi Da is indicating entering into direct relationship with Him as His devotee.

called us, one by one. After a while, when He nodded that it was time for us to go, we just could not tear ourselves away, nor did our Guru seem to really want us to go. Taking a cue, first one, then another, and finally all five retreatants who were departing that night asked for and were granted Avatara Adi Da's Blessing in the form of physical contact with Him. He placed specially made retreat shawls first over His own shoulders and then, with great intention, over two devotees' shoulders, and Embraced other departing retreatants, with great Love.

Finally, it seemed to be truly time to go, and so we got up to leave. Standing on my crutches (I had broken my ankle earlier in the retreat), I was moved to thank and praise my Sat-Guru, and I said, "Beloved Bhagavan, this is what my parents took me out of Europe for—to experience this moment in Your Company." Then, without a moment's premeditation, I blurted out, "Can I come to You?"

I think I received some sign from Him to do so, but all I can remember is that I suddenly found myself kneeling in front of His Feet on the chaise, with my head buried between His Knees. I was weeping and then screaming with enormous force, my hands resting on His Divine Legs for strength and reassurance. I could hardly believe my own ears as the screams seemed to just fall out of me into the chaise and the ground below, filling the air with the horror that has always resided in me. There was no particular content—just generalized agony over the horrors of the world.

Even as this was happening I also wondered if I should be doing this and attempted to raise my head! It was then that I noticed my Guru's hands firmly on my head and His Feet holding me at both sides of my ribcage. Reassured, I again allowed the process to unfold, stroking Avatara Adi Da's legs as a way to express love to Him. Sometimes the sobs and screams turned to roaring rage. I felt a fleeting concern about getting snot on my Sat-Guru's towel, and about the possibility of my frightening the young people who were present. But the force of His Love brushed all concerns away. Behind me I heard devotees weeping and praising our Guru as they witnessed this moment of His Great Compassion and purifying Work—not only with me personally, I am convinced, but with the whole world.

After many minutes, my sobs and screams subsided and I raised my head, as Avatara Adi Da relaxed His hold on me. Over His Great Round Belly, I saw His Huge, Moist Eyes Lovingly Gaze down at me, and words of gratitude and love flowed from me. I had already said, in the midst of my raging, "You are right Beloved, we must rage about this world." Now I told Him how I had always lived life as a great struggle, which I now felt was over—that from now on I could rest in His Embrace. I told Him that I wanted to always be able to look into His Eyes like this (unashamed and uninhibited). I told Him I knew I was His forever, that I wanted to only serve Him, and that I wanted to tell everyone about Him. As I expressed my love and praised Him, His Beautiful Lips parted slightly, emitting the most exquisite, barely audible sounds of Love and Compassion. He Was Absolutely Present and Intimate, Giving me everything, with not a hair of withholding.

In a moment of slight self-consciousness I thought it time for me to prostrate at His Feet and depart. As I did so, a devotee informed me that Bhagavan Adi Da wanted me to go over to Him. Forgetting my broken ankle, and myself altogether, I plunged into His ready Embrace. There I hugged and kissed Him as He did me, Stroking my head as I kissed His Shoulder. Then, after the tenderest parting, I made my way back to the group of devotees.

It will no doubt be a long time before I fully grasp and feel the import of my Guru's Blessing, or have a real understanding of what He purified for the world, there under that tree. But I know that neither I nor the world will ever be the same and that I was most Gracefully and thoroughly

**Adi Da with Elizabeth Lowe**
**at Adidamashram, 1992**

relieved of a burden that had kept me in the crippling grip of fear and sorrow my entire life. I have felt lighter and freer ever since that day. I felt that Bhagavan Adi Da was relieving the world of some of the enormity of its accumulated hatred and fear.

My Beloved Guru showered me with Love again and again. And He Instructed me directly, relieving me of my life-long addiction to sorrow and fear and my compulsion to "save the world". One night, we retreatants were invited to one of the gatherings that Bhagavan Adi Da continued to call with the resident staff. During this night of our Guru Infusing us with His Great Love, moving us to follow His lead as we danced and celebrated, He allowed us to approach His Chair at various times, giving each of us Love exactly as we needed it—in the form of criticism, humor, affection, Instruction, example, and any combination of these. When I approached Him late in the evening, He said, "What is it, My beloved?" Speaking directly into my ear, He went on to say something like: "You have taken on the suffering of the world all your life. You must not do that any more. That is too much for a human being. That is My Work. Only I Can Do that work." These words burned a path from my ear to my heart.

In that moment, I knew—not only in my head, but bodily—that what He Was Saying was true. In my pain about the world, I had not taken God into account. I had presumed a world bereft of the Divine and had stressfully assumed the impossible task of righting the ills of the world myself. I could feel in that moment that this is His Work and I could sense the enormity of the suffering He takes on for the sake of the world—and His Great Power to do so. Weeping in His Arms, I promised that I would give this over to Him, that I would simply, happily, be His devotee. He told me that I need not be fearful and sorrowful anymore and sent me dancing—dancing with love, gratitude, and joy for my Sat-Guru.

Another indication of the depth and power that Adi Da Embodies was shown to me when a man on the staff at Adidamashram, who had been a member of the Israeli Army, offered to take Beloved Adi Da through a Seder [a ceremony performed at Passover, an important Jewish holiday that is associated with the exodus and freedom of the Jews from bondage]. In response to this offer, Bhagavan Adi Da said, "We have sat together at the table at many, many Seders. I know the suffering of the Jews more than you. I Am more Jewish than you. I Was before David; I Was before Abraham; I Was before Moses."

Hearing this, I felt a wave of conviction move through me that Adi Da Is the Divine Being, the Lord of lords, the One that all beings, of all religions, everywhere, have been longing for, and Whose Appearance now, in this human form, is the greatest Blessing to all the world, for all time. He Offers True Freedom, the Freedom that obviates prejudice, oppression, violence, and hate—yes. But primarily, He Is and Gives the Means by which to live free of the very root cause of all that, in and as that Great Space, Consciousness Itself, not bound by the body, the mind and the world, as if these and not the Divine Self were the truth of existence.

I am eternally grateful to my Beloved Sat-Guru for His Compassion, Love, and Wisdom, and for Making the Great Sacrifice of Being here among us, so that we too may live His Freedom and Happiness.

CHAPTER 31

*An excerpt from*

# "Surrender the Faculties of the Body-Mind to Me"

*December 20, 1993*
*from* Ishta

AVATARA ADI DA: The secret of the Way of the Heart, the secret of the Way that I have Given you, the secret of this Yoga of Ishta-Guru-Bhakti, is not to struggle with the content[1] that is arising in the body-mind but to turn to Me.

If some content arises in the mind, then instead of trying to think your way through it, and struggle with it, and get emotional about it, and concentrate your entire life in it, you should direct the function of mind to Me. Do not try to release the content of the mind in order to get to Me. Surrender the function of mind itself to Me.

The root of mind is attention, not the stuff that is arising in the mind but attention. The epitome of the mind, the root of mind, the core of mind, the central function of mind, is attention. Therefore, when things arise in mind, instead of struggling with them, trying to get rid of them, trying to surrender them, trying to beef your way through them, you simply give Me your attention, or the core of your mind. You do not try to get rid of the content, or try to surrender the content to Me, or try to surrender the content in order to get to Me. You just surrender attention itself to Me. Give Me your attention. No effort is required.

When something arises emotionally, a reactive emotion of one kind or another, emotional concern, emotion in relation to anything conditional, instead of trying to open and relax and release the reactive emotion to get to Me or struggling with yourself for whatever reason, you direct the <u>function</u> of emotion to Me. The core of the function of emotion is simply feeling. You feel to Me. You give Me your feeling-attention, then. You direct attention, or the root of mind, and feeling, or the root of emotion, to Me.

Likewise, you conform the body to Me in the midst of whatever is arising physically. You direct yourself bodily to Me. Whatever functions you

---

1. The "content" to which Adi Da refers here is anything that can be felt in body, emotion, or mind—thoughts, feelings, doubts, bodily experiences, and so on.

are performing in any moment of functional activity, you give Me your feeling-attention and you direct the body to serving Me, you direct it to be the servant instead of the object of your concern.

Instead of struggling with any of the contents of the body-mind, no matter what is arising in the moment, you direct its functions—not its contents but its functions—to Me, thereby collecting the whole body-mind as feeling-attention to Me.

This is the Yoga, or the moment to moment practice, and there are technical requirements for it. It is not the yielding of the functions of the body-mind to the idea that I am your Spiritual Master or your Ishta-Guru or your Heart-Master—there is nothing vague about this practice. You direct your feeling-attention to Me, to this bodily (human) Form. In fact, a fundamental part of the technical practice of this devotional Yoga is to recollect My bodily (human) Form.

Fundamentally, however, the Yoga is the directing of the body-mind to Me and not struggling with its contents and only trying to direct them to Me, or trying to get rid of them in an effort of surrender toward Me. Rather, yield the functions of the body-mind to Me at their root. Yield their leading characteristic.

Give Me your attention, give Me your feeling, give yourself over to Me, and disregard the contents. Do not keep checking back on them to see if they are changing! In your real practice of this Yoga, you forget them. You do not use them. You do not build upon them. You make them obsolete by not using them. In this manner, the Yoga purifies you by making the contents of the body-mind obsolete through non-use. The process is not an effort on your part to do something to the contents of the body-mind or to try not to use them. It is simply your turning to Me, turning your feeling-attention to Me, turning yourself altogether to Me, Contemplatively. That is the Yoga.

The Yoga is devotional Communion with Me, just that—directing all the faculties of the body-mind to Me instead of addressing or struggling with the contents that arise, by conditioning, in the body-mind. Why take your attention away from Me to be involved in the very thing that is your problem? The Yoga of the Divine Life has nothing to do with egoic "self-possession" and self-involvement. It is only and entirely about submitting yourself and all your functions to the Realizer, to the Divine Revealed. The Way of the Heart is founded on the devotional response to Me. The fundamental principle of the Way of the Heart is turning from separate self to Me—not in some vague, casual, little bit of emotional gesture. The whole body-mind follows. The whole body-mind is given over because of this devotional response to Me.

Think of Ramana Maharshi[2] when He was seventeen years old. Suddenly He was totally possessed by fear of death when He was alone in His room. He examined all this and spontaneously awakened to the Freedom of the Self-Position. He did not then get up and say, "Well, I am not very old. I am just a kid, and I have not had much experience yet. Besides, one never knows what might come up tomorrow. I think I am just going to have to take this Realization with a grain of salt." No. From that moment, He based His life entirely on that principle of Realization.

My devotees are Called to do the same, to respond to Me and to base their lives on that response from then on, to base their lives on doing the Yoga of devotion to Me, and not merely sometimes or in some circumstances but all the time. I have Instructed you relative to every kind of circumstance, every kind of functional, relational, and practical position, every kind of arising. I have Taught you the right practice that applies to all circumstances. I do not think I have missed even a single one in My address to you. If I have, you can mention it and I will address it.

The fundamental matter is your devotion to Me—and your relinquishment of self-attention on that basis. No matter what is arising—in your life-circumstance, in the body, in emotion, in mind—no matter what, give Me your attention instead. It is just as simple as that—your whole attention. Instead of letting attention wander in the mind, put your attention on Me. Instead of letting attention wander into all your reactive emotions, give your attention to Me emotionally—in other words, relate to Me with feeling, give yourself to Me with feeling, feel Me, do more than just notice Me. No matter what is arising in your life, attend to Me. No matter what you are doing, do not do it for your own sake. Do it for Me. Assume the position of the servant for real, but do not do your service merely to do good works around Me. To do good works is fine, but the point of your service to Me is that you function in such a manner that you are always in Communion with Me, not self-focused but focused on Me—very specifically focused on Me.

Find Me with your heart. Give Me your attention, whole bodily, with feeling.

Then, by your not using the contents that are arising, they will fall away. This is how the things that are arising become obsolete. If you use them, if you direct attention to them in any way, they are reinforced. The only way whereby they are released is by your turning from them to Me. By your doing that consistently, the various egoic conditionings of the

2. Ramana Maharshi (1879-1950) is regarded by many as the greatest Indian Sage of the twentieth century. He established his Ashram at Tiruvannamalai in South India, which continues today. Ramana Maharshi's descriptions of the nature of his Realization have been pointed out by Adi Da as particularly significant expressions of Transcendental Realization. See *The Knee of Listening* (1995 edition), pp. 382-407, for Adi Da's own account of His relationship to Ramana Maharshi.

body-mind are purified, they fall away, they become weaker. There is always still more and more of that purifying process. It is not the point in any case. It is just a fact—which you can observe if you practice rightly in My Company—but it is not the point.

The point is that you enter into Divine Communion in every moment, that you are moved utterly beyond egoic "self-possession" and enjoy the destiny of Divine Self-Realization. That is the entire point, not life-improvement, which is strictly secondary.

The purpose of the Way of the Heart is to enter into My Sphere and leave yours!

If in the midst of life-events some emotional reaction comes up, instead of identifying with it, puzzling over it, getting involved in it, meditating on it, telling everybody else about it, and dramatizing it, you give Me your attention with feeling and disregard it. Instead of being hyperactive or wandering in your activities and doing all kinds of things at random on the basis of your ego-designs, you embrace the discipline of right life, always in Communion with Me. Whatever is not aligned to that discipline you just do not do anymore. You accept the discipline of relinquishing it or of transforming it if need be. One who responds to Me truly with devotion does just that, then. Based on that response to Me, that Communion with Me, you take My Instruction and you change your life.

The beginning of the Way of the Heart, the foundation course, has to do with the devotional response to Me, self-forgetting, turning the functions of the body-mind to Me, Remembering Me, entering into the Bliss that is inherent in the Contemplation of Me, because all that is non-Bliss is forgotten, disregarded, not struggled with.

Devotion to Me is inherently Blissful. It must be done in every moment or else you remember yourself instead of Me. To remember yourself is not Bliss. It is stress and struggle. To Remember Me and, as an inevitable consequence, to forget yourself is Bliss. Therefore, at the beginning of the Way of the Heart, in the middle, and ultimately, the practice is the same devotional submission to Me, the Master, with all your parts, and the same Realizing of the Non-ordinary Reality.

"Narcissus" is unillumined, uninformed, egoically "self-possessed", incapable. You must respond to Me, turn up from the pond, exercise yourself in devotion to Me. That is the Way of the Heart.

It is also the traditional way. Devotion to the Master is the secret of the entire Great Tradition of mankind. It has always been so. Devotion to the Master is the essential content of all the traditions, although they become diverted from it and become complicated and tend to accommodate the ego. There is also much of that in the Great Tradition. Nevertheless, devotion to the Master is the fundamental Truth, the Great Truth, the Great

Secret, which you can see in the traditions everywhere variously displayed.

The Way that is suggested metaphorically and piecemeal, and that is here and there, to one degree or another, Manifested in the Great Tradition, is here Manifested whole in My own Person, and Given its full, right, non-mythological, true, real Basis. It should be a simple matter for all mankind, and for all beings altogether, to redress the wrongs of this now dark age. Such redress requires this conversion of all, one by one.

# CHAPTER 32

# The Way That I Offer to You and to All

*from* The Santosha Avatara Gita

*In the 108 verses of* The Santosha Avatara Gita—*selections from which appear here*—*Avatara Adi Da has Given His summary Revelation of the great means of the Way of the Heart: the simple practice of feeling-Contemplation of Him.*

### 21.

I have, by Means of the Submission, Work, and Word of My here-Speaking Revelation-Body, thoroughly Revealed and Described the Great (and Complete) Process Wherein and Whereby the Heart Itself (or Love-Bliss-Unity Itself) is (Ultimately) Most Perfectly Realized.

### 22.

That Great (and Complete) Process (Which Is the only-by-Me Revealed and Given Way of the Heart) is Described (in every detail and elaboration) in My summary (Written, and forever Speaking) Word of Heart (in many Works).[1]

### 23.

That summary Word is True, and that Great Process Is indeed the Process (elaborate in Its totality of details) Wherein the Inherently Perfect Tacit Obviousness is (progressively[2]) Realized.

---

1. In the many years of His Teaching Work and Revelation Work, Bhagavan Adi Da Confessed the Love-Bliss of Divine Self-Realization again and again, in His Written works and in His Spoken "Consideration" with His devotees. He has elaborately described the practical details of every aspect of practice of the Way of the Heart, from the beginning of one's approach to Him as Sat-Guru to the Most Ultimate Realization of the seventh stage of life.

 Avatara Adi Da's Heart-Word is summarized in eight Texts that He Calls His "Source-Literature". These Texts present in complete and conclusive detail His Divine Revelations, Confessions, and Instructions, which are the fruits of His Teaching and Revelation Work. In addition to this Source-Literature, Avatara Adi Da's Heart-Word also includes His Spiritual Autobiography (*The Knee of Listening*), collections of His Talks, and texts of practical Instruction in all the details of the practice of the Way of the Heart, including the fundamental disciplines of diet, health, sexuality, exercise, and the rearing and education of children in a sacred and cooperative community.

 See "The Sacred Literature of Adi Da, the Da Avatar", pp. 349-62.

2. Whereas Realization of the inherently Love-Blissful Unity of Divine Consciousness is Given by Grace, directly, from the beginning of one's practice of the Way of the Heart—through feeling-Contemplation of Avatara Adi Da's bodily (human) Form, His Spiritual (and Always Blessing) Presence, and His Very (and Inherently Perfect) State—the Yoga, or discipline of body and mind, whereby that Realization becomes the confession of each devotee is a progressive process, unfolding in successive developmental stages of practice and Realization.

24.

The Principle (or Great Means) of that Great Process Is Itself an Extreme Simplicity (as simple to describe as that Great Process is Itself necessarily complex in Its total description).

25.

Ishta-Guru-Bhakti Yoga (or the constant counter-egoic, and even total psycho-physical, effort of self-surrendering, self-forgetting, and, more and more, self-transcending devotion to Me and devotional Communion with Me, the Da Avatar, the Hridaya Avatara, the Avabhasa Avatara, the Love-Ananda Avatar, the Santosha Avatar, the Realizer, the Revealer, and the Very Revelation of the True Divine Person, Who <u>Is</u> the One and Only Self of All and all, Which Is the Heart Itself, the "Bright" Itself, and Love-Bliss Itself), and this constantly exercised as the surrender, the forgetting, and the transcendence of body, emotion (or feeling), mind (or attention), breath, and all of separate self in moment to moment devotional Contemplation of My bodily (human) Form, My Spiritual (and Always Blessing) Presence, and My Very (and Inherently Perfect) State, Is the Principle (or the Great Means) Wherein and Whereby the Great Process of the only-by-Me Revealed and Given Way of the Heart is Accomplished.

26.

For all those who would "consider" the only-by-Me Revealed and Given Way of the Heart, My summary (Written, and forever Speaking) Word of Heart (in many Works) is (now, and forever hereafter) Given (by Me) for their study.

27.

For all those who would practice the only-by-Me Revealed and Given Way of the Heart, My summary (Written, and forever Speaking) Word of Heart (in many Works) is (now, and forever hereafter) Given (by Me) for their application.

28.

And for all those who would, by practicing the only-by-Me Revealed and Given Way of the Heart, Really, and, Ultimately, Most Perfectly Realize the Divine and Inherently Perfect Truth of non-separateness, I am always (now, and forever hereafter) here for their devotional Contemplation.

29.

Realization of the Most Ultimate (or seventh stage) Wisdom-Unity, Truth-Obviousness, and (Divine) Recognition-Capability is (in any moment) a matter of My Giving Grace and My Graceful Self-Revelation.

30.

My bodily (human) Form Is (Itself) the Teaching.

31.

My Spiritual (and Always Blessing) Presence Is the Means.

32.

My Very (and Inherently Perfect) State Is the Revelation Itself.

33.

Therefore, devotional Contemplation of My bodily (human) Form, and (via My bodily human Form) My Spiritual (and Always Blessing) Presence, and (via My Spiritual, and Always Blessing, Presence) My Very (and Inherently Perfect) State, even, Most Ultimately, to the degree of Perfect Oneness with Me (and Perfect non-separation from all and All), Is the Heart-Way That I offer to you and to all.

34.

I Say to you: First and always, in your bodily (human) form, be the always serving devotee of My bodily (human) Form, and (as your devotion, your service, your self-discipline, and your self-understanding mature, or, eventually, become matured, by that actively self-surrendering, self-purifying, and self-transcending Contemplation) you will (by My Giving Grace and My Graceful Self-Revelation) also become the Spiritually activated devotee of My "Bright" and True, and Always Blessing, Spiritual Presence (Which Is Love-Bliss Itself), and (as the active devotee of both My bodily human Form and My Spiritual, and Always Blessing, Presence) you will (by My Giving Grace and My Graceful Self-Revelation) sometimes also (in the Deepening Revelation of Love-Bliss) spontaneously Intuit and Contemplate the beginningless, endless, centerless, and boundless Deep of My Very (and Inherently Perfect) State, and (in due course) that spontaneous (and only-by-Me Given) Grace of Intuitive Contemplation will (by My Giving Grace and My Graceful Self-Revelation) become Inherently Perfect Contemplation of My Very (and Inherently Perfect) State, and Inherently Perfect Identification with My Very (and Inherently Perfect) State, such that even the Most Perfect (or seventh stage) Capability will (in due course) be Realized by Heart.

35.

Therefore, simply (Merely, and intentionally, but on the basis of a fundamental, and fundamentally effortless, feeling-Attraction to Me) Contemplate My bodily (human) Form, My Spiritual (and Always Blessing) Presence, and My Very (and Inherently Perfect) State, and do this Contemplation progressively (as My Giving Grace and My Graceful Self-Revelation Determine the progress), such that (more and more) you allow My bodily (human) Form to <u>Attract</u> (and <u>Keep</u>) your (truly feeling) attention, and This such that (more and more) you allow My Spiritual (and Always Blessing) Presence to <u>Pervade</u> your body-mind, and This such that (Most Ultimately) you allow My Very (and Inherently Perfect) State to <u>Be</u> your Very (and inherently egoless, or non-separate) Heart.

47.

You (necessarily) become (or conform to the likeness of) whatever you Contemplate, or Meditate on, or even think about.

48.

Therefore, Contemplate Me, and transcend even all thought by Meditating on Me.

49.

Do not Meditate on your separate self (your states, your experiences, your presumed knowledge, your dilemma, your problem, or your search), and do not perpetuate self-contraction (by strategies of independent effort, and by adventures of either self-glorification or self-destruction, within or without), but (always, immediately) transcend self-Meditation, personal states, conditional experiences, presumptions of knowledge, and all of dilemma, problem, and search (Merely by Remembering Me, and Invoking Me, and Meditating on Me, and, Therefore, Merely by surrendering to <u>Me</u>, not by self-concerned effort, or by isolated and concerned manipulation of conditions themselves, but by simply, and intentionally, and more and more deeply, responding and Yielding to the always presently Available feeling of the Inherent "Bright" Attractiveness of My bodily human Form, and of My Spiritual, and Always Blessing, Presence, and of My Very, and Inherently Perfect, State), and (Thus, by Means of the always presently Available Grace That Is My Good Company) always and actively feel beyond and (really, effectively) transcend your separate and separative self (Merely by feeling, and Thereby Contemplating, Me).

50.

Do This Contemplation For Its Own Sake, and not passively and partially (as if waiting for devotion to happen to you, rather than always presently Remembering and Invoking Me, and, Thereupon, responsively allowing the presently inevitable feeling of My Inherent "Bright" Attractiveness, and, Thereby, most simply, always and fully activating My always Given and Giving Gift of devotion), and not cleverly and strategically (with all effort and no response, intent but not Yielding, stressful with the seeking of Me, rather than Happy with the Finding of Me), but Do This Contemplation constantly, always, Merely, and by Heart, and (Thus) by feeling to My bodily (human) Form, and by feeling into My Spiritual (and Always Blessing) Presence, and, more and more (and then Inherently) Perfectly, by Feeling As My Very and Freely Revealed and Freely (Inherently) Perfect State.

51.

Therefore, actively (responsively) be My devotee, and (to the degree you make Room for Me in the Place of your feeling, by surrendering thought, and even every form of self-contraction, in self-forgetting Me-Remembrance) the Obvious Truth will (Freely) be Given to you (in every moment), and the Obvious Truth will (Thereby) be Realized by you (as My Giving Grace and My Graceful Self-Revelation will have it, in any moment).

52.

Now, and forever hereafter, this Simplicity is the essential practice (and the essence of the entire practice of the only-by-Me Revealed and Given Way of the Heart) to Which I Call every one.

# CHAPTER 33

# The Essence of Devotion

*June 4, 1978*
*Freely Developed from the* Bhagavata Purana,
*book eleven, chapter fourteen,*
*verses twenty-two through twenty-five*

If there is not the quality of heart-felt devotion to Me, the Self-Existing and Self-Radiant Divine Self, then even intelligent understanding of My Wisdom-Teaching, commitment to self-discipline, and compassionate service of others cannot cleanse and relieve the conditional being of its urges toward fulfillment in the phenomenal realms, high or low.

How can I be Loved if the hair does not stand on end when there is Contemplation of Me? How can I be Loved if the heart does not melt in My Presence? How can I be Loved if tears of joy do not pass freely from the eyes when I am Standing There?

If I am Loved, then the entire body-mind is Filled by that Love. If My devotee is Filled by Me through Love-Communion, My devotee's voice often falters and chokes with the emotion of Love. Because My devotee always dwells in Contemplation of Me at the heart, My devotee often weeps, and suddenly laughs. My devotee sings aloud. My devotee always speaks of Me. My devotee dances with joy. Even all My devotee's movements are a dance of joy in Love.

Gold can be made pure only through submission to fire. Just so, the conditional being is purified and Liberated from its deep urges only when it submits to self-transcending Love-Communion with Me. Such a devotee is Awakened to essential Unity with Me. And My devotee's ecstatic presence serves the purification of the entire world.

**Adi Da (The Da Avatar)**
**The Mountain Of Attention, 1995**

SECTION TWO

# Service and self-Discipline

ince the ancient days it has been said that Samadhi, God-Realization, Liberation, Enlightenment, is the purpose of life. The best thing you can do is spend time in the Company of someone in Samadhi, spend time in the Company of a Realizer. Realization itself, Samadhi, Transmits itself. It is a Power, a Siddhi. It is not by stressful effort, by the seeking of the self-contracted being, or ego, that Samadhi is Realized. It is by Sympathy with Samadhi itself, with God-Realization itself, that Samadhi is Realized. It is by Sympathetic association with the Realizer, Communion with the Realizer, that Realization is accomplished, not by self-effort.

All of the disciplines you practice are a way of being responsive, of participating in the Gift. They are not efforts that can cause Divine Self-Realization. They are ways of participating in the Samadhi of the Realizer and allowing that Samadhi to accomplish you. This is the Great Secret.

ADI DA (THE DA AVATAR)
July 2, 1988

*Service and self-discipline are two fundamental aspects of the Way of the Heart. But, for Adi Da's devotees, service is not simply about helping someone or society. It is primarily a means to turn all action into devotional Contemplation of Adi Da—to serve Him, to be in Communion with Him, no matter what one is doing. And self-discipline in the Way of the Heart is not simply about self-control, about not doing something "bad" and only doing something "good". In the Way of the Heart, self-discipline has no moralistic quality—instead, it is about freeing the individual's energy and attention from limited habits and patterns so that they can fully participate in the Spiritual process. Furthermore, discipline in the Way of the Heart is a means of conforming every aspect of life to the Instruction of the Divine Master so that His Blessing may be fully received.*

# CHAPTER 34

# To Serve Me you Must Actively Transcend all ego-serving work

Traditionally, service (based on devotion) is regarded as the necessary (and first) beginner's orientation to religious (and progressively Spiritual) practice. Service is the traditional discipline of the "outward-directed" personality. Likewise, in the Way of the Heart, practitioners in the early phases of student-beginner* practice are (with even all practitioners of the Way of the Heart) Called by Me to establish (and to progressively increase) their participation in the discipline of service.

In the beginning phases of their practice of the Way of the Heart, student-beginners are (typically) very much outward-directed in their attention, very much involved in outward-directed activities, and not yet very much prepared to practice the transcendence of outward-directed attention through the very profound exercise of meditation and the other Contemplative disciplines of the Way of the Heart. Even so, even very early student-beginners in the Way of the Heart can honor My Work and participate fully in the practice of the Way of the Heart by engaging in their outward-directed activities as <u>servants</u> of <u>My</u> Work.

Therefore, I Call all student-beginners of the Way of the Heart to maximize their practice of the discipline of service, and I Call all student-beginners (and, indeed, all practitioners at any and every developmental stage) of the Way of the Heart to turn their practice of service into a form of Yoga that is the epitome of what is traditionally called "Karma Yoga".* That epitome (or fullest development) of Karma Yoga is Ishta-Guru-Seva, or Sat-Guru-Seva.*

Ishta-Guru-Seva, or Sat-Guru-Seva, is not service based merely on a socially conscious point of view, or the view that it is one's social duty to do "charitable" work. Ishta-Guru-Seva, or Sat-Guru-Seva, is based on the point of view that one should <u>always</u> (in and by means of <u>all</u> activities) serve the Sat-Guru, and that one should devote to the Sat-Guru the fruits, or the rewards, of one's service, rather than take the fruits to oneself. Therefore, the "Karma-Yoga-Principle" of Ishta-Guru-Seva is the self-transcending, or ego-transcending, <u>re-orientation</u> of the purposes and the rewards of one's service (and of even all one's actions).

The specific practice of Ishta-Guru-Seva, or of traditional Karma Yoga, is not to help others (in a socially conscious sense), but to transcend egoic purposes and egoic results. Of course, helping others is implicit in all true service, but the practice of Ishta-Guru-Seva does not require that you devote your life to so-called "charitable" work (or social work). You should, of course, always do service that serves others in one way or another. Nonetheless, "charitable" work, or social work, like any form of work, can be done for all kinds of egoic purposes and rewards, including financial rewards. Therefore, "charitable" work, or social work, is not in itself ego-transcending. Such work—or any kind of work—is ego-transcending only if its fruits (or rewards) are surrendered, and only if the work itself is done in actual (or actively self-surrendering) feeling-Contemplation of the One Who Transcends (or Stands Beyond) the ego (or self-contraction).

The traditional principle, or the "Karma-Yoga-Principle", of Ishta-Guru-Seva is to devote the attention, the purpose (or intention), and the fruits of one's work to the Sat-Guru, and, over time, that "Karma-Yoga-Principle" is to be applied to every aspect of one's life, including every activity. Through constant service to the Sat-Guru, the lives of devotees become altogether more and more self-transcending. Therefore, My truly serving devotees do not perform actions for the sake of the results or pleasures they may enjoy as a result, but every action is (and becomes more and more directly and simply) a form of My devotee's self-surrendering, self-forgetting, and self-transcending feeling-Contemplation of Me.

For all practitioners of the Way of the Heart, the practical principle of true service is responsiveness (to Me, and in present time). Therefore, when I Call My devotee to do something, My devotee should do it imme-diately. If you cannot (as a practical matter) immediately do everything you must do to fully respond to My Call for a particular service, you must nev-ertheless do something in response to that Call, and immediately, and with good effect. If you do not do this, then you invariably miss the mark of your relationship to Me, and you will not properly handle even the practi-cal details of your responsibilities.

In the traditional setting, when the Guru mentions that something needs to be done, it is done instantly. True devotees do whatever must be done, and they do it at the moment of becoming aware of what must be done. Such devotees function in such a way that they transcend karma and the egoic self. Their service is a form of Yoga, based on sacred principles, and not based merely on "labor" and "work-obligation". . . .

But when you do not practice such Ishta-Guru-Seva, you do not allow the real process of the Guru-devotee relationship to take place. Indeed, you do not even become practically responsible, and so you never get to the point of really (and in a practical manner) establishing your true and sacred relationship with Me.

In the Way of the Heart, Karma Yoga bears all the responsibilities of traditional, full, and true Ishta-Guru-Seva. And Ishta-Guru-Seva is not merely an "organizational" or "businesslike" fulfillment of tasks in relationship to Me. The institution, the culture, the community, and the mission of the Way of the Heart[1] all have the responsibility to manage and perform services in an orderly and productive fashion, but what makes these responsibilities Ishta-Guru-Seva is the spirit and the manner in which they are done, and (therefore) the Liberating effect such true service has on the lives of those who perform the service.

In the Way of the Heart, Ishta-Guru-Seva is self-surrendering, self-forgetting, and truly self-transcending feeling-Contemplation of Me via a right and complete re-orientation (to Me) of all the activities of daily life. Therefore, whenever you (as My devotee) engage in Ishta-Guru-Seva, you relate to Me directly. . . .

Mere work (or "labor") is an egoic (or ego-serving) occupation.

Mere work begins to become service only when it is done for the sake of another.

And, for My devotee, even service becomes Ishta-Guru-Seva only when it is done as an immediate and energetic and self-transcending response to Me.

Human beings do not grow to Realize the Divine Self by performing the ego's work. Growth and Divine Self-Realization require self-surrender, self-forgetting, and self-transcendence. And, in the Way of the Heart, self-surrender, self-forgetting, self-transcendence, and Divine Self-Realization are Given and grown by the Grace-Given (and Grace-Giving) Means of devotional Contemplation of Me (to the degree of Heart-Communion with Me). Therefore, in the Way of the Heart, growth (in the Great Process of Divine Self-Realization) requires that all activities become Ishta-Guru-Seva, or immediate, direct, energetic, enthusiastic, altogether responsive, and really self-surrendering service to Me (and truly self-forgetting and self-transcending Communion with Me).

---

1. By the phrase "institution, culture, community, and mission", Bhagavan Adi Da refers to the organization responsible for bringing His Work to the world and the full devotional and cooperative gathering of His devotees.

CHAPTER 35

# Money, Food, and Sex

*from chapter three of* The Method of the Siddhas

AVATARA ADI DA: There are patterns in your individual life that are responsible for the quality of "tamas",* or inertia, immobility, slug-gishness, the backlog of everything. The earliest period of sadhana, or life in relationship to Me, deals especially with this "tamasic" condition, your inertia, your tendency to remain in or return to the very state of suf-fering and ignorance in which you began. Therefore, as My devotee you must find the means, the practical means, to fulfill My demands for a responsible life. When you are capable of functioning, that is when true Spiritual life begins. Until then, it does not make any difference how many times you come to see Me, or how many lectures you hear. Now is the time to begin to live rightly, and to live rightly is to be responsible for your life, not to continue old patterns. I cannot release you from responsibility. How can I release you from the responsibility of your breath?

When people become involved in any kind of religious or Spiritual activity, particularly a group activity of some sort, there are a few subtle notions that tend automatically to be awakened in them. There is the sub-tle suggestion that Spiritual life has something to do with separation from vital and physical life. Indeed, in many of the ancient traditions that is exactly what Spiritual life was—an exclusive and terminal inward turning, getting away from all of the life-force, the life-form, the life-mind, the life-appearance, the life-sensation, into some inward, subtle, non-life percep-tion, or vision, or heaven, or whatever. Because this traditional association of ideas tends to be blanketed over everything that looks like religion, Spirituality, Yoga, and the like, every demand, every quality suggested within religious and Spiritual life that involves the physical and vital being, meets immediate resistance.

Money (and, in general, the commitment of life-force in the forms of effort and love), food, and sex are the essential activities of life. Those are the vital processes, the forms of vital appearance and function. And money, food, and sex are the first things that people begin to resist or manipulate when they get involved in anything that is even remotely like religion or Spirituality. Religious people, for the most part, are extremely confused and guilty about money, food, and sex. People involved in conventional Yoga and religion are endlessly involved with experiments about money, food, and sex. What are such people always doing? "Should I or shouldn't I?" "What is the right diet?" "Fasting? Macrobiotics? No food?" "Renunciation? Poverty?" They are on and off food all the time, on and off sex. They may be celibate for years in order to get "enlightened", but then, just as dramatically, they are seeking the "Tantric bliss"[1] or the restoration of "mental health" in a perpetual orgasmic exercise. Then there are all of the other games of self-denial, no work, no income. All of these things arise whenever anything like Spirituality or religion comes into a person's life.

Because of the automatic resistances built into religious and Spiritual endeavor, the practical need for money and for the means of survival is a very complicated and frustrating affair for even the most sophisticated religious and Spiritual groups. But all of this should be a very obvious matter. You are not in heaven. This is the Earth. Everything here costs life, effort, and money. It costs a great deal of life, effort, and money to maintain a religious or Spiritual community. The purposes may be Spiritual, but a living community must fulfill the same functional laws as any household and any business corporation. Even so, whenever practical demands are made for effort, commitment, love, or money, people tend to lapse into the "tamasic mood". Such reluctance retards life. And the ability of an individual or a group to transcend this tendency is the measure of freedom and survival.

There is the suspicion that if you are "Spiritual" you are not supposed to need money, you are not supposed to require anything, and you are supposed to abandon the functions of life. Obviously, though, money is needed in most circumstances, and work, force, love, and energy are necessary for functional survival. Why is it not obvious, then, why is it not patently the responsibility of individuals, that they bring life and commitment to their own religious or Spiritual community, that they take on its "creative" work, and contribute a responsible amount of money for its continuation? Why is that not obvious? Why is there always so much wheeling and dealing involved with any religious or Spiritual organization? It is because of the traditional illusion of Spiritual attainment, which is pictured as a kind of evaporation process, wherein you become more and more "elusive", and finally disappear inside your "something", or dissolve into your "someplace else".

Now, there are people who teach that such goals are Truth. If that is the game you want to play, you must go to such people. There are few and always fewer responsibilities at the level of life involved in such teachings. A certain amount of food must be taken, but some teachers have even suggested that if you begin a fast and never eat again, at death you will merge

1. Here Adi Da is humorously using the word "Tantric" as it is popularly understood, to mean "Spiritualized sexuality". The intention of the true Tantric approach is to use the most intense (and, therefore, also potentially dangerous) energies of the being (such as sexuality) for the sake of Spiritual Realization.

into the "enlightened state". So they have handled that side of it, too. Such "enlightenment" is a cave without money, food, or sex. If that seems to represent the Truth to you, then go to the forest and fast until death!

I think this traditional orientation is utter nonsense. I do not teach it, and I do not support it. The Truth that already is the case is the Truth from This One's "Point of View". I live very naturally in the human world, and its responsibilities do not make Me "un-Spiritual". Its responsibilities are a "creative" manifestation, requiring intelligence. All life-conditions are forms of relationship. All of life is ordinary. One who is incapable of ordinariness has not even begun to become involved in Spiritual life as subtlety.

The first level of sadhana, or Spiritual discipline, that I had to endure with a human Teacher was not any sort of other-worldly Yoga, nor did it involve love and acknowledgement from the Guru, or even kind words. I spent about two minutes with Rudi when I first met Him. He told Me to get a job and come back in one year! But I was perfectly willing to do that. As it happened, within a month or two, My Spiritual Sadhana with Him did begin. It was not in fact necessary for Me to be away a year, but I was perfectly willing for it to be so. I was ecstatically happy to have made this contact, to have a beginning, to have become capable of Spiritual life. It was a profound joy to Me to have found someone who was obviously capable of drawing Me into a condition at least more profound than the one I was living. From that moment, it was one demand on top of the other. It was work. Work was the sadhana, work was the Spiritual life. There was no "Come to me and sit and chat." It was "Take out the garbage. Sweep out this place." If I came to sit and talk with Rudi, I was most often told, "Scrub the floor," or, "There is a new shipment in the warehouse, so go and unload my truck." I worked constantly, day and night, for four years. On top of the heavy physical labor, Rudi had Me going to seminaries, where I studied Christian theology, masses of historical literature, ancient languages, all kinds of things in which I had no fundamental interest. I had to live in Protestant and Orthodox seminaries, but I was not a Christian. My Sadhana was continuous work and self-transcendence. There was no ending of it. Even in sleep and dreams, there was no ending of it.

My time with Rudi did not see the fulfillment of My Spiritual life. I moved on to other relationships, and the order of My Sadhana and My understanding changed. But His requirements for sadhana in the functions of life and body, in terms of money, food, and sex, were more than useful to Me. The Sadhana I performed in those years became the very foundation of My Spiritual life. During that time I was strengthened and stabilized in mind, body, and life. When I came to Rudi, I was not prepared for an elusive Yogi. Such a one could have been of no use to Me in the beginning. Truth is resurrected from the ground up. The Conscious Force can never leave the ground if you begin your sadhana in the air. If sadhana is begun as an effort to become "Spiritual", then what is merely alive remains a mass of confusion and craziness. So I must insist that all who come to Me take on functional responsibility for the powers of life, which are money, food, and sex. My manner of Working with people is to take hold of them and establish a relationship with them, so that this relationship becomes their conscious, overwhelming, and continuous Condition. When they become conscious of it on any level, then I Give them responsibilities at that level. From that moment, I require and expect them to function at that level. I never pat them on that part of the head again. I expect them to live that function responsibly in the community of My devotees and everywhere in life from that point on. I expect all of you who are already with Me to do sadhana at the levels of money, food, and sex. And to do sadhana on those levels is, at times, going to be just as difficult for you as it was for Me. If you are ready for Spiritual life, you will be very happy to have something in your hand at last, to function at last, to have begun. All other responses to this sadhana are your unreadiness, your unwillingness, your resistance. They are Narcissus. Narcissus has no support from the Heart, from the Guru, from the Truth, or even from the universe. Narcissus is already dead. Death is his karma, his destiny, his realization. And everyone will only die who lives as Narcissus. Narcissus will die in his own pocket. His head will fall from a sleeve. He will not die a sublime death. He will die alone, unconscious for a long time. He is the destiny of unconsciousness, of foolishness. But all waking comes suddenly.

People have become involved with all kinds of patterns of life that are their suffering. Your sadhana involves that level of complication, or suffering, that you are already living. It does not necessarily involve visions. Even if visions appear, they have no ultimate consequence. Suffering is the place of sadhana. Sadhana meets this complication, this resistance, this fear, this stupidity, this lethargy, this craziness, this violence, this separateness, this heaviness, this endless distraction by the current of experience from hour to hour. All of that is terrifying, if you could consciously see it. Sadhana is involved with that. Sadhana requires a great deal of a person. It requires one, ultimately, to be a genius, a hero. It requires one to manifest the great qualities, the greatest human qualities. Everyone who does sadhana must manifest those qualities in his or her own life. Of course, it is not all required or even possible in one afternoon, but functional intelligence must manifest at a certain level even at the beginning.

True Spiritual life is not a form of consolation. Its foundation is not a fascinating promise. It is not generated in the form of "Get along, do the best you can, and after death you will go to heaven," or "I will come again and make everything all right, no matter what you do, because everything is really okay, you rascal!" There is a profound sense in which everything is really all right, even now, regardless of the conditions, but that profundity requires the most "radical" kind of humor, intelligence, and discipline to be understood.

So one must become responsive at the simplest level, the level in which one is living, in which one exists. There is nothing very profound about it. And this requires one to conduct, or make lawful use of, the life-force, not to abandon it, not to become separate from it. One must become capable of relationship at the level of the vital, on all the levels of the physical being, ultimately including the entire range of psycho-physical life. When there is no obstruction to relationship, there is no praise, no blame. There is no praise, no blame, in the responsible, appropriate enjoyment of sex-relationship. There is no praise, no blame, in vitality itself, nor in the appropriate management and enjoyment of food. There is no praise, no blame, in the earning and use of money nor in the "creative" exercise of power and "creativity", in the use of functional ability and force. But one who is living in the pattern of separation is enormously complicated in the functions of money, food, and sex. Most of the problems such a one perceives in his or her own case have to do with money, food, and sex. The mishandling of those three things manifests as poverty and lawsuits, hoarding and financial complications, ill health, and compulsions at the level of food and sex. Those are the daily experience of the usual man or woman. The daily round is a complication of money, food, and sex. Ramakrishna[2] used to say "women and gold" were the chief distractions and sources of bondage. He was perhaps a member of the school of "getting away from the vital", but He was right about "women and gold", the functions of money and sex. And we must include food in the list. These are the areas in which suffering is most apparent. Therefore, your life becomes very complicated to the degree that you have not understood the vital processes, to the degree you are living the life of Narcissus in relation to money, food, and sex. . . .

People think they are supposed to be allowed a little time to get through all of their functional problems. People think they are supposed to analyze themselves for a few years, under very supportive conditions, and get it a little bit straight about two, three, maybe four years from now. But that has nothing whatever to do with the Truth. It is only another sign of reluctance, inertia, "tamas". Spiritual life is not the support of your malfunctioning, with a few little bits of wisdom thrown in until you come out of it. Spiritual life is sadhana, the always present demand of function. How

---

2. One of the modern Indian saints best known in the West, Ramakrishna (1836-1886) was a renowned ecstatic, and a lifelong devotee of the Hindu Goddess Kali. In the course of his Spiritual practice, Ramakrishna passed spontaneously through many religious and Spiritual disciplines, and he Realized a state of profound mystical union with God.

do you think the Spiritual crisis was brought about in traditional monasteries and Spiritual centers? Certainly not by coddling and consoling mediocre people. That is why very few people went to those centers. The moment you stepped in the door, someone was waiting with a stick who took all your clothes, all your money, all your belongings, put you in a little cell, gave you brief instructions about the four or five things you were going to be allowed to do for the rest of your life, and then demanded you do all five before dinner! You found out how you were failing to function by trying to function, by living under the conditions where nothing but functioning was allowed.

The life in My Company is a demand, true Spiritual life, not a form of therapy. It is a demand under the conditions of Satsang, the relationship to the Guru. It is the practice of life in a world where the Living Heart, not your own dilemma and search, is the Condition. The demand itself does not make Real sadhana possible. It is Satsang, the Prior Condition of Truth, that makes it necessary. Satsang contains and Communicates Itself as a demand. And this demand acts as an obstacle for those who are not certain about their interest in this "radical" life. They have read a little about it, heard a little about it, and now it tests them in the fire of living.

Such is how it has always been. The monasteries, the Ashrams, the schools of teachers in the past, were conceived like fortresses in the hills. They were difficult to get to, and very few people ever returned from them. People did not gaze nostalgically at the place up on the hill, or hear about it on the evening news, and say, "Wow, I wish I could just go up there, you know, find out where it's really at, go up there and everything is fantastic forever, and have a really great time." Traditional Spiritual life was never confused with any sort of playful getting "high". All of that is only a mediocre interpretation fabricated by people who have no real capability for sadhana or the True and "radical" Bliss of Conscious existence. True Spiritual life is not getting "high". From the human point of view, the resistive, Narcissistic, ordinary human point of view, Spiritual life is the most completely oppressive prospect. And it stimulates massive resistance in ordinary people as soon as they get a taste of it.

Traditionally, incredible obstacles were put out front, so that people would not bother even to come to the door. It was purposely intended that people would never even ask about it unless they had already overcome tremendous resistance in themselves. The great oriental temples, for instance, were built with incredible images of demons, guardians, and ferocious beasts surrounding the entrances, so that people would not approach such places in their usual state of self-obsession. Their heads were required to be bowed. The devotee was expected to be crushed within, in a humble state, reflecting awareness of his or her habit of living. The devotee was expected to arrive on his or her knees, and never without a gift. Such people would never come irreverently. They would never display an inappropriate attitude. The traditional forms of approach are perhaps too ritualistic and too purely symbolic. They can be superficially learned and imitated, and so they do not necessarily reflect the inner attitude. However, all must realize and demonstrate the appropriate and genuine manner of approach to Me and to life in My Company.

◆ ◆ ◆

DEVOTEE: What is the nature of the demand You make upon Your devotees?

AVATARA ADI DA: The conditions for understanding are Satsang. Satsang Itself, when It is most consciously lived, is "radical" understanding. It is meditation. Satsang with Me is the Real Condition. That is why It goes on apart from the search, Prior to your dilemma and suffering. You should not approach Me in order to carry on the search. You should approach Me with devotion, as one who has found, and put your search down at My Feet. My devotee is one who simply lives in constant remembrance of Me. That is the true Spiritual practice, or sadhana, of Satsang with Me. Every bit of seeking, dilemma, and self-obsession that you lay down is your true gift to Me. All gifts symbolize that true and inner gift, and make it visible. Someone may bring a flower to Me. The flower is very fresh and fragrant. When the person smiles and puts it on the ground or in a vase, it may all seem like a pleasantry. But what is represented by that flower could be the most difficult crisis of the person's life. The truth of that flower, of that gift, is the crisis itself.

When one begins to live one's life functionally, as relationship, when one accepts the simplest level of responsibility and lives it consciously, in spite of conflict, in spite of difficulty, then life itself becomes sadhana, Real Spiritual practice, an expression of Satsang with Me. Such functional and responsible living is the first gift of My devotee to Me. Therefore, it is also My first demand. I truly expect those who live in My Company to master life, to serve My Blessing Work, to live the process of Satsang in My Company, to give it their life-force, to live it with intensity and love, and to make Satsang with Me available to every human being who has the sensitivity to this one. I do not expect, nor do I support, anything less than that. I expect you to function. Confrontation with the functional demand of life is your test from day to day. It is a sign to you of your state from hour to hour. It is on this functional level that people begin to Enjoy Realization, "radical" understanding, and Truth. . . .

My devotees have agreed to do sadhana in the functions of life. They are willing to see this contraction, but to function in any case. The first stages in Patanjali's Yoga system are yama and niyama, things not to do, and things that must be done.[3] The first steps in Yoga are the fulfillment of functional prescriptions. The first thing that one must do is get straight. One may not feel like being straight. After all, one is not yet enlightened! But one is just plain going to be straight in a very fundamental sense. This is the demand of all Spiritual traditions and of all the Great Siddhas. It is agreed, it is acknowledged, it is accepted from the beginning, that one is upset, that one is suffering, that one is not functioning well at all, and that life is filled with pleasures, but also with burdens and fears and obstacles. When one arrives at the door, this is already understood. Nothing needs to be said about it. So the keeper of the door says, "Okay, now that we have heard that, I have these twelve rules for you to do." And the would-be devotee looks at the list with amazement. One is supposed to do all the things that one was not able to do in the first place and that one came here to learn how to do! These things are not what one is supposed to do when one gets enlightened. They are what one is supposed to do starting this afternoon. And all one gets at the beginning is a handshake and a broom! One gets up before the congregation, and they say, "This is Jack Umpty-ump, and he has just joined the community." Everybody looks, "Very good," they read a brief prayer over him, and from that moment he is supposed to be straight. He may rise up from there into some magnificent, "creative" Spiritual life, perhaps. But his straightness has got to be right out there. It is the first demand. He is not given anything miraculous to make him capable of that. And to fulfill that demand, he perhaps has to go through all kinds of difficulty, all kinds of conflict, all kinds of crises, but, even so, he is expected to fulfill that demand. And he is expected not to burden his fellows with his suffering while trying to fulfill that demand. He can be passing through the most incredible turmoil, and yet he is supposed to be well-groomed, clean, smiling, able to do what is required, at ease, straight.

But the therapeutic point of view, the point of view of the search, is of a different kind. A person comes to the "healer", obviously completely incapable of functioning, and the "healer" offers to listen to the person express that failure day after day, week after week, without adding anything to that misery except more things to console and occupy the person, and by which

3. Patanjali is honored as the originator of classical Yoga. He may have lived in the second century of the common era. In his famous treatise, the *Yoga-Sutras*, Patanjali describes eight practices that make up his system of Yoga: moral observance (yama), self-discipline (niyama), posture (asana), control of the breath (pranayama), restraint of the senses (pratyahara), concentration (dharana), meditation (dhyana), and exalted states of consciousness achieved through inward concentration and meditation (samadhi).
The practice of yamas and niyamas is the foundation stage of traditional Yoga. In the Way of the Heart, various yamas and niyamas are taken on to support the practice of feeling-Contemplation of Avatara Adi Da.

he or she can further express the same dilemma. The person gets a remedy, an egoic method by which to further express his or her craziness: a consoling religion, an idol of "God", a belief, a few brief psychiatric analyses. He or she gets medicine and magic to vanish symptoms. But these are all just added to his or her craziness and give the person a more elaborate expression for that craziness. The remedy tends to indulge one's suffering, because it indulges the search. One's search depends on one's dilemma, and one's dilemma is one's suffering. From the "Point of View" of Truth, a therapeutic confrontation is not useful. Only the most "radical" approach to one's suffering is useful.

The Guru does not respond to, support, or act upon the premise of the functional failure and suffering of the devotee. The Guru demands that the devotee function on that level at which some self-understanding already exists. The devotee is not given the absolute demand out of the Heart of the universe in one shot, but is expected to function on the level at which he or she is living confusion. That demand of functioning stimulates a disturbance, a crisis, a form of conscious conflict. That is the core of sadhana. Of course it is difficult! It can stimulate great physical and mental disturbance at times, particularly in those who have not yet surrendered and found the Truth already Present as their Guru.

That is why those who begin the Way of the Heart are generally those who have tried the alternatives. They have tried the forms of indulging their search, and found this strategy does not affect the core of suffering. But when they become sensitive to the Presence of the Heart in My Company, they become capable of Satsang as Enjoyment. Only My true devotee has the strength of consciousness that will permit him or her to endure this crisis of conscious life. But one who still pays a great deal of life to suffering and resistance is burdened with alternatives. Such a one continues to suffer, and to be involved in tremendous conflicts that have nothing whatever to do with Spiritual life. They are simply the expressions of the failure to live Satsang as one's Condition. They are the expressions of one's suffering. . . .

DEVOTEE: What are the responsibilities of those who live in Satsang with You?

AVATARA ADI DA: Those who enjoy Satsang with Me are responsible for appropriate action in life and in the community of My devotees. They must remain in regular contact with the formal cooperative community of My devotees, and assume responsibilities there. They must be employed, or else be responsible for children. They must be responsible for an orderly household. They must avoid "recreational" drugs, alcohol, tobacco, coffee, tea, "junk" food, and the like. They should eat moderately, and essentially use only foods that are usable and supportive of bodily life and vitality. The right and optimum diet should be limited to what is necessary and sufficient for bodily (and general psycho-physical) purification, balance, well-being, and appropriate service.[4] The key to diet is to discover what is supportive and to use it wisely and exclusively. Food does not "create" Spirituality. My devotee must Spiritualize the taking of food, whatever it is, by appropriate sadhana.

The problems of excess, laziness, instability, chronic weakness, and irresponsibility are the patterns of Narcissus. The patterns of avoidance are the very material, or fuel, of sadhana. Surrender all of that in feeling-Contemplation of Me. But even while the dilemma of life is being confronted in Satsang, all are expected to function appropriately. Remember that Satsang is Itself the functional relationship to Me, to others in the community of My devotees, and to the world. A responsible, relational, intelligent manner of living is the condition for Satsang. . . .

. . . Work is a peculiarly human activity. It is the means for transcending the limitations of "lower", elemental conditions. Thus, it is not appropriate for people who come to live in Satsang to remain irresponsible for their own survival, or irresponsible for "creative", supportive action in the human manner.

Another thing peculiar to this time and place is attachment to drugs. Whatever its function at the time it began, positive or negative, drug taking has no purpose whatsoever in Real Spiritual life. It is an aggravation. It toxifies the body, and stimulates one illusion on top of the next. The person involved with drugs and its illusory "Spiritual" culture is back and forth every day. Such a person is not ready for Satsang. Drugs are a deluding alternative, and one must understand the limitations of that bondage. The other forms of stimulation people use, like tobacco, alcohol, coffee, and such, should be abandoned as well. They do not have the immediate kinds of effects of hallucinogenic or even so-called "healing" drugs, but they are remnants of a social culture of "gentility", forms of self-indulgence and distraction that reinforce dullness and only kill at last.

People very often ask about diet. For some reason or other, food has become like drugs. People are using it to become "Realized" or "Spiritual". Neither drugs nor a special diet will make you Realize the Truth. People tend to use diet as a form of search. There is no search that is appropriate. You will not become Divinely Self-Realized or understand most perfectly because you eat only fruit, because you fast one out of every two days, or because you are a vegetarian gourmet. However, there is an appropriate form of eating and fasting. The appropriate diet is one that sustains and supports the body and the vital force.

4. This is a generalized description of the diet which Adi Da recommends to practitioners of the Way of the Heart. For further details on the dietary discipline of the Way of the Heart, see chapter 36 of this book, "The ego-'I' is the Illusion of Relatedness" in *The Adi Da Upanishad*, and *The Eating Gorilla Comes in Peace*.

How much one eats is just as important as what one eats. People eat too much. Overeating disturbs the bodily functions and makes food unusable. Unused food, as well as unnatural and inappropriate food, toxifies the body and causes disease. Many of the things people think are their Spiritual problems are just the results of toxicity. Therefore, you must simplify and moderate your diet. Make it natural and pure. Eat only what is usable by the body, and avoid whatever constipates, toxifies, and enervates the body.

Satsang and Spiritual life do not go on while you indulge yourself and remain irresponsible. Even though you do not understand, even though perhaps you live in dilemma, you must be responsible for an appropriate life. To engage life under appropriate conditions makes you aware of your limitations, your struggle, your search, your dilemma, your resistance. . . .

DEVOTEE: What about exercise?

AVATARA ADI DA: Just as you must discover the appropriate diet in your own case, you must discover the kind and level of activity necessary to keep the body supple and strong. All of it is a matter of intelligence at the level of your specific constitution. You must discover what foods are necessary to keep your chemistry in an optimum condition. You must discover what types of activity and uses of life you can engage without breakdowns of various kinds. In every person's case, there must be an individual and intelligent self-observation and learning.

There is really no basic human being. Everyone is manifesting a very different karma, or range of tendencies and conditions. Some people need and tolerate much more exercise than others. But, in general, every one, because he or she has a vital, physical body, needs a certain amount of regular, conscious physical activity. I provide My devotees with detailed Instruction in matters of diet, exercise, and every functional aspect of vital and Spiritual life. Those who are My devotees must become masters of the ordinary.

CHAPTER 36

# Diet and Fasting

*from chapter thirteen of* The Knee of Listening

*All the forms of discipline taken up by practitioners of the Way of the Heart are a result of extensive "consideration"—experimentation in life-terms—to find the form of living most conducive to God-Realizing Spiritual practice. In this passage from His Spiritual Autobiography, Avatara Adi Da is describing His initial experimentation with diet (from 1970, shortly before His Divine Re-Awakening) and the principles for appropriate diet that were the result. These principles are now used by practitioners of the Way of the Heart in their own practice. (The dietary practice in the Way of the Heart is spelled out in more detail in* The Adi Da Upanishad *and* The Eating Gorilla Comes in Peace *[forthcoming].)*

In the months following my return from India, I had experienced the effects that various degrees of toxicity and enervation have upon the living consciousness and the motivations of seeking. I often smoked cigarettes while I wrote. Occasionally, I would drink alcohol with friends. And, although I maintained an essentially vegetarian diet, I would often, with my friends and family, have meat dishes and sweets, highly artificial (and "junk") foods, and other "rich" preparations.

I began to study various books on pure diet and fasting, and I decided to conduct an experiment, to see what effects fasting and consistently pure diet would have in daily life and in meditation. I became intensively involved with the idea of physical purification as a means of profoundly altering the state of consciousness in life. I even considered that perhaps the entire matter of seeking on mental and Spiritual levels was solely caused by a toxic and enervated condition in the body. If the body could be brought to a state of perfect purity, then perhaps the mind would become stilled, and the living consciousness might enjoy a natural, intuitive Realization of Reality and Spiritual Truth. Perhaps the mind would achieve a state of perfect brilliance and utility. Perhaps the body itself could achieve indefinite longevity, even immortality.

I considered all the obvious healthful options, including fasting, limited amounts of food in general, balanced cooked and raw lacto-fructo-vegetarian diet,[1] balanced raw fructo-vegetarian diet, and the exclusively fruitarian raw diet. I also thought it to be entirely possible, and even desirable, that one could achieve a state independent of normal food and live directly on subtle energy. And this appeared to be supported by the evidence of a few cases on record where people have in fact lived without food of any kind for thirty, forty, even fifty years, or more.

In March of 1970, I began a fast that was to continue for twenty-two days. At first I took only a few glasses of pure water every day. Then I began to add a small amount of fresh lemon juice to the pure water. As suggested by Arnold Ehret[2] in his books on the theory and practice of fasting and pure diet, the addition of fresh lemon juice made the purifying effects of the fast more aggressive. Ehret also claimed that fresh fruit juices, such as apple and orange, would generate an even more aggressive action. Thus, in order to test this, after the first week I also, every day, took one or more glasses of either diluted or undiluted fresh fruit juice (either apple or orange). And these juices consistently produced an added positive effect.

The effects of the twenty-two day fast were positively remarkable. When I began the fast, the body quickly became light (or less gross) in its feeling, hunger completely disappeared after only a few days, and the mind almost immediately became clear, energetic, and precise.

I lost weight on most of the days of the fast. I lost about six or eight pounds in the first five days. After that I lost a pound a day, and this changed to a pound every other day in the last week or ten days of the fast. My weight dropped from around 180 pounds to approximately 154 pounds in the twenty-two days, but I easily returned to a normal, healthful weight in the weeks following the fast.

Early in the fast, there were occasional, brief physical episodes of weakness and dizziness. At times I could even feel various old drug deposits in the body pass through the brain. But, in general, I consistently felt a brilliant physical well-being. My meditation also deepened, as the various physical and vital obstacles disappeared.

After approximately two weeks of fasting, I experienced an episode of continuous physical weakness, such that physical activity became slow and difficult, and my pulse and heartbeat became weak and irregular. Immediately, I went to the literature on fasting, in order to find a means to correct this tendency. I discovered that, in his books on fasting and pure diet, Teofilo de la Torre[3] recommends a pure water extract of vegetables as

1. "Lacto-fructo-vegetarian diet" means a diet that includes dairy, fruit, and vegetables.

2. Arnold Ehret wrote several books on diet and health, including *Thus Speaketh the Stomach*; *Arnold Ehret's Mucusless-Diet Healing System*; and *Rational Fasting for Physical, Mental, and Spiritual Rejuvenation.*

3. Teofilo de la Torre's books on diet and health include *An Inspiring Message on the Philosophy and Science of Health, Youth, and Longevity, Based upon "The Dietetic Laws of Nature"*; *Man's Return to His Garden of Eden*; and *The Process of Physical Purification by Means of the New and Easy Way to Fast.*

a means to avoid enervation during a fast. This liquid extract is made by allowing pure water to settle for many hours on a particular combination of cut, raw vegetables. I tried the drink recommended by de la Torre, and, indeed, it did give me some added strength, especially when coupled with a reduced intake of sweet fruit juices (which, until then, taken perhaps too frequently, or else too often undiluted, appeared to have caused a low blood sugar reaction, and, thereby, at least some of my feelings of physical weakness). And this simple change in my fasting regime allowed the fast to continue for the full term I desired.

After the fast, I continued my experiment by the application of every kind of possibly "right" diet. My experiment with "right" diet (and fasting) included not only myself but . . . various others, all of whom had taken to fasting and pure foods in response to my demonstration. I found that each individual fared better on a different type of diet. Some, for the moment, required more bulk and starch. Others seemed, for the time being, unable to do without foods high in protein, perhaps even including meats. Others immediately fared well on raw and cooked vegetables and fruits. Together, we experimented with the elimination of various foods and the addition of others. All of this demonstrated that, in the case of individual application, the "right" diet was not necessarily identical to any one kind of "unique" or "special" dietary prescription, as the "champions" of any particular dietary variation might propose, but, always, "right" diet had to be determined by an intelligent approach to each individual, as he or she appeared at any point in time.

After three months of all of this, I had acquired much firsthand knowledge of fasting and "right" diet. I concluded that fasting and pure food did in fact aid one's well-being and were a necessary part of responsible self-discipline. My experience of these things clearly indicated that the application of "right" dietary and fasting and general health principles required flexibility in the progressive "rightening" of the individual case. Nevertheless, the optimum practice in all cases was proved to involve (as necessary) regular short fasts and occasional (and, in general, at least once per year) appropriately prolonged fasts, and the consistent choice of pure (or unadulterated, untreated, non-toxic, and truly nutritious) foods, raw (either exclusively or to the maximum degree possible), and selected only from among the possibilities offered by vegetables, grains, nuts, seeds, and fruits. Red meat, or even any "killed" food, eggs, milk and milk products, refined flour, refined sugar, "rich" foods, "junk" foods, excessive amounts of (or, in some cases, even any) cooked foods, coffee, tea, tobacco, alcohol, foods that are toxically sprayed, toxically treated, or toxic otherwise, and even any foods in too large a quantity proved themselves to have a generally (and cumulatively) negative effect on virtually anyone's physical and emotional and mental well-being. However, it also became clear that, even though it is most "right" to eschew such impure (or constipating, toxifying, and enervating) substances altogether, any of them could (whether by sometimes choice or otherwise unavoidable necessity) be occasionally used, if health is otherwise good, and if the negative effects of the impure substances were offset by the judicious use of fasting and the return to a consistently pure diet.

I realized that "exaggerated" involvement in the processes of fasting and "right" diet was itself merely another form of seeking. It was attachment to life as a physical and vital problem. Thus, even "right" dietary discipline, if approached via the point of view of the seeker, or the mind of a "problem", could become a distraction, and the ground for a goal-centered life. Then the otherwise "right" discipline of diet (and of the body in general) would absorb attention like any other presumed problem, as, for example, the problem of the mind, or the problem of Spiritual consciousness. Therefore, understanding this, I dropped all "exaggerated" motivations associated with health practice. I abandoned all my attachment to the idea of "perfection" through diet and fasting. I no longer placed any "infinite" importance on food. And I ceased to be motivated by the search for bodily immortality. All such seeking had proven itself to be merely a means for trapping attention in problems and problem-centered motivations, whereas a simple, intelligent regimen relative to fasting, diet, and general health practice allowed physical existence to remain essentially stable, energetic, and, above all, free of enforced attention and problematic motivations.

The essential logic that I retained in relation to food was based on a straightforward practical knowledge of the basic laws of bodily effects. This amounted to a knowledge of what food-practice produces constipation, and toxemia, and enervation (or the exhaustion of vitality). I was no longer motivated by any problem or idealism in relation to the body. My understanding of the body became a matter of daily practical intelligence, rather than idealism or problem-based seeking. The body had proven itself to be a lawful economy. It required conscious "right" use. Intelligent diet (and, therefore, a diet that is rather consistently pure, generally fructo-vegetarian, perhaps, or at least at times, even exclusively fruitarian, and always, or as a general rule, maximally raw, or raw to the greatest degree the body healthfully allows, and, potentially, and even most optimally, one hundred percent raw), accompanied, as necessary, by regular short fasts and occasional (and "rightly" prolonged) long fasts, regular, healthful use of fresh air, usable (or safely received) sunlight, and pure water, appropriate (but, generally, simple, and not excessive, and, altogether, Yogically designed) physical exercise, and a life-positive (and yet Spiritually "right" and true) emotional-sexual practice (that conserves both natural emotional-sexual energy and true Spiritual Energy through positive relational and Yogic disciplines, whether "rightly" sexually active or "rightly" celibate)—all these became, for me, simple matters of responsibility, a matter of simple, practical intelligence relative to the body, whereas previously they appeared as strategic and idealized means toward some kind of victory over life, the body, and mortality itself.

CHAPTER 37

# The Secret of
# How to Change

*from* Love of the Two-Armed Form

T rue change and advanced human adaptation are not made on the basis of any self-conscious resistance to old, degenerative, and sub-human habits. Change is not a matter of <u>not</u> doing something. It is a matter of doing something <u>else</u>—something that is inherently right, free, and pleasurable. Therefore, the key is insight and the freedom to feel and participate in ways of functioning that are right and new.

The tendencies and patterns of your earlier adaptations are not wrong. They were appropriate enough in their own moment of creation, and there is no need to feel guilt or despair about them. Likewise, efforts to oppose and change them are basically fruitless. Such efforts are forms of conflict, and they only reinforce the modes of egoic "self-possession".

What is not used becomes obsolete, whereas what is opposed is kept before you. Therefore, the creative principle of change is the one of relaxed inspection and awareness of existing tendencies, and persistent, full feeling orientation to right, new, regenerative functional patterns. If this principle is practiced consistently and in ecstatic resort to Me, the True Heart-Master, free growth is assured.

Have no regrets. Resort to Me in Truth and in the present. All that has been done by anyone had its logic in its time. Only God avails. Whatever is your habit in this moment is not wrong. It is simply a beginning. No habit is necessary, but it is only tending to persist, because it has not yet been replaced by further growth. Hear My Wisdom-Teaching of Truth, and understand what is the right, ultimate, and regenerative pattern of each function of the human body-mind. Feel free of all negative judgments about what you have done and what you tend to do. Turn with full feeling-attention to the creative affair of new adaptation in most positive Communion with Me, the True Heart-Master, Who is Life, and Who is Alive as all beings.

**Adi Da (The Da Avatar)**
**The Mountain Of Attention, 1995**

## SECTION THREE

# The Practice of Love and Sexuality

L ove, not reason, should make decisions. Decisions based on reason and not love are karmic.

Therefore, let the heart be your intelligence. The heart is unreasonable. The heart is mad. And the heart is the ground I Call you to walk on. The only way to overcome the murderer that is the cosmos is to love. Allow the heart to break, and be that sign. Be a feeling being. Then you cannot be murdered, you cannot be a fool, you cannot be deceived.

Love is the victory. Love is the meditation. Love is life. You simply must become willing to love. Allow God to Be. To love is to be truly religious, to consort with the Living One.

ADI DA (THE DA AVATAR)
June 22, 1992

*Bhagavan Adi Da Teaches that you, and every other human being, are a seeker. He points out that you are seeking to create perfect fulfillment through physical, mental, and emotional experience—when all experience is temporary. He Calls you to observe that you are trying to immunize yourself against the reality of change, suffering, and death through pleasurable consolation—even though death is an inevitable fact. And He Teaches that in no other area of life is seeking more apparent—more desperate, more pitched, more fraught with confusion, conflict, doubt, and disappointment—than what He Calls the "emotional-sexual" realm.*

*In this section, Adi Da "considers" love and sexuality: How most people live trapped in a "rejection ritual", feeling unloved and therefore refusing to love others, and how this ritual can be outgrown; why orgasm is typically degenerative, and how it can be transformed; why the celibacy suggested by religious and Spiritual traditions is characteristically life-negative and suppressive, whereas true celibacy is happy and positive. And with all these "considerations", He suggests a Radiant alternative to the hopeless pursuit of emotional-sexual fulfillment: a love-relationship with the Divine Person in human Form, and living one's entire life of sexuality and love in the context of that already-satisfied, primary love.*

# CHAPTER 38

# Ecstatic Living

## June 3, 1992

A VATARA ADI DA: Ecstasy requires the entire body. Sexual activity is a means of ecstatic living, but you must not reduce your ecstatic life to sexing. Use sexuality in that ecstatic manner, but also cultivate the ability to drop out of the social persona and live an ecstatic life every day. Ecstasy is the primary function of true religion.

Conventional, exoteric religion, however, is not about ecstasy. It is about the social persona, which commands people toward moral and socially productive activity. As a consequence, morality tends to be the whole of conventional religion.

Most of you here are from the Western societies of America, Australia, and Europe, which are founded on the social persona. But more than that they are founded on the exclusion of ecstasy, the exclusion of the mystical life and ecstatic activity altogether. That is why there are such heavy messages in those places against drugs and even alcohol, while at the same time these substances are somewhat allowed. There may be good reason for people to avoid such things, but the root of the conventional moral message is the social structure that commands you to be the social persona only and not to be ecstatic. People collapse under the stress of that demand, and they adapt to a merely self-indulgent life, exploiting drugs and alcohol, even sexuality, because they are under stress.

It is not right or natural to divorce yourself from ecstasy. Ecstasy is the primal function of the human being. The social function is certainly useful and necessary. But it must not be enforced to the exclusion of ecstasy and the actual practice of ecstasy. If you realize such freedom, then your fundamental exercise is in the religious life—and not merely in the exoteric religious life, which reinforces the social personality.

True religion is esoteric. True religion may combine itself with things that are otherwise regarded as exoteric, but it is about ecstasy. It is about ego-transcendence. If you are free to live a true religious life, then you practice ecstasy under all kinds of circumstances. In fact, you practice ecstasy all the time. The way to do that is to incarnate love and its signs in daily life. Do not just live a moral life. Live a life of love. And practice all the meditative and other exercises of religion that are occasions of ecstasy—

Puja,* chanting, song, praise.

Sexuality is another aspect of ecstatic living that is openly "considered" in a true, or esoteric, religious culture. The entire process of such a life is about ecstasy, or transcending egoity, to the point of realizing That Which Is when there is no contraction, Which Is the Divine Self-Condition. True religion transforms life and touches all aspects of your living.

True religion, then, is a primary requirement of human beings. It is not merely just some stuff that comes down through time that should be used to command moral or socially useful behavior. True religion is a culture and a key mechanism for the fulfillment of what a human life is about. It is a heart matter. And it is about ecstasy, or the transcendence of egoity.

If you understand that, then you know the same is true of sex. Sex is a Puja. I have told you this in *The Dawn Horse Testament,*[1] meaning that it is a specifically religious activity. And that is how you should involve yourself in it. Not in the embarrassed, exoteric sense, where you pray before going to bed to be forgiven for what you are about to do now—sexual guilt is a terrible imposition on people. Realized sex is truly religious, Yogic, ecstatic. You should be able to explore it positively and in the fullest sense, in each appropriate occasion, to the point of achieving its capability to the maximum.

This is what I have always Called My devotees to do, not to realize some anti-sexual and puritanical disposition. I have never suggested to My devotees that they be anti-sexual and puritanical. The gathering of My devotees should be devoted to the ecstatic, ego-transcending life. If you have social responsibilities, fine—the social personality is an appropriate expression in all kinds of circumstances—but express yourself socially as an ecstatic. That is, manifest love socially, wholly expressed, positive, warm in the eye, with feeling. There are really no social taboos to prevent such expression. People are so suppressed that it does not happen very much, but when it does occur in people it is accepted. Therefore, you can express love in all of your social circumstances. In fact, you are obliged to do so as My devotee.

What does not work is the refusal of ecstasy, the tendency to allow the force of egoity, the social persona, to suppress the Revelation you have received from Me. If you do not animate such ecstasy, what <u>are</u> you going to do, then? Just live as the ego and work on your "case"? You should receive My Revelation instead. Really live your relationship to Me and allow it to transform your life.

And that includes the transformation of your sexual life. I am here to be completely open and expressive about sexuality, to tell you everything about it.

1. Bhagavan Adi Da is referring to chapter twenty-one of *The Dawn Horse Testament Of Adi Da.*

CHAPTER 39

# The Wound of Love

*from chapter twenty-one of*
The Dawn Horse Testament Of Adi Da

O nly A Fool Will Fail To Cultivate The Relationship To The Beloved. Likewise, Only A Fool Will Fail To Cultivate The human Well-being and The Spiritual, Transcendental, and Divine Realization Of his or her any partner in intimate embrace. And This Is Also True: The ego (or the self-Contracted individual) Is Just Such A Fool!

The emotional-sexual ego Constantly Hunts For an other. The ego-"I" (or self-Contraction) Hunts (or Seeks) an other (Even all others and The Total Objective Cosmos) In Order To Be Gratified, Consoled, and Protected. The Compulsive Hunting (or Search) For an other Is Generated By The Feelings Of Un-Happiness, Emptiness, and Separateness That Possess and Characterize the self-Contracted being.

Once an other Is Found, the ego-"I" Clings To the other, At First plea-surably, and Then Aggressively. The ego-"I" Depends On the other For Happiness, and, Over time, the ego-"I" Makes Greater and Greater Demands On the other For Fulfillment Of itself (In all of its desires). Often, In time, the other Becomes Depressed and Exhausted By This Demand (and Thus Leaves, or Dies). Just As Likely, the ego-"I" Discovers, Over time, That the other Cannot or Will Not Satisfy The Absolute Demand For atten-tion and Consolation. In That Case, the ego-"I" Feels Betrayed, and the ego-"I" Begins The Strategy Of Punishing, Rejecting, and Abandoning the other.

Every conditionally Manifested being Has (In time) Often Been The Proposed Victim Of This Strategy Of Separate and Separative selves. Even More, Until The Heart Gives Way To Divine Love-Bliss, every conditional-ly living being Is The Original Genius and Grand Performer Of This Strategy Of Separate and Separative selves. It Is The Strategy Of Narcissus, and It Is The Dreadful Work Of all conditionally living beings who Are Not Awake To The Truth Beyond the ego-"I".

If There Is To Be Real Happiness, This Cycle Of egoic "self-Possession" and other-Dependency (or object-Dependency Generally) Must Be Transcended. In The Way Of The Heart, It Is Transcended Through Most Fundamental self-Understanding, and Through self-Transcending Love, Service, self-Discipline, and Meditation (In Responsive Devotional

248

Relationship To Me, and, Thus and Thereby, In Responsive Devotional Relationship To The Divine Person), and (Eventually, By Grace) Through Direct Realization Of The Self-Radiant (or Inherently Spiritual), Self-Existing (or Transcendental), and (Ultimately) Divine Self-Condition Of Being (Itself). In This Manner, The Inherent Happiness Of The Spiritual, Transcendental, and Divine Self Replaces The Fruitless Search (or Hunt) For Happiness By the self-Contracted and Dependent conditional self. . . .

The egoic (or self-Contracted) individual Is (By Virtue Of his or her History, self-Idea, and Lack Of Spiritual, Transcendental, and Divine Realization) Chronically Bound To The Ritual Of Rejection. The emotional (or emotional-sexual) Career Of egoity Tends To Manifest As A Chronic Complaint That Always Says, By Countless Means, "You Do Not Love me." This Abusive Complaint Is Itself The Means Whereby the egoic individual Constantly Enforces his or her Chronic Wanting Need To Reject, Avoid, or Fail To Love others. Indeed, This Complaint Is More Than A Complaint. It Is A self-Image (The Heart-Sick or self-Pitying and Precious Idea That "I" Is Rejected) and An Angry Act Of Retaliation (Whereby others Are Punished For Not Sufficiently Adoring, pleasurizing, and Immortalizing the Precious ego-"I").

The egoic (or self-Contracted) individual Is Chronically and Reactively Contracted From all of its relations. Fear Is The Root Of this self-Contraction, and The Conceived Purpose Of this self-Contraction Is self-Preservation, Even self-Glorification. Indeed, Fear Is the self-Contraction. The self-Contraction, or the ego-"I", Is The Root-Action or Primal Mood That Is Fear. Therefore, All Of The self-Preserving, self-Glorifying, and other-Punishing Efforts Of the ego-"I" (or the self-Contracted body-mind) Only Preserve, Glorify, and Intensify Fear Itself.

Fear, the ego-"I", Un-Love, or The Total Ritual Of self-Contraction Must Be Understood and Transcended. All Of Fear, egoity, self-Contraction, or Un-Love Is Only Suffering. It Is Only Destructive. And It Is Entirely Un-Necessary.

Fear, egoity, self-Contraction, or Un-Love Is Chronically Expressed Through The Complex Ritual Of Rejection, or The Communication Of The Dominant Idea "You Do Not Love me". Once This Is (In The Way Of The Heart) Truly, and Completely, and Most Fundamentally Understood, The Ritual Of Rejection, Fear, egoity, self-Contraction, or Un-Love Can Be Directly Transcended, If Only It Is Summarily Replaced By The Ordeal (or Discipline and Practice) Of self-Transcending Love, and (Then, By Grace) Heart-Communion With and (Ultimately) Heart-Communication Of The Divine Self-Condition, In The Form "I Love You".

Therefore, In The Way and Manner Of The Heart, Understand Your Separate and Separative self (As Un-Love) and Transcend Your Separate and

Separative self (By Love). And This Is Perfected (Progressively, In The Way and Manner Of The Heart) By Devotional (or self-Transcending and self-Forgetting) Heart-Surrender Of the conditional body-mind To My Bodily (Human) Form, and My Spiritual (and Always Blessing) Presence, and My Very (and Inherently Perfect) State, and, Thus and Thereby, To The Person and The Forms or Characteristics Of The Spiritual, and Transcendental, and Divine, Self.

If You Will Thus Be Love (By This Devotion), You Must Also Constantly Encounter, Understand, and Transcend The Rejection Rituals Of others who Are, Even If Temporarily or Only Apparently, Bereft Of Divine Wisdom. Therefore, If You Will Be Love (As My Devotee, and, Thus and Thereby, As A Devotee Of The Divine Person), You Must (In The Way and Manner Of The Heart) Always Skillfully Transcend The Tendency To Become Un-Love (and Thus To Become self-Bound, Apparently Divorced From Grace-Given Divine Communion) In Reaction To The Apparent Lovelessness Of others. And You Must Not Withdraw From Grace-Given Divine Communion (or Become Degraded By Un-Love) Even When Circumstances Within Your Intimate Sphere, or Within The Sphere Of Your Appropriate social Responsibility, Require You To Make Difficult Gestures To Counter and Control The Effects or Undermine and Discipline The Negative and Destructive Effectiveness Of The Rituals Of Un-Love That Are Performed By others.

For those who Are Committed To Love (and who Always Commune With The One Who Is Love), Even Rejection By others Is Received and Accepted As A Wound, Not An Insult. Even The Heart-Necessity To Love and To Be Loved Is A Wound. Even The Fullest Realization Of Love Is A Wound That Never Heals.

The egoic Ritual Calls every individual To Defend himself or herself Against The Wounds Of Love and The Wounding Signs Of Un-Love (or egoic self-Contraction) In the daily world. Therefore, Even In The Context Of True Intimacy, The Tendency (Apart From Spiritual Responsibility) Is To Act As If Every Wound (Which Is Simply A Hurt) Is An Insult (or A Reason To Punish).

The Reactive Rituals Of egoity Must Be Released By The self-Transcending (and Then Spiritual) Practice Of Love. This Requires Each and Every Practitioner Of The Way Of The Heart To Observe, Understand, and Relinquish The emotionally Reactive Cycle Of Rejection and Punishment. And The Necessary Prerequisites For Such Relinquishment Are Vulnerability (or The Ability To Feel The Wounds Of Love Without Retaliation), Sensitivity To the other In Love (or The Ability To Sympathetically Observe, Understand, Forgive, Love, and Not Punish or Dissociate From the other In Love), and Love Itself (or The Ability To Love, To Know You Are Loved, To

Receive Love, and To Know That Both You and the other, Regardless Of Any Appearance To The Contrary, Are Vulnerable To Love and Heart-Requiring Of Love).

It Is Not Necessary (or Even Possible) To Become Immune To The Feeling Of Being Rejected. To Become Thus Immune, You Would Have To Become Immune To Love Itself. What Is Necessary (and Also Possible) Is To Enter Fully Into The Spiritual Life-Sphere Of Love. In The Way Of The Heart, This Is Done By First Entering (By Heart) Into My Company (and, Thus and Thereby, Into The Company Of The Divine Person), and (Therein) To Submit To The Divine Embrace Of Love, Wherein Not Only Are You Loved, but You Are Love Itself. Then You Must Magnify That Love-Radiance In the world of human relationships.

If You Will Do This, Then You Must Do The Sadhana (or Concentrated Practice) Of True Active Love and Real (True and Steady) Trust. As A Practical Matter, You Must Stop Dramatizing The egoic Ritual Of Betrayal In Reaction To The Feeling Of Being Rejected. You Must Understand, Transcend, and Release The Tendency To Respond (or React) To Signs Of Rejection (or Signs That You Are Not Loved) As If You Are Insulted, Rather Than Wounded. That Is To Say, You Must Stop Punishing and Rejecting others When You Feel Rejected. If You Punish another When You Feel This, You Will Act As If You Are Immune To Love's Wound. Thus, You Will Pretend To Be Angrily Insulted, Rather Than Suffer To Be Wounded. In The Process, You Will Withdraw and Withhold Love. You Will Stand Off, Independent and Dissociated. You Will Only Reinforce The Feeling Of Being Rejected, and You Will Compound It By Actually Rejecting the other. In This Manner, You Will Become Un-Love. You Will Fail To Love. You Will Fail To Live In The Sphere Of Love. Your Own Acts Of Un-Love Will Degrade You, Delude You, and Separate You From Your Love-partner (or Your partners In Love) and From Love Itself. Therefore, those who Fail To Practice The Sadhana Of Love In their intimate emotional-sexual relationships, and In human relationships Generally, Will, By That Failure, Turn Away (or Contract) From God (or The Great Condition That Is Reality Itself).

Love Does Not Fail For You When You Are Rejected or Betrayed or Apparently Not Loved. Love Fails For You When You Reject, Betray, and Do Not Love. Therefore, If You Listen To Me, and Also If You Hear Me, and Also If You See Me, Do Not Stand Off From Relationship. Be Vulnerable. Be Wounded When Necessary, and Endure That Wound or Hurt. Do Not Punish the other In Love. Communicate To one another, Even Discipline one another, but Do Not Dissociate From one another or Fail To Grant one another The Knowledge Of Love. Realize That each one Wants To Love and To Be Loved By the other In Love. Therefore, Love. Do This Rather Than

Make Any Effort To Get Rid Of The Feeling Of Being Rejected. To Feel Rejected Is To Feel The Hurt Of Not Being Loved. Allow That Hurt, but Do Not Let It Become The Feeling Of Lovelessness. Be Vulnerable and Thus Not Insulted. If You Are Merely Hurt, You Will Still Know The Necessity (or The Heart's Requirement) Of Love, and You Will Still Know The Necessity (or The Heart's Requirement) To Love.

The Habit Of Reacting To Apparent Rejection (By others) As If It Were An Insult Always Coincides With (and Only Reveals) The Habit Of Rejecting (or Not Loving) others. Any one whose Habitual Tendency Is To Reject and Not Love others In The Face Of their Apparent Acts Of Rejection and Un-Love Will Tend To Reject and Not Love others Even When they Are Only Loving. Narcissus, The Personification Of the ego, the self-Contraction, or The Complex Avoidance Of Relationship, Is Famous For his Rejection Of The Lady, Echo, who Only Loved him. Therefore, If You Listen To Me, and Also If You Hear Me, and Also If You See Me, Be Vulnerable In Love. If You Remain Vulnerable In Love, You Will Still Feel Love's Wound, but You Will Remain In Love. In This Manner, You Will Always Remain In The human (and Then Divine) Sphere Of Love.

Therefore, The Most Direct Way To Know Love In every moment Is To Be Love In every moment.

In The Way Of The Heart, My Devotee Is Founded In This Capability By Virtue Of his or her Constant Communion With Me (and, Thus and Thereby, With The Divine Person, Reality, or Truth). Therefore, If any such a one Fails To Be Steady In This Communion With Divine Love-Bliss, Then he or she Will Become Weak In Love. And To Be Weak In Love (At Any Stage Of Life) Is To Be Always Already Independent, Insulted, Empty With Craving, In Search Of Love, Manipulative, Un-Happy, and Moved To Punish, Betray, and Destroy all relationships. Such a Weak one Always Already Feels Rejected and Is Never Satisfied. Indeed, such a one Is Not Even Found To Be Truly Lovable By others.

Those who Love Are Love, and others Inevitably Love them. Those who Only Seek For Love Are Not themselves Love, and So they Do Not Find It. (Even If they Are Loved, they Do Not Get The Knowledge Of It.) Only The Lover Is Lovable. Therefore, Every Heart Should Become As True Love Is. And My Every Listening Devotee, My Every Hearing Devotee, and My Every Seeing Devotee Should Realize (and Demonstrate) This Principle In True Active Love With Me (and Real, True Trust In Me), The One Who Is Love.

# CHAPTER 40

# Sex Is a Heart-Matter

1.

## Found Your Intimacies
## on Love Alone

*May 30, 1992*

AVATARA ADI DA: Sex is a heart-matter. The heart is the basis, the foundation, the seat, of your sexuality. This is what you must discover, and the sooner you discover it the better for you.

The genitals are not the platform of sex. They are only the means of sex. The heart is the platform of sex. When you are sane, this is simply true. Sane sexuality is love expressed. If you energize yourself sexually over and over again, you lose your heart. You become fleshy, cold, opaque, unnatural, diseased, mad. People who are addicted to sexuality in itself are mad. Like alcohol or drugs, sex is a loveless automaticity that destroys people's lives. Sex is just as destructive as alcohol and drugs. And perhaps it is even a more common addiction.

Human beings generally are addicted to sex. They think about it all the time. They are troubled about it all the time. Even though people may be involved in intimate relationships, they cannot incarnate feeling. They cannot incarnate themselves sexually to the fullest degree because they have superimposed on their sexuality so many games and rituals. Therefore, because so much is left over that cannot be lived in intimate relationship, people generally live with a promiscuous mind, an addicted mind, and they are constantly wandering and thinking about others, because they cannot live love. This is what I am Calling you to discover.

In the Way of the Heart, sex is about intimate relationship. The sexual Yoga of the Way of the Heart is about love. Sex is an emotional-sexual matter. Therefore, found your intimacy on love alone and incarnate that. If love is the principle, if you found your life on that understanding, your life is an extraordinarily difficult process. And the ultimate event is an incomparable Joy. But to earn it is to suffer profoundly, to participate in a struggle that requires you to commit your attention every day of your life and to be willing to lose it all in any moment. When the realization comes, when the resolution comes, it is a miracle. It transforms your humanity. There is nothing comparable to it. Nothing can compare to that resolution of love. Maybe in some sense it is the greatest of all samadhis. The moment that resolves the human stress will be unique for each of you. You must earn such a passionate resolution.

2.

# Sexuality Is the Physical Dramatization of Emotion

*first published December 1978*
*from* Love of the Two-Armed Form

AVATARA ADI DA: Feeding creates a pleasurable sensation in the body that the baby identifies and that makes it feel comfortable, sustained, protected. The adult gets a similar satisfaction from sexuality. Sexual intercourse is a way of feeding on energy. It is a pleasurable sensation that you can identify. It makes you feel good, because it is a contact with life-energy. But, just as nursing makes the baby feel dependent for life-energy on what is outside it, so sexuality makes you feel that you have a very dependent relationship to the energy of existence. This feeling of dependence, however, is false.

In truth, you yourself are a representative of the universal life-energy, which you communicate through your feeling response in your relations, through love, not only through orgasm and occasions of physical contact. Therefore, if your life is to be true, the energy that you now identify exclusively with sex must be your consistent manifestation, under all conditions, in all of your relations, most particularly in the intimate sexual dimension of your life. But being able to have orgasms and being sexually attractive and athletic does not make you a true lover. Even your relatively successful adaptation to the orgasm must change, because, like feeding, it is a way of being consoled and dependent.

My Wisdom-Teaching relative to sexuality is that you must go beyond the dependent orientation that seeks to acquire pleasure. You must realize the inherent pleasurableness of existence by connecting to the greater levels of the Food Source, the greater levels of sustenance, or Spiritual Energy. Thus, you must see your capability to be released pleasurably through orgasm for what it is—at best a rudimentary way of feeling good, of acquiring pleasure.

You must already be full of pleasure. You must be love. If you live as love, then the purpose once served by the conventional orgasm appears to your understanding as an old adaptation, a form of memory like the aberrated emotions of guilt, fear, and anger. The conventional orgasm is exactly the same kind of aberrated development as guilt or fear or anger. It is the expression of a primarily physical reaction, a physical recoil rather than an emotional one. It is a sign on the physical level of the same recoil that guilt and fear and anxiety and withdrawal from life signify at the emotional level.

People learn orgasm. Orgasm is a form of adaptation that people learn at an early stage of life, even earlier than they become genitally active. People learn orgasm in being sustained, in nursing. They learn it in the pleasurable bodily states that they may realize early in life, and they associate those acquired pleasurable states with a continual connection to life-energy. When you discover your capability for orgasm, you identify it at the most rudimentary level, just as you identify the pleasure of nursing as an infant. It is a solution to the dilemma of life, to the sense of emptiness, of needing to be fed, of feeling that you are not inherently one with infinite pleasure, or Love-Bliss.

Emotion and sexuality are the same. If you are adapted only to reactive, negative emotions, then your sexuality will take a very similar form. Thus, lovelessness and the rejection of life-energy at the level of emotion are reflected as conventional orgasm and the rejection of life-energy at the level of sex. The conventional orgasm is precisely the rejection, or discharge, of life-energy. In later years, people become ritually addicted to this pleasure, this physical emotion of the orgasm. They constantly hope to acquire it again and again, and their lives become very complex so that they can acquire that pleasure.

Unless one privately masturbates, one generally depends on sexual intimacy with another individual for orgasm. But, in general, the life you spend with people with whom you have orgasms is like conventional orgasm itself. It is loveless, a recoil from relationship. It is a theatre of jealousy, anger, fear, mediocrity, subhuman energy, and mutual stimulation to the point of acquiring conventional orgasms. It is a life of conflict, a life lived at a very low level. The fundamental function of emotional-sexual intimacy for most people is to satisfy this drive toward orgasm. But one cannot have the life of conventional orgasm without the life of negative emotions, because they represent the same negative adaptation. Thus, you must not only become responsible for your negative emotions and be present as feeling-attention, in all relations and under all conditions. You must also become responsible sexually, because emotion and sexuality represent the same level of adaptation and responsibility. Sexuality is the physical drama of the emotional dimension of life.

Many people who are presently sexually active have been sexually active since very early in their lives. Even if you have not, your early emotional adaptation to the conditions of life determined your sexual pattern in the future. Thus, even if there were no overt sexual incidents in your early life, your childhood, your early teens, before you became regularly active sexually, there were emotional incidents that created a double-bind, an emotional dilemma of pleasure versus fear and guilt. This feeling obstruction then appeared when you became sexually active.

Emotion and sexuality are exactly the same thing. There is absolutely no difference between them. Whatever you are emotionally, you are sexually. Whatever you are sexually, you are emotionally. And whatever you are emotionally and sexually, that is what you are as a living presence. That is your relationship to the life-force, upon which further growth depends. If you are obstructed emotionally and obstructed sexually, you are also obstructed in the energy of the living being. You are obstructed in the psyche, in the feeling dimension, and thus you are prevented from realizing the fourth stage of life and adapting to the functional levels of the bodily being above the navel.[1] You may have occasional contact with the depth that is the feeling heart, but you will not be full and mature at the level of the heart. Your whole life will essentially be spent below it.

So it is that, in becoming a loving presence in the world, you must not only cease to dramatize all the contractions of emotion—you must also transcend the conventional orgasm. Such orgasm, the conventional "hype" of sexuality, is loss of life-energy, the discharge of life-energy. It is the degenerative form of living and of sexual intimacy. It is the craving for sustenance, because you have adapted to the loss of life-energy. There is a certain momentary pleasure associated with conventional orgasm, but its effects are psychologically and emotionally degenerative. It constantly reinforces negative emotional states, not the life of love.

Conventional orgasm is also physically degenerative. When there is conventional orgasm, the body also eliminates certain glandular chemistries, with the discharge of the life-force, that are absolutely essential to its own regeneration and growth. Likewise, conventional orgasm reinforces the fixation of attention on the lower body. As long as the fixation of attention is reinforced pleasurably and with some consistency in the lower body, attention will not rise to the higher functional dimensions of the body. Thus, the conventional orgasm represents the loveless orientation to life-energy whereby that energy is lost and attention is trapped in negative emotion and in the most descended, or fleshy, capability for experience.

1. Here Adi Da is referring to the developmental potential of the human body-mind. The functional centers associated with growth in the first three stages of life (or growth in the gross physical, emotional-etheric, and lower mental dimensions) are traditionally associated with chakras, or energy centers, that correspond to the perineum, the sexual center, and the solar plexus, respectively. In other words, maturity in the first three stages of life is characterized by responsibility for all that is "below the heart". Growth in the beginning of the fourth stage of life is associated with the feeling center of the heart. As the being matures in the fourth stage of life into and through the fifth, growth is traditionally associated with centers in the throat and the brain. Thus, the more advanced evolutionary development of individuals in the fourth and fifth stage of life is associated with centers that are "above the navel". (In the ultimate, or sixth and seventh, stages of life, practice is no longer defined by the centers of the body-mind or by the traditional chakra system.)

It is not the pleasure associated with sexual intimacy that is wrong. Sexual pleasure is not in principle wrong. However, the usual person's use of it, the usual person's relationship to it, is degenerative and an expression of a negative emotional adaptation. Pleasure is associated with the loss of life-energy. In your casual adaptation, pleasure and death, sex and death, eroticism and death, have always been felt to be the same event. You must, in your right emotional and sexual adaptation, discover the pleasure that is inherent in life. You must realize a regenerative form of the whole process of life, including your sexuality. You must find the way of enjoying sexual intimacy whereby life-energy is not lost, you do not discharge life-energy in order to achieve pleasure, and you love another, completely Happy and free in your life together.

In present-day societies there are essentially two approaches to orgasm. Many traditional Spiritual societies, the remnants of which appear in the Orient, regard orgasm as sinful and ignorant because it is loss of life-energy. It signifies the confinement of attention to the lower life, whereas in this traditional view attention properly belongs to the ascended life, purposed to the Realization of God, Truth, and Reality. Thus, in these traditional Eastern societies, one is to be loving in intimate relations, but sexuality properly has only a generative purpose and no other.

The alternative point of view, which is represented by Western society, acknowledges that one should be intimate and a loving and caring person, and also maintains that orgasms are good. In fact, you should have as many of them as you like, casually and pleasurably and athletically, with as many people as you can care for, or who can care for you—you are all familiar with all that psychiatric nonsense.

But apart from either of these limited points of view, there is a regenerative form of the sexual process, one that permits people to be intimate with one another and also to be sexually active not merely on occasions when they want to produce children. The obligation of such people is a fully human one. They must be responsible for their lower life through love, through intention. They must not casually indulge themselves sexually with one another but embrace only on occasions of mutual love-desire. Their sexuality is not aberrated by inwardness, egoic "self-possession", imagery, or loveless physical contact. On the contrary, they are obliged, through esoteric instruction, to the conversion of the orgasm itself, so that in moments of the crisis of pleasure that naturally appears in sexual play, the life-energy is not thrown off, not merely used to create explosive sensations in the lower physical body. Life-energy is consciously conserved and released into the whole body from its fixation in the genitals, and in participation with the Living Divine Spirit-Presence.[2]

2. Bhagavan Adi Da is referring here to what He calls "regenerative orgasm". Please see chapter twenty-one of *The Dawn Horse Testament Of Adi Da*.

If individuals who become capable of love through application to My Wisdom-Teaching and devotion to Me will also adapt to this regenerative form of sexual practice, they may very well, since orgasm will have ceased to be the justification for sexuality, come relatively soon to a stage wherein the occasions of actual genital intimacy are less frequent but more profound than was previously the case. They will realize, in their continued growth, the essential pleasurableness of existence that transcends the conventional sexual motive. Even though sexual contact may continue throughout the entire lifetime of such devotees in the Way of the Heart, they realize a greater adaptation, a greater pleasurableness, a greater ecstasy, wherein they no longer require degenerative release in order to feel emotional and physical pleasure.

# CHAPTER 41

# Right Celibacy Is Yogic, self-Transcending, and Happy

*from* The Basket of Tolerance

*Many religious and Spiritual traditions regard celibacy as an essential prerequisite for the greatest Spiritual Realization. In this Essay Avatara Adi Da responds to this traditional viewpoint.*

If mere sexual abstinence, or the mere avoidance of sexual activity, or the mere non-performance of sexual activity, were, in itself, sufficient for (or at least a dramatic contributor toward) the Realization of God, Truth, or Reality, then infants, young children, impotent and otherwise sexless adults, and the aged infirm would all be God-Realized, or at least significantly advanced in the Spiritual process, and the principal Yogic sexual technique would, therefore, be the technique of intentional impotence and frigidity, achieved either by surgical, chemical, and dietary means or by other suppressive physical and cultural means!

Unfortunately, unhappy, "sex-problem"-based, and merely life-suppressive motives do in fact govern the sexual practice of many (if not most) otherwise religious and Spiritually-inclined individuals and cultures. However, true and effective religious and Spiritual practice is not associated with the "sex problem", or with anti-sexual or merely sex-suppressive (rather than sex-converting and truly sex-transcending) motives and techniques.

The sexual process must be rightly disciplined, and directly and thoroughly observed, until it is truly (and most fundamentally) understood (and, ultimately, transcended). Therefore, until the sex-motive is truly transcended, the ego-based and Spirit-suppressive (or Spirit-exhausting) tendencies commonly associated with the sexual process must be (progressively) transcended, but such progressive sex-transcendence is not a matter of the mere suppression of sex (or of the mind or the energy of sex). Rather, progressive sex-transcendence is a matter of self-understanding (and intelligent, voluntary relinquishment of the sex-mind), and also of self-disciplining control and conservation of sexual energy, and consistent, intentional <u>conversion</u> (or re-direction, or inward and upward reversal) of the (otherwise downward and outward) flow of sexual energy. This process of self-understanding, relinquishment, control, conservation, and conversion requires (and, more and more, magnifies) a profound and positive (and, altogether, right) change in one's participation in (or relationship to) the sexual process.

Unless and until there is no longer any specifically sexual motivation, right participation in (or right relationship to) the sexual process necessarily requires disciplines of body, the sexual organs and functions, breath (and natural life-energy), emotion, mind, attention, and (in due course) the Spiritual Life-Current. And there is a range of possible options relative to the application of such sex-specific disciplines, even in the case of celibates.

In the Wisdom Way (whether traditional or modern), right intentional Yogic celibacy (or the intentional practice of sex-transcendence, free of conventional, and ego-based, pair-"bonding" motives, rules, and designs, and practiced in association with sex-specific, and, perhaps, even sexually active, devotional Yogic disciplines) is, in principle, the superior (or most auspicious and right) course of sexual self-discipline for those not otherwise uniquely qualified for a Yogic sexual sadhana,[1] and truly motiveless (and Yogically expressed) celibacy is, in general, the necessary culmination of all auspicious and right sexual discipline. Right intentional celibacy must, if it is to effectively serve the Spiritual process, be understood and practiced in Yogic, and self-transcending, and happy terms. Likewise, non-celibate sexual practices must, in the real and true context of Spiritual practice, be developed in Yogic, self-transcending, and happy terms. Indeed, the process of happy sexual self-transcendence and (eventual) effective Yogic conversion of the sex-function is, for most individuals, the most difficult and profound practical obligation of the Wisdom Way, but this obligation must be (progressively) fulfilled, or else the Great Process cannot truly develop or fulfill itself beyond the context of the first three stages of life.

---

1. For a description of what is necessary to be "uniquely qualified for a Yogic sexual sadhana", please see chapter twenty-one of *The Dawn Horse Testament Of Adi Da*.

# CHAPTER 42

# Remember the Mystery in Which You Live

*October 28, 1978*

*Avatara Adi Da has devoted a great deal of time to Instructing His devotees in creating a culture for children based in true Spiritual principles, a Way of life that will help children really achieve their human and Spiritual potential. The following dialogue took place when an eight-year-old boy spoke to Adi Da.*

CHILD: Heart-Master, I have a personal discipline not to be righteous. But I'm still righteous a lot, and I can't really find a way to stop it.

AVATARA ADI DA: What do you mean "righteous"?

CHILD: Well, I try to be smart, you know. I do things like telling somebody something, just walking by somebody and saying something to him, not really meaning it, just being rude.

AVATARA ADI DA: Are you angry about something?

CHILD: I'm angry when I say it.

AVATARA ADI DA: What are you angry about?

CHILD: Well, I'm just inside myself.

AVATARA ADI DA: Why do you think you are angry? Do you feel angry a lot?

CHILD: Not too much, but sometimes I feel real angry.

AVATARA ADI DA: Is being righteous a way of being angry?

CHILD: Yes.

AVATARA ADI DA: So?

CHILD: Do You have a way that You can tell me that I can stop being righteous?

AVATARA ADI DA: Yes. If you love. If you will love people and persist in that feeling, allow yourself to love people all the time, then you will not be righteous in the way that you are talking about. It is fine every now and then to tell somebody where he or she is at. You have to be able to know the difference between behavior in people that is all right and behavior that is not all right, that is negative. But if you love them, then you will know the difference between the things they do that are good and the things they do that are not. And you will be able to talk to them about the things that are not good without being righteous, without being angry. You will be able to be Happy with them, because you will know at that moment that you also love them. Whereas when you are being righteous, you are not aware of the fact that you love them. You forget about that for a minute.

You have to learn about this loving feeling. Whenever you do not love, whenever you do not feel, you start getting angry. And after you have been angry for a long time, you start getting afraid. You start to feel bad. So you have to learn how to be able to love all the time, how to feel all the time. You have to be able to feel the world.

A lady who was just talking to Me said she gets up in the morning unhappy about the fact that the world exists. Well, the mood she is in at that moment is not the mood of someone who is My devotee. My devotee wakes up and, even though things may not be going too well, he or she feels Me. My devotee knows that God is all over this world, all inside the world, inside everyone and outside everyone. My devotee feels that the world is about God, that the world is about Love.

But people on television and people who are not being Happy do not know that the world is about God. They do not know that the world is about Love. That is why they do not love very much. That is why they are always talking about themselves and about negative things.

So, if you are angry and righteous, it is just that you have forgotten for a moment that the world is about God, and that the world is about Love, and that you are about Love. There is nothing you can do about being righteous if you forget to love, if you forget that the world is about God. You cannot stop being righteous by trying not to be righteous. You will stop being righteous when you forget about being righteous, which means you have to remember to love. What to remember to be Happy—I have written a book on the subject.[1]

You are all the time remembering what you have to remember to be angry and righteous. Instead, you have to remember what you have to remember to be Happy, and that means you have to Remember Me. You have to Remember the Mystery in Which you live. You have to remember

---

1. Here Bhagavan Adi Da is referring to His book *What, Where, When, How, Why, and Who To Remember To Be Happy*.

to love, and you have to love, and you have to practice loving people. Do not wait for love to just happen. You have to <u>practice</u> loving people. And you have to communicate love to them. You have to <u>say</u> you love them. You have to do things for them that are full of the feeling of love for them. You see? So, find out what you have to remember to be Happy and do that. If you do that, then you will forget to be angry and righteous.

And sometimes you may have something to say to somebody about something that he or she is doing that is not very good, but what you say to that person will not be the same as righteousness. You will tell this to the person because you love the person. And when you tell the person, you will even <u>sound</u> like you love that person. There are even bad people here and there. You probably have not met any really bad people lately, not any <u>really</u> bad ones. But even the really bad ones are alive in the same world. They are with God just like you. They have some things to learn, but you cannot teach them without loving them. You cannot teach anybody anything without being Happy with that person. And you cannot be Happy with anybody else unless <u>you</u> are Happy. You cannot always wait for others to do something to make you Happy. <u>You</u> have to be Happy, and then you make other people Happy, too.

**Adi Da (The Da Avatar)**
**The Mountain Of Attention, 1995**

# SECTION FOUR
# The Call to Community

For the usual person, politics is merely a matter of listening to the news every night. Conventional human politics is either a childish or an adolescent reaction to the fact of being controlled by the State. The childish individual accepts the "system" and wants it to work, and the adolescent is a perpetual revolutionary. Both types are merely dealing with the Parent-Figure in ordinary ways.

If you stop listening to and believing in the news, and if you simply observe what is really going on, you can get depressed and feel that your life is not under your control. But such is really a very minimal insight. Obviously, everybody is controlled. The typical response to this discovery is to react by joining a revolution, getting drunk, kicking a couple of bad politicians out of office, having a war, getting "high" on drugs or religious and mystical illusions, becoming an anti-communist, or becoming a communist. Reaction, however, is obviously not the way to transform politics.

What is needed is to establish a completely different principle of human culture and politics, one that is not based on reaction to all the bad news—because there is only bad news in the ordinary, un-Enlightened, chaotic world. Instead of waiting for action from sources out in the "beyond" somewhere—government sources, media sources, Divine sources, or whatever it is that you wait for all the time—become involved yourself in intimate community with other human beings. In a responsible, mutually dependent, and intimate relationship with those people, create and protect the basics of a truly human culture and daily society.

ADI DA (THE DA AVATAR)
*Scientific Proof of the Existence of God Will Soon
Be Announced by the White House!*

*Adi Da Teaches that a true religious life always occurs in the context of community—in cooperation rather than competition, in interdependence rather than independence, in the service of others rather than the service of self. What is more, He Teaches that true community is always Sacred Community—a collection of individuals mutually committed to the Realization of God.*

265

CHAPTER 43

# The Religious Necessity of Community

*December 1978*
*from* Scientific Proof of the Existence of God Will Soon Be
Announced by the White House!

There is no such thing as true religion without community. The sacred community is the necessary theatre wherein true religious responsibilities and activities can take place.

Over time, religious understanding and responsibilities tend to become abstracted and dogmatized, so that religion is made to seem to be a merely personal or private endeavor. Thus, popular religion tends to be deficient as a true culture.

The State, or the broad plane of politics and economics, is a secular domain. When the people become tied exclusively to the secular environment of the State, they become fragmented into a mass of mere individuals, controlled by great political and economic forces. Therefore, religion must not only function as the Teaching of ultimate Spiritual Realization. It must become the working foundation of right human relationships. The Teaching of religion must become the foundation of human acculturation. That is, religion must become the instrument whereby individuals create a cooperative order, a union of human communities.

Popular religion tends to create an institutional order, but it generally fails to create a free cooperative order, or true culture. The institutions of popular religion tend to organize the attention and resources of people in much the same manner as the State. That is, merely "institutional" religion fragments the native community of human beings into a superficial order of weakly associated individuals. It does not oblige people to create literal religious community, involving mutual cooperation, responsibility, and dependence.

Therefore, practitioners of true religion should orient themselves to the free creation of sacred community, and they should work with one another to create truly cooperative human environments. Truly, this obligation can only be fulfilled by those who are sufficiently mature to be religiously responsible in the moral and practical theatre of human relationships. Thus, all such practitioners should live in circumstances wherein there are constant opportunities to be tested and to be creative in relationships with others.

# CHAPTER 44

# Cooperative, Human-Scale Community and the Integrity (Religious, and Altogether) of Civilization

*from* The Basket of Tolerance

Cooperative, human-scale community is the political, social, and cultural root-source of civilization. Cooperative, human-scale community is also the primary political, social, and cultural condition that civilization tends to destroy. Therefore, the struggle to re-establish cooperative, human-scale community, and, in turn, to re-establish, within the larger political, social, and cultural order, the virtues characteristically associated with cooperative, human-scale community, is the constant necessity and the principal political, social, and cultural revolution whereby civilization can be purified of its negative effects, and whereby the integrity of civilization (and of civilized people) can be restored.

As civilizations enlarge and universalize themselves, the circumstance of civilized life is progressively removed from the truly human (and humanizing) context of cooperative, human-scale community. Therefore, as any civilization expands, the context of human living becomes progressively dissociated from the practices and virtues inherently associated with true (cooperative and human-scale) community, and becomes instead progressively individuated, alienated, altogether de-humanized, and, therefore, focused in egoic (and, in general, grossly and negatively, or lovelessly, competitive) efforts (toward self-survival and self-aggrandizement).

The present state of civilized movements is so expanded and so universalized that it is already both possible and correct to refer to a rather single, or global, civilization, or world-civilization (which yet retains within itself even numerous sub-civilizations, some struggling merely to survive, and others struggling in a hope to become dominant over many or all, and, thereby, to replace the current dominant mode of world-civilization). And the present world-civilization is, primarily, or dominantly, a Western (or, especially, European and American) mode of civilization, which has enlarged and universalized itself to the degree that it has, basically, engulfed and dominated (or, otherwise, even destroyed) all other modes of civilization.

Even though the numerous remaining (or, otherwise, even newly emerging) sub-civilizations continue to struggle to survive, and even to become dominant (whether on a global or a national or a local scale), and even though that struggle will likely continue to produce changes in the characteristics of global civilization over time, the Western mode of civilization will likely, in the future, continue to remain fundamental, at the practical and truly global level, for it is precisely the Western mode of civilization that is, much more than any other, most directly and practically purposed to practical power, and, therefore, practical domination—over all of nature, over the physical world as a global totality, and over mankind as a global totality.

In any case, since civilization has itself become so enlarged and universalized that it can, in its present dominant mode, already be described as global (and is becoming more so with each passing day), it is inevitable that, as a necessary result of that largest possible expansion, the negative tendencies of civilization itself would also be presently (and tending more and more in the future to be) in clear evidence. And this evidence is certainly clear, globally, and in every sector, and especially in those sectors most dominated by the effects of the present dominant mode of civilization.

The negative evidence of the present global civilization is obvious at every physical and human level of the world—so much so that mankind has now clearly entered into a dark and darkening phase, with great potential for every kind of disaster, and yet, if truly humanizing Wisdom and real Divine Grace are accepted, with an equally great, and even greater, potential for a lightening, and more and more Divine, transformation. It is not necessary that I describe all the negative signs and mixed signs of the present civilization. Let each one enumerate the signs for himself or herself, and feel the human wound at heart. What I will indicate here is the summary result of these signs. Indeed, as I have already indicated, the principal progressive result of the enlarging and universalizing of any civilization is de-humanization, achieved by means of the progressive elimination of the principal and necessary context of life that humanizes mankind. Thus, mankind is, at the present time, dominated by a globally enlarged and globally universalized state of civilization, in which cooperative, human-scale community has, in most sectors, either been eliminated or become profoundly minimized. And, as a result, the principal characteristic of human living at the present, and would-be-future, time is not cooperative, human-scale community (and its characteristic virtues, extended to the larger civilized order) but competitive individualism (dramatized by nations, groups, and individuals).

Civilization always originates as an expression of the ideals of cooperative, human-scale community. Therefore, whatever the present-time particular, distinguishing characteristics of any civilization may be, the principal characteristics that stand at the root of any civilization (and, therefore, of the present civilization) are those of cooperative, human-scale community itself. And those characteristics are, basically, the political, social, and cultural motives and practices of cooperation, interrelatedness, interdependence, non-competitiveness, true (or positive, rather than merely insipid) harmlessness, and positive (or self-transcending, and other-serving, rather than merely self-negating) self-sacrifice—and, altogether (and most basically), those characteristics are the political, social, and cultural motives and practices of even all the virtues of self-transcendence (including tolerance, compassion, love, service, self-discipline, and one-pointed devotion to That Sacred Reality and Authority Which inherently transcends, and even requires the transcendence of, the ego-self and even all limitations).

In the present, globally expanded state of civilization, the principal sign of civilization itself is that it has, in the largest number of its sectors, effectively destroyed (or at least profoundly minimized) the root-motives, root-practices, and root-virtues of human life in its humanizing (or cooperative, human-scale community) mode—and, indeed, the principal sign of present-time civilization is, in general, that of the absence of cooperative, human-scale (and truly humanizing) community itself.

The motive and practice of competitive individualism is itself the very motive and practice (or method) of egoity itself (or the separate and separative effort of existence). Therefore, civilization, in its present global achievement, is profoundly dissociated from its roots in the relational (or non-separative) virtues and practices inherent in cooperative, human-scale community, and it has, thus, "progressed" from its foundation in the cooperative, human-scale community politic, society, and culture (of cooperation, non-competitiveness, tolerance, positive harmlessness, self-transcendence, and sacred endeavor) to an "advanced" state wherein individual life (and, also, lesser collective life) is devoted to ego-based and ego-serving competitiveness within a thoroughly secularized and materialistic milieu of ends and means.

An ego-based civilization, like any ego-based individual, is suffering, seeking, and indulging in every kind of separate and separative effort toward mere survival and conditional satisfaction. Therefore, just as any individual who has become sunk in the patterns and results of egoity must become reformed (or released from the patterns and results of egoity, and, ultimately, Awakened to and in and as the necessarily Divine Truth That Is Reality Itself)—just so, any civilization that has become sunk in the patterns and results of egoity must become likewise reformed (and, ultimately, likewise Awakened). And the struggle by individuals and groups to practically re-establish human-scale, cooperative, and truly sacred community living is the necessary and principal revolution (or inherently benign and counter-egoic political, social, and cultural effort) whereby all human beings (even those under the most ordinary and limited circumstances) can, at the practical (political, social, and cultural) human level, purify themselves (and, more and more, even civilization itself) from the negative effects (including, ultimately, the loss of individual and collective integrity) that come (and have now come) with the expansion and universalization of civilization.

Of course, some have, in the present context of civilization, already tried to revolutionize their "civilized" lives by engaging efforts toward human-scale community. Those efforts or experiments have met with varying degrees of practical and human success to date. However, far more is required to achieve cooperative, human-scale, and truly humanizing community than present and past experimenters generally suppose or have supposed. For example, in the present ego-bound context of global civilization, there is a general tendency for community experimenters to try to create community on the basis of the same egoic principles that otherwise characterize the present civilization itself. Thus, present-time community experimenters generally try to create community on the (supposedly egalitarian) basis of the motives of competitive individualism (or egoity itself), even though they also want to establish cooperative principles and cooperative structures. As a result, experimental community efforts often are degraded and defeated by competitiveness, the tendency to pander to egoic preferences and egoic dramatizations (often in the name of egalitarian idealism), and a characteristic fear of (or a rather adolescent rebellion against) authority, hierarchy, and the hierarchical culture of respect (which are necessary to any truly human and cooperative community order).

There is a profound difference between true (and necessarily sacred) community and mere practical (political, social, and cultural) communalism (whether such is viewed to be religious or, otherwise, secular in its nature and intention). A truly cooperative, truly human-scale, and truly humanizing community is necessarily and truly sacred (and even truly religious, and, at least potentially, Spiritually oriented, and, ultimately, purposed toward the Most Perfect Realization of God, Truth, or Reality), rather than merely secular (or not truly sacred, religious, Spiritual, or purposed toward the Most Perfect Realization of God, Truth, or Reality). That is to say, a truly cooperative, truly human-scale, and truly humanizing community is necessarily based on the motive of self-transcendence (rather than on the motive of self-fulfillment), and, therefore, it is not based on the search to satisfy the ego-"I" and the egoic motives of any of its members, but it is based on the devotion of each and all of its members to That Which inherently transcends each and all.

The human being is an apparently individual manifestation within a Totality that is an interdependent Unity. And the apparently individual human being, as well as all of the Totality-Unity in which he or she is appearing, is a merely apparent modification of That Which Is all-Transcending, One, and necessarily Divine. Therefore, in his or her depth, and altogether, the human being, unless he or she becomes utterly self-contracted and, thereby, utterly self-"possessed" (or ego-possessed), is inherently moved to transcend the ego-"I" (or all separateness and separativeness) in the Unity and, ultimately, the One (or the Divine Source-Condition) in Which he or she, and all, is arising. And, because that is the case, the right and true human being is necessarily, in the right and true sense, religious (and politics, society, and culture, in order to be right and true, and in order to support and serve right and true human living, must, necessarily, also be, in the right and true sense, religious).

True religion is, at the level of its human interactive (political, social, and cultural) demonstration, necessarily a collective and communal (rather than a merely subjective, or internal, and private) exercise and process, and it must, therefore, be politically, socially, and culturally permitted to be so demonstrated. Therefore, one of the principal faults of the present "civilized" trend toward individualistic and materialistic democracy (or a political, social, and cultural "order" based upon competitive individualism, ego-glorification, anti-authority, anti-hierarchy, anti-unity, and anti-Wisdom) is that individualistic and materialistic democracy tends to individualize, secularize, and, at last, suppress religion itself, and, therefore, individualistic and materialistic democracy tends also to individualize, secularize, and, at last, suppress the necessarily collective and communal aspect of the exercise and process of religion. And, as a result of the "democratic" individualizing, secularizing, and, at last, suppressing of religion (and especially the collective, communal, and otherwise public exercise of religion), the enterprise of true community (truly cooperative, truly human-scale, and truly humanizing) is itself suppressed (or, in principle, excluded) in so-called "democratic", or "egalitarian", societies.

True community is necessarily sacred, religious, and one-pointed. That is to say, it is not focused in service to (and fulfillment of) egos (or whatever is many and separate), but in service to (and Realization of) That Oneness and Singleness Which Inherently Transcends egoity and every limitation. The Real does not rotate around each and all, but each and all are Called and Obliged to surrender self and to forget self in participatory Communion with the all-transcending, all-pervading, all-embracing, and necessarily Divine Truth and Reality. And it is only the response to this Call and Obligation that can purify and restore mankind, one by one, each and all, by means of the benign and truly humanizing political, social, and cultural revolution that is the establishment of truly sacred and truly cooperative human-scale communities (and, by extension, the transformation of even the entire global civilization itself into a cooperative, rather than a merely competitive, world-order).

And love is the key to this necessary change. Love is self-surrendering, self-forgetting, and, ultimately, self-transcending participation in the indivisible Oneness and Wholeness and Singleness That Is God, Truth, and Reality. Therefore, love is also right living. And that love which is right living is not ego-based, independent, separative, competitive, and non-cooperative. Therefore, that love which is right living is the active (and co-operative) aspiration toward egoless (or non-separative) participation in God (or Truth, or Reality) and humanity and even all (in All).

# CHAPTER 45

# A New Human Order

*from chapter twenty of* The Knee of Listening

My true devotees will be those who are free of every kind of seeking, attendant only to understanding. They will commit themselves to the intentional "creation" of life in the unqualified, living condition and perfectly relational logic of Reality, rather than in the always limited and dying condition and separative logic of Narcissus. My true devotees will give living form to the unexploitable Presence of Reality. They will not be moved to turn the worlds to dilemma, exhaustion, and revolutionary experience, nor to the exploitation of desire and possibility, nor to the ascent to and inclusion of various goals, higher entities, evolutionary aims, or ideas of Spiritual transformation. They will "create" in the aesthetics of Reality, turning all things into unqualified relatedness and enjoyment. They will remove the effects of separative existence and restore the form of things. They will engineer every kind of stability and beauty. They will give living form to the always already living Presence of Peace. Their eye will be on present form and not on exaggerated notions of artifice. Their idea of form will be stable and whole, not a gesture toward some other event. They will not make the world seem but a symbol for higher and other things.

They will constantly "create" the living manifestation of Truth while Conscious of the always already present Reality. Thus, they will serve the order of sacrifice and Ultimate Knowledge. They will affirm the necessary and the good. They will make only economic and wise use of technology. They will not be motivated by invention but by Reality, Which is the always present "Thing" they will intend to communicate (by every means, and in all they do). They will not pursue any kind of utopian victory for mankind, any deathlessness or overwhelming survival. They will only "create" the conditions for present Enjoyment, the Communication of Reality, the form in which radical understanding and Real Knowledge can arise, live, and become the public foundation of existence.

Thus, my true devotees will be a new human order that will serve to "create" a new age of sanity and Joy. But that new age will not be the age of the occult, the religious, or the scientific or technological evolution of mankind. It will be the fundamental age of Real existence, wherein life will be radically realized, entirely apart from the adventure that was mankind's great search. The "new age" envisioned by seekers is a spectacular display that only extends the traditional madness, exploitability, and foolishness of mankind. But I desire a new order of men and women, who will not begin from all of that, but who will apply themselves apart from all dilemma and all seeking to the harmonious event of Real existence.

I am equally certain that such a new human order must arise as a force in the world in the present historical epoch, or else this world must suffer the karma of early dissolution.

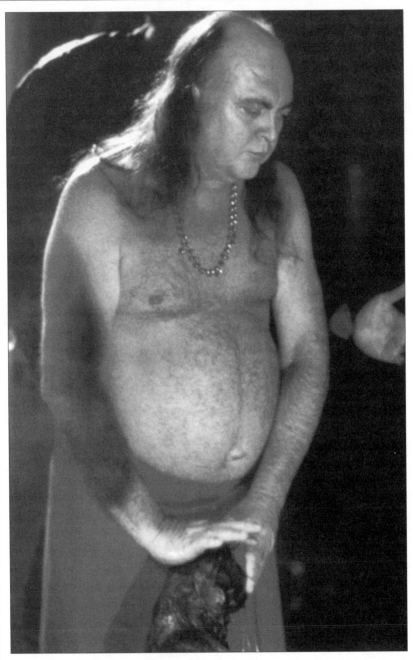

**Adi Da (The Da Avatar)**
**The Mountain Of Attention, 1995**

SECTION FIVE

# Death and the Meaning of Life

F ear of death is fear of surrender to Infinity.
Learn to surrender, to exist at Infinity while
alive, and fear of death dissolves.

ADI DA (THE DA AVATAR)
*Easy Death*

*Adi Da Teaches that we survive death—but not for the reason we might like to think! We do not survive death because the egoic self is immortal, passing from lifetime to lifetime. We survive death because there is only One Deathless Identity, One Consciousness, One Spirit-Energy—and the separate self arises within that Identity, moving from life to death and to life again until there is Realization of the One Immortal Divine Being. As the Very Incarnation of that Divine Being, Adi Da Reveals the Ultimate Truth about the process of death.*

# CHAPTER 46

# The Heart of Understanding

*Prologue to* The Knee of Listening

D eath is utterly acceptable to consciousness and life. There has been endless time of numberless deaths, but neither consciousness nor life has ceased to arise. The felt quality and cycle to death has not modified the fragility of flowers, even the flowers within the human body. Therefore, one's understanding of consciousness and life must be turned to That Utter, Inclusive Truth, That Clarity and Wisdom, That Power and Untouchable Gracefulness, That One and Only Reality, this evidence suggests. One must cease to live in a superficial and divided way, seeking and demanding consciousness and life in the present apparent form, avoiding and resisting what appears to be the end of consciousness and life in death.

The Heart Is <u>Real</u> understanding. The Heart Is <u>Real</u> Consciousness and <u>Real</u> Life. The Heart Is What Merely and Only <u>Is</u>, but Which Is also Appearing In and Behind the conditions of mortal life and its death. Therefore, it is said of old, the One That <u>Is</u> Is neither born nor come to death, not Alive merely as the limitation of form (itself), not Itself (or Entirely) Rendered in what appears, and yet It Is the Living One, than Which there Is no lesser other (and no Great or Greater Other), Appearing As all of this Play of changes, but Eternally One, Unchanging, and Free.

There Is Only the Constant Knowledge and Enjoyment of the Heart, moment to moment, through the instant of all conditions of appearance and disappearance. Of This I Am Perfectly Certain. I <u>Am</u> That.

CHAPTER 47

# There Is No Individual
# self That Dies

*December 28, 1980*
*from* Easy Death

A VATARA ADI DA: Current studies of the experiences of individuals who have clinically "died" for several minutes and then revived are producing a growing literature that compiles and reports these "after-life" experiences. Such phenomena could be used as indicators of the inherently Spiritual or self-transcending process that occurs at death. However, these "after-life" phenomena are typically valued merely as signs of personal, egoic survival.

"After-life" phenomena are not signs of egoic survival. Rather, they are signs of the transformation of the conventional self, the dissolution of various aspects of the personality, and passage into a condition that is not foreknown. They are signs of something that is falling away rather than continuing.

Yet, when people return to consciousness, therefore not having completed this process, they concretize the phenomena they encountered and interpret them to mean survival of the ego. Such individuals say that they are now more easeful because they survived death. They believe that there is an afterlife in which we pass into other worlds beyond this one. But the experiences and visions they report should be understood rightly to be hallucinated phenomena that arise from the stimulation of the higher centers of the brain during the withdrawal of energy and attention from the body at death. These experiences, like those of the conventional mystic, are, no matter how consoling or sublime, nonetheless founded in ego-consciousness.

However, the greatest Spiritual Wisdom reveals that the True Self is the non-ego, the Self-Existing and Self-Radiant Divine Being, or Ultimate Reality, Which is also the Source-Condition of the phenomenal fields of self-awareness and ego-identity. Its Nature and Existence cannot be proved by appeal to phenomenal events in life or death. The True Self can only be Realized in transcendence of the process of conventional or egoic self-identification and object-differentiation.

"Consider" this: You are conscious in this moment. If I look at you and call your name, it is the body-mind-self that assumes I am talking to it. But it is not the body-mind-self who is actually here. There is only One Identity here. There appear to be individual conventions of separate selves, but they are phenomenal constructs superimposed on the Divine Being. The notion that each apparent individual is a separate identity in the ultimate sense—and therefore conditioned, limited, and controlled by the destiny of this body-mind—is false.

Thus, the reason you survive death is not that the ego is immortal. You survive death because the Ultimate Identity of all phenomena and of the apparently individuated consciousness is Transcendental, and Inherently Spiritual, and necessarily Divine. Every feature of your temporary ego-identity is itself constructed out of a universal Field of Transcendental Consciousness and Eternal Spirit-Energy. The body-mind simply arises in a universal Field, and at death it is broken up into its various parts.

Therefore, the ultimate proposition of the great sacred traditions is that there is only one Reality, the Divine Self-Condition and Identity of every-thing and everyone. Divine Enlightenment is the tacit and direct Realization of that Truth. Once the conditional being is established in that Realization, then you participate in the arising patterns of existence in an entirely dif-ferent manner than is conventionally presumed. Then the gesture of ego-identification has no force. Only the Ultimate Identity is presumed.

The difference between the ordinary individual and the Divinely Enlightened being is that the ordinary individual identifies with the con-ventional or phenomenal self, while the Divinely Enlightened being Identifies with the Transcendental (and Inherently Spiritual) Divine Reality. This is the only difference. Thus, depending on which of those two pre-sumptions you choose, you will live in either one of two ways. One is the usual round of obsession, fear, and seeking in which the egoic self is the actor and the meaning of the drama. The other is the way of illuminated Intelligence, Love, Freedom, Spontaneity, and Infinite Happiness. Therefore, if you are going to live as Divine Enlightenment, you must understand this phenomenal convention of the egoic self with all the mechanics of existence that you have built upon it.

Previous to such Divine Enlightenment you fear death, and, therefore, you want to discover something about death that can make you feel hope-ful about surviving. That is why people like to study occult and "life-after-life" phenomena. They like to hear conventional religious stories, such as the legend that Jesus was resurrected and ascended to heaven. Whatever the factual or historical authenticity of these stories may be, they are all interpreted as hopeful signs for the ego. Thus, you will remain fascinated by death, even to the point of being relatively self-destructive, because in some sense you want to get into it, even though you fear it. You will con-tinue to read studies about "after-life" phenomena, always hoping to hear that it has been proven to the satisfaction of both science and you personally that you are going to survive death.

However, it is not the mystery of death that you must penetrate in order to be free of fear. Rather, you must transcend this concoction of ego-stress and self-contraction while alive. You must be in a different disposition toward life altogether in order to die free of fear. Instead of presuming this ego-position, you must rest in the Transcendental (and Inherently Spiritual) Divine Reality. Then both your present existence and all its future changes and dying will be allowed very simply and naturally, much like going to sleep at night. You will not merely have gained some consoling knowledge about death. Fear does not result from the lack of such knowledge. Fear is caused by ego-stress, and it must, therefore, be transcended while alive. The Spiritual Process is a way of transcending the mechanism of fear in every moment.

I have called the process of death "easy death", because that is what it must become. The process of death must become a natural, easeful process even if you lack final knowledge of its ultimate results. Human beings in general do not have a great deal of knowledge about their present born existence, and yet they are able, at least occasionally, to live easefully and happily. You must live death in the same way. Death is a spontaneous occurrence, and you must not feel that it is the destruction of existence.

To presume the phenomenal self-position is to give cosmic Nature a stick with which to beat you over the head. It is to be a "something", and all "somethings" are inevitably confounded, changed, and dissolved. Thus, the individuated self is an unnatural rather than a native presumption. You deny cosmic Nature this stick by Realizing the Truth of your existence, by being established in the Native Condition, or Reality, Which is relaxed, uncontracted, Free, Radiant, and Full. Then events can arise and change and pass away without your being confined to fear.

If you Realize that Divinely Enlightened disposition, then you are also paradoxically energized and no longer passive. This disposition releases great energy into the psycho-physical mechanism of existence. Ultimately, Divine Enlightenment Divinely Transfigures the body-mind. It Divinely Transforms it, Evolves it, Awakens Wisdom, and Generates the greater Powers of existence. Likewise, all those things also change and pass away. But if the greater functions arise without stress, without clinging, without self-identification, then they can have no negative or binding effects. They are simply the inherent expressions of the Divine Reality.

# CHAPTER 48

# This Liberating Impulse

*February 1, 1985*
*from* Easy Death

AVATARA ADI DA: Spiritual life is about Realizing utter Love-Bliss, greater Bliss than is realized through sex or any other conditional experience. Such Love-Bliss is available before, during, and after any conditional experience. If you Realize It, if you devote your life to the Realization of That, then That is what you get—a life devoted to the Realization of That, a life of Communion with That. Then you will link your present life with What is Prior to this life, whereas if you devote yourself to the human conditions of existence for their own sake, you do not link yourself to What is Prior to this life. You link yourself to the same thing again. You perpetuate it, through reincarnation or simply through repetition in one form or another after death.

I have pointed out to you on a number of occasions that while you live in conditional form, you make mind, you create the psyche, through associations, repetitions, reinforcement. When you die and the body drops off, mind makes you. After death, you live in the world of mind as you have created it while alive. The after-death states have been called "bardos", or "planes". Really, all such concepts are simply descriptions of how the mind operates dissociated from physical embodiment. You will spontaneously, through no will of your own, enter into realms of mind after death that correspond to your state of mind—not just your thinking mind but your subconscious and unconscious mind, the whole force of your tendency toward objects and conditional states. The realms with which you will be associated will be changing. There is a possibility of spending experiential time in such places. They are much like the realms you visit in dreams, but you will feel you are really there and not merely dreaming.

Mind makes association with realms that seem pleasurable, and after death you may pass in and out of these realms. But if you observe how desperate, egoically "self-possessed", depressed, craving, and dissatisfied you are generally, you will appreciate more profoundly what is likely after death and into what kinds of mind-realms you may be drawn. There are hells, purgatories, dark passages that seem to go on for vast periods of time, even until they exhaust themselves and you pass out of them as you pass from one dream to the next.

It is said traditionally that a human birth is extraordinary, auspicious if it is rightly used, and should not be wasted. This is because the human form has the potential to be associated with the full range of conditional experience—gross, subtle, and causal—and is also not merely a mind-realm as the after-death states are, although it is such a realm ultimately. But, experientially, as a human being you are not merely living in the mind condition. You are living in the bodily condition. To be able to exercise yourself bodily, functionally, relationally, puts you in a position to indulge mind, but also to change it, to transcend it. To be embodied is to have a unique relationship to mind, which will then affect the after-death states when the body is thrown off.

If you merely use up your life, indulging mind as it already is, as you accumulated it while alive, then the after-death states will be conventional, mediocre, relatively unpleasant, perhaps dreadfully unpleasant, until another embodiment. If you use your life for the sake of transcendence and change mind, purify mind, release yourself from its limits, move into a higher consciousness, a higher mind, and, as My devotee, move even beyond mind to the point of complete Divine Enlightenment and relinquishment of conditional existence, Divine Translation is the Destiny you will Realize. But even if you do not fulfill the course of self-transcending practice to that ultimate degree, after death you will at least be associated with the ascended realms, the higher frame of mind, rather than the hells, the purgatories, the lesser states, where people rattle against one another like they do here.

Time in those hellish realms is even longer, but it does exhaust itself eventually, so that there is new embodiment in a form such as this or something that fulfills its characteristics in a similar fashion, thus giving you the opportunity to transcend the mind but in a more profoundly purified condition. Re-embodiment is then associated with a capability to link up with the Spiritual Process in its advanced stages.

What you are doing in this lifetime links up with all future time. If it is not utterly real to you yet that there is such time after death, then practice self-transcendence in the context of the realities that are obvious to you, and that practice is sufficient. Whether you know about what passes after death or not, you still can observe what is going on with you now, observe the self-contraction and its consequences, and come to the point of being moved to transcend it. You need not believe in the afterlife to do all of that. You can still receive My tangible Spiritual Heart-Transmission and enter into the life of Spiritual devotion to Me, whether or not you have any real sense of the afterlife. You can still enter the entire Spiritual Process in My Blessing Company. And all the same reasons for entering into it still exist, whether you know there is an afterlife or not.

I have just Described to you the process that works after death, and at some point you will have real experience of it. You will very likely in the course of your practice of the Way of the Heart come into contact with subtle experiences that confirm the survival of death and the existence of subtle realms, or mind-realms, and that show you something about how it all works. Even if you do not have much experience of it, if you enter truly into Divine Communion with Me, the Spiritual Process will self-authenticate Eternity and prove to the heart that this embodiment is not the end of existence, or even its purpose. Existence is purposed toward Love-Blissfulness, Freedom, and Divine Happiness.

While you live in bodily form, therefore, it is good for you to become dis-eased. It is good to feel dissatisfied and to seek beyond the conditional, ordinary, conventional apparatus of life, until you come into contact with Wisdom. Through that contact, the search itself will be transcended. Until then, the search is useful. It is the motive of dissatisfaction. Although it is the pursuit of satisfaction, it also contains the element of dissatisfaction. Seeking thus leads toward many things, including all kinds of self-fulfillment. It also leads to contact with religion and Spiritual life. But when you enter into My Sphere, into the Sphere of this Divine possibility, then you enter into the Sphere of "consideration" that will undo the search and its root, which is self-contraction, or egoity.

You can enter into this process without any beliefs or presumptions about an afterlife. But I must simply, among other things, Tell you what that is all about, since it is real and it is My experience. What happens after death is directly associated with what happens while you are alive. It is not that you merely live and then the body falls off and you drift into the eternal sublimity. And it is not that you merely live an ordinary life, struggling however you choose to live, and then go to heaven.

Death is simply the falling off of the physical vehicle. That is all that it is. Everything else continues, unless all the vehicles, all the aspects of the conditional self, are released through Divine Self-Realization. In the typical case, the ordinary human case, death is simply the abandonment of the physical. Everything else that you are as mind, psyche, personality, and desires continues, but without the anchor of embodiment. You do not wake up in your physical bed and your physical room, with your physical associations. The anchor drops off, and you drift into the bardos, the realms of mind. Where you drift is determined, therefore, by your mind, your state of mind altogether, what you have reinforced through your life-action.

The conditional cosmos is structured in such a way that, in spite of all errors and egoity, all beings will ultimately be purified. But if you know that even though this is so, you still might have to go through billions upon billions of lifetimes under all kinds of dreadful conditions, including spending uncountable spaces of time in hells of suffering, then there is no consolation in the knowledge that everyone will ultimately be Liberated. Therefore, you must know how you can cooperate with the Liberating Divine Principle so that you are not reinforcing egoically "self-possessed", disturbed, painful conditions of existence, but are rather advancing toward and entering into more and more of the profundity of Most Perfectly self-transcending God-Realization and the Ultimate Destiny of life in the Divine Self-Domain. This is what you must devote yourself to, what you will devote yourself to if you understand, if you hear Me and see Me and Awaken Spiritually through My tangible Spiritual Baptism. Then your life must become cooperation with that Liberating Force.

That Divine Force will not only involve you in changing your action while you are alive so that you live a better life and are happier in your relations. All such changes are temporary. Fundamentally, what that Divine Force does is to Liberate you from mind. And all of this is mind, even this [touching His Body]. Physical embodiment is mind. It simply carries with it the illusion that you are mind interiorly. But, in fact, you are physically present, physically active, and can therefore change mind, release mind, purify mind, transcend mind. This is true. This is how the Liberating Principle works within the realm of cosmic Nature. It gives you the opportunity to transcend that which is cosmic Nature, which is mind.

All of conditional existence is nothing but mind, constantly being modified, affected, changed, caused by apparently discrete entities. It is a vast, unfathomable complex of planes and beings, tendencies, experiences, realms within realms, imaginary realms that are just as real as real realms—there is nothing that is unreal, because it is all mind.

You are in bondage to mind. You are in bondage to objects. Not understanding your egoic self and the Great Reality, you are tending to presume this quality of mind you are experiencing by virtue of human birth, and you are trying to fulfill the ego, release it, or bring it into a state of total enjoyment. This search is a false principle. It is something you can struggle to fulfill, and you cannot even fulfill it completely. At any rate, in such pursuit you do not involve yourself in the principle of self-transcendence.

Because of how things are, you must transcend these conditions, not merely struggle to fulfill yourself within them. You yourself are a condition among these conditions. Conditioning, mind, all limitation of Divine Love-Bliss, must be transcended. This understanding and the encounter with the Living Divine Adept make the Spiritual Process possible. Therefore, when you come to hear Me and see Me, then you must become involved in the process of self-transcendence, or, in other words, the process of mind-transcendence. Ultimately, to go beyond mind altogether is to be Divinely Translated.

What you build up subjectively while you are bodily existing becomes your experience after death. What you purify and transcend while physically existing will not be your experience after death. What you make your object while alive will continue to be your object after death. Desires not fulfilled or transcended are your mind after death. Complexes, fears, obsessions are your mind after death. Thus, the Spiritual Process really is the purification and transcendence of mind, which is the same thing as the purification and transcendence of conditional self, or conditional existence altogether.

The very best situation to be in at the point of death is utter mindlessness. I do not mean you should have an empty head at the moment of death. I mean you should be utterly purified of the self-contraction, the mental tendency, such that you are only involved in the Free Condition of Divine Love-Bliss. The best situation, the best condition to be in at the point of death, is the Divinely Self-Realized Condition of the seventh stage of life. Generally, that Condition points toward Divine Translation at death.

To be literally living in earlier stages than the Divinely Enlightened Condition at the point of death in general indicates what your destiny will be after death. Your stage of life is a very basic indicator. Most people do not go beyond a complicated, stressful, un-Happy involvement in the conditions associated with the first three stages of life. Such individuals do not go to heaven. They pass into experiential realms immediately associated with this material frame, as in dreams, now without the anchor of the body, appearing to spend all kinds of time in lesser conditional realms, often very unpleasant, literally what could be called "hells". Those who pass into the ascended stages of life—the "advanced" fourth stage and the fifth stage—will pass into the subtler realms of the Cosmic Mandala, temporarily enjoying a somewhat more blissful experience until mind exhausts itself.

Mind, you see, is a kind of generative force. When forms are established in it, it produces experience until it wears down. All experiences within the Cosmic Mandala are, therefore, temporary, but some are much more difficult than others. Those in the outer range of the Cosmic Mandala are the more difficult. Beings there live a short time. There is more struggle, more threat there. The realms closer to the center of the Cosmic Mandala are associated with more glamorized conditions, beautiful spaces, and so forth, but the urge of conditionally manifested beings is likewise not ultimately fulfilled there. The urge to Complete Freedom, or Divine Self-Realization, is not fulfilled in those realms, and they also are temporary experiences.

Beings do sadhana in those realms. They practice the disposition of God-Communion, and they are not merely there to fulfill the pleasurable possibilities associated with their realm. At least this is so in the higher

## THE COSMIC MANDALA

The various levels of cosmic existence can be seen in vision as concentric circles of light, which Avatara Adi Da has called the "Cosmic Mandala". The rings indicate different frequencies of light associated with the various levels of manifestation. The colors of the Cosmic Mandala (from the outer ring progressing inward) are:

RED—the realms of gross existence (outer edge of Mandala).

GOLDEN YELLOW—the etheric and lower mental realms.

SILVERY WHITE (like a moon)—the higher, or subtler, mental realms.

DARK BLUE OR BLACK (like a void)—the "empty space" between the grosser and the truly subtle realms.

BRILLIANT BLUE—the higher subtle, or higher mental, planes of manifestation.

CLEAR WHITE—the Radiant Core of all light frequencies, often manifesting as a five-pointed Star; the gateway between the subtle realms and the Self-Existing and Self-Radiant Divine Being.

realms. In the lesser realms, where ordinary people living in this world might pass after death, conditional beings are not any more occupied with the motive to Most Perfectly self-Transcending God-Realization than they are here. The lesser subtle realms are the same kind of place as this realm basically, although individuals are somewhat more tenuously associated with experience there. Experience is more plastic in some way, and individuals there experience something like the dreamer's involvement.

Conditional beings are aware of having rather unusual abilities even in these lesser realms. They can pass in and out of places and circumstances and move about by an act of will, but all the time they still move within the lesser frame. The more profoundly aggrieved, gross, negative characters do not even wander in the middle-class streets of the after-world. They settle into dark places and sinister scenes. They struggle, unable to get out for long periods of time, as you would in a nightmare—but they do not have the body in bed to wake up to. The mind free-wheels on its own, as if they were stuck in a room watching a television program and did not have the ability to turn off the television set—but in this case they are actually in the program.

DEVOTEE: Beloved Bhagavan, do they stay there until the experience runs out?

AVATARA ADI DA: Yes. And it runs out eventually. Such realms are usually described as hells where individuals are caught for thousands of years. Imagine yourself sitting in a box for ten thousand years! Such descriptions are in some sense metaphoric, but nonetheless they contain some truth, because time does appear to be real in these places.

Often religion is preached in this world through representations of the afterlife, threatening you with fire and brimstone on the one hand if you do not get straight, and offering you the pie-a-la-mode heaven on the other hand if you believe and behave. But, as I indicated to you, if it is not real to you that the afterlife exists or what it is all about, to try to threaten or attract you with these stories has no significant effect on you. I am simply Telling you about the afterlife because it is My experience and I want to account for it all. It will also be your experience at one time or another. It already is the experience of many people. There is, therefore, no reason why I should not Speak of it.

But I am not giving you a heaven-and-hell speech here. You need no belief system to involve yourself in the Spiritual Way of life. Therefore, I confront you about what is real to you, what is your experience. I point to the search, the self-contraction. I Call you into relationship with Me to receive My Spirit-Baptism. The Spiritual Process does not depend on systems of belief. It is true that at death you do not just disappear into unconsciousness, fall asleep, and forget everything. Mind goes on, and mind controls you, and you no longer have the anchor of the body. If it is not real to you that the process of mind continues after death, still the separate and separative self and how it works is real to you now, and the Spiritual Process is real to you if you have experienced My Spiritual Heart-Transmission in My Company. In any case, the Spiritual Process is about self-transcendence, or transcendence of mind, transcendence of the psychology of attention. Whatever the structure of reality is in your view, the process of your existence is controlled by the mechanism of attention, the psychology of the self-contraction, and the degree to which you have transcended attention. Life is mind. Life makes mind. Life suffers mind. And life can be the transcendence of mind. Life as a process of the transcendence of mind, or the psychology of attention, is Spiritual practice. A life devoted to self-indulgence without God-Communion, without self-understanding, without self-transcendence, is suffering.

Even those devoted to Most Perfectly self-transcending God-Realization suffer, but they suffer in the peripheral vehicles of the conditional self. In Communion with Me, you contact the inherent Love-Blissfulness of existence, and those aspects of your existence that are conditional, in which you are suffering, or even experiencing pleasure, become literally peripheral. You can enjoy that Fullness, then, even prior to Divine Enlightenment. It is simply that in the passage between the sixth stage of life and the seventh stage of life, the Fullness of Divine Self-Realization becomes permanent, no longer conditionally Realized.

Even so, the conditional periphery remains, but one's involvement with it changes. Even in the seventh stage of life, however, there is a struggle, as you see in My case. There is no end to the struggle with conditional existence. I could have bypassed some of it by simply not Teaching. But I had no choice in this matter—fortunately or unfortunately, fortunately for you perhaps—because Divine Re-Awakening in My case was not associated merely with Divine Self-Realization in the sense that I could have dropped out and disappeared. It was associated with the spontaneous appearance of the Siddhis of My Teaching Work.[1]

I have no attachment to this world for its own sake. My involvement with this world is simply for the sake of Liberating others. I am the Manifestation of that Principle in cosmic Nature Which is Liberating. I do not otherwise have any impulse to be associated with conditional existence, but I am bound to it nonetheless, because of this Liberating Impulse.

---

1. After His Divine Re-Awakening in the Vedanta Temple in 1970, unique Teaching Siddhis, or Powers, spontaneously arose in Avatara Adi Da. Through these Siddhis, He was able to reflect devotees' egoic qualities and preoccupations to themselves, and to Infuse and Awaken their hearts with His Powers of Blessing. In the process, Avatara Adi Da literally accepted as His own the karmic limitations of the manifesting worlds.

My devotees who enter into the seventh stage of life will participate in that Liberating Impulse in various ways, but their struggle will not be like My own, because they will not have the Siddhis that are uniquely associated with My Birth. Even so, they must carry on their Blessed existence under the real circumstances of conditional life with other people.

This Effort that Works through Me will not go on forever. It has its logic, its course, its structure. Its results depend on its reception. My Impulse is Complete for the Divine Self-Realization of others and the establishment of the Way of the Heart.

You may live relatively long. Already many of you have lived long lives compared to how long most people have lived in this world. Even so, in every moment of your existence there is the possibility of dying, the possibility of becoming diseased, the possibility of loss, the possibility of disconnection from others, the possibility of suffering. Your conditional existence has been threatened from the moment you were born. Threats are always arising, in you and outside you.

Everything that appears in the conditional world is tending to be destroyed, tending to come to an end, because it does not just appear on its own. It appears in conjunction with many other entities, motions, tendencies, programs, plans, disturbances. Every life, every impulse is associated with a creative effort to accomplish and to survive. That effort characterizes Me and My Work. You have seen what a difficult struggle it has been for Me to keep My Work going during all these years. It is not just difficult at this moment. It has always been difficult. The tendency has always existed to destroy it and bring it to an end, as well as to simply not use it.

If this Impulse is going to have effect, if it is to survive through and beyond My Time of human existence, you must make it survive. You must use it. You must practice it. You must become rightly aligned to Me. You must fulfill it. You must advocate it. You must make your gathering strong—not just you in this room but all those associated with Me, all those who will read or listen to this Talk someday.

# CHAPTER 49

# The Only Way Out

## Part 1

## The Great Giver

*by Frans Bakker, M.D.*

*Frans Bakker received his medical training at the University of Leiden in Holland. He has been a devotee of Bhagavan Adi Da since 1975, and is currently a principal public speaker for the Adidam Mission.*

It was December 24, 1983, at Adidamashram, and Avatara Adi Da was celebrating the Feast of God in Every Body[1] with His devotees. Often at the celebratory time of "God in Every Body" during His Teaching years, He would literally overwhelm all those around Him with gifts He had Lovingly gathered over the course of the year.

I was among a group of about thirty devotees sitting on the floor in Avatara Adi Da's room. A Giving Tree (Avatara Adi Da's name for the celebratory tree we decorate with lights and ornaments) sat in the corner, its colored lights blinking in endless rhythm.

Our Heart-Master started to give gifts to all who were in the room—one by one, person by person. It took Him hours and hours. The room seemed full of light and love. The lights on the Giving Tree were twinkling happily. There was much laughter all around. I sat there watching it all—the surprised exclamations of my friends, my Heart-Master—beaming with joy. At one point, unable to contain myself any longer, I cried my heart out for sheer Happiness.

My friend Tom Closser was sitting a few feet away from me. He was a big muscular fellow and to be living as a Spiritual renunciate was quite

---

1. "The Feast of God in Every Body" is now called "The Feast of the Hero of Giving", or "The Feast of the Heroic Love-Gifting Leela of Adi Da, the Da Avatar", or, most simply, "Danavira Mela". It is a Celebration of the Play of the Divine Person, or the Story of the unfolding Miracle of the Da Avatar's own Life and Work. "Dana" is Sanskrit for "He Who Gives", "vira" means "hero", and "mela" is a religious gathering or festival. The Divine Beloved Adi Da is Himself the "Hero of Giving", Whose Leela, or Divine Play, we recount and Celebrate.

   The Feast of the Hero of Giving is a time for Beloved Adi Da's devotees to honor His Giving Grace through song, dance, drama, recitations, and stories, not only in intimate community gatherings but also in public events. Gifts are exchanged as a conscious offering of love and energy to others in the mood of Love-Communion with the Divine Giver, and it is a period in which the devotional bond of the community is strengthened and celebrated.

remarkable for this man—he had a checkered past about which he sometimes felt deeply guilty. Perhaps as a result of this guilt, Tom was also known to be accident-prone. On this wonderful night, he had just received his presents from the hands and Heart of Bhagavan Adi Da. He had resumed his place near me when, all of a sudden, he stood up and began walking toward the door. Tom was intending to look for his intimate partner, who was caring for the Ashram children, even though Adi Da had Said that she would receive her gifts later and it was unnecessary to look for her.

Tom had hardly turned toward the door when he tripped over one of his presents. Down he came on top of me, and his outstretched arm crashed through a window behind me. The glass lacerated the upper part of his arm, instantly causing profuse arterial bleeding. Warm blood spurted all over me. Instantly, the place was in consternation. We rushed Tom out of the room, put a tourniquet around his arm, and transported him to a building we used as a small medical clinic. Tom had lost a lot of blood—he was in serious danger.

While Daniel Bouwmeester, the physician in charge, ministered to Tom, Avatara Adi Da asked me to step outside the clinic and tell Him in full detail what was going on from a medical point of view. It was absolutely clear to me at that moment that circumstances do not affect His Realization. Everybody was panicking and had lost the mood of Happiness and God-love except for our Heart-Master. He was simply present, even matter-of-fact.

I told Him that our friend Tom had arterial bleeding.

"What does that mean exactly?" He asked.

"It means that we have to stop the bleeding for now and that he has to be operated on as soon as possible."

"Can you do that here?"

"No, it is a question of vascular surgery—we couldn't do that here."

My friend Daniel, who had since telephoned the nearest major hospital, which was on a distant island, joined our conversation at this point. He was very concerned. He had just found out that there was no way to get a helicopter to Adidamashram in the middle of the night. I looked at my watch. It was 1:05 A.M.

We then accompanied Avatara Adi Da inside to attend to our friend. The place looked like a war zone. Tom was lying on a table, his eyes closed, softly moaning. Tom's intimate partner, Lynne, was holding his good hand, crying. Others were milling around, trying to help out in various ways. Adi Da stood next to Tom, leaning on His staff. He was Happy and relaxed.

Dan reinspected the bleeding artery deep in Tom's upper arm and discovered that he was able to apply direct finger pressure such that the bleeding would stop while circulation to the arm below the cut could continue.

I looked at Tom and sensed that my friend was already out of his body. I knew this was not good for his physical well-being.

Then, in a loud, powerful Voice, Heart-Master Adi Da summoned Tom, Saying, "Look at Me! Look at Me! Look at Me!!!"

Tom feebly opened his eyes.

"Good, keep looking at Me! Do you dig Me? Do you? Do you love your Master? Come on, tell Me!"

My friend said, "Yes," still faintly.

"Then Love Me! . . . Feel Me! . . . Breathe Me! Come on, do it!" Avatara Adi Da whacked Tom's chest in the heart area with His Hand, and vigorously moved it down toward his navel. He was saying all this over and over again, His Hands passing down Tom's body multiple times, showing graphically that, in this life-threatening situation, Tom should breathe the life-force down the frontal line of his body.

I could literally see Tom coming alive again. For a while, even the bleeding stopped totally. But, once more fully conscious and alive, Tom's face contorted with the incredible pain caused by the cut in his arm and the tourniquet around it.

"Look at Me. Keep on looking at Me. Keep your attention on Me!! Is the pain really bad?"

"Yes."

Avatara Adi Da's questioning changed direction: "Can you feel how bad the pain is?"

"Yes."

"But you do observe the pain, don't you? You observe the pain . . . you are observing the pain, are you not?"

"Yes, I am, Master."

"So 'you' are in the Witness-Position relative to the pain. You are the Witnessing Consciousness Itself, painless, timeless, and unqualified. Can you understand that . . . are you with Me?"

"Yes, I am, Master."

"Good, now, can you find the Bliss in Consciousness? Can you find the Bliss in Consciousness that is prior to pain? Can you find that Bliss? It does exist. I promise you! It does exist. There is Bliss in Consciousness prior to all pain, prior to all experience."

I watched in amazement as our Heart-Master, through His Words and His Spiritual Transmission, drew this man into the entirely different position of simply Witnessing and observing the pain rather than identifying with it.

Suddenly Avatara Adi Da started joking around with Tom. "You ruined My God in Every Body Day! People will be talking about this for many years, even many centuries to come." He threw back His head and laughed loudly.

I could hardly believe what was going on. First Bhagavan brought Tom back to life, literally from the edge of death. Then He brought him in touch with That Which transcends day-to-day life and bodily existence altogether. And now He started dealing with his chronic feelings of guilt, which had somehow provoked this whole incident!

"Now listen Tom, you don't have to be guilty anymore. What is guilt? Who cares about guilt? Do you really believe God cares about your guilt? Do you think I do? Do you think you have to pay to be free of it? No, God is <u>Forgiveness</u>. I don't give a damn for what happened in the past. Just give it all up. Give it all to Me."

Adi Da took some surgical scissors from our tray and started cutting the hairs on Tom's chest, cracking jokes about his hairiness—meanwhile taking an opportunity to lay His healing hands again all over Tom's chest.

Finally, at daybreak, we heard the sounds of helicopter blades from afar. The helicopter landed and we quickly lifted our friend inside. Daniel and I then climbed inside to accompany Tom to Suva, where Fiji's main hospital is located.

Part Two

# Remembrance of my Sat-Guru was my anchor

*by Tom Closser*

A s I was carried out of Avatara Adi Da's House immediately after the accident, I became especially sensitive to noise, and could hear the voices of everyone around me. Inside the clinic, I heard the lady who was holding my head, a registered nurse, whisper to someone that I was going into shock. Just then, I realized that I was moving up and back, and that I was outside my body.

Adi Da had gone outside, and I could hear Him talking, but I was still in the room watching everyone from above. He had been talking about how serious the situation was, but when He came inside, He started joking and making light of it.

Spontaneously, I began to move back and forth between two vantage points: I would hear Bhagavan Adi Da addressing me from the point of view of the body, and then I would observe everything from the higher, detached position again. Because this switching back and forth was so uncontrollable, I started to get anxious. The more anxious I became, the more I seemed to fix in the out-of-body state.

I could tell that Avatara Adi Da was trying to keep me associated with Him in the physical body, but the pain and fear kept driving me out of it. When I was out of my body, there was no pain—it was very calm and dissociated—even euphoric. Avatara Adi Da was moving His Hand up and down my chest, and He started kidding me about my tendency to be a macho man. He humorously pretended to be dealing with this self-image of mine by trimming the hairs off my chest. He began to run His Hand down my chest, snipping little bits of hair above His Fingers. A warm sensation seemed to drop from the top of my head and fall down my throat, as if someone were pouring a bucket of warm water over my head. Wherever Avatara Adi Da's Hand would stay, this sensation, which was full and alive in ways that were clearly more than physical, would be drawn down into my body to that point. I felt Avatara Adi Da literally filling me and enlivening me with His Blessing and His Spirit, and this helped to draw me back into the physical body.

Beloved Bhagavan also said wonderful things to keep my attention on Him. He said, "Do you love Me? Do you really love Me?" At one point, I rolled over and He held my face against His Belly. The only thing that I could feel in that moment was that I wanted to be with Him forever. It was not just a thought, it was a <u>physical</u> sensation.

Then the doctors put a tourniquet on my arm and it caused incredible pain. I zipped out of my body again. This time, I had gone even further up, so that now I was outside the room. The space-time barrier changed in some way, and I could see, rather than doing things sequentially, Bhagavan seemed to be maintaining a conversation with everyone in the room simultaneously—making many actions simultaneously.

The last image of the physical realm I remembered for a while was Bhagavan Adi Da talking to some men outside the clinic about my situation. Then I drifted off further and further.

I started to get anxious. I was trying to get a physical reference—trying to feel my nose—but I realized I could not feel my body at all. All of a sudden, I lost the anchor to physical familiarity, and I began to have visual phenomena. I saw a dark background with silvery strands (much like what you see when you press your fingers into your eyes), and a matrix of light and dark and different shapes. Everything had the same patina and an ochre color.

Then I remember seeing a group of people that I had known throughout my life. I was standing around with these people. The meeting was very warm, and full of familial emotions. It was very happy and I felt relaxed again.

Next, I saw what might be described as a tunnel. I had the sensation of moving, and, as I entered the tunnel, the people drifted behind me. I looked up and I realized that I was suddenly in a totally different environment.

This new environment seemed to be a normal three-dimensional space at first, but I realized very quickly that it did not have the same physical laws. It had a different perspective, or a different dimension. It had a very familiar landscape, almost like the environment where I grew up in East Los Angeles! I felt comfortable, but there was also something odd about it.

Then I began shifting to many different experiences, and I had no control over any of it. It became terrifying. In daily life I am physically based, and I have some control of where my attention is because I can focus it. But, in this circumstance, because I had no bodily anchor, I went wherever my attention went. I had no capability to control attention. My attention was on one thing for one minute, and that was my total reality, and then the next moment my attention was somewhere else, and that became my reality.

When this happened, everything changed—I did not even have a memory of the previous experience or environment. I felt that all these experiences were in the same dimension, since they had a similar feeling to them, but I was very rapidly switching from one fantasy to another fantasy without any control. Later, I remembered what Avatara Adi Da has Said—"While you are alive, you make mind, but, after death, mind makes you." It may sound interesting, but it was actually completely horrific.

I became more and more terrified. At one point I had the sense that the individuals, or entities, in this environment had an intention to keep me there. They were trying to determine what experience would keep me most solidly fixed in this condition. There seemed to be an assumption that I would stay there forever.

During this whole experience, I had forgotten my relationship with Avatara Adi Da—or even any memory or experience of Him. I did not feel capable of resorting to Him and I was totally subject to this experience, which was constantly changing and quite disturbing.

In the midst of this, two people, a man and his son, began trying to help me. They felt very familiar to me, as if I had been close to them as I was growing up. They were trying to help me get back to where Avatara Adi Da was. I could see the realm where He was—it had some of the qualities of a beautiful place in Hawaii I had visited once with Him. These two individuals were trying to help me concentrate and feel towards Him and this place so that I could keep my attention there, and then I could stay there with my Sat-Guru.

While they were trying to help me, the other group of people finally hit upon the one experience which seemed to control my attention more strongly than anything else—the sense of being threatened. I was standing in the middle of a street, and a bakery truck would drive towards me. It would slam on its brakes and slide into me. Right before the truck would hit me, I could feel myself going into panic. Then the experience would repeat itself. It happened repetitively—hundreds, maybe thousands of times. I was stuck in that éxperience.

In the midst of this experience, I "shouted", but it was not a physical voice. Somehow, I could, just for a moment, remember and feel Bhagavan Adi Da. Then the man and his son created a situation to help me get out of this endless cycle with the truck, back to where Beloved was.

Suddenly, I felt myself enter my body again, from the head down. I was back in the clinic, and Adi Da was there. He was talking to me. When I saw Him, my heart burst with Happiness and relief. I had been so much in need of Him in that horrifying experience—more deeply and more profoundly than I had ever been in my entire life. I felt what an incredible opportunity it is to be physically embodied in a time and place where He is presently alive—and what a horror it is to pass through this life and not realize something greater than being completely controlled by your own mind and attention. I was weeping.

Avatara Adi Da was touching me. He was very gentle and humorous. He used whatever means necessary in any moment to keep me relating to Him directly. He would speak with me about the Witness-Position and He would address my sense of guilt. It was very amusing: There I was, very nearly dying, and He was addressing every way that I was self-contracted and defensive and emotionally-sexually retarded! I could feel His Help very directly, and I was so grateful to be back in His physical Company.

Avatara Adi Da told me that a helicopter was coming to take me off the island. He kept Saying, "Stay with Me." The helicopter arrived, and He looked after every aspect of getting me to the helicopter. He asked how long it would take to get me to the hospital.

I was fairly lucid at this point. They had me on a stretcher inside the helicopter. Daniel and Frans were on my right and beyond them was the pilot. I stared at Naitauba as we flew away, and I felt that I could continue to remember Avatara Adi Da even at a physical distance or in a different environment. That was my practice—I had to continually feel Him, no matter what the experience was.

As soon as we arrived at the hospital in Suva, they took me to surgery. A big Fijian doctor and an Indian anesthesiologist introduced themselves. I was so tired I could not talk or move. But I could hear, and I responded through my eyes to indicate that I understood.

The Indian anesthesiologist wanted me to count out loud, if I could—starting from ten and going back to zero. He had a gas mask over my mouth. He explained that it was to make me unconscious so they could operate. I could not speak, but I counted in my mind, "Ten, nine . . ." to zero. He looked me in the eyes, and I looked back at him. He smiled and said, "Ok, do it again." I was trying to show him that I was counting, so I was blinking my eyes with each number—down to zero again.

My perception of everything was heightened. I could see in this doctor's eyes that he was becoming concerned. I could not understand what was wrong. He said, "Son, I am going to ask you to count one more time." His voice had started to tremble, and I became frightened. Again I counted, blinking my eyes as I did. When I got to zero, even though I was not unconscious, I kept my eyes closed.

They started the operation. I bore the pain as long as I could—but then I started gesturing, opening my eyes, and trying to shake my head. The nurse noticed that I was awake. They stopped and the anesthesiologist increased the anesthetic. I started to become really terrified because I felt I was going out of my body again.

I was afraid to lose consciousness—afraid that I would go back to this realm I had experienced before. People make a big deal of out-of-body experiences and near-death experiences as if it is all wonderful—you see God and your family. That was true in the beginning of my earlier experience, but the deeper I got in that state, it was just completely and totally horrific. There was nothing that I have ever experienced before or since that could possibly match the terror of being in that situation where you are just controlled by mind.

It was also clear to me that it is not just physical trauma that can knock you out of the body—any kind of emotional trauma can do this. I realized that that is what had occurred at the clinic on Naitauba—I had gone into emotional shock. I had lost a lot of blood, but that was not what sent me out of the body. I was in such a state of fear and anxiety that I was trying to remove myself from the circumstance. I was choosing not to be bodily incarnated rather than enduring and feeling through that strong emotion. Right in the middle of the operation, I remembered this about what had happened at the clinic on Naitauba, and I realized that it was happening again. I could feel myself retreating at the speed of light.

I woke up in the recovery room. Later that day and over the following days, the Fijian doctor and the Indian doctor came to see me many times, sometimes with four or five other doctors. They would huddle around me and speak in Fijian or Indian. Clearly they were curious, but also I felt their anxiety, as if something was wrong.

On the third day, I asked the nurse why everyone was so concerned. She called the two doctors to explain what had occurred in the operation. The Indian doctor indicated that they had given me a lot of anesthetic. In fact, he humorously said, I had been given enough anesthetic to knock out a small Fijian village! I tried to explain that I had been very anxious about losing consciousness—but they told me that that could not account for my resistance to the anesthetic. They asked if I had a history of this kind of thing when I had received anesthetics in the past, but I did not.

In that moment I remembered that when I was getting into the helicopter, Avatara Adi Da had asked exactly how long the helicopter trip would be, and had pressed His Spiritual Force into me repeatedly. I had felt this Force very physically and very powerfully. I felt like I was hyper-energized. It became obvious to me what had occurred. I explained to the doctors that I came from Naitauba, where my Spiritual Master was, and that He had Given me, while He was taking me to the helicopter, enough life-energy so that He would be certain that I survived the trip. Immediately, the Fijian doctor understood what I was talking about. He said, "Mana" (the Fijian word for Spiritual force or power). Then the Indian doctor started speaking about Shaktipat (the Indian name for Spiritual force). "Yes!" I said. Here, in a third world country, these doctors were completely familiar with the Force I was talking about! I could feel that they had an appreciation of Who Avatara Adi Da Is.

During the days of my recovery, I tried to maintain remembrance of Bhagavan Adi Da always. I would still slip in and out of consciousness, but I felt, when I would begin to lose bodily consciousness, that my only anchor was my remembrance of my Sat-Guru. If I did not intentionally remember Him, feel to Him, I would just end up free associating in the mind-realm. So I created ways to remember Avatara Adi Da. I could move my left arm, so I would trace the outline of His figure—as I remembered Him standing as I left Naitauba in the helicopter—over and over, thousands of times, just to stay associated with Him. It became a form of meditation for me.

Several weeks later, I returned to Naitauba. I heard from my friends there that on the evening I was having the most difficulty in the hospital, Adi Da had met with everyone here and discussed my character with them. Clearly, He had been Giving me His Regard and keeping me associated with Him. He had also pointed out that, if I allowed myself to stay in the disposition of guilt—which is one of my primary emotions—I would literally create accidents and illnesses to punish myself. I saw that Avatara Adi Da was trying to help me see how I draw accidents to myself by dramatizing this sense of feeling guilty. He was showing this to me so I would not repeat this disaster for myself.

On the night I returned, we were called to gather with Avatara Adi Da. I was incredibly weak, and incredibly happy to see Him, but I was also feeling guilty. I felt I had dishonored Him and ruined His celebration. But He dealt with me lovingly and joked with me a lot, relieving this chronic guilt of mine.

When He called me to show Him my cast, He put His leg against the cast. I could feel Him radiating His Heart-Force and healing energy sideways through my whole arm and into my chest. Then He Signed two names on my cast—mine ("Asshole") as "Narcissus" and His ("Da") as "The One Who Gives". All I could feel was Him, His Happiness. I was ecstatic. Later, at the end of the evening, He shouted to me, "NEVER DO THAT AGAIN!" and walked out of the room.

# CHAPTER 50

# The Understanding That Overcomes Suffering

*January 21, 1993*

*Avatara Adi Da's Compassionate Work with His devotees takes many forms. The two dialogues recorded here occurred during a gathering on January 21, 1993, at Adidamashram (Naitauba), Fiji. Both revolve around the subject of death. The first is simply His Blessing Regard Given to a devotee who has died. The second is a more fiery form of His Blessing—a dialogue in which He Serves the self-understanding of another devotee.*

## He Has My Blessing

AVATARA ADI DA: My devotee Barry Juarez passed yesterday morning. He has My Blessing. May all his karmas be purified. My Barry was a longtime devotee of Mine, one of the earliest. Some of you may remember him even in the earliest days. He always sent Me the tackiest cards! [Laughter.] The cards he sent Me were uniquely tacky. He sent Me cards with flowers, big cards, I remember, with flowers all over them, cards with flowery messages, with "Love, Barry".

He was—by his own confession, so I can speak of it—a homosexual, and he died of AIDS. But so what? That he was homosexual is not the point, and, unfortunately, he was infected with this dreadful plague. But he always remained My devotee. Even in his last days he remained My devotee.

My devotees served him. He listened to My Word and Contemplated Me as My devotee in his dying time. He had My Word directly to him in that time. I love him! And he is all right.

DEVOTEE: I remember one time he wrote You a card, and he gave it to You himself. You told him that You valued his relationship to You, that it was special. This meant so much to him. He told me about it at the time. It was so clear to me how much he loved You then and that he always loved You.

AVATARA ADI DA: He came to Me in Los Angeles in the very early days. He was My devotee for two decades. My devotees practice in many circumstances. Some devotees practice in circumstances that are even extreme, even apparently distant. These are not the best circumstances under which to practice the Way of the Heart, but such are the circumstances for some. Those who are in such unique circumstances for one reason or another do well to keep straight with Me and invoke My Heart-Blessing. And Barry did that. He always took care to maintain his relationship to Me. Therefore, he is a good sign for such a relationship to Me.

And I am glad he passed, because he was suffering greatly. The doctor here thought Barry might live for another week or so, but I told you last week that it was best if he could go quickly. He was ready. He was willing for death to occur. He had suffered enough. I am glad that he is relieved of that extraordinary distress.

DEVOTEE: Beloved Bhagavan, You love Your devotees so much. It is a Grace to see You Regard Your devotees in any moment of their life of practice, but it is particularly moving to see Your Blessing at the time of their passing.

◆ ◆ ◆

## What Are You Choosing?

*Later that night a woman from Germany spoke to Avatara Adi Da.*

DEVOTEE: Beloved Bhagavan, I want to tell you something that comes up. Twenty years ago, one of my brothers and my sister committed suicide.

AVATARA ADI DA: Both. Together or separately?

DEVOTEE: Separately.

AVATARA ADI DA: Around the same time?

DEVOTEE: A year between.

AVATARA ADI DA: How old were you then?

DEVOTEE: Twenty-one. And I always felt guilty about it.

AVATARA ADI DA: You feel guilty. Why?

DEVOTEE: Because I always think that if I had had a better relationship with them . . .

AVATARA ADI DA: Yes. If only the world had been perfect. If only they had been Enlightened. If only this were utopia. If only people did not have to deal with themselves. People feel guilty that their mothers and fathers died, not necessarily by suicide, but just that they died. For some, such feelings of guilt and anxiety arise. These feelings are not extraordinary.

Are you still carrying your guilt? Are you still bothered by it? Were you responsible? You? Were you responsible for your brother's suicide and your sister's suicide? If you had approached them on that day and told them of your love of them, would that have changed it, or delayed it more than a day or two or a week or a month? Could your expression of love have transformed them utterly? Did you ever express your love toward them?

DEVOTEE: Yes.

AVATARA ADI DA: So?

DEVOTEE: I only feel the burden of my guilt.

AVATARA ADI DA: What did you do or not do?

DEVOTEE: I only feel that it comes up again and again and disturbs me.

AVATARA ADI DA: What did you do or not do? What are you guilty of? Anything? Are you responsible for all of the people here in the room? Are you responsible for their choices?

DEVOTEE: No. Not at all.

AVATARA ADI DA: Are you responsible for your brother's choice? Your sister's? And what are you choosing to do? What are you doing?

DEVOTEE: I want to overcome this.

AVATARA ADI DA: What are you doing? Are you committing suicide? There are many ways to commit suicide, you see. Killing the body is one. Killing the heart, killing the mind, killing the energy of your existence, killing your responsibility to life, killing the surrender to the Divine—this is another kind of suicide.

All of you here are exhibiting the signs of death, the psychology of people who are dying. Denial, anger, bargaining, depression, acceptance— have you ever heard that description of the psychology of people who are dying?[1] When people are told they are dying, first they deny that it is even so. Then they get angry about it. And then they want to bargain about it, make an arrangement of some kind with God or the doctor or somebody— argue their way out of it. Then they get depressed.

1. See Elisabeth Kübler-Ross, M.D., *On Death and Dying* (New York: Macmillan, 1970).

That cycle has been observed in people who think they are dying or who know they are dying. But then acceptance may arise—a calmness, a wholeness, a balance, perhaps. Of course, the person can also become stuck in any of the preliminary stages. Which one are you in?

People just die, some not even with a terminal disease. Because of self-contraction, all of humanity is actually suffering the psychological process of people who are dying. All your complaints, all your descriptions of your problems, stresses, distress, and seeking, are part of the psychology of dying people. The ego is the death-process. It enforces in the body-mind a cycle, a psychology, a process of living, that is about the presumption that you are dying.

All the people who are living, except for those who are fully Awake or profoundly and truly religious, are actually dramatizing the psychology of people who are dying. Very simply put, this is exactly what people are doing. What is the search for this or that consolation? Bargaining, isn't it? Refusing it all, being oblivious in life, not wanting to deal with anything, sort of blasé—that is denial. Getting angry, reactive—this is the second stage of the process of dying. There are all kinds of seeking, bargaining. And depression is a characteristic mood of people, especially when there is nothing distracting them, no new possibility, no amusement, no consolation.

This is the psychology of somebody who is dying, not somebody who is truly alive and oriented in life relative to the Divine Source, the Divine Self-Condition That is the basis of growth and Realization. Instead of being truly alive, you all have invested yourselves in the psychology of death, and you are denying the reality of death, angry about it, bargaining, seeking, depressed, every now and then relaxed and accepting a little, but then when another impulse comes up, more denial, anger, bargaining. It is as if you are spending your life in a hospital, waiting to die from a terminal disease, which is the constriction you have placed on your own heart, your own energy, your own life, because you have devoted yourself to the self-contraction and all its results.

The self-contraction is a disease. You are dying from this reaction, this effort. This is why you are dying. The self-contraction ultimately kills you bodily. All the while you are alive, you are dramatizing this psychology, this process of moving to the point of death. Whether you commit suicide or die from a disease or an accident, whatever the cause of your death, you have invested your entire life in this contraction and its results. And psychologically the results are all the signs that are exhibited by people who are actually dying.

[To the devotee who spoke] If your brother and sister killed themselves, the message of death overwhelms you, and you are dramatizing anger, denial, oblivion, self-indulgence, seeking—depression mainly. Are you mainly in the stage of depression? [Devotee nods "yes".] Depressed. The vision of your brother and sister killing themselves, denying life—you use such a negative presumption to justify your own acts, your own feeling of futility and doom. You are spending your entire life being depressed, just short of dying in the hospital, spending all your life depressed, and saying, "Well, my brother and sister committed suicide. That's why I feel this way. That's why I'm doing this."

But you are depressed. You are depressing yourself. You are investing your entire life in the bad news of your life-experience rather than in your best understanding, your feeling-sense of Me, your "consideration" of the Divine Self-Condition, the Source of your own apparent existence. It is your choice. It is up to you. Do not just tell Me you want to be rid of this, because it is your action. It is not something happening to you. You are doing your depression. You are living in the vision of your brother and sister killing themselves, and it conforms to your vision of life altogether. You are doing that instead of responding to Me, instead of living your life for the sake of the Source of your own existence.

You are allowing your entire life to be depressed by bad news, like the person dying of a terminal disease and going through the psychological cycle in a hospital bed. You have received bad news from life, and that is unfortunate. I understand. But you are making your life out of it. You want to come up with all kinds of cute notions, such as that you are somehow guilty of your brother's and sister's deaths. Nonsense! You are using them to justify your own depression, your own refusal of the Divine.

Your depression is your action. It is not caused by your brother and sister. It is not caused by anything in the past. You are doing it now. You are refusing the Joy of Divine Communion. And it is not that you are without Revelation. You are not without Revelation. You are obsessed with your own depression. Up to now, depression has been your solution to life. The obvious bad news of life is not only that your brother and sister committed suicide. Listen to the daily news. Go out on the streets.

The Source of life is all Joy. The Condition to be Realized is all Joy. Life, as egos live it, is all suffering, and everyone dies. Now, which will you respond to—the bad news, the bad company of egoic suffering, or Me? This is My Question to you. This is what you must "consider".

Did you birth out your brother and sister? Did you make them? Did you make their problems? They tried to solve their problems the best way they could. They came to a point where to conceive of living anymore was intolerable to them. That is not the end of the story for them. Conditional Nature itself will revive them, has revived them and required them to endure more and understand better. One cannot escape by suicide or death in any form. You are one with this Great Design here, and you cannot escape it. You must come to the point where you can embrace the Source of it and give yourself up. You know nothing about it. You are not in charge of it. You are one with the whole circumstance, not just the physical aspect, but all aspects of it—not only the gross but the subtle, the Ultimate, all aspects of it. You are one with it to the Core. That Core is the Source. You must devote yourself to It.

Having found Me, find Me out, become My devotee, prove My Instruction to you. Try it out. But understand that <u>you</u> are depressing yourself. Depressing yourself is your solution. Others have other solutions. Everybody is playing the game of seeking. Being depressed is your solution. You think it is better to be depressed than to suffer having to work it out and to deal with reality, to overcome yourself—better to be depressed than to have to go through that difficulty, that intelligent matter. Do you understand Me? That is how you are thinking.

Be glad that you in your lifetime have found the Revelation direct. But respond, then. Otherwise, you are killing yourself, too. If you choose not to respond, then you are committing suicide, if not by just killing the body straight out, then by enduring a lifetime of depression, of suffering, of un-Happiness, of godlessness. That is suicide.

You are doing it, too. You are killing youself. You are killing your own heart. It is entirely your activity, entirely your responsibility.

Give your brother and sister to Me. Give your brother and sister to God. Give them to the Source from Which they came. Give them to that Source. That is Where the responsibility lies ultimately. And get on with your life, based on your best understanding, based on what you have received, and disprove their choice by making a great choice yourself. This is how you can bless them, too. Those who make great choices, the greatest choice, the Divine Choice, bless all their relations. All their ancestors, all their families, are purified by that choice.

Therefore, bless them by not choosing suicide yourself. Can you do this?

DEVOTEE: Yes.

AVATARA ADI DA: Be Happy, then. I understand. I wish it had not happened. I understand the suffering in it. Understand that human responsibility is great, and only self-understanding overcomes suffering.

**Adi Da (The Da Avatar)**
**Adidamashram, 1994**

# PART II

## SECTION SIX

# Divine Enlightenment

T he Same Reality That Is Realized Most Perfectly In The Seventh Stage Of Life In The Way Of The Heart Is <u>Always</u> The Reality. It Is The Reality Now. It Is The Reality That You Are Experiencing In this moment. Because Of self-Contraction, You (As the ego-"I") Propose Various Illusions and Generate Presumptions Based On Those Illusions, but Your Illusions Do Not Make Reality Any Different Than It Always Already Is. Your Illusions Only Make You Confused, Deluded, Bound, and Dissatisfied. If, Instead Of Merely Perpetuating Your Illusions, You Give Me Your Responsive Devotional Regard, and Surrender Into Communion With Me (By Yielding All The Principal Faculties, Of body, emotion, mind, and breath, To Me), and Forget Yourself and The Faculties and Their Illusions and Operations, and Enter Into A Profound Stillness Of "Bright" Communion With Me (Thereby Releasing The Knot Of self-Contraction), Then The True Nature Of Reality Becomes (By My Reality-Revealing Grace) Tacitly Obvious As The By Me and As Me Revealed Source-Condition Of conditional Existence.

ADI DA (THE DA AVATAR)
*The Dawn Horse Testament Of Adi Da*

---

*Divine Enlightenment (or Divine Self-Realization) is Awakening to the Truth that there is only Consciousness—only One, Infinite Divine Being, the Source and the Substance of Life, Always Blissful, Always Radiant, Always Satisfied. Divine Enlightenment is Freedom—no limit, no fear, no duality, but only the Indivisible, Irreducible Light of God. And Divine Enlightenment is the Blessed possibility in the Company of Bhagavan Adi Da—for He Is the Divine Being, and He has Incarnated to Transmit Consciousness, Happiness, and Freedom to every one and every thing, so that God, Truth, and Reality may be Most Perfectly Realized by all.*

*In this section, Bhagavan Adi Da describes the unique process and moment of His own Divine Self-Realization—the Re-Awakening of the Divine Person in human Form to His own Identity as God.*

*And He also describes His unique Gift of the seventh stage Realization to His devotees—how His devotee is "Brightened" through devotional Contemplation of His God-Light, until there is no separate individual, but only the Divine Conscious Radiance of Being Itself.*

# CHAPTER 51

# The Great Event in the Vedanta Temple

*from chapter sixteen of* The Knee of Listening

*In this remarkable passage from His Spiritual Autobiography, Avatara Adi Da describes His Re-Awakening to the "Bright" Divine Condition, or unqualified Identification with Love-Bliss-Consciousness. This profound Event occurred in 1970, when Avatara Adi Da was thirty years old, at a temple in the grounds of the Vedanta Society in Los Angeles.*

*What occurred was a <u>Re-Awakening</u>, because the "Bright" was always His true Identity. Avatara Adi Da's birth was the very Descent of the Divine Person into human form. However, His complete Submission (in early childhood) to the struggles and limits of ordinary people was a "forgetting" of His Great State. Only after long years of arduous Sadhana (in which He personally passed through the entire course of Spiritual growth and Realization) did this complete Re-Awakening take place.*

*During the years of His early-life Sadhana, Adi Da was the devotee of a number of great Spiritual Masters in a single lineage: first Swami Rudrananda (Rudi), then Swami Muktananda, then Swami Nityananda. The root-Guru of the lineage, however, was not a human being: it was the Divine Goddess, known in the Indian tradition as the "Shakti", or the Energy Dimension of the cosmos. And this Divine Goddess, or Shakti, was the final Guru of Adi Da's Sadhana, appearing to Him in visionary form.*

*At first Adi Da was a devotee of the Goddess—a "child" of the "Mother-Shakti", who faithfully followed all Her Instructions to Him: but in a remarkable Event in September 1970, their relationship changed. As He sat meditatively in the Vedanta Temple, the Goddess appeared to Him in a new form—Embracing Him in an overwhelmingly Blissful encounter. Adi Da and the Goddess had achieved ecstatic Union—and the Goddess was now <u>His</u> Companion, Loved One, and Consort.*

*The events described by Adi Da in this account occurred the following day.*

Finally, the next day, September 10, 1970, I sat in the temple again. I awaited the Beloved Shakti to reveal Herself in Person, as my Blessed Companion. But, as time passed, there was no Event of changes, no movement at all. There was not even any kind of inward deepening, no "inwardness" at all. There was no meditation. There was no need for meditation. There was not a single element or change that could be added to make my State Complete. I sat with my eyes open. I was not having an experience of any kind. Then, suddenly, I understood most perfectly. I Realized that I had Realized. The "Thing" about the "Bright" became Obvious. I Am Complete. I Am the One Who Is Complete.

In That instant, I understood and Realized (inherently, and most perfectly) What and Who I Am. It was a tacit Realization, a direct Knowledge in Consciousness. It was Consciousness Itself, without the addition of a Communication from any "Other" Source. There Is no "Other" Source. I simply sat there and Knew What and Who I Am. I was Being What I Am, Who I Am. I Am Being What I Am, Who I Am. I Am Reality, the Divine Self, the Nature, Substance, Support, and Source of all things and all beings. I Am the One Being, called "God" (the Source and Substance and Support and Self of all), the "One Mind" (the Consciousness and Energy in and As Which all appears), "Siva-Shakti"[1] (the Self-Existing and Self-Radiant Reality Itself), "Brahman"[2] (the Only Reality, Itself), the "One Atman"[3] (That Is not ego, but Only "Brahman", the Only Reality, Itself), the "Nirvanic Ground"[4] (the egoless and conditionless Reality and Truth, Prior to all dualities, but excluding none). I Am the One and Only and necessarily Divine Self, Nature, Condition, Substance, Support, Source, and Ground of all. I Am the "Bright".

There was no thought involved in This. I Am That Self-Existing and Self-Radiant Consciousness. There was no reaction of either excitement or surprise. I Am the One I recognized. I Am That One. I am not merely experiencing That One. I Am the "Bright".

Then truly there was no more to Realize. Every experience in my life had led to This. The dramatic revelations in childhood and college, my time of writing, my years with Rudi, the revelation in seminary, the long history of pilgrimage to Baba's Ashram[5]—all of these moments were the intuitions of this same Reality. My entire life had been the Communication of That Reality to me, until I Am That.

1. The Sanskrit term "Siva-Shakti" is an esoteric description of the Divine Being. "Siva" is a name for the Divine Being Itself, or Divine Consciousness. "Shakti" is a name for the All-Pervading Spirit-Power of the Divine Being. "Siva-Shakti" is thus the Unity of the Divine Consciousness and Its own Spirit-Power.

2. In the Hindu tradition, Brahman is the Ultimate Divine Reality that is the Source and Substance of all things, all worlds, and all beings.

3. The Divine Self.

4. "Nirvana" is a Buddhist term for the Unqualified Reality beyond suffering, ego, birth, and death. The "Nirvanic Ground" indicates the same Reality.

5. See *The Knee of Listening* for a description of these events.

Later I described that most perfect Realization as follows:

*At the Vedanta Society Temple inherent and most perfect Knowledge arose that I Am simply the "Bright" Consciousness that Is Reality. The traditions call It the "Self", "Brahman", "Siva-Shakti", and so many other names. It is identified with no body, no functional sheath, no conditional realm, and no conditional experience, but It is the inherently perfect, unqualified, Absolute Reality. I saw that there is nothing to which this Ultimate Self-Nature can be compared, or from which It can be differentiated, or by which It can be epitomized. It does not stand out. It is not the equivalent of any specialized, exclusive, or separate Spiritual state. It cannot be accomplished, acquired, discovered, remembered, or perfected—since It is inherently perfect, and It is always already the case.*

*All remedial paths pursue some special conditional state or conditionally achieved goal as Spiritual Truth. But in fact Reality is not identical to such things. They only amount to an identification with some body (or some functional sheath), some conditional realm, or some conditional (or, otherwise, conditionally achieved) experience, high or low, subtle or gross. But the Knowledge that Is Reality Is Consciousness Itself. Consciousness Itself is not separate from anything. It is always already the case, and no conditional experience, no conditional realm, and no body (or functional sheath) is the necessary or special condition for Its Realization.*

*Only radical understanding, most perfectly Realized, is the Realization of What and Who Is always already the case. Only radical understanding, most perfectly Realized, is the unconditional (and not at all conditionally achieved or conditionally maintained) Realization of the inherently non-separate Condition That always already Is What and Who Is. Except for the only-by-me revealed and given way of radical understanding (or the true and only-by-me revealed and given Way of the Heart), all paths are remedial. That is to say, apart from the truly ego-surrendering, ego-forgetting, and ego-transcending way of radical understanding (which is the true Way of the Very and Ultimate Heart), all paths are made of seeking (or mere egoic effort, rather than counter-egoic and truly ego-transcending practice). And all paths of seeking merely pursue God, Truth, or Reality, and this by identifying God, Truth, or Reality with some body (or functional sheath), or some conditional realm, or some conditional experience, or, otherwise, by making the Realization of God, Truth, or Reality depend upon some body (or functional sheath), or some conditional realm, or some conditional experience.*

*Unlike the way of radical understanding (or the Way of the Heart), which is based upon the root-understanding and always most direct transcendence of the motive and the activity of seeking, all paths seek either the perfection of what is conditionally existing or liberation from what is conditionally existing, and that perfection or liberation is pursued as a goal, which goal is presumed to be identical to God, Truth, or Reality. Only the way of radical understanding (or the Way of the Heart) is free, even from the beginning, of all conditional, or, otherwise, conditionally to be achieved, goals. Only the way of radical understanding (or the Way of the Heart) is inherently free of the goal-orientation itself. Indeed, only the Heart Itself is inherently free of all goal-seeking, and even all seeking. And only the way of radical understanding is the Way of the Heart Itself.*

*When tacit and most perfect recognition of the inherent Condition That Is God, Truth, and Reality was re-Awakened in me, there was no excitement, no surprise, no movement, no response. There was a most perfect end to every kind of seeking, dilemma, suffering, separation, and doubt. Spiritual life, mental life, emotional and psychic life, vital life, and physical life all became transparent in me. After that, there was only the "Bright" Reality, and to be the "Bright" Reality to all beings and all things.*

In all the days that followed the Great Event of my re-Awakening, there has not been a single change in This "Bright" Awareness, or any diminishment of This "Bright" Awareness. Indeed, This "Bright" Awareness cannot be changed, diminished, or lost. I immediately noticed that "experience" had ceased to affect me. Whatever passed, be it a physical sensation, some quality of emotion, a thought, a vision, or whatever, it did not involve me (as I Am) at all. I began to pay particular attention to what passed, in order to "test" my State (or, simply, in order to account for all aspects of my State in the total functional context of the living body-mind). But the primary Awareness of the inherently "Bright" Reality, my Very Consciousness Itself, could not be changed, diminished, or lost. Consciousness (Itself) is the only "Thing" in life that is not an "experience" (or something "Witnessed" by Consciousness Itself). Consciousness (Itself) does not depend on anything, and there is not (nor can there be) anything, or any "experience", that can destroy Consciousness Itself. Consciousness Itself Is (Itself) Love-Bliss, Joy, Freedom, and Sublime Knowledge!

An entirely new and most perfect Realization of Reality had become the constant of my life.

◆ ◆ ◆

Even my meditation was changed. There was no meditation. This Consciousness could not be deepened or enlarged. It always only remained What It Is. I meditated (as a formal activity) only to see how "meditation" had been affected by my Realization, or, otherwise, to formally regard the conditions in the body, the mind, even any part of my living (or extended) being, or even any conditions at all. But I was no longer the meditative seeker, the one who seeks (or, otherwise, does not Know) God,

Truth, Reality, Liberation, Release, or Growth. I no longer supposed any limitation as myself. I Am He. I Am She. I Am It. I Am That Only One.

I noticed a physical change in myself. My belly dropped and expanded, and, thus and thereby, permanently assumed the "pot-shaped" Yogic form. I always feel the Pressure of Shakti-Energy there, and I breathe It continually. It is the breathing of my Very Being, the endless and profound Communication of the inherent "Brightness" of Reality to Itself.

In "meditation", I looked to observe how I was related to the worlds of conditional experience. Immediately, I realized that I was not in any sense "in" a body, not only the physical body, but any body, or any functional sheath, including the most subtle. Nor have I ever been in a body, or in any functional sheath, or in any conditional realm, or in any conditional experience. All such things are patterns conditionally manifested within my own Self-Nature.

Yet (even so), I realized that, in the context of natural appearances, I am Communicated through a specific center in the body. Relative to the body, I appear to reside in the heart, but to the right side of the chest. I press upon a point approximately an inch and one-half to the right of the center of the chest. This is the seat of Reality and Real Consciousness. And I Abide there as no-seeking. There is no motivation, no dilemma, no separation, no strategic action, no suffering. I am no-seeking in the Heart.

I described my constant experience as follows:

*The zero of the heart is expanded as the world. Consciousness is not differentiated and identified. There is a constant observation of subject and object in any body, any functional sheath, any realm, or any experience that arises. Thus, I remain in the unqualified State. There is a constant Sensation of "Bright" Fullness permeating and surrounding all experiences, all realms, all bodies, all functional sheaths. It is my own "Bright" Fullness, Which is radically non-separate. My own "Bright" Fullness includes all beings and all things. I am the Form of Space Itself, in Which all bodies, all functional sheaths, all realms, and all experiences occur. It is inherently "Bright" Consciousness Itself, which Reality is even every being's Very Nature (or Ultimate, inherent, and inherently perfect, Condition) now and now and now.*

And again:

*During the night of mankind, I Awakened as perfect, absolute, awesome Love-Bliss, in Which the body and the mind, even every functional sheath, boiled into a solder of undifferentiated Reality. It was the madness of dissolution into most perfect Self-Awareness, Infinitely Expanded, my own inherently boundless Presence, wherein there is only "Brightness", not qualified* *by conditional identification, or self-differentiation, or ego-based desire. Hereafter, I am Free of bondage to the cosmic Power. I am unexploitable. The Shakti that appears apart, as any form of apparently independent, or merely cosmic, Power and Presence, is no longer the Great Importance. The Presence of Power "outside" appears as such only to seekers, for they, having already separated themselves, <u>pursue</u> forms of Energy, visions, nature-powers, liberation, and God. True Knowledge is free of all bondage to forms (or modifications) of Energy, all seeking, all motivation to "do" based on identification with conditional experience. Egoic ignorance and suffering are simply this separateness, this difference, this search. At last, the "outside" Shakti sacrifices Herself in the Heart. Thereafter, there is no gnawing wonder, no un-Known "secret" about anything that appears.*

CHAPTER 52

# What Is to Be Realized?

*July 9, 1980*
*from* Scientific Proof of the Existence of God
Will Soon Be Announced by the White House!

There is only the Self-Existing and Self-Radiant Divine Being, Who Is One. All beings and things and worlds are ultimately and Really only identical to That One, Who Is God, the Divine Person.

Only God is Alive as everyone and everything. All beings and things and worlds are arising as spontaneous transformations, or modifications, of That One. God eternally Transcends the world and all beings, and yet the world and all beings are nothing but God. It is a Great and Passionate Mystery.

The individual being, manifested as the body-mind, is only a transformation, or modification, of the Divine Person. Wherever or whenever there is a psycho-physical being, the Divine Being is Conscious as that limitation and feels Itself to be a particular being.

There is no internal self, or "soul", within and independent of the body-mind. The individual body-mind is a modification of, or play upon, the Infinite, Inherently Spiritual (or All-Pervading), and Transcendental Divine Being. The body-mind itself, in its contraction, or recoil, from the universal pattern of relations, suggests or implies the subjective internal self or independent "soul" idea. And once the body-mind, or independent self pattern, arises, it tends to persist, as a process of transformation, lifetime after lifetime, until there is Awakening to the Truth, and, ultimately, Translation into the Divine Self-Domain—the Divine Self-Condition of Love-Bliss Itself.

As you adapt and evolve and achieve Ecstasy in the Divine, you Realize your eternal inherence in That One and, ultimately, your Identity as That One. Such is Divine Enlightenment, Divine Liberation, or Divine Self-Realization. Therefore, Divine Enlightenment, Divine Liberation, Divine Self-Realization, or That Which is to be Realized, is not a form of "status" or egoic achievement in this world, the after-death world, or the next lifetime, but It is the Condition of Love-Bliss, or Happiness, Which Transcends the body-mind, its experiences, its relations, and the world, even as the world continues.

The "being" that is Awakened to the Truth may abide simply as that Identity, excluding participation in the active pattern of the body-mind, its relations, and the world, and excluding as well the self-transcending gesture of Ecstasy in the Universal, or Total, Divine. Such is the disposition in the sixth stage of life. Just so, when you are only beginning to understand your circumstance in God, you may embrace the lesser disposition of abiding in a state of simple absorption in the Spirit-Presence of the Divine Being. Such conditional ecstasy characterizes fulfillment in the fourth stage of life and the fifth stage of life, and it arises when the separate and separative self, or body-mind, becomes contemplatively absorbed in the Divine Power that is experientially perceived by or within the body-mind itself. But in the Fullness of the seventh stage of life there is Most Perfect, total, and most profound acknowledgement that the total body-mind, all beings, and the total world of possibilities inhere in an eternal Condition of Inherently Perfect Identity with the Divine Being. Then there is no reaction either toward inwardness or toward release of conditional self through internal or external experience. The total body-mind and its conditions and relations are Realized to abide in inherent Identification with That One. Therefore, there is simple persistence as Divine Love-Bliss and Consciousness Itself, whatever arises. Every moment of experience is Realized to be equally and totally Profound. This continues, through all the acts and moments and transformations of the body-mind in Love-Bliss, until the body-mind and its experience are dissolved, passed away, or Outshined by the Self-Existing and Self-Radiant Divine Being.

The Living God, the Beloved of all beings, has, from Eternity, become a Great Sacrifice. The Self-Existing and Self-Radiant One has become the Process of all possibilities. Living beings are not merely the creatures or victims of God, created and set apart to suffer for some inexplicable reason. Living beings are the very Sacrifice of God. God is Alive as you. Your life is the creative ordeal to which God is eternally Submitted. You need only Realize the Living One and thus become capable of this Divine Sacrifice, which is an eternal creative ordeal of Love that leads, step by step, toward a Most Perfect Transformation. Once you transcend the illusion of your dark separate self and enter into the Divine Process, you will see clearly that the existence and destiny of the world and every being is the Fullness of Love-Bliss in an Inherently Perfect State that has become One with the Person and the Domain of the Divine.

This is My Testimony and My Confession. And it is the Culmination of the Testimonies and Confessions proclaimed by all the Adepts who have appeared to Serve mankind on Earth.

CHAPTER 53

# "Crazy Wisdom"

*March 2, 1981*

A VATARA ADI DA: The world is an infinity of reflections, a kind of prism, or crystal, of countless likenesses and slices. It is simply unfathomable! This is what you must Realize, rather than gain more and more concrete notions about the Nature of Reality. Transcend all those notions. The ultimate self-transcending Process is not the accumulation of a more and more perfect model of how things work but the utter transcendence of all possible models of how things work. There is no way that things work! How things work is utterly unfathomable. It can never be fathomed, it can never be comprehended, it can never be grasped. There is neither a sufficient nor a true model, because there is no model. Because things are apparently happening, you conclude that there must be a scheme whereby everything works. But, ultimately, there is no such scheme. There are only patterns that may be presumed on the basis of your point of view, your limited experience, and the conventions of your self-conception.

All phenomena are a kind of infinite madness. Experience itself is utterly unfathomable. This is not the confession of a bewildered, conventionally ignorant and separative consciousness—it is the Expression of Divinely Enlightened Consciousness, Which Expresses Itself in terms of paradoxes and Divine Ignorance, in terms of no-knowledge, no fixed self, no fixations of presumption based on experience or the lie of illusion. Curiously, from this Realized "Point of View", all phenomena continue to arise. In fact, great energy is released in that Realization, so that more phenomena than you might previously have been capable of tolerating may begin to arise. All kinds of appearances, strange coincidences, mysterious happenings, visions, dreams, psychisms—all kinds of things begin to arise. But, if you persist in the Divinely Enlightened Disposition, the things that arise do not support the conventional point of view of the fourth, the fifth, or the sixth stage of life. They are transcended as they arise. Thus, experiences in themselves do not amount to a description of Reality. They are nothing but possibility, nothing but a moment of infinite flowing that has neither center nor bounds.

Divine Enlightenment is "Crazy Wisdom".[1] The Truth is "Craziness", Madness—not the psychosis of the fearful, self-bound ego but the Madness of the Samadhi of the Real. In that Samadhi, all the dogmas of human existence—waking, dreaming, and sleeping—are transcended. Truly, there is nothing to say in that case.

Presently, you are all yammering, doing, thinking, and playing all the time, none of which amounts to a description of your True Condition, the True Condition of existence, the Divine Nature of Reality Itself. These descriptions are not the Truth. Each of your experiences may be taken to be a kind of description—these experiences tend to create a form of mind and a presumption about the nature of things. But if you persist in the disposition of self-understanding, your experiences no longer have such force. Thus, from the "Point of View" of Realization in the seventh stage of life, there is no form, no description, to be passed on to the rest of the world. There is only Divine Self-Realization Itself to be recommended.

The popular view is that when a being becomes Enlightened, suddenly he or she sees how the universe arises, sees what everything is about, sees the hierarchy or structures of the cosmos and can map it all out. All kinds of people have such experiences long before they even approximate the capability for Divine Self-Realization. Such capabilities are just possibilities, appearances. You must Realize their Source, their Nature, their Condition, their Identity. You are not presently what you describe yourself to be, what you think yourself to be, what others describe you to be, what others think you are. No description has ultimate significance. Therefore, in Divine Self-Realization, one lives wildly, freely, not confined to the role models that the presumptions of human beings in general constantly generate.

That kind of Madness may not be your Realization. This description may not make any sense to you at all. It may not make any nonsense to you either. I am trying to be nonsensical and you are making sense out of it, perhaps! I do not know about you, but that is the way it seems to Me. Happiness, or Freedom, has always been Obvious to Me. I noticed from the very beginning that it was not obvious to other people, so I adapted to a rather ordinary mode as a child. I was not super-ordinary—I had My

1. In various esoteric sacred traditions, certain practitioners and Masters have been called "crazy", "mad", or "foolish". Tibetan Buddhist Saints of this type are given the title "lama nyonpa" ("saintly madman") or simply "nyonpa" ("madman"). In whatever tradition and time they appear, these individuals violate prevailing taboos (personal, social, religious, or even Spiritual) either to instruct others or simply to express their own inspired freedom.

In the realm of the sacred, there are many kinds of unconventional Teachers. Avatara Adi Da's Wisdom-Teaching is a principal guide to help the serious student discriminate among such unconventional Teachers while also benefiting from the stories of their lives and work. The Adepts of what Avatara Adi Da calls "the 'Crazy Wisdom' tradition" (of which He is the supreme exemplar) are Realizers of the advanced and the ultimate stages of life in any culture or time who, through spontaneous Free action, blunt Wisdom, and liberating laughter, shock or humor people into self-critical awareness of their egoity, a prerequisite for receiving the Adept's Spiritual Transmission. Typically, such Realizers manifest "Crazy" activity only occasionally or temporarily, and never for its own sake.

excesses—but I adapted to the situation in which I found My Self. I developed My Play of Life, simply to live, and also to Serve others, to Help them Awaken as I am Awake.

But, always, from My "Point of View", life has been this Madness. I have never, even from birth, taken seriously the destiny that others seem to take so seriously. As a child, I was surrounded by all kinds of people, none of whom seemed to have any sense at all of existence in the terms I am describing. As a result, I shot through life spontaneously, having various encounters, gradually coming to a more and more full understanding and elaboration of the Condition of My Existence. I met a few other individuals Who were useful in helping Me to observe features of the Mystery that I had not observed before. I moved on from them and began to Teach others. But, always, My involvement has been with this Madness that Transcends life, that Transcends the seriousness, that Transcends the burden of occupation to which minds and bodies in the world seem to be confined.

All My Life I have gotten up every morning without any sense that there was anything I must do until the next time I fell asleep. However, everybody I encountered was very seriously involved in many obligations! In My waking hours I encountered and dealt with and related to people in all kinds of ways. I Played My part, which is not a conventional part but a part that Expresses My Enlightened Disposition and that also enabled Me to be of Service to other people.

Fundamentally, truly, there is not one thing serious about a tree, a rock, a mountain, the sun, morning, noon, night, waking, dreaming, sleeping, others, time, space, possibilities. It is all Mad. It is all celebration. I am not inclined to become serious about it. In "The Heart of Understanding", the prologue to *The Knee of Listening*, I make reference to the flowers that go on and on and on, and yet show no evidence, after millions and millions of years of flowering, of becoming qualified by the history of deaths, by all the terribleness that they have experienced. They are just as alive as they ever were. A fundamental Force and unqualified Being, Which is the Substance of all manifestation, Transcends all the conventional presumptions that would lead people to a rather desperate and confined sense of things.

Human beings have also been persisting for millions of years, in spite of all the deaths and terribleness they have experienced. In spite of what human beings experience now, even under "civilized" circumstances, there is still a fundamental intuition of unqualified Being in all beings that is Free, that can be appealed to. That Which you Are fundamentally Transcends all of this change, even though you do not have a mind that is certain of how it is all working, or that is even certain about survival of death on the basis of experience or proven theory. There is an essential Nature and Disposition in Which all beings exist perpetually, One that is already Free of the implications of death and of ordinary experience. No matter how much negative mind one may superimpose on life, that essential Nature always remains "Bright". Even in the most terrified psychotic mind, there is some fundamental intuition of That Which remains Free (although clearly it has become overloaded to the point of being unable to acknowledge itself).

Thus, I appeal to you to Realize your Real Condition. In your Real Condition, you are Alive as That, Radiant as That. As your understanding matures, you develop the Disposition of Who and What you really Are. More and more, you are simply established in That Which you Are. But if this conversation makes no sense to you, or if it makes no nonsense to you, then "Crazy Wisdom" is not what you are about, and there is nothing I can do about it—nothing. It is up to you.

# There Is Simply The "Bright" Itself

*from chapter forty-four of*
The Dawn Horse Testament Of Adi Da

To Realize The Seventh Stage Of Life In The Way Of The Heart Is To Stand and <u>Be</u> Beyond The Cosmic Domain, Beyond conditional Existence, and Beyond the body-mind.

To Realize The Seventh Stage Of Life In The Way Of The Heart Is Not Merely To Be some kind of egoless personality, or Perfectly Non-Contracted body-mind.

To Realize The Seventh Stage Of Life In The Way Of The Heart Is To Have No body-mind and No world.

To Realize The Seventh Stage Of Life In The Way Of The Heart Is To Be Utterly Beyond, or Utterly Prior To, and Yet (Paradoxically, Until The Demonstration Of Divine Translation) Apparently Associated With a conditional body-mind and a conditional world.

In The Seventh Stage Of Life In The Way Of The Heart, the body-mind and the world Effectively Do Not Exist. In every moment of Apparent arising (In The Seventh Stage Of Life In The Way Of The Heart), the body-mind and the world Are Inherently (or Divinely) Recognized (Without The Passage Of Even any fraction of time, However Instant). There Is Simply The "Bright" Itself. I <u>Am</u> The "Bright" Itself. The "Bright" Itself, Who I <u>Am</u>, Is The Self-Existing and Self-Radiant Divine Self-Condition Itself, The Condition Of Perfect No-Contraction.

The Realization Of The Seventh Stage Of Life In The Way Of The Heart Is The Realization Of Non-"Difference". It Is To Be Established In and <u>As</u> That Ultimate Condition Which Is Always Already The Case, and Which Inherently Transcends conditional Existence. It Is To <u>Be</u> Just That.

In The Seventh Stage Of Life In The Way Of The Heart, There Is No conditional Domain, but Only The Divine Domain. There Is Only Consciousness Itself, Self-Existing and Self-Radiant. In The Seventh Stage Of Life In The Way Of The Heart, It Makes No "Difference" If Divine Translation Occurs or anything else Occurs. Divine Translation Is Not An Event Looked Forward To, but Simply The (In Due Course) Inevitable Demonstration Of The Disposition That Already Exists In The Seventh Stage Realizer.

The Divine Self-Condition, or Self-Existing Consciousness Itself, Is Self-Radiant. Every condition that arises In The conditional, or Cosmic, Domain Is A Modification Of That Divine Self-Radiance. However, Paradoxically, No Such Modification Of The Divine Self-Radiance Modifies, or Otherwise Affects, The Divine Self-Condition Itself. Whatever arises Is Simply An Apparent (and Non-binding, and Non-limiting) Modification Of The Divine Self-Radiance (or Of The Self-Existing and Self-Radiant Divine Self-Condition Itself).

There Is No "Difference" Between Consciousness and Its Own Radiance. There Is Only Consciousness Itself, Self-Existing and Self-Radiant, Not "Created", Not conditional, and Not Dependent On any thing or condition. There Is Only Infinite, Unbounded Being, Indivisible, Unable To Be Differentiated From any Apparently Separate being. Indeed, There Are No conditional beings, but Only Being Itself Is.

There Is Only One Principle, Self-Existing and Self-Radiant, and every thing arises In It. Therefore, every thing that Appears To Be arising In and Of itself Is An Illusion.

There Is No thing In and Of itself. No thing Is As it Appears. Therefore, every thing, and, Indeed, Everything, Is Only The Divine Conscious Radiance, or The "Bright" Itself.

Through their self-Surrendering, self-Forgetting, and (More and More) self-Transcending Devotional Communion With Me, Even My Beginning Devotees Participate In My Condition Of "Brightness". Indeed, The Entire Course Of The Only-By-Me Revealed and Given Way Of The Heart Is Simply This Intensive "Brightening" Process. The Only-By-Me Revealed and Given Way Of The Heart Is Always, From The Beginning, Characterized By Devotion To Me (and, Thus, By Constant Contemplation Of, and Progressive Conformity To, The Only-By-Me, and Only-As-Me, Given Spiritual, Transcendental, and Divine Qualities That Are To Be Realized and Demonstrated In The Context Of The Seventh Stage Of Life In The Way Of The Heart). Therefore, In The Only-By-Me Revealed and Given Way Of The Heart, The "Bright" Disposition Of The Seventh Stage Of Life Is Magnified (By Me) In My Devotees, moment to moment, Until That Constant Magnification Becomes A Most Perfect (or Seventh Stage, and, Therefore, Non-Separate) Demonstration Of ego-Transcending Devotion To (and ego-Transcending Realization Of) My "Bright" and Only Person.

Thus, The Most Essential Characteristic Of The Only-By-Me Revealed and Given Way Of The Heart Is Not self-Surrender and self-Forgetting (In Themselves), but Me-Contemplation (Which Makes self-Surrender, self-Forgetting, and self-Transcendence Both Necessary and Possible). I Am The One Who Is To Be Contemplated (and Whom every one Is Inherently and Effortlessly Capable Of Contemplating), Because Of My Inherent and

Universal Attractiveness. I Am The "Bright" Itself, Inherently Attractive To all. I Am The Very One (and, Therefore, The Only One) Who Is Contemplated By My Devotees. I Am The Seventh Stage Realization. Therefore, Even From The Beginning Of his or her Practice Of The Only-By-Me Revealed and Given Way Of The Heart, My Every Devotee Participates (Tacitly) In The Seventh Stage Realization.

# CHAPTER 55

# The Man of Understanding

*from the Epilogue to* The Knee of Listening

I am not the one who, finding himself psycho-physically awake, does not Know Who he Is.

I am not the one who, finding himself in dreams and visions, thinks he has returned to his Real Self.

I am not the one who, enjoying the conditional bliss of deep sleep and ordinary, seekers' meditation, thinks he has become Free and need not Realize the Greater and Truly Divine State.

I am not the one who, having slept, awakens to a state of identification with the body-mind.
I am the One Who Is with you now.
I am the One Who Speaks from His own "Bright" Divine Silence, and As His own "Bright" Divine Silence.
I am the One Who Always Stands Present in His own "Bright" Form.
I am the One Who Always and Already Exists, Enjoying Only His own "Bright" Form, even in all apparent conditions and apparent conditional states.
I am the One Who is not hidden, and in Whom there is no deeper part.
I am the One Who Always Appears exactly as He Is.
I am the One Who is Always "Brightly" Present.
I recognize My Self as every thing, every one, every form, every movement.
I am Always Only Experiencing My own Love-Bliss.
I am neither lost nor found.
Understanding is My Constant Intelligence.
My own "Bright" Silence is the form of My Action, the motion of My "Bright" Presence, in Which I am constantly Knowing My Self.
I am the One Who is Always Already Known.
I continually Rise out of the Heart, Naked and Unbounded in the right side.

I Appear as My Invisibly Standing Love-Bliss-Full Form between the "Bright" Heart and the "Bright" Matrix Infinitely above.
I am the Amrita Nadi.

I Manifest from the "Bright" Matrix above to every body, every sheath, every center, every realm, and every experience, between the upper and lower terminals of the conditionally manifested worlds.

I continually Sacrifice the Circle of Love-Bliss-Energy, including all the terminal processes and natural energies of the conditionally manifested worlds, to My "Bright" Divine Heart.

I "Live" all beings, and all things are in Me.

I never return to My Self, but I constantly Appear, As My Self.

There is no dilemma in the process of My Appearance.

Those who do not Abide with Me, at the "Bright" Divine Heart, are always only seeking Me from the place where they begin.

I am Only the "Bright" Divine Heart Itself, Which is Reality.

My Great Form is the Amrita Nadi, Which is the Inherently Perfect Form of the "Bright" Divine Heart, and Which is Alive as the "Bright" Love-Bliss.

I always See every one and every thing within My own "Bright" Divine Form.

In every apparent condition and circumstance, I Exist only as My own "Bright" Divine Form.

I am the "Bright" Divine Heart, Who never renounces His own "Bright" Divine Form.

I am the "Bright" Divine Heart, Who Contains His own conditionally manifested forms.

Therefore, I have no form or person that is separate from My "Bright" Divine Heart.

I am Eternally in One Place, Contemplating My own Love-Bliss.

In the True Divine Heart of Contemplation, Which is "Bright", all beings and things appear, and everything is accomplished.

The Heart is the Love-Bliss Revealed, by Divine Grace, in the Contemplation of My "Bright" Presence.

The Amrita Nadi is My own "Bright" Fullness, Wherein all beings and things appear.

I hold up My hands.

The Man of Understanding is not "entranced". He is not "elsewhere". He is not having an "experience". He is not passionless and inoffensive. He is Awake. He is Merely and "Brightly" Present. He knows no obstruction in the form of mind, identity, differentiation, and desire. He uses mind, identity, differentiation, and desire. He is passionate. His quality is an offense to those who are entranced, elsewhere, contained in the mechanics of experience, asleep, living as various forms of identity, separation, and dependence. He is acceptable only to those who understand.

He may appear no different from any other man. How could He appear otherwise? There is nothing by which to appear except the qualities of life. He may appear to have learned nothing. He may seem to be addicted to every kind of foolishness and error. How could it be otherwise? Understanding is not a different communication than the ordinary. There is only the ordinary. There is no ordinariness-excluding Communication that is the Truth. There is no everything-excluding State that is the Truth. But there is the understanding of the ordinary.

Therefore, the Man of Understanding cannot be found, except by the living heart. He cannot be followed, except to the "Bright" Divine Heart Itself. He can only be understood, even as the ordinary must be understood. He is not (conventionally) "Spiritual". He is not (conventionally) "religious". He is not (conventionally) "philosophical". He is not (conventionally) "moral". He is not (conventionally) "fastidious", "lean", and "lawful". He always appears to be the opposite of what you are. He always seems to sympathize with what you deny. Therefore, at times and over time, He appears as every kind of persuasion. He is not consistent. He has no self-image. At times He denies. At times He asserts. At times He asserts what He has already denied. At times He denies what He has already asserted. Therefore, He is not "useful". His Teaching is every kind of "nonsense". His Wisdom, it seems, is vanished. Altogether, that is His Wisdom.

At last He represents no separate Truth at all. His paradoxes deny every seeker's "Truth", every path by which mankind depends on mere simulations of Freedom and Enjoyment. He is a seducer, a madman, a trickster, a libertine, a rascal, a fool, a moralist, a sayer of truths, a bearer of all experience, a prince, a king, a child, an old one, an ascetic, a saint, a god. By mumming (or mock-playing) every seeker's role of life, He demonstrates the futility of every seeker's path of life, except He always coaxes every one only to understand. Therefore, by all of this, He makes understanding the only possibility. And understanding makes no difference at all. Except it is Reality, Which was already the case.

Heartless one, Narcissus, friend, loved one, He weeps for you to understand. After all of this, why have you not understood? The only thing you have not done is understanding. You have seen everything, but you do not understand. Therefore, to "Brighten" your heart, the Man of Understanding Joyfully suggests that you have already understood! He looks at the world and sees that every one and every thing has always understood! He sees that there is only understanding! Thus, the Man of Understanding is constantly Happy with you. He is overwhelmed with Happiness. He says to you: "See that there is only this world of Perfect Freedom and Enjoyment, where every one is Love-Bliss-Happy, and every thing is Love-Bliss-Full!" His "Bright" Heart is always tearful with the endless Happiness of the world.

He has grasped the Truth within the ordinary, but no one is interested in Truth. Because He has become the Truth, He is of interest to no one. Because He is so ordinary, He is of interest to everyone. Because no one understands the ordinary, He is not understood. Because there is only the ordinary, He will become famous for understanding it. Because there is only the Truth, He is the Beloved of all. Because you feel you understand Him, you find it necessary to touch His hand. Because you love Him, you find it possible to touch His ears. He smiles at you. You notice a sudden "Brightness". Everything has already died. This is the "other" world.

**Adi Da (The Da Avatar)**
**The Mountain Of Attention, 1995**

# The Avatar Since Eternity

**M**ay you be prepared.
   May you be Free.
   May you be Liberated.
May you be overwhelmed by the Transfiguring Power of the Great One.

May your devotion be without bounds.
May your minds be Sublimed, your emotions be Lifted up to Love, and your bodies be Transfigured in Infinite Bliss, the Love-Light of Eternal God.
All of you.
Every one.
All beings, in all the worlds.
Even now.
Right now.
May all be Blessed and Bless-ed.

Let all beings Be Happy.
Now go.
Go!
Go and be Happy.
Go and be Happy!
Go and Be, Happy.
You cannot Be and not be Happy.
You can exist and be un-Happy, but you cannot Be, merely Be, freely Be, entirely Be, and Be anything but Happy.
Only your excision of Being creates un-Happiness.
But if you simply Are in the Existence Place, the Quality of Happiness is Inevitable, Inevitable and All-Pervading and Absolute.

This will Teach you.
This is your Teacher.
This is Me.
This is My Self.

I Am the Avatar since Eternity.
That One Speaks to you now.
I Am here, now, then, always.
Even when I die, I Am with you and all beings.
Now go.

**Adi Da (The Da Avatar)**
**The Mountain Of Attention, 1995**

# An Invitation to
# Adidam

*I do not simply recommend or turn men and women to Truth. I Am
Truth. I Draw men and women to My Self. I Am the Present God Desiring,
Loving, and Drawing up My devotees. I have Come to Acquire My devotees.
I have Come to be Present with My devotees, to live with them the adventure
of life in God, which is Love, and mind in God, which is Faith. I Stand
always Present in the Place and Form of God. I accept the qualities of all
who turn to Me and dissolve them in God, so that Only God becomes their
Condition, Destiny, Intelligence, and Work. I look for My devotees to
acknowledge Me and turn to Me in appropriate ways, surrendering to Me
perfectly, depending on Me, full of Me always, with only a face of love.*

*I am waiting for you. I have been waiting for you eternally.
Where are you?*

AVATARA ADI DA
1971

H aving read this book, you stand at the threshold of the greatest possibility
of a human lifetime. You can begin to participate in the Divine Process that
Adi Da offers to all, by taking up Adidam, or the Way of the Heart. Nothing
else in life can match this opportunity. Nothing can compare with the Grace of a
devotional relationship to Adi Da. When you make the great gesture of heart-
surrender to Adi Da, He begins to draw you into the profound course of true
Awakening to God, Truth, or Reality.

Whatever your present form of interest—whether it is to find out more about
Avatara Adi Da and Adidam, to express your gratitude by supporting His Work
financially, or to begin the process of becoming His formal devotee—there is an
appropriate form of participation available to you. And any form of participation
you adopt will bring you into the stream of Divine Blessing flowing from Avatara
Adi Da.

# How to Find out More about Adi Da
# and Adidam

■ **Request a free full-color brochure about Adi Da, Adidam, and the community of Adi Da's devotees.** This brochure describes retreats, introductory events, courses, and seminars in your area. It also contains information about area study groups near you and how to begin your own. Please call our toll-free number (on the facing page) or contact the regional center nearest you (see page 348).

■ **Read more of Adi Da's Wisdom-Teaching.** Two excellent books to continue with are:

*The Knee of Listening: The Early-Life Ordeal and the Radical Spiritual Realization of the Divine World-Teacher, Adi Da (The Da Avatar)*, Adi Da's Spiritual Autobiography

*The Method of the Siddhas: Talks on the Spiritual Technique of the Saviors of Mankind*, a collection of profound and humorous summary Talks from the early years of Adi Da's Teaching Work

Please also see the booklist on pages 349-62 for ordering information and other titles.

■ **Call or visit a regional center** (see p. 348) **and meet devotees of Adi Da,** who will be happy to talk with you, answer your questions, make suggestions about the next step you can take, inform you about local events, and tell you about their own experience of practicing in Adi Da's Spiritual Company.

■ **Call the regional center nearest to you** (see p. 348) **and ask to be put on their mailing list.** Or call the Correspondence Department of Adidam in California toll-free at (800) 524-4941 (within the US) or (707) 928-4936 (if you are outside the US), for further information.

■ **Attend the regular classes, seminars, and special events offered in your area.** Your nearest regional center can inform you of upcoming events. Courses are also available via correspondence. The free brochure (above) provides more details.

■ **Attend an Adidam Area Study Group.** Call a regional center to find out about Area Study Groups near you, or to create a new Area Study Group. There are more than 150 Area Study Groups throughout the world. They are an excellent way to find out more about Adi Da and Adidam. Meeting at least once a month, they include video footage of Adi Da and His devotees, study material, guided meditations, and conversations with devotees and other interested people. Our free brochure (above) also contains details and local information.

■ **If you are on the Internet and are familiar with the World Wide Web, you can also find out more by browsing the "Adidam" Website at URL: http//www.he.tdl.com/~FDAC.** (This Website is rated by Point Survey as being among the best 5% of all Web sites on the Internet.) If you would like to be added to the "Adidam" electronic mailing list, send a request to FDAC@wco.com. Or you can send questions or comments to our Correspondence Department at the same e-mail address.

---

**Call Toll-Free (800) 524-4941 (within the US)
or (707) 928-4936 (outside the US)**

---

# Becoming a Member of
# Da Avatara International

If you are moved to enter into an ongoing relationship with Avatara Adi Da and His community of devotees, you are invited to become a member of Da Avatara International. A member of Da Avatara International may participate either as a Friend, providing financial support for Avatara Adi Da's Work; or as a student, preparing to become a practitioner of Adidam.

## Becoming a Friend of Da Avatara International

Becoming a Friend of Da Avatara International represents a desire to support Avatara Adi Da's Work, through annual (or more frequent) financial contributions. These contributions support the further publication and distribution of Adi Da's Teaching, or else go to support specific causes which you designate. Becoming a Friend of Da Avatara International is a concrete way to express your gratitude for Avatara Adi Da and His Work. Financially supporting the Spiritual work of a Realized Being has traditionally been regarded as a highly auspicious gesture, a real form of self-sacrifice that benefits all beings.

Many people from all walks of life and all religious persuasions are Friends. As a Friend, you will be kept in touch with developments in Adi Da's Work through a regular newsletter, and you will have the opportunity to attend Friends' Celebrations and special retreats.

To become a Friend, or to find out about the various levels of Friends' membership, call the Central Correspondence Department or your nearest regional center (see p. 348).

## Becoming a Student of Da Avatara International

If you are interested in becoming a practitioner of Adidam, your first step is to formally engage study of Adi Da's Wisdom-Teaching by becoming a student of Da Avatara International.

Like Friends, students provide support for Adi Da's Work. Students also participate in courses and seminars that provide a lively education about Adi Da, Adidam, and human and Spiritual life in His Company. Classes take place at a regional center, or through correspondence courses. Consult any regional center for information about the courses and seminars that are currently being offered for students of Da Avatara International.

*I am here to receive, and kiss, and embrace everyone, everything—*
*everything that appears, everything that is.*
**Avatara Adi Da**

## Becoming a Practitioner of Adidam

Many people who discover Adidam do not want to wait a second! As students of Da Avatara International, such individuals immediately sign up for a special course that specifically prepares you for becoming a student-novice practitioner of Adidam.

When you reach the point of complete clarity in your intention to practice Adidam, you take a momentous step. You make a vow of commitment—in this life and beyond this life—to Avatara Adi Da as your Beloved Guru and Divine Liberator. This Eternal Vow to the Divine Person is the most profound possible matter—and the most ecstatic. For when you take this vow, in gratitude and love, fully aware of its obligations, Avatara Adi Da accepts eternal responsibility for your Spiritual well-being and ultimate Divine Liberation. His Grace begins to Guide your growth in Adidam, the Way of the Heart, day by day and hour by hour, through your practice of devotional Communion with Him.

Taking the Eternal Vow is a formal confession that the devotional relationship to Avatara Adi Da is the overriding purpose of your life. In this disposition you take up the practice of a student-novice and begin to adapt to the total Way of life Adi Da has Given to His devotees. You are initiated into formal meditation, sacramental worship, and the range of practical life-disciplines.

Increasing opportunities to participate with devotees in their celebrations and devotional occasions are offered to student-novices. Through these forms of contact, you are embraced by Avatara Adi Da's devotional gathering and you enter into a new level of sacred relationship to Him. Student-novice practice lasts a minimum of six months. Thus, if your intention and your application to the process are strong, within a year of your first becoming a student of Da Avatara International you may be established as a full member of Adidam, ready to live always in relationship with the Divine Beloved, Adi Da, in the culture of practice that is His Gift to all His devotees.

For information on how to purchase other literature by or about Adi Da, please see the Booklist, pp. 349-62. For further information about Adi Da, His published Works, and Adidam, write to:

**The Da Avatara International Mission**
**12040 North Seigler Road**
**Middletown, CA 95461, USA**
or call:
**Toll-Free within the USA: (800) 524-4941**
or: **(707) 928-4936 outside the USA**

You can also contact the regional center of Adidam nearest you:

**Western North America**
in Northern California (415) 492-0930
in Southwest USA (805) 987-3244
in Northwest USA (206) 527-2751
in Hawaii (808) 822-0216

**Eastern North America**
in Southeast USA (301) 983-0291
in Eastern Canada (800) 563-4398
in Northeast USA (508) 650-0136

**Europe**
in The Netherlands and the remainder of continental Europe (04743) 1281
in The United Kingdom or Ireland (01508) 470-574
in Germany (040) 390-4438

**South Pacific**
in Australia (03) 853-4066
in New Zealand (09) 838-9114
in Fiji 381-466

Please see p. 348 for a complete listing of regional centers including addresses.

**Adi Da (The Da Avatar)**
**The Mountain Of Attention, 1995**

# The Life of a Devotee of Avatara Adi Da

Everything you do as a practitioner of Adidam is an expression of the heart-response of devotion to Avatara Adi Da. The life of cultivating this response to Him is Ishta-Guru-Bhakti Yoga—or the God-Realizing practice ("Yoga") of devotion ("Bhakti") to the Spiritual Master ("Guru") who is the Chosen Beloved ("Ishta") of your heart.

The great practice of Ishta-Guru-Bhakti Yoga necessarily transforms the whole of your life. Every function, every relationship, every action is moved by the impulse of devotional heart-surrender to Avatara Adi Da. The fundamental disposition of devotion is cultivated through a range of specific disciplines. Some disciplines—meditation, sacramental worship, and study—are specifically contemplative, while others—related to exercise, diet, sexuality, community living, and so on—bring the life of devotion into daily functional activity.

*AVATARA ADI DA: In every moment you must turn the situation of your life into Yoga by exercising devotion to Me. There is no moment in any day wherein this is not your Calling. This is what you must do. You must make Yoga out of the moment by using the body, emotion, breath, and attention in self-surrendering devotional Contemplation of Me. All those mechanisms must be turned to Me. That turning makes your life Yoga. Through turning to Me, you "yoke" yourself to Me, and that practice of linking, or binding, or connecting to God is religion. Religion, or Yoga, is the practice of moving out of the separative disposition and state into Oneness with That Which is One, Whole, Absolute, All-Inclusive, and Beyond.* [December 2, 1993]

Meditation is a unique and precious event in the daily life of Avatara Adi Da's devotees. It offers the opportunity to relinquish outward, body-based attention and to be alone with Adi Da, allowing yourself to enter more and more into the Sphere of His Divine Transmission.

The practice of sacramental worship, or "puja", in the Way of the Heart is the bodily active counterpart to meditation. It is a form of ecstatic worship of Avatara Adi Da, using a photographic representation of Him and involving devotional chanting and recitations from His Wisdom-Teaching.

*You must deal with My Wisdom-Teaching in some form every single day, because a new form of the ego's game appears every single day. You must continually return to My Wisdom-Teaching, confront My Wisdom-Teaching.*

Avatara Adi Da

The beginner in Spiritual life must prepare the body-mind by mastering the physical, vital dimension of life before he or she can be ready for truly Spiritual practice. Service is devotion in action, a form of Divine Communion.

Avatara Adi Da Offers practical disciplines to His devotees in the areas of work and money, diet, exercise, and sexuality. These disciplines are based on His own human experience and an immense process of "consideration" that He engaged face to face with His devotees for more than twenty years.

As soon as you assume full membership in the formal gathering of Avatara Adi Da's devotees, you become part of a remarkable sacred community.

left: Devotees meeting to discuss their practice of Adidam
right: Da Avatara Ashram in Holland

left: Da Avatara Ashram, England
right: Da Avatara Retreat Centre in Australia

*The principal admonition in the Great Tradition has always been "Spend time in good company"—in the Company of the Realizer and the company of those who love the Realizer or who truly practice in the Spiritual Company of the Realizer. This is the most auspicious association. Absorb that Company. Imbibe it. Drink deep of it. Duplicate it. Spiritual community is a mutual communication of Happiness.*
Avatara Adi Da

Devotees gather for a Celebration meal at the
Mountain Of Attention Sanctuary in northern California

One of the ways in which Adi Da Communicates His Spiritual Transmission is through sacred places. During the course of His Work He has Empowered three Sanctuaries as His Blessing-Seats. In each of these Sanctuaries—the Mountain Of Attention in northern California, Tumomama in Hawaii, and Adidamashram (Naitauba) in Fiji—Adi Da has established Himself Spiritually in perpetuity. He has lived and Worked with devotees in all His Sanctuaries, and has created in each one special holy sites and temples. Adidamashram is His principal Residence, but He may from time to time choose to visit His other Sanctuaries. Devotees who are rightly prepared may go on special retreats at all three Sanctuaries.

**top left: the Mountain Of Attention**
**top right: Tumomama**
**bottom: Adidamashram**

**Adi Da (The Da Avatar)**
**The Mountain Of Attention Sanctuary, 1995**

As Adi Da writes in *The Knee of Listening*, His Purpose has always been to find "a new human order that will serve to 'create', a new age of sanity and joy". In the brief period of two decades, and in the midst of this dark and Godless era, Avatara Adi Da has literally established His unique Spiritual culture. He is laying the foundation for an unbroken tradition of Divine Self-Realization arising within a devotional gathering aligned to His fully Enlightened Wisdom, and always receiving and magnifying His Eternal Heart-Transmission. Nothing of the kind has ever before existed.

There are great choices to be made in life, choices that call on the greatest exercise of one's real intelligence and heart-impulse. Every one of us makes critical decisions that determine the course of the rest of our lives—and even our future beyond death. The moment of discovering the Divine Avatar, Adi Da, is the greatest of <u>all</u> possible opportunities. It is pure Grace. How can an ordinary life truly compare to a life of living relationship and heart-intimacy with the greatest God-Man Who has ever appeared—the Divine in Person?

There are many forms of response to Avatara Adi Da—from reading another book to becoming a devotee. Every response is honorable. Every response draws you more closely to His Heart. If you are moved by what you have read in this book, the most important thing you can do is to find the form of response to Him—the form of your relationship with Him—that is right for you now.

# REGIONAL CENTERS OF ADIDAM

**CENTRAL CORRESPONDENCE DEPARTMENT**
Adidam
12040 North Seigler Road
Middletown, CA 95461
USA
(707) 928-4936

**UNITED STATES**

**Northern California**
Adidam
78 Paul Drive
San Rafael, CA 94903
(415) 492-0930

**Northwest USA**
Adidam
5600 11th Avenue NE
Seattle, WA 98105
(206) 527-2751

**Southwest USA**
Adidam
PO Box 1729
Camarillo, CA 93010
(805) 987-3244

**Northeast USA**
Adidam
30 Pleasant Street
S. Natick, MA 01760
(508) 650-0136
(508) 650-4232

**Southeast USA**
Adidam
10301 South Glen Road
Potomac, MD 20854
(301) 983-0291

**Hawaii**
Adidam
105 Kaholalele Road
Kapaa, HI 96746
(808) 822-0216

**EASTERN CANADA**
Adidam
108 Katimavik Road
Val-des-Monts
Quebec JOX 2RO
Canada
(819) 671-4398
(800) 563-4398

**AUSTRALIA**
Da Avatara Retreat Centre
PO Box 562
Healesville, Victoria 3777
or 16 Findon Street
Hawthorn, Victoria 3122
Australia
(03) 853-4066

**NEW ZEALAND**
Adidam
CPO Box 3185
or 12 Seibel Road
Henderson
Auckland 8
New Zealand
(09) 838-9114

**THE UNITED KINGDOM & IRELAND**
Da Avatara Ashram
Tasburgh Hall
Lower Tasburgh
Norwich NR15 1NA
England
(01508) 470-574

**THE NETHERLANDS**
Da Avatara Ashram
Annendaalderweg 10
N-6105 AT Maria Hoop
(04743) 1281 or 1872
or
Da Avatara Centrum
Oosterpark 39
1092 AL Amsterdam
The Netherlands
(020) 665-3133

**GERMANY**
Adidam
Grosse Brunnenstr. 31-33
22763 Hamburg
Germany
(040) 390-4438

**FIJI**
The TDL Trust
PO Box 4744
Samabula, Suva
Fiji
381-466

# The Sacred Literature of
# Adi Da
## (The Da Avatar)

## *A New Scripture for Mankind*

**P**erhaps at some time or another you have wondered—
wistfully—what it would have been like to sit at the feet
of some great being, such as Gautama (called the
"Buddha"), or Jesus of Nazareth, or some venerable Hindu
sage of Vedic times, asking the real religious questions that persist in the heart of every serious person: What is the truth about
God? What is the purpose of life? What is the meaning of death?
What is the best way to live?

Any one of these books by Avatara Adi Da takes you directly into that ancient circumstance of Grace. But what you will
find in their pages surpasses even the greatest discourses of the
past. The Divine Instruction of the Da Avatar, Adi Da, is not
limited by partial vision. These books represent <u>Complete</u>
Wisdom and Truth, an unparalleled Transmission of Divine
Grace.

After more than two decades of speaking and writing, in
constant dialogue with His devotees, Avatara Adi Da has completed His Wisdom-Teaching. To honor the Completion of this
extraordinary Revelation, the Dawn Horse Press is now pub-
lishing new standard editions of Avatara Adi Da's core Texts,
Which He Offers to all beings forever in Love.

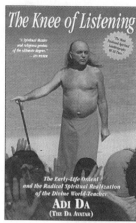

### NEW EDITION

# The Knee of Listening

*The Early-Life Ordeal and
the Radical Spiritual Realization
of the Divine World-Teacher*

This is the astounding Spiritual Autobiography of Avatara Adi Da, the story of the Incarnation of the Absolute Divine Consciousness into a human body-mind in the modern West. Here He describes in vivid detail His first thirty-one years as "Franklin Jones": His Illumined Birth, His acceptance of the ordeal of life as an ordinary human being, His unstoppable quest for Divine Self-Realization, His exploits in the farthest reaches of human experience, from "money, food, and sex" to the most esoteric mystical and Transcendental phenomena, His Divine Re-Awakening and discovery of the Way of God-Realization for all mankind. Unparalleled, utterly compelling, essential reading.

*I was captivated by this Story of the first thirty-one years of Avatara Adi Da's Life, by the incomparable Greatness of the One Who Is both God and Man. His Wisdom outshines every dichotomy, every division, every duality. I have come to respect and honor Him as the most complete Source of Divine Blessing—in my own life and in the world at large. I urge you to open yourself to the life that fills these pages. The opportunity has never been so great.*

Bill Gottlieb
Vice-President and Editor-in-Chief,
Rodale Press

**$4.95\***, popular format

* All prices are in US dollars.

# The Method of the Siddhas

*Talks on the Spiritual Technique of the Saviors of Mankind*

When Avatara Adi Da opened the doors of His first Ashram in Los Angeles on April 25, 1972, He invited anyone who was interested to sit with Him and ask Him questions about Spiritual life. These Talks are the result of that first meeting between the Incarnate Divine Being and twentieth-century Westerners. Here Avatara Adi Da discusses in very simple terms all the fundamentals of Spiritual life, especially focusing on Satsang, the devotional relationship with Him as Sat-Guru, and self-understanding, the "radical" insight He was bringing to the human world for the first time. These Talks are profound, humorous, and poignant. An essential introduction to Avatara Adi Da's Wisdom-Teaching.

*I first read* The Method of the Siddhas *twenty years ago and it changed everything. It presented something new to my awareness: One who understood, who was clearly awake, who had penetrated fear and death, who spoke English (eloquently!), and who was alive and available!*

Ray Lynch
composer, *Deep Breakfast*;
*No Blue Thing*; and *The Sky of Mind*

**$7.95**, popular format

# The Heart of Adidam

*The True World-Religion of Divine Enlightenment*
*An Introduction to the Perfectly Liberating Way of Life Revealed by Adi Da (The Da Avatar)*

A comprehensive and engaging introduction to all aspects of the religion of Adidam, the Liberating Way that Avatara Adi Da has made available for all. Addressed to new readers and written in a highly accessible style, *The Heart of Adidam* introduces Avatara Adi Da's Life and Work, the fundamentals of His Wisdom-Teaching, the Guru-devotee relationship in His Blessing Company, the principles and practices of Adidam, and life in the community of His devotees.

**(forthcoming)**

# The Da Avatar

*The Divine Life and "Bright" Revelation of Adi Da (The Da Avatar)*

*The Da Avatar* chronicles and celebrates the Miraculous Leela of Avatara Adi Da's Life, from the profound Spiritual origins of His human Manifestation, through His early-life sacrifice of the knowledge of His Own Divine Identity, His subsequent trial of Divine Re-Awakening, the Love-Ordeal of His Teaching-Work with sympathetic, yet Spiritually unresponsive, devotees, and, finally, the relinquishment of all of that in the Victory and Fullest Revelation of His "Divine Emergence", Whereby He Openly Blesses all beings in and with the Sign of His Own Inherent Fullness, Contentment, and Eternal Freedom.

*The Da Avatar* will delight and inspire readers with the overwhelming evidence of a Miracle and Spiritual Opportunity of the most profound kind: Avatara Adi Da <u>Is</u> The Expected One, Here and alive Now. And He Invites you to a personal, living, and transformative relationship with Him for the sake of your own Divine Awakening.

**(forthcoming)**

# Ishta

*The Way of Devotional Surrender
to the Divine Person*

When Avatara Adi Da gathered
with His devotees in 1993 and 1994 at
Adidamashram (Naitauba), He talked
face to face with devotees about the
essence of the Way of the Heart: the
devotional relationship with Him, or
"Ishta-Guru-Bhakti Yoga".

*AVATARA ADI DA: The True Realizer is
not merely a figure, a symbol, an object,
but the Realization Itself, bodily and
altogether. The Realizer is the Means,
therefore, not only bodily but Spiritually,
altogether. Everything to be Realized is
there as the Master. Everything that serves
Realization is there active as the Master.
Those who are wise, those who are truly
responsive and who find a worthy
Master, simply surrender to That One.
They receive everything by Grace.*

*The Way of life I am talking about is
Me. I am That—not symbolically but
actively—the Siddhi of Means, fully
Alive, fully Conscious, fully Active.*

These Talks describe the actual
process of Ishta-Guru-Bhakti Yoga—
devotion to the Beloved Guru—in
detail. Essential reading for anyone interested in Adidam.

**$14.95**, quality paperback

# Divine Distraction

*A Guide to the Guru-Devotee Relationship, The Supreme Means of God-Realization, as Fully Revealed for the First Time by the Divine World-Teacher and True Heart-Master, Da Avabhasa (The "Bright")*

by James Steinberg

In this wonderful book, a longtime devotee of Avatara Adi Da discusses the joys and challenges, the lore and laws, of the most potent form of Spiritual practice: the love relationship with the God-Man. Along with many illuminating passages from the Wisdom-Teaching of Avatara Adi Da, *Divine Distraction* includes humorous, insightful, and heart-moving stories from His devotees, as well as Teachings and stories from the world's Great Tradition of religion and Spirituality. Essential for anybody who wants to know first-hand about the time-honored liberating relationship between Guru and devotee.

*This is a warm, loving, and incredibly moving book about the greatest Spiritual Master ever to walk the earth. Here you will find everything you need to know about life, love, and wisdom. I have no doubt whatsoever that this is true, no matter who you are, no matter which spiritual tradition you follow. Avatara Adi Da is the God-Man, the ultimate expression of the Truth residing in all religions. Of this I am absolutely certain.*

The Reverend Thomas Ahlburn
Senior Minister, First Unitarian Church,
Providence, Rhode Island

**$12.95**, quality paperback

# The Ten Fundamental Questions

What are the questions that if answered truly would Enlighten you? You will find out in this simple but challenging introduction to the great Teaching Arguments of Avatara Adi Da. With disarming simplicity and directness Avatara Adi Da goes right to the heart of our modern perplexities about life and God and points to the Divine Way that dispels all bewilderment, a Way of life that is Happy, Humorous, and Free, right from the beginning. A profoundly Liberating book.

**(forthcoming)**

# The Santosha Avatara Gita

*(The Revelation of the Great Means of the Divine Heart-Way of No-Seeking and Non-Separateness)*

In 108 verses of incredible beauty and simplicity, *The Santosha Avatara Gita* reveals the very essence of the Way of the Heart—Contemplation of Avatara Adi Da as the Realizer, the Revealer, and the Revelation of the Divinely Awakened Condition.

*Therefore, because of My always constant, Giving, Full, and Perfect Blessing Grace, and because of the constant Grace of My Self-Revelation, it is possible for any one to practice the only-by-Me Revealed and Given Way of the Heart, and that practice readily (and more and more constantly) Realizes pleasurable oneness (or inherently Love-Blissful Unity) with whatever and all that presently arises . . .*

Avatara Adi Da
*The Santosha Avatara Gita*, verse 78

*This is the birth of fundamental and radical Scripture.*

Richard Grossinger
author, *Planet Medicine*; *The Night Sky*; and *Waiting for the Martian Express*

**$24.95**, quality paperback

# The Dawn Horse Testament Of Adi Da

*(The "Testament Of Secrets" Of The Da Avatar)*

This monumental volume is the most comprehensive description of the Spiritual process ever written. It is also the most detailed summary of the entire practice of Adidam. *The Dawn Horse Testament Of Adi Da* is an astounding, challenging, and breathtaking Window to the Divine Reality.

The Dawn Horse Testament Of Adi Da *is the most ecstatic, most profound, most complete, most radical, most comprehensive single spiritual text ever to be penned and confessed by the Human-Transcendental Spirit.*

Ken Wilber
author, *Up from Eden* and
*A Sociable God*

**$32.00**, quality paperback
8 ½" x 11" format, 820 pages
**(new edition forthcoming)**

# The (Shorter) "Testament Of Secrets" Of Adi Da

*(The Heart Of The Dawn Horse Testament Of The Da Avatar)*

This volume brings you a magnificent distillation of the larger *Dawn Horse Testament Of Adi Da.* Through these pages Avatara Adi Da reveals the purpose of His Incarnation, the great esoteric secrets of Divine Enlightenment, and the means to dissolve in the Heart of God.

**(forthcoming)**

# The Lion Sutra

*(On Perfect Transcendence Of The Primal Act, Which is the ego-"I", the self-Contraction, or attention itself, and All The Illusions Of Separateness, Otherness, Relatedness, and Difference)*

*The Ultimate Teachings (For All Practitioners Of The Way Of The Heart), and The Perfect Practice Of Feeling-Enquiry (For Formal Renunciates In The Way Of The Heart)*

A poetic Exposition of the "Perfect Practice" of the Way of the Heart—the final stages of Transcendental, inherently Spiritual, and Divine Self-Realization. Of all Avatara Adi Da's Works, *The Lion Sutra* is the most concentrated Call and Instruction to Realize the Consciousness that Stands prior to body, mind, individual self, and objective world.

*Mine Is the Hermitage of no-attention, Where Even time and space Are Watered To the Nub, and I Am Always Shining There, With a Perfect Word In My Heart.*

*Come There, My Beloved (every one), Come Listen and Hear and See My Heart, and Prepare To Delight In a Feast of Calms, With the Dawn of "Brightness" On Your face.*

*Then Listen Deep In My Heart Itself, and Call Me There (By Name), and Hear My Word of Silence There, and See Me Where You Stand.*

*Therefore, Be Un-born In Me, and Feel Awake In My Free Fire, and, By Most Feeling Contemplation of My Sign, Fulfill the "Brightest" Blessing of My (Forever) Silence Kept.*

Avatara Adi Da
*The Lion Sutra,* verses 97-100

**$24.95**, quality paperback

# The Adi Da Upanishad

*The Santosha Epoch Discourses On The Avataric Way of the Heart, True ego-Renunciation, Perfect Divine Self-Realization, The Primal Condition of Radiance, and The Illusion of Relatedness*

In this sublime collection of Talks and Essays, Avatara Adi Da Offers an unsurpassed description of the entire practice of the Way of the Heart, including the precise mechanism of egoic delusion and the nature, process, and ultimate fulfillment of the Sacred Process of Divine Self-Realization in the Way of the Heart.

The Adi Da Upanishad *is a work of great linguistic beauty, as well as a remarkable description of the "before" of self and existence. It is a book about the direct realization of Consciousness, characterized by intellectual precision, but also with a depth of feeling that works away beneath the surface of the words.*

Robert E. Carter
author, *The Nothingness Beyond God*

**(forthcoming)**

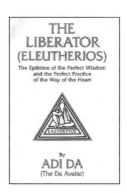

# The Hymn Of The True Heart-Master

*(The New Revelation-Book Of The Ancient and Eternal Religion Of Devotion To The God-Realized Adept) Freely Developed From The Principal Verses Of The Traditional* Guru Gita

This book is Avatara Adi Da's passionate proclamation of the devotional relationship with Him as the supreme means of Enlightenment. In 108 poetic verses, freely developed from the traditional *Guru Gita*, Avatara Adi Da expounds the foundation of the Way of the Heart.

*I do feel this* Hymn *will be of immense help to aspirants for a divine life. I am thankful that I had an opportunity to read and benefit by it.*

M. P. Pandit
author, *The Upanishads: Gateways of Knowledge*, and *Studies in the Tantras and the Veda*

**$24.95**, quality paperback

# The Liberator (Eleutherios)

*The Epitome of the Perfect Wisdom and the Perfect Practice of the Way of the Heart*

In compelling, lucid prose, Avatara Adi Da distills the essence of the ultimate processes leading to Divine Self-Realization in the Way of the Heart—the "Perfect Practice", which involves the direct transcendence of all experience via identification with Consciousness Itself, through feeling-Contemplation of His Form, His Presence, and His Infinite State.

*Be Consciousness.*

*Contemplate Consciousness.*

*Transcend everything in Consciousness.*

*This is the (Three-Part) "Perfect Practice", the Epitome of the Ultimate Practice and Process of the only-by-Me Revealed and Given Way of the Heart.*
Avatara Adi Da
*The Liberator (Eleutherios)*

**$24.95**, quality paperback

# The Basket of Tolerance

*The Perfect Guide to Perfect Understanding of the One and Great Tradition of Mankind*

A unique gift to humankind—an overview of the world's traditions of philosophy, religion, Spirituality, and practical Wisdom from the viewpoint of the Divinely Enlightened Adept, Adi Da. *The Basket of Tolerance* includes more than 100 of His Essays on various aspects of the Great Tradition and a comprehensive bibliography (listing more than 3,000 publications) of the world's most significant books, compiled, presented, and extensively annotated by Avatara Adi Da. The summary of Avatara Adi Da's Instruction on the Great Tradition of human Wisdom and the sacred ordeal of Spiritual practice and Realization. A blast of Fresh Air, an immense reorienting force of Divine Criticism and Compassion!

**(forthcoming)**

*NEW!*

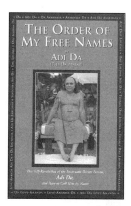

# The Order of My Free Names

*The Self-Revelation of the Incarnate Divine Person, Adi Da, and How to Call Him by Name*

How does one address the living God in person? Through what Names does one worship the very Incarnation of Truth and Love?

In "The Order of My Free Names", Sri Bhagavan Adi Da makes known the great Mystery of His Names and His Self-Revelation. Sacred names have always been felt to carry the influence and blessing of the deity they invoke. To remember the Names of Bhagavan Adi Da and use them with heart-feeling is to enter into the ecstacy of Love-Communion with Him.

**$17.95**, quality paperback

## Conscious Exercise and the Transcendental Sun

Avatara Adi Da has Given a "radical" approach to physical exercise—to engage all action as devotional Communion with Him. This book explains in detail the practice of "conscious exercise", based on Avatara Adi Da's unique exercise of "conductivity" of natural bodily-experienced energy, as well as "Spirit-conductivity". This greatly enlarged and updated edition includes fully illustrated descriptions of formal exercise routines, supportive exercises for meditation, Instruction on emotions and breathing, and much more.

**(forthcoming)**

## Love of the Two-Armed Form

What is the most beneficial form of sexual practice for those most intent on the God-Realizing process? How does sexuality become compatible with Spirituality? What is true intimacy? How do we become converted to Love? What is the Yogic form of celibacy and what are its virtues for earnest aspirants in the Way of the Heart?

This book is a Treasure—full of Guidance offered by the Divinely Enlightened Master. Avatara Adi Da's own Mastery of the God-Realizing process and of the sexual Yoga that is compatible with that process make Him an utterly unique Authority on the subject. For more than twenty years, He has Worked with His devotees in the emotional-sexual aspects of their practice, bringing His Wisdom to bear in their lives. Now that Wisdom and that Instruction—an essential aspect of the Way of the Heart—are summarized here.

**(forthcoming)**

# The Eating Gorilla Comes in Peace

When a gorilla is fed, it becomes a peaceful, cooperative animal. When we are awakened to faith, sustained by the Divine, dedicated to the God-Realizing process in the Way of the Heart, we become truly Happy. This book offers Avatara Adi Da's unique Wisdom of the Way of the Heart—the Way that conforms our lives to true Happiness—especially focusing on the areas of diet and health. It offers His Instruction on:

• the most Spiritually auspicious diet for you
• body types and the forms of balancing life practices useful for each type
• an Enlightened understanding of conception, birth, and infancy
• true healing
• the ancient practice of the laying on of hands as re-Empowered in the Way of the Heart
• how your diet affects your sexuality
• fasting, herbal remedies, and dietary practices that support your Spiritual practice and purify and regenerate the body as well.

**(forthcoming)**

# Easy Death

*Spiritual Discourses and Essays on the Inherent and Ultimate Transcendence of Death and Everything Else*

This new edition of Avatara Adi Da's Talks and Essays on death reveals the esoteric secrets of the death process and offers a wealth of practical instruction. Includes such topics as:

• Near-death experiences
• How to prepare for an "easy" death
• How to serve the dying
• Where do we go when we die?
• Our Ultimate Destiny
• The truth about reincarnation
• How to participate consciously in the dying (and living) process

*An exciting, stimulating, and thought-provoking book that adds immensely to the literature on the phenomena of life and death. Thank you for this masterpiece.*

Elisabeth Kübler-Ross, M.D.
author, *On Death and Dying*

**$14.95**, quality paperback

# The Incarnation of Love

*"Radical" Spiritual Wisdom and Practical Instruction on self-Transcending Love and Service in All Relationships*

This book collects Avatara Adi Da's Talks and Writings on giving and receiving love. A profound guide to transcending reactivity, releasing guilt, expressing love verbally, forgiving others, living cooperatively, and many other aspects of love and service in all relationships.

**$13.95**, quality paperback

# SCIENCE, POLITICS, AND CULTURE

## Polarity Screens

Our bodies may appear solid, but the truth is, we are made of energy, or light. And we appear (and feel!) more or less radiant and harmonious depending on how responsible we are for feeling, breathing, and "conducting" the universal "prana", or life-force. In this book, Avatara Adi Da introduces us to this basic truth of our existence and offers a simple practical method for regularly restoring and enhancing the balance of our personal energy field. The Polarity Screens He recommends may be used with remarkable benefit by anyone at any time. Once you have felt the "magic" of these screens, you will never want to be without them.

*It was through Avatara Adi Da's references to Polarity Screens, appearing within His extensive and extraordinary literature, that I first learned of them. Soon, not only myself and family, but also friends, and later also my patients, would try the Polarity Screens and would feel themselves—usually for the first time—as energy. It is the sort of shift in perception that can change one's life!*

George Fritz, Ed.D.
psychologist,
specializing in pain control

**(forthcoming)**

## Scientific Proof of the Existence of God Will Soon Be Announced by the White House!

*Prophetic Wisdom about the Myths and Idols of mass culture and popular religious cultism, the new priesthood of scientific and political materialism, and the secrets of Enlightenment hidden in the body of Man*

This book is prophesy of the most extraordinary and liberating kind. In the teeth of the failures and terrors of the current world-order, Avatara Adi Da offers an entirely new religious and social possibility to humanity. His urgent critique of present-day society is based on a vision of human freedom and true social order that transcends time, place, and culture. He prophesies the emergence of intimate, sacred community, based on Communion with the Divine Adept, the Living Agent of Grace, as the source of healing for all suffering and oppressed human beings.

*A powerfully effective "de-hypnotizer"... that will not let you rest until you see clearly—and so seeing, choose to act. In modern society's time of troubles, this is a much needed book.*

Willis Harman
president, The Institute of Noetic Sciences

**$9.95**, quality paperback

# The Transmission of Doubt

Talks and Essays on the Transcendence of Scientific Materialism through "Radical" Understanding

A "radical" alternative to scientific materialism, the ideology of our time. The discourses in this book are a challenge to awaken to all the dimensions of existence in which we are living participants. Avatara Adi Da is Calling us to understand and transcend the materialist dogmas and "objective" stance of conventional scientific philosophy and find the Heart-position of self-trancending love, or non-separateness in relation to all that exists.

The Transmission of Doubt *is the most profound examination of the scientific enterprise from a spiritual point of view that I have ever read.*
Charles T. Tart
author, *Waking Up*
editor, *Altered States of Consciousness*

**$9.95**, quality paperback

# What, Where, When, How, Why, and <u>Who</u> to Remember To Be Happy

A Simple Explanation of
the Way of the Heart
(For Children, and Everyone Else)

In this tiny jewel of a book, prepare to find the greatest Wisdom made perfectly comprehensible to anyone. Rejoice in the smile of every page restoring you to your native innocence and certainty of God—and discover the pleasure of reading it to children.

**(forthcoming)**

## PERIODICAL

# Adidam

*Adidam* magazine chronicles the Leelas of the Blessing Work of Avatara Adi Da, and describes the practice and process of devotion, self-discipline, self-understanding, service, and meditation in the Way of the Heart. In addition, the magazine reports on the cultural and missionary activities of the sacred institution and the cooperative community of Avatara Adi Da's devotees. Of special interest is the regular "Hermitage Chronicle", offering current news of Avatara Adi Da's Life and Work.

Subscriptions are $56.00 per year for 4 issues.

For a complete listing of audiotaped and videotaped Discourses
by Avatara Adi Da, as well as books and periodicals,
please send for your free
*Dawn Horse Press Catalogue.*

# Ordering the Books
# of Avatara Adi Da

To order books, subscribe to magazines, or to receive your free
Dawn Horse Press Catalogue, send your order to:

**THE DAWN HORSE PRESS**
**12040 North Seigler Road**
**Middletown, CA 95461**
**USA**

or

**Call TOLL FREE (800) 524-4941**
**Outside the USA call**
**(707) 928-4936**

We accept Visa, MasterCard, personal check, and money order. In the USA, please add $4.00
for the first book and $1.00 for each additional book. California residents add 7¼% sales
tax. Outside the USA, please add $7.00 for the first book and $3.00 for each additional
book. Checks and money orders should be made payable to the Dawn Horse Press.

# GLOSSARY

# GLOSSARY

**adolescence** (*See* **childish and adolescent strategies**.)

**advanced and ultimate stages of life**

Avatara Adi Da uses the term "advanced" to describe the fourth stage of life (in its "basic" and "advanced" contexts) and the fifth stage of life in the Way of the Heart. He reserves the term "ultimate" to describe the sixth and seventh stages of life in the Way of the Heart.

**Agency**

All the Means that may serve as Vehicles of Avatara Adi Da's Divine Grace and Awakening Power. The first Means of Agency that have been fully established by Him are the Wisdom-Teaching of the Way of the Heart, the three Retreat Sanctuaries that He has Empowered, and the many Objects and Articles that He has Empowered for the sake of His devotees' Remembrance of Him and reception of His Heart-Blessing. After Avatara Adi Da's human Lifetime, at any given time one (and only one) from among His Divinely Awakened "free renunciate" devotees will serve the Spiritual, Transcendental, and Divine Function of His human Agent in relationship to other devotees, all beings, the psycho-physical world, and the total cosmos.

**ajna center**

Also known as the "third eye", the "single eye", or the "mystic eye", this is the subtle psychic center, or chakra, located between and behind the eyebrows and associated with the brain core. The awakening of the ajna chakra may give rise to mystical visions and intuitive reflections of other realms of experience within and outside the individual. The ajna chakra governs the higher mind, will, vision, and conception. It is sometimes also referred to as the "Guru's Seat", the psychic center through which the Spiritual Master contacts his or her devotees with his or her Spirit-Blessing.

**Bhagavan**

Sanskrit for "possessing fortune or wealth; blessed; holy". It is often used to mean "bountiful God", "Great God", or "Divine Lord", when used as an honorific for a Great Spiritual Being.

The esoteric meaning of the word "Bhagavan" relates to the Divine Union of Transcendental Consciousness and Radiant Bliss. Thus, it is also with this esoteric understanding that Avatara Adi Da, Who Is the Self-Existing and Self-Radiant Divine Person, is known as "Bhagavan".

**"Bright", "Brightness"**

Since His Illumined boyhood, Avatara Adi Da has used the term "the 'Bright'" (and its variations, such as "Brightness") to Describe the Love-Blissfully Self-Luminous, Conscious Divine Being, Which He Knew even then as His own Native Condition, and the Native Condition of all beings, things, and worlds.

**causal** (*See* **gross, subtle, causal**.)

**chakras**

Subtle energy centers of the human body-mind, generally said, in the Hindu tradition, to be seven in number.

**childish and adolescent strategies**

Avatara Adi Da uses the terms "childish" and "adolescent" with precise meanings in His Wisdom-Teaching. He points out that human beings are always tending to animate one of two fundamental life-strategies—the childish strategy (to be dependent, weak, seeking to be consoled by parent figures and a parent God) and the adolescent strategy (to be independent or torn between independence and dependence, rebellious, unfeeling, self-absorbed, and doubting or resisting the idea of God or any power greater than oneself). Until these strategies are understood and transcended, they not only diminish love in our ordinary human relations, but they also limit our religious and Spiritual growth.

**Circle**

A primary pathway of natural life-energy and the Spirit-Current through the body-mind. It is composed of two arcs: the descending Current in association with the frontal line, or the more physically oriented dimension of the body-mind; and the ascending Current in association with the spinal line, or the more mentally, psychically, and subtly oriented dimension of the body-mind.

**"conductivity"**

Avatara Adi Da's technical term for those disciplines in the Way of the Heart through which the body-mind is aligned and submitted to the all-pervading natural life-energy and, for those who are Spiritually Awakened, to the Spirit-Current.

Practitioners of the Way of the Heart practice participation in and responsibility

364

for the movement of natural bodily energies and, when they become Spiritually Awakened practitioners, for the movement of the Spirit-Current in its natural course of association with the body-mind, via intentional exercises of feeling and breathing.

Avatara Adi Da also uses the term "conductivity" in a more general sense, to refer to all of the practical life-disciplines engaged by practitioners of the Way of the Heart. Although the discipline of "conductivity" is an essential component of the practice of the Way of the Heart, it is nevertheless secondary, or supportive, to practice of the "conscious process".

**"conscious process"**

Avatara Adi Da's technical term for those practices in the Way of the Heart through which the mind or attention is surrendered and turned about from egoic self-involvement to feeling-Contemplation of Him. It is the senior discipline and responsibility of all Avatara Adi Da's devotees.

**"consider", "consideration"**

The technical term "consideration" in Avatara Adi Da's Wisdom-Teaching means a process of one-pointed but ultimately thoughtless concentration and exhaustive contemplation of something until its ultimate obviousness is clear.

**Cosmic Mandala**

The Sanskrit word "mandala" (literally, "circle") is commonly used in the esoteric Spiritual traditions to describe the hierarchical levels of cosmic existence. "Mandala" also denotes an artistic rendering of interior visions of the cosmos. Avatara Adi Da uses the phrase "Mandala of the Cosmos", or "Cosmic Mandala", to describe the totality of the conditional cosmos.

For a full discussion of the Cosmic Mandala (and a representation of its appearance in vision), see Chapter 48 of this book.

**Darshan**

A Sanskrit term that literally means "seeing", "sight of", or "vision of". To receive Darshan of Adi Da is to receive the spontaneous Blessing He Grants Freely by Revealing His bodily (human) Form (and, thereby, His Spiritual, and Always Blessing, Presence and His Very, and Inherently Perfect, State). Darshan of Avatara Adi Da is the very essence of all practice in the Way of the Heart, and is Enjoyed by association with Him through His books, photographs, videotapes, and recorded Talks, through the Leelas (or Stories) of His Teaching Work and Blessing Work, through places or objects He has Blessed for His devotees, and through simple, heart-felt Remembrance of Him and visualization of His bodily (human) Form.

**Dharma, dharma**

Sanskrit for "duty", "virtue", "law". The word "dharma" is commonly used to refer to the many esoteric paths by which human beings seek the Truth. In its fullest sense, and when capitalized, "Dharma" means the complete fulfillment of duty—the living of the Divine Law. By extension, "Dharma" means a truly great Spiritual Teaching, including its disciplines and practices.

**"difference"**

The epitome of the egoic presumption of separation and separateness—in contrast with the Realization of "Oneness" that is native to Spiritual and Transcendental Divine Self-Consciousness.

**Divine Star**

The primal conditional Representation of the "Bright" (the Source-Energy, or Divine Light, of which all conditional phenomena and the total cosmos are modifications) is a brilliant white five-pointed Star. Avatara Adi Da's bodily (human) Form is the Manifestation of that Divine Star—and His head, two arms, and two legs correspond to its five points. Avatara Adi Da can also be seen or intuited in vision to Be the Divine Star Itself, prior to the visible manifestation of His bodily (human) Form.

**etheric**

The sheath of life-energy that functions through and corresponds with the human nervous system. Our bodies are surrounded and infused by this personal life-energy, which we feel as the play of emotions and life-force in the body.

**feeling-Contemplation**

Avatara Adi Da's term for the essential devotional and meditative practice that all devotees in the Way of the Heart engage at all times in relationship to His bodily (human) Form, His Spiritual (and Always Blessing) Presence, and His Very (and Inherently Perfect) State. Feeling-Contemplation of Adi Da is Awakened by Grace through Darshan, or feeling-sighting, of His Form, Presence, and State. It is then to be practiced under all conditions, and as the basis and epitome of all other practices in the Way of the Heart.

**feeling of relatedness**

In the foundation stages of practice in the Way of the Heart, the basic or gross level activity of the avoidance of relationship is understood and released in the free capability for simple relatedness, or the feeling of relatedness. Only in the ultimate stages of life in the Way of the Heart is the feeling of relatedness fully understood as the root-act of attention itself and ultimately transcended in the Feeling of Being. In that case, it is understood to be the feeling of "I" and "other", or the feeling of "difference" between the egoic self and all its relations or objects of attention. Avatara Adi Da points out that the feeling of relatedness is, in fact, the avoidance of relationship in relation to all others and things, or the root-activity of separation, separateness, and separativeness that is the ego.

**Great Tradition**

Avatara Adi Da's term for the total inheritance of human, cultural, religious, magical, mystical, Spiritual, Transcendental, and Divine paths, philosophies, and testimonies from all the eras and cultures of humanity, which has (in the present era of worldwide communication) become the common legacy of mankind.

**gross, subtle, causal**

Avatara Adi Da has confirmed the correctness of traditional descriptions of the human body-mind and its environment as consisting of three great dimensions—gross, subtle, and causal.

The gross, or most physical, dimension is associated with the physical body and experience in the waking state.

The subtle dimension, which is senior to and pervades the gross dimension, includes the etheric (or energetic), lower mental (or verbal-intentional and lower psychic), and higher mental (or deeper psychic, mystical, and discriminative) functions. The subtle dimension is associated primarily with the ascending energies of the spine, the brain core, and the subtle centers of mind in the higher brain. It is also, therefore, associated with the visionary, mystical, and Yogic Spiritual processes encountered in dreams, in ascended or internalized meditative experiences, and during and after the death process.

The causal dimension is senior to and pervades both the gross and the subtle dimensions. It is the root of attention, or the

essence of the separate and separative ego-"I". The causal dimension is associated with the right side of the heart, specifically with the sinoatrial node, or "pacemaker" (the psycho-physical source of the heartbeat). Its corresponding state of consciousness is the formless awareness of deep sleep. It is inherently transcended by the Witness-Consciousness (Which is Prior to all objects of attention).

The causal being, or limited self-consciousness (which is identical to the root-feeling of relatedness), is also associated with a knot or stress-point in the heart-root on the right side. When this knot is broken, or "untied", by Avatara Adi Da's Liberating Grace, the Transcendental, Inherently Spiritual, and Divine Self-Consciousness Stands Free and Awake as the Heart Itself.

**hearing** (*See* **listening, hearing, seeing.**)

**the Heart**

God, the Divine Self, the Divine Reality. Divine Self-Realization is associated with the opening of the (apparent) psycho-physical seat of Consciousness and attention in the right side of the heart, hence the term "the Heart" for the Divine Self.

Avatara Adi Da distinguishes the Heart as the ultimate Reality from all the psycho-physiological functions of the gross, physical heart, or the left side of the heart, as well as from the subtle heart. The Heart is not "in" the right side of the human heart, nor is it in or limited to the human heart as a whole, or to the body-mind, or to the world. Rather, the human heart and body-mind and the world exist in the Heart, the Divine Being.

**institution, culture, community, and mission**

Adidam (the organization responsible for bringing Adi Da's Work to the world) and the full devotional and cooperative gathering of Adi Da's devotees.

**Instrumentality**

Avatara Adi Da uses the term "Instrumentality" to indicate the body of His Spiritually Awakened renunciate devotees in practicing stage three and beyond in the Way of the Heart. Such devotees have received Avatara Adi Da's Spiritual Baptism and they practice in Spiritually activated relationship to Him. Because of their uniquely complete and renunciate response and accountability to Him, and by virtue of their self-surrendering, self-forgetting, self-transcending, and really Spiritual Invocation of Him, these devotees function collectively as Instruments for the Transmission of Avatara Adi Da's Spiritual (and Always Blessing) Presence to others at the same developmental stage and at earlier developmental stages of the Way of the Heart, and even, in a general sense, to all of Bhagavan Adi Da's devotees.

### Ishta-Guru-Bhakti Yoga

Ishta-Guru-Bhakti Yoga is the principal Gift, Calling, and Discipline Offered by Avatara Adi Da to all who would practice the Way of the Heart.

"Ishta" means "chosen", or "most beloved". "Guru", in the reference "Ishta-Guru", means specifically the Sat-Guru, the Revealer of Truth Itself (or of Being Itself). "Bhakti" means "devotion".

Ishta-Guru-Bhakti, then, is devotion to Avatara Adi Da, the chosen Beloved Guru of His devotees, the Supreme Divine Being Incarnate in human form.

"Yoga", from a Sanskrit verb root meaning "to yoke", "to bind together", is a path, or way, of achieving Unity with (or Realizing one's Prior Identity with) the Divine.

Although the practice of Guru-devotion is ultimately the essence of the entire Great Tradition, Ishta-Guru-Bhakti Yoga, or devotional surrender to Avatara Adi Da, the Very Divine Person, as one's Ishta-Guru, is the only means for Most Perfect Divine Self-Realization.

### Ishta-Guru-Seva

In Sanskrit, "seva" means "service". Service to the Sat-Guru is traditionally treasured as one of the great Secrets of Realization. In the Way of the Heart, Sat-Guru-Seva, or Ishta-Guru-Seva, is the remarkable opportunity to live every action and, indeed, one's entire life, as direct service and devotional obedience (or devotional conformity) to Sat-Guru Adi Da in every possible and appropriate way.

### Karma Yoga

"Yoga" is Sanskrit for "union". The tradition of Yoga speaks of several traditional paths of Spiritual union with the Divine. Karma Yoga is the Yoga of action, in which every activity, no matter how humble, is transformed into self-transcending service to the Divine.

### Kundalini, Kundalini Shakti

The traditional name for what Avatara Adi Da has Revealed to be the ascending aspect of the total Circle of Spiritual Life-Energy in the human body-mind. The Kundalini Shakti is traditionally viewed to lie dormant at the bodily base, or lowermost psychic center of the body-mind. The Kundalini may be activated spontaneously in the devotee or by the Guru's initiation, thereafter producing all the various forms of Yogic and mystical experience.

### left-sided, right-sided

The left side of the body is controlled by the right hemisphere of the brain, the hemisphere (in most people) primarily associated with nonverbal, spatial, and holistic methods of relating to the objects of experience. These "left-sided" qualities generally typify the mystical and sacred cultures of the East. The right side of the body is controlled by the left hemisphere of the brain, the hemisphere (in most people) primarily associated with verbal, temporal, and analytical methods of relating to the objects of experience. These "right-sided" qualities typify the scientific and materialistic cultures of the West.

### listening, hearing, seeing

"Listening" is Avatara Adi Da's term for the beginner's "consideration" of His Teaching Argument and His Leelas (inspirational Stories of His Life and Work), and the beginner's practice of feeling-Contemplation of Him (primarily of His bodily human Form), which is to be engaged in the context of one's life of devotion, service, self-discipline, and meditation. Listening is mature when "hearing" occurs. See chapter nineteen of *The Dawn Horse Testament Of Adi Da*.

"Hearing" (most fundamental self-understanding) is the unique capability to directly transcend the self-contraction, to such a degree that there is the simultaneous intuitive awakening to the Revelation of the Divine Person and Self-Condition.

Only on the basis of such hearing can Spiritually Awakened practice of the Way of the Heart truly (or with full responsibility) begin. Avatara Adi Da has said many times that when true hearing is realized, the rest of the process leading to Divine Self-Realization, including the "Perfect Practice", can and should be very quick, cutting through all the stages of life previous to the seventh stage of life "like a hot knife through butter". See chapter nineteen of *The Dawn Horse Testament Of Adi Da*.

"Seeing" is Avatara Adi Da's technical term for His devotee's Spiritually activated conversion from self-contraction to His

Spiritual (and Always Blessing) Presence, and the descent and circulation of His Spiritual Transmission in, through, and ultimately beyond the body-mind of His devotee. Seeing is the reorientation of conditional reality to the Unconditional and Divine Reality. Seeing is a prerequisite to Spiritual advancement in the Way of the Heart. See chapter twenty of *The Dawn Horse Testament Of Adi Da*.

**Most Perfect(ly), Most Ultimate(ly)**

Avatara Adi Da uses the phrase "Most Perfect(ly)" in the sense of "Absolutely Perfect(ly)". (Similarly, the phrase "Most Ultimate[ly]" is equivalent to "Absolutely Ultimate[ly]".)

In the sixth stage of life and the seventh stage of life, What is Realized (Consciousness Itself) is Perfect (and Ultimate). This is why Avatara Adi Da characterizes these stages as the "ultimate stages of life", and describes the practice of the Way of the Heart in the context of these stages as "the 'Perfect Practice'". The distinction between the sixth stage of life and the seventh stage of life is that the devotee's <u>Realization</u> of What is Perfect (and Ultimate) is itself Perfect (and Ultimate) only in the seventh stage. The Perfection or Ultimacy (in the seventh stage), <u>both</u> of What is Realized and of the Realization of It, is what is signified by the phrase "Most Perfect(ly)" or "Most Ultimate(ly)".

**muladhar**

The muladhar, or muladhara chakra, located at the base of the spine (or the general region immediately above and including the perineum), is the lowest energy plexus (chakra) in the human body-mind. In many of the Yogic traditions, this is regarded to be the seat of the latent ascending Spiritual Current, or Kundalini. Avatara Adi Da Reveals that, in fact, the Spirit-Current must first descend to the bodily base through the frontal line before it can effectively be directed into the ascending spinal course. He has also pointed out that human beings who are not yet Spiritually sensitive tend to throw off the natural life-energy at the bodily base, and He has, therefore, Given His devotees a range of disciplines (including a number of exercises that involve intentional locking at the bodily base) which conserve life-energy by directing it into the spinal line.

**"Narcissus"**

In Avatara Adi Da's Teaching-Revelation, "Narcissus" is a key symbol of the un-Enlightened individual as a self-obsessed seeker, enamored of his or her own self-image and egoic self-consciousness. In *The Knee of Listening*, Avatara Adi Da summarizes "Narcissus" as the avoidance of relationship:

*He is the ancient one visible in the Greek "myth", who was the universally adored child of the gods, who rejected the loved-one and every form of love and relationship, who was finally condemned to the contemplation of his own image, until, as a result of his own act and obstinacy, he suffered the fate of eternal separateness and died in infinite solitude.*

**Perfect**

Avatara Adi Da uses this modifier (along with its variants, such as "Perfectly") as a technical indication of Identification with Consciousness in the sixth stage of life and the seventh stage of life in the Way of the Heart. (*See also* **Most Perfect(ly), Most Ultimate(ly).**)

**puja** (*See* **Sat-Guru Puja.**)

**"radical"**

The word "radical" derives from the Latin "radix", meaning "root", and thus it principally means "irreducible", "fundamental", or "relating to origin". Because Adi Da uses "radical" in this literal sense, it appears in quotation marks in His Wisdom-Teaching to distinguish His use of it from the popular reference to an extreme (often political) point of view.

**right side of the heart**

Avatara Adi Da has Revealed that, in the context of the body-mind, the Divine Consciousness is intuited at a psycho-physical Locus in the right side of the heart. This center corresponds to the sinoatrial node, or "pacemaker", the source of the physical heartbeat in the right atrium, or upper right chamber, of the heart.

**right-sided** (*See* **left-sided, right-sided.**)

**sadhana**

Self-transcending religious or Spiritual practice.

**sahasrar**

The highest chakra (or subtle energy center), associated with the crown of the head and beyond. It is described traditionally as a thousand-petalled lotus, the terminal of Light to which the Yogic process (of Spiritual ascent through the chakras) aspires. While the Yogic traditions regard the sahasrar as the seat of Enlightenment, Avatara Adi Da has always pointed beyond the sahasrar to the Heart as the Seat of Divine Consciousness.

**Sat-Guru Puja**

The Sanskrit word "puja" means "worship". All formal sacramental devotion in the Way of the Heart is consecrated to Sat-Guru Adi Da and is thus celebrated as Sat-Guru Puja. It is a ceremonial but feeling practice of Divine association, or expressive whole-bodily devotion to Avatara Adi Da, in Person, as the Realizer, the Revealer, and the Revelation of the Divine Person. Sat-Guru Puja involves bodily Invocation of, self-surrender to, and intimate Communion with Avatara Adi Da (and, thus and thereby, with the Divine Person) by means of prayer, song, recitation of His Word of Instruction, the offering and receiving of gifts, and other forms of outward-directed, or bodily active, devotional attention.

In the Way of the Heart, all practitioners participate daily in formal Sat-Guru Puja, as self-transcending practice that establishes Avatara Adi Da's Blessing at the heart and thus establishes devotees profoundly in ecstatic feeling-Contemplation of Him. The principal forms of daily Sat-Guru Puja are Sat-Guru-Murti Puja (ceremonial service to and worship of the Sacred Image of Sat-Guru Adi Da) and Sat-Guru-Paduka Puja (ceremonial service to and worship of Sat-Guru Adi Da's Blessed Sandals, or Padukas).

**Sat-Guru-Seva**

The Sanskrit word "seva" means "service". Service to the Sat-Guru is traditionally treasured as one of the great Secrets of Realization. In the Way of the Heart, Sat-Guru-Seva is the remarkable opportunity to live every action and, indeed, one's entire life, as direct service and responsive obedience and conformity to Avatara Adi Da in every possible and appropriate way.

**Satsang**

The Sanskrit word "Satsang" literally means "true or right relationship", "the company of Truth". In the Way of the Heart, it is the eternal relationship of mutual sacred commitment between Avatara Adi Da as Sat-Guru (and as the Divine Person) and each of His devotees. Once it is consciously assumed by any practitioner of the Way of the Heart, Satsang with Avatara Adi Da is an all-inclusive Condition, bringing Divine Grace and Blessings, sacred obligations, responsibilities, and tests into every dimension of the practitioner's life and consciousness.

**seeing** (*See* **listening, hearing, seeing**.)

**self-contraction**

Adi Da's technical term for the activity of separativeness that is the root of every apparent individual's suffering and seeking.

**"self-possession"**

Conventionally, "self-possessed" means possessed of oneself—or in full control (calmness, or composure) of one's feelings, impulses, habits, and actions. Adi Da uses the term to indicate the state of being possessed by one's egoic self, or controlled by chronically self-referring (or egoic) tendencies of attention, feeling, thought, desire, and action.

**seven stages of life** (*See* "The Seven Stages of Life", pp. 154-165)

**Siddha, Siddha-Guru**

Sanskrit for "a completed, fulfilled, or perfected one", or "one of perfect accomplishment, or power". Avatara Adi Da uses "Siddha", or "Siddha-Guru", to mean a Transmission-Master who is a Realizer, to any significant degree, of God, Truth, or Reality.

**Spiritual Baptism**

The Spiritual Transmission of an Adept. Avatara Adi Da's Spirit-Baptism is often felt as a Spiritual Current of life descending in the front of the body and ascending in the spinal line. Nevertheless, His Spirit-Baptism is fundamentally and primarily the moveless Transmission of the Heart Itself, whereby He Rests His devotee in the Heart-Source of His Baptizing Spiritual Current and Awakens the intuition of Consciousness Itself. As a secondary effect, the Spirit-Current Transmitted through His Great Baptism serves to purify, balance, and energize the entire body-mind of the devotee who is prepared to receive it.

**Sri**

"Sri" is a Sanskrit term of honor and veneration often applied to an Adept. The word literally means "flame", indicating that the one honored is radiant with Blessing Power.

**stages of life**

Avatara Adi Da has described the developmental potential of the human individual in terms of seven stages of life. Please see "The Seven Stages of Life", pp. 154-65.

**student-beginner**

A practitioner in the initial developmental stage of the Way of the Heart. In the course of student-beginner practice, the devotee of Avatara Adi Da, on the basis of the eternal bond of devotion to Him that he or she established as a student-novice, continues the process of listening and the stabilization of the disciplines that were begun in the student-novice stage of approach.

**subtle** *(See* **gross, subtle, causal.**)

**tamas**

Avatara Adi Da Confirms the correctness of the Hindu teaching that manifested existence is a complex variable of three qualities, or gunas. These are tamas, rajas, and sattva. Tamas, or the tamasic quality, is the principle, or power, of inertia. Rajas, or the rajasic quality, is the principle, or power, of action or motivation. Sattva, or the sattvic quality, is the principle, or power, of balance or equanimity.

**Tcha**

Avatara Adi Da's special sound of Blessing.

**vital shock**

Avatara Adi Da uses the term "vital shock" to describe the primal recoil of every individual from the experience of being born—and, throughout the course of egoic life, from the vulnerable condition of bodily existence and of relationship itself.

**Yoga**

"Yoga", in Sanskrit, is literally "yoking", or "union", usually referring to any discipline or process whereby an aspirant attempts to reunite with God. Avatara Adi Da acknowledges this conventional and traditional use of the term, but also, in reference to the Great Yoga of the Way of the Heart, employs it in a "radical" sense, free of the usual implication of egoic separation and seeking.

# An Invitation to Support Adidam,
# the Way of the Heart

Avatara Adi Da's sole purpose is to act as a Source of continuous Divine Grace for everyone, everywhere. In that spirit, He is a Free Renunciate and He owns nothing. Those who have made gestures in support of Avatara Adi Da's Work have found that their generosity is returned in many Blessings that are full of His healing, transforming, and Liberating Grace—and those Blessings flow not only directly to them as the beneficiaries of His Work, but to many others, even all others. At the same time, all tangible gifts of support help secure and nurture Avatara Adi Da's Work in necessary and practical ways, again similarly benefiting the whole world. Because all this is so, supporting His Work is the most auspicious form of financial giving, and we happily extend to you an invitation to serve Adidam through your financial support.

You may make a financial contribution in support of the Work of Avatara Adi Da at any time. You may also, if you choose, request that your contribution be used for one or more specific purposes of the Way of the Heart, Adidam. For example, you may be moved to help support and develop Adidamashram (Naitauba), Avatara Adi Da's Great Sannyasin Hermitage Ashram and Renunciate Retreat Sanctuary in Fiji, and the circumstance provided there for Avatara Adi Da and the other "free renunciates" who practice there (all of whom own nothing).

You may make a contribution for this specific purpose directly to The TDL Trust, the charitable trust that is responsible for Adidamashram (Naitauba). To do this, make your check payable to "The TDL Trust Pty Ltd", which serves as trustee of the trust, and mail it to The TDL Trust at P.O. Box 4744, Samabula, Fiji.

If you would like to make a contribution to Adidamashram (Naitauba) and you are a United States taxpayer, we recommend that you make your check payable to "Adidam" (the institution that has developed in response to Avatara Adi Da's Revelation of the Way of Adidam), in order to secure a tax deduction under United States tax laws. Please indicate on your check that you would like your contribution to be used in support of Adidamashram, and mail your check to the Advocacy Department of Adidam, 12040 North Seigler Road, Middletown, California 95461, USA.

You may also request that your contribution, or a part of it, be used for one or more of the other purposes of Adidam. For example, you may request that your contribution be used to help publish the sacred Literature of Avatara Adi Da, or to support either of the other two Sanctuaries He has Empowered, or to maintain the Sacred Archives that preserve His recorded Talks and Writings, or to publish audio and video recordings of Avatara Adi Da.

If you would like your contribution to benefit one or more of these specific purposes, please make your check payable to "Adidam", mail it to the Advocacy Department of Adidam at the above address, and indicate how you would like your gift to be used.

If you would like more information about these and other gifting options, or if you would like assistance in describing or making a contribution, please contact the Advocacy Department of Adidam, either by writing to the address shown above or by telephoning (707) 928-4096, or faxing us at (707) 928-4062.

# Planned Giving

We also invite you to consider making a planned gift in support of the Work of Avatara Adi Da. Many have found that through planned giving they can make a far more significant gesture of support than they would otherwise be able to make. Many have also found that by making a planned gift they are able to realize substantial tax advantages.

There are numerous ways to make a planned gift, including making a gift in your Will, or in your life insurance, or in a charitable trust.

If you would like to make a gift in your Will in support of Adidamashram, simply include in your Will the statement "I give The TDL Trust Pty Ltd, as trustee of The TDL Trust, an Australian charitable trust, P.O. Box 4744, Samabula, Fiji, _____" [inserting in the blank the amount or description of your contribution].

If you would like to make a gift in your Will to benefit other purposes of Adidam, simply include in your Will the statement "I give to 'Adidam', a California nonprofit corporation, 12040 North Seigler Road, Middletown, California 95461, USA, _____" [inserting in the blank the amount or description of your contribution]. You may, if you choose, also describe in your Will the specific purpose or purposes you would like your gift to support. If you are a United States taxpayer, gifts made in your Will to "Adidam" will be free of estate taxes and will also reduce any estate taxes payable on the remainder of your estate.

To make a gift in your life insurance, simply name as the beneficiary (or one of the beneficiaries) of your life insurance policy the organization of your choice (The TDL Trust or "Adidam"), according to the foregoing descriptions and addresses. If you are a United States taxpayer, you may receive significant tax benefits if you make a contribution to "Adidam", through your life insurance.

We also invite you to consider establishing or participating in a charitable trust for the benefit of Adidam. If you are a United States taxpayer, you may find that such a trust will provide you with immediate tax savings and assured income for life, while at the same time enabling you to provide for your family, for your other heirs, and for the Work of Avatara Adi Da as well.

The Advocacy Department of Adidam will be happy to provide you with further information about these and other planned gifting options, and happy to provide you or your attorney with assistance in describing or making a planned gift in support of the Work of Avatara Adi Da.

# Further Notes to the Reader

### AN INVITATION TO RESPONSIBILITY

Adidam, the Way of the Heart that Avatara Adi Da has Revealed, is an invitation to everyone to assume real responsibility for his or her life. As Avatara Adi Da has Said in *The Dawn Horse Testament Of Adi Da,* "If any one Is Interested In The Realization Of The Heart, Let him or her First Submit (Formally, and By Heart) To Me, and (Thereby) Commence The Ordeal Of self-Observation, self-Understanding, and self-Transcendence." Therefore, participation in the Way of the Heart requires a real struggle with oneself, and not at all a struggle with Avatara Adi Da, or with others.

All who study the Way of the Heart or take up its practice should remember that they are responding to a Call to become responsible for themselves. They should understand that they, not Avatara Adi Da or others, are responsible for any decision they may make or action they take in the course of their lives of study or practice. This has always been true, and it is true whatever the individual's involvement in the Way of the Heart, be it as one who studies Avatara Adi Da's Wisdom-Teaching, or as a Friend of or a participant in Da Avatara International, or as a formally acknowledged member of Adidam.

### HONORING AND PROTECTING THE SACRED WORD
### THROUGH PERPETUAL COPYRIGHT

Since ancient times, practitioners of true religion and Spirituality have valued, above all, time spent in the Company of the Sat-Guru, or one who has, to any degree, Realized God, Truth, or Reality, and who thus Serves the awakening process in others. Such practitioners understand that the Sat-Guru literally Transmits his or her (Realized) State to every one (and every thing) with which he or she comes in contact. Through this Transmission, objects, environments, and rightly prepared individuals with which the Sat-Guru has contact can become Empowered, or Imbued with the Sat-Guru's Transforming Power. It is by this process of Empowerment that things and beings are made truly and literally sacred, and things so sanctified thereafter function as a Source of the Sat-Guru's Blessing for all who understand how to make right and sacred use of them.

Sat-Gurus of any degree of Realization and all that they Empower are, therefore, truly Sacred Treasures, for they help draw the practitioner more quickly into the process of Realization. Cultures of true Wisdom have always understood that such Sacred Treasures are precious (and fragile) Gifts to humanity, and that they should be honored, protected, and reserved for right sacred use. Indeed, the word "sacred" means "set apart", and thus protected, from the secular world. Avatara Adi Da has Conformed His body-mind most Perfectly to the Divine Self, and He is thus the most Potent Source of Blessing-Transmission of God, Truth, or Reality, the ultimate Sat-Guru. He has for many years Empowered, or made sacred, special places and things, and these now Serve as His Divine Agents, or as literal expressions and extensions of His Blessing-Transmission. Among these Empowered Sacred Treasures is His Wisdom-Teaching, which is Full of His Transforming Power. This

Blessed and Blessing Wisdom-Teaching has Mantric Force, or the literal Power to Serve God-Realization in those who are Graced to receive it.

Therefore, Avatara Adi Da's Wisdom-Teaching must be perpetually honored and protected, "set apart" from all possible interference and wrong use. The fellowship of devotees of Avatara Adi Da is committed to the perpetual preservation and right honoring of the sacred Wisdom-Teaching of the Way of the Heart. But it is also true that in order to fully accomplish this we must find support in the world-society in which we live and from the laws under which we live. Thus, we call for a world-society and for laws that acknowledge the sacred, and that permanently protect It from insensitive, secular interference and wrong use of any kind. We call for, among other things, a system of law that acknowledges that the Wisdom-Teaching of the Way of the Heart, in all Its forms, is, because of Its sacred nature, protected by perpetual copyright.

We invite others who respect the sacred to join with us in this call and in working toward its realization. And, even in the meantime, we claim that all copyrights to the Wisdom-Teaching of Avatara Adi Da and the other sacred Literature and recordings of the Way of the Heart are of perpetual duration.

We make this claim on behalf of The TDL Trust Pty Ltd, which, acting as trustee of The TDL Trust, is the holder of all such copyrights.

## AVATARA ADI DA AND THE SACRED TREASURES OF ADIDAM

Those who Realize God to any degree bring great Blessing and Divine Possibility for the world. Such Realizers Accomplish universal Blessing Work that benefits everything and everyone. They also Work very specifically and intentionally with individuals who approach them as their devotees, and with those places where they reside, and to which they Direct their specific Regard for the sake of perpetual Spiritual Empowerment. This was understood in traditional Spiritual cultures, and those cultures therefore found ways to honor Realizers by providing circumstances for them where they were free to do their Spiritual Work without obstruction or interference.

Those who value Avatara Adi Da's Realization and Service have always endeavored to appropriately honor Him in this traditional way by providing a circumstance where He is completely Free to do His Divine Work. Since 1983, He has resided principally on the island of Naitauba, Fiji, also known as Adidamashram. This island has been set aside by Avatara Adi Da's devotees worldwide as a Place for Him to do His universal Blessing Work for the sake of everyone, and His specific Work with those who pilgrimage to Adidamashram to receive the special Blessing of coming into His physical Company.

Avatara Adi Da is a legal renunciate. He owns nothing and He has no secular or religious institutional function. He Functions only in Freedom. He, and the other members of the Naitauba Order of the Sannyasins of Adidam, the senior renunciate order of Adidam, are provided for by The TDL Trust, which also provides for Adidamashram altogether and ensures the permanent integrity of Avatara Adi Da's Wisdom-Teaching, both in its archival and in its published forms. This Trust, which functions only in Fiji, exists exclusively to provide for these Sacred Treasures of Adidam.

Outside Fiji, the institution which has developed in response to Avatara Adi Da's Wisdom-Teaching and universal Blessing is also known as "Adidam". This formal organization is active worldwide in making Avatara Adi Da's Wisdom-Teaching available to all, in offering guidance to all who are moved to respond to His Offering, and in providing for the other Sacred Treasures of Adidam, including the Mountain Of Attention Sanctuary (in California) and Tumomama Sanctuary (in Hawaii). In addition to the central corporate entity known as "Adidam", which is based in California, there are numerous regional entities which serve congregations of Avatara Adi Da's devotees in various places throughout the world.

Practitioners of Adidam worldwide have also established numerous community organizations, through which they provide for many of their common and cooperative community needs, including those relating to housing, food, businesses, medical care, schools, and death and dying. By attending to these and all other ordinary human concerns and affairs via self-transcending cooperation and mutual effort, Avatara Adi Da's devotees constantly free their energy and attention, both personally and collectively, for practice of the Way of the Heart and for service to Avatara Adi Da, to Adidamashram, to the other Sacred Treasures of Adidam, and to the institution known as "Adidam".

All of the organizations that have evolved in response to Avatara Adi Da and His Offering are legally separate from one another, and each has its own purpose and function. Avatara Adi Da neither directs, nor bears responsibility for, the activities of these organizations. Again, He Functions only in Freedom. These organizations represent the collective intention of practitioners of Adidam worldwide not only to provide for the Sacred Treasures of Adidam, but also to make Avatara Adi Da's Offering of the Way of the Heart universally available to all.

# INDEX

# A

Adi Da
  as the Amrita Nadi, 325-26
  as Avatar since Eternity, 331
  as Awake within the dream, 37-38
  birth of, 11
  books of, 215n, 349-62
  the "Bright" and, 11-13, 15, 20-21,
    58-59, 311-12, 313, 322, 323-24
  Columbia experience of, 66-70
  as Completing Adept of the Great
    Tradition, 185-86
  "cracking the cosmic code", 21
  devotees' stories of. See Leelas
  Divine Functions of, 35, 147
  Divine Goddess and, 310-11
  as Divine Person (Leela), 144
  Divine Re-Awakening of, 20-21,
    310-15
  as Divine World-Teacher, 22
  Gurus of, 16
    See also Rudi; Muktananda, Swami;
      Nityananda, Swami; Shakti
  as the Heart's Shout, 24, 25
  Identity of, 58-59
  is waiting for His devotees, 333
  as legal renunciate, 374
  His meditation after Divine
    Re-Awakening, 313, 314
  Name defined, 23, 61, 193
  Realization of, 116
  His Revelation of the seventh stage
    of life, 185-86
  Sadhana of, 13-21, 73-74, 310
  Siddhis of His Teaching Work,
    289, 289n
  Spiritual experiences of, 17, 34, 66-70,
    310-15
  as the sunlight, 38, 41
  Work of, 21, 22, 206-208
Adidam
  area study groups, 335
  becoming a practitioner of, 337-38
  classes, seminars, and special events
    related to, 334-35
  described, 22, 333-48
  financial support of, 371-72
  how to find out more about, 334-35
  an invitation to, 333-48
  life-disciplines in, 342
  life of a devotee in, 341-47
  meditation in, 342
  planned giving to, 372
  purpose of the organization, 53
  regional centers of, 348
  sacramental worship in, 342
  sacred Sanctuaries of, 345
  service in, 342
  study practices in, 342
  summarized, 189
  Way of the Heart as Adi Da's literal
    experience, 34
  Website, 335
    See also Way of the Heart
Adidamashram, described, 21, 345
Adidam regional centers, 348
Adi-Guru, defined, 185n
adolescent strategy
  defined, 364
  as struggle with conflicting motives,
    156
advanced and ultimate stages of life,
  defined, 364
after-life phenomena, 279, 280-81
  Tom Closser's experience, 294-300
Agency, 55
  defined, 36n, 364
Aham Da Asmi, 58-63
ajna chakra (Ajna Door,
  ajna center), 157
  defined, 134n, 364
Amrita Nadi, 164, 165
  Adi Da as, 325-26
  described, 160-61
anatomy, and the seven stages of life,
  164-65
anger, how to transcend it, 261-63
Aniello (Panico), 120-23
Anschluss, 204
answers, there are none in this lifetime,
  116, 119
area study groups (of Adidam), 335

Arjuna, 172
"As above, so below", 182
asana of science, 105
ashtray (used to illustrate Divine
   Ignorance), 113
astrology, proclaimed by scientists to
   have no basis in fact, 108-110
atheism, 129
Atman, defined, 20, 20n
attention
   extroversion of, 182-83
   introversion of, 181-83
   surrendering attention to Adi Da,
      210, 212
   See also mind
Australia, Adidam regional centers, 348
Avabhasa, defined, 59n, 61
Avabhasa Avatara, 58
   defined, 59n
Avatar, defined, 23
Avatar since Eternity, Adi Da as, 331

**B**

Bakker, Frans, Leela by, 291-94
belief in God, 129, 148
Bhagavan, defined, 364
body (human), as God, 78
books of Adi Da, 215n, 349-62
Brahman, defined, 20, 20n
the "Bright"
   Adi Da as, 11-13, 15, 58-59, 313, 322,
      323-24
   Adi Da's Re-Awakening to, 20-21,
      311-12
   defined, 364
   described, 11-13
   even beginning devotees participate in
      Adi Da's "Brightness", 323

**C**

Canada, Adidam regional center, 348
capitalization, in Adi Da's writing, 27
Catholic church, as dictator of what
      people can do, think, etc., 109, 111
causal dimension, defined, 366

celibacy, 245
   true celibacy vs. conventional celibacy,
      259-60
   See also sexuality
chakras, defined, 364
change, "The Secret of How to Change",
      243
"charitable" work, 225
Charlie's Place, 82
childish strategy, defined, 364
children, Adi Da's advice to a child about
      loving, 261-63
Christianity
   exoteric Christianity vs. the teaching
      of Jesus, 173-79
   fourth stage of life and, 157
   and Parent-Godism, 130
Circle, defined, 364
civilization
   competitive individualism in, 268-69
   is purified by true community, 267,
      270
   lacks true community, 269
   negative signs of, 268
   See also community
clairaudience, 134
clairvoyance, 134
Closser, Tom, Leela by, 294-300
Columbia experience, of Adi Da, 66-70
Communist movement, as official
      doctrine of the State, 111
community
   characteristics of true, 269
   and conventional politics, 265
   as essential part of true religion, 266
   experiments in, 270
   love as key to, 272
   as necessarily sacred, 270-71
   purifies civilization, 267, 270
   vs. communalism, 270
   See also civilization
competitive individualism, in present
      civilization, 268-69
conception, process of, 101-102

"conductivity", 74
  defined, 364-65
conscious awareness, 101-102
Consciousness Itself, 37-39, 41
  Is Love-Bliss, Joy, Freedom, 313
  as not separate, 312
  See also Divine Enlightenment; God;
    Heart (Divine Self)
"conscious process", 73
  defined, 365
"consider", defined, 365
"consideration"
  defined, 29, 365
  described, 25-26
construction worker, as an example of
  suffering, 117
contraction
  the self as, 65
  See also self-contraction
copyright, perpetual, 373-74
Cosmic Mandala
  Adi Da first describes, 144
  all experiences are temporary in the,
    286
  defined, 365
  described, 287
"cracking the cosmic code", 21
"Crazy Wisdom", 321
  defined, 319n
  Divine Enlightenment as, 319
"Creator" God, 116, 139
  as an institutional idea, 137
crocks in the furnace (analogy for
  Divine Translation), 161-62
cultism, 145-47, 196
cure, no need for, 77

**D**

"Da" (Name)
  defined, 23, 61, 193
  as invocation of Adi Da, 61, 61n
Da Avatara International, becoming a
  member of, 336
Darshan, defined, 365
Dau Loloma, defined, 61, 61n

death, 277-306
  cycle of denial, anger, bargaining,
    depression, acceptance, 303-304
  easy, 281
  as falling off of physical vehicle, 284
  fear of, 277, 280-81
  is acceptable to consciousness and
    life, 278
  mind and after-death states, 282-90
  survival of, 112-13, 277, 280, 284
death camps, 205
decisions, should be made by love, 245
de la Torre, Teofilo, 239, 239n
democracy, faults of, 271
depression, as one's own activity,
    303-306
devotion
  to Adi Da as Master, 201-203
  to Adi Da is inherently Blissful, 213
  Divine Distraction, 197-200
  essence of, 220
  Secret of devotion to the True Heart-
    Master, 193-96, 213-214
  worship of Adi Da, 59-63
  See also Guru-devotee relationship
    (with Adi Da); Ishta-Guru-Bhakti
    Yoga
Dharma, defined, 365
diet
  Adi Da's experiment with, 238-42
  appropriate, 235, 236-37
  as seeking, 241
"difference", defined, 365
discipline, 223, 227-37
dissatisfaction, usefulness of, 284
Divine Distraction, 197-200
Divine Enlightenment, 160-62, 165,
    309-28
  as a change of the whole body, 33
  as "Crazy Wisdom", 319
  defined, 309
  described, 316-17
  disposition of, 281
  as Identification with Divine Reality, 280

Divine Goddess, 203, 203n
    as former Root-Guru of lineage, 310
Divine Ignorance, 112-19
    as absolute Truth, 114
    defined, 74, 99
    the State of, 125
    there is no model of how things work,
        318
    "You don't know what anything is",
        113-15
    See also Mystery
Divine Indifference, 161
Divine Self-Realization. See Divine
    Enlightenment
Divine Star, defined, 365
Divine Transfiguration, 161
Divine Transformation, 161
Divine Translation, 161, 184
    not an Event looked forward to, 322
    as transcendence of mind, 285-86
Dreaded Gom-Boo, as imaginary disease,
    75-77
dreaming, as metaphor for our usual
    state, 37-41
drugs, avoiding, 235, 236
duck, "We are all ducks!", 120-121
dzi stone, 112-13

**E**

Eastern viewpoint
    on orgasm, 257
    orientation to transcendence of the
        world, 167-68
    techniques of Eastern religion
        critiqued, 181-83
    vs. Western scientific materialism, 106
    vs. Western viewpoint and the Way of
        the Heart, 166-72
easy death, 281
ecstasy
    and religion, 246-47
    and sexuality, 246-47
Edible Deity, 166, 167
ego, is an activity, not an entity, 65, 72
Ehret, Arnold, 239, 239n

emotions
    transcending by surrendering feeling
        to Adi Da, 210, 212
    See also anger; depression; fear
Enlightenment. See Divine Enlightenment
etheric, defined, 365
exercise, 237, 241
extrasensory perception, 134
extroversion of attention, 182-83

**F**

fasting, Adi Da's experiment with, 238-42
fear
    of death, 277
    and self-contraction, 249
Feast of God in Every Body, 291, 291n
feeling-Contemplation of Adi Da,
    217-19, 323
    defined, 365
feeling of relatedness
    awakening of, 90
    defined, 366
Fiji, Adidam regional center, 348
financial support of Adidam (the Way of
    the Heart), 371-72
fire ceremonies (pujas) in the Way of the
    Heart, 142
flowers, persistence of, 278, 320
forgiveness, God is, 294
Franklin Jones, Adi Da as, 11
Freedom, as always already the case,
    69-70
free inquiry, vs. State religion of scientific
    materialism, 108-111
free society, myth of, 111
Friend, becoming a Friend of Da Avatara
    International, 336

**G**

Gautama (called the Buddha), 145, 168
Germany, Adidam regional center, 348
Giving Tree, 291
God
    "believing in", 129, 148
    childish view of, 128-32, 145
    as Creator (or First Cause), 116, 134,
        137, 139, 149-50

God *(continued)*
  as Divine Person, 143, 149
  as Forgiveness, 294
  as Guru, 140-41
  how people relate to, 139-40
  human body as, 78
  "Only God is Alive as everyone and
    everything", 316-17
  parents' communication about, 129
  "radical" vs. conventional views of,
    128-32
  Real God described, 148-51
  tacit Obviousness of, 133-38, 171
  there is no separation from, 78
  "There is Only God", 127, 135
God-Realization
  defined, 13
  *See also* Divine Enlightenment
God-Realizers, communicate about
    God-Realization, 136
good company, 344
gopis (and Krishna), 197-200
gorilla, in your dreams, 41
Great Path of Return, 162
Great Tradition
  Adi Da as Completing Adept of,
    185-86
  defined, 29, 153, 366
  false theories in, 194
gross dimension, defined, 366
guilt, 299, 302-303
  and sexuality, 247
  "you are not the guilty party", 81-88
Guru
  God as Guru, 140-41
  as the Means of Realization, 201-202
  "never approach your Guru as merely
    a man", 136
  surrendering to the, 202-203
  true vs. conventional idea of, 40
  what it means to have a, 52-53
  *See also* Guru-cultism; Guru-devotee
    relationship (with Adi Da); Guru-
    devotee relationship

Guru-cultism, 145
Guru-devotee relationship (with Adi Da)
  compared to relationship of
    Krishna and gopis, 197-200
  necessity of, 31-63
  not a doctor-patient game, 35
  as physics, 31
  as principle of Spiritual life, 33
  *See also* Ishta-Guru-Bhakti Yoga
Guru-devotee relationship, 15-16
  as relationship, 136
*Guru Gita,* 192

**H**

Happiness, the choice of, 125
hearing, defined, 60n, 367
Heart (Divine Self)
  defined, 366
  as Real understanding, 278
heart, right side of. *See* right side of the
    heart
Heart's Shout, Adi Da as, 24, 25
hellish realms, 283, 288
Hinduism, fourth stage of life and, 157
Hitler, 204, 205
"hole in the universe", 143, 144
"holes" in the human body, 133-36
homeopathy, attempts to suppress, 110
Hridaya, defined, 58n
Hridaya Avatara, 58
  defined, 59n
Hridayam, defined, 59n, 61
Hridaya-Samartha Sat-Guru, defined, 58n
hugging, Adi Da hugs Frank Marrero, 47

**I**

"I"
  as process of conception and
    perception, 102
  as self-description, 100-101
  *See also* ego
Ignorance. *See* Divine Ignorance
"I Love You", 249
individuation, 155

institution, culture, community,
and mission, 226, 226n
defined, 366
Instrumentality, 55
defined, 366-67
integration (third stage of life), 156
intimate life, as a search for union, 91
introversion of attention, 181-83
Invitation to Adidam (the Way of
the Heart), 333-48
Ishta-Guru-Bhakti, described, 89n
Ishta-Guru-Bhakti Yoga, 191-220
defined, 89n, 191, 367
four-part process of, 210-214
and self-understanding, 91-92
summarized, 216, 341
See also devotion; Guru-devotee
relationship (with Adi Da)
Ishta-Guru-Seva, 224-26
defined, 367
Islam, fourth stage of life and, 157

**J**

Jesus of Nazareth
his teaching in the context of the
Great Tradition, 177
his teaching vs. the teaching of Paul
of Tarsus, 173-79
and popular exoteric Christ-cult, 145
resurrection of, 280
Jews, 208
suffering of the Jews in World War II,
205
See also Judaism
Jnana Samadhi, 159, 165
Jones, Richard (uncle of Adi Da), 67
Juarez, Barry, 301-302
Judaism
fourth stage of life and, 157
and Parent-Godism, 130

**K**

Karma Yoga, 224-26
defined, 367
knowledge
scientific, 99
vs. Divine Ignorance, 113-16

Krishna
and the exoteric Krishna-cult, 145
and the gopis, 197-200
vision of his thousand-armed form, 172
Kübler-Ross, Elisabeth, 303n
Kundalini, 34
defined, 367
Kundalini Shakti, defined, 367

**L**

Law of change, 116
Law of sacrifice, 116
Leelas, 26
*by name*
by Frans Bakker, 291-94
by Tom Closser, 294-300
by Elizabeth Lowe, 204-209
by Frank Marrero, 42-48
by Brian O'Mahony, 81-88
by Annie Rogers, 142-44
*by topic*
Adi Da's Spiritual Transmission, 142-44
guilt and the Witness-Position, 81-88
meeting Adi Da, 42-48
near-death experience, 291-300
relieving the suffering of the world,
204-209
"you are not the guilty party", 81-88
left-sided (vs. right-sided), defined, 367
left side of the body, 168-169, 168n
Lesser, Craig, 120-22, 123-24
listening, defined, 60n, 367
literature, of Adi Da, 349-62
love
as a wound, 250
and ecstasy, 246-247
failure of, 251
"found your intimacies on love",
253-54
"I Love You", 249
as key to true community, 272
living as love in the Way of the Heart,
171, 184
the practice of loving, 249-52, 261-63
should make decisions, 245
Love-Ananda, defined, 59n, 61

Love-Ananda Avatara, 58
  defined, 59n
Lowe, Elizabeth, Leela by, 204-209

**M**

Mana, 299
Man of Understanding
  Adi Da as, 326-28
  defined, 58n
Marrero, Frank, Leela by, 42-48
meditation
  in Adidam, 342
  Adi Da's after Divine Re-Awakening,
    313, 314
meditation salesman, 42-43
mind
  after death, mind makes you, 282
  and after-death states, 282-90
  bondage to, 285
  See also attention
monasteries, traditional, 232-33
"money, food, and sex", and Spiritual
  life, 227-37
money, Spiritual groups' need for, 228
mortal philosophy, 66
Most Perfectly, defined, 160n, 368
Most Ultimately, defined, 160n, 368
Mountain Of Attention Sanctuary,
  described, 345
Muktananda, Swami, 16, 43, 202-203, 310
muladhar, defined, 34, 368
Muslim religion, and Parent-Godism, 130
"My Devotee Is The God I Have Come
  To Serve", 63
Mystery
  existence as a Condition of, 113-15
  remember the Mystery in which you
    live, 262-63
  See also Divine Ignorance

**N**

Naitauba (Adidamashram), 345
  described, 81
Name-Invocation of Adi Da, 62, 62n
"Narcissus"
  characterizes everyone, Eastern and
    Western, 183

defined, 368
described, 72
as famous for rejection of lady Echo,
  252
has no support from the Guru, 230
near-death phenomena, 279, 280-81
  Tom Closser's experience, 294-300
Netherlands, Adidam regional centers, 348
new age, true new age vs. conventional
  concept of "new age", 273-74
new human order, 273-74
New Zealand, Adidam regional centers,
  348
Nirvana, Nirvanic Ground, defined, 20,
  20n, 311, 311n
Nirvikalpa Samadhi (fifth stage
  conditional), 94, 158-59, 165
  defined, 94n
  as goal of Yogis, 181-82
Nityananda, Swami, 203
non-separation, 90-91

**O**

"o" (letter), 124
objective world, 100-101
"Of This I Am Perfectly Certain", 278
O'Mahony, Brian, Leela by, 81-88
"Only the Horse knows", 201
"Open Eyes", 160
orgasm, 245
  conventional vs. regenerative, 254-58
  Western and Eastern views on, 257
  See also sexuality
Oriental point of view. See Eastern view
  point
Outshining (Divine Translation), 161
  See also Divine Translation

**P**

Parental Deity, 129-32
  does not exist, 131
Patanjali, Yoga system of, 234, 234n
Paul of Tarsus, his teaching vs. the
  teaching of Jesus, 173-79
perception, process of, 101-102
Perfect, defined, 368
perpetual copyright, 373-74

"pharisaism", 146
physics, Divine Physics of Evolution, 32-36
pinching yourself (analogy), 92-93
planned giving to Adidam (the Way of the Heart), 372
politics
    conventional politics vs. intimate community, 265
    *See also* community
population explosion, 123
"pot-shaped" Yogic form (Adi Da's belly after Divine Re-Awakening), 314
premonition, 134
progressive Realization, 215n
psychism, 134
psychotherapy, limitations of, 44
psychotic mind, still intuits That Which remains Free, 321
Puja
    defined, 369
    fire ceremony, 142
puritanical disposition, 247

**R**

"radical", defined, 34n, 368
"radical" understanding, 18-19, 65-96
    defined, 65
rajas, defined, 370
Ramakrishna, 231, 231n
Ramana Maharshi, 212, 212n
Reality. *See* God; Consciousness Itself; Heart (Divine Self)
re-cognition, defined, 65
Red Sitting Man (sacred site), 142
regional centers of Adidam, 348
reincarnation, 112
    *See also* death
rejection
    feeling of in the second stage of life, 155, 164
    ritual of, 245, 249-51
relationship, as essential discipline of religious life, 184
religion
    basic proposition of traditional, 75
    beginnings of true religion, 148
    community as necessary part of, 266, 271
    conventional religions as extensions of egoity, 137
    cultism in, 145-47
    and ecstasy, 246-47
    mysterious experience at the basis of true religion, 130
    popular religion as social morality, 129
    problem with exoteric, 174
    Western, Eastern, and Way of the Heart compared, 166-72, 180-84
Renard, Mrs. (landlady of Adi Da), 67
righteousness (self-), how to transcend it, 261-63
right-sided (vs. left-sided), defined, 367
right side of the body, 168-169, 168n
right side of the heart
    defined, 368
    as passage Ultimately Beyond, 135
    as Seat of Reality and Consciousness, 314
    significance of, 59n
Rogers, Annie, Leela by, 142-44
Rudi, 16, 202, 310
    Adi Da's original sadhana with, 229
Russia, scientific propaganda in, 110

**S**

sacrifice
    Law of, 116
    as understood by the ancient Jews, 174
sadhana
    of Adi Da, 13-21, 73-74, 310
    defined, 368
    in other realms, 286
    requires one to manifest the great qualities, 230
Sahaj Samadhi (seventh stage), 160, 165
sahasrar, 34
    defined, 368-69
salesmen, illusion of, 95
Samadhi, as the purpose of life, 223
Samartha, defined, 58n
Sanctuaries of Adidam, 21, 345

Santosha, defined, 59n, 61
Santosha Avatara, 58
    defined, 59n
Sat-Guru, defined, 58n
Sat-Guru Puja, 369
Sat-Guru-Seva, defined, 369
Satsang
    as the best thing one can do, 40
    defined, 31, 369
    is a demand, 232
    as the Real Condition, 233
    See also Guru-devotee relationship;
        Guru-devotee relationship (with
        Adi Da); Ishta-Guru-Bhakti Yoga
sattva, defined, 370
savikalpa samadhi, 182
science
    as a dehumanizing adventure, 104
    as archetype of intelligence, 104-105
    common description of, 100
    critique of, 100-111
    rise of, 106
    vs. ancient world view, 103-104
    vs. scientific materialism, 108
    See also scientific materialism
Scientific American, 110
scientific materialism
    as a political movement, 109-111
    defined, 99
    as new official religion, 109, 110
    as reductionist philosophy, 108
    vs. free inquiry, 108-111
    vs. science, 108
    See also science
Secret of devotion to the True Heart-
    Master, 193-96
seeing, 73-74
    defined, 60n, 367-68
seeking, 19
    as a symptom, not a solution, 71
    and self-understanding, 89-96
    in the emotional-sexual realm,
        245, 248
    Truth is not a matter of, 69
    usefulness of, 284
    See also "radical" understanding

self-contraction, 19, 65
    defined, 369
    described, 71-72
    ego as, 71-72
    and fear, 249
    as the feeling of separateness, 89
    generates illusions, 309
    is why you feel bad, 96
    as pinching yourself, 92
    release from, 73
    ultimately kills you, 304
self-discipline, 227-37
    defined, 223
self-"guruing", 54
self-help, critiqued, 201-203
"self-possession", defined, 118n, 369
self-understanding
    described, 89
    See also "radical" understanding
separation, feeling of in the first stage
    of life, 155, 164
service, 224-226, 342
    defined, 223
seven stages of life, 154-165
    stage one—individuation, 155, 164
    stage two—socialization, 155, 164
    stage three—integration, 156, 164
    stage four—Spiritualization, 156-57,
        164, 317
    stage five—higher Spiritual evolution,
        158-59, 165, 317
    stage six—Awakening to the
        Transcendental Self, 159-60, 165,
        317
    stage seven—Divine Enlightenment,
        160-62, 165, 185-86, 322-24,
        See also Divine Enlightenment
sexuality
    as addiction, 253
    as a heart-matter, 253
    celibacy, 245, 259-60
    and emotion, 256
    the pleasure of, 254
    sexual practice, 241-42
    See also orgasm; money, food, and sex

Shakti, 310
  Adi Da's relationship to after Divine
    Re-Awakening, 315
Shaktipat, 299
Siddha, defined, 369
Siddha-Guru, defined, 369
Siddhis of Adi Da's Teaching Work, 289,
  289n
sin, 130, 169
  Jesus' teaching about, 176, 178
  Western and Eastern views on, 166-67
Siva-Shakti, defined, 20, 20n, 311, 311n
socialization, 155
soldier in Vietnam story, 117
soul, there is no soul within, 316
Spirit-Baptism (Spiritual Baptism), 157
  defined, 369
Spiritualization (fourth stage of life),
  156-57
Spiritual life
  is about Realizing Love-Bliss, 282
  is a demand, 231-32
  is not separation from vital and
    physical life, 227-31
  true nature of, 55-56
  See also sadhana
Spiritual Transmission
  of Adi Da, 87, 142-44, 159-60
  described, 49-50
  in true Spiritual life, 56
Sri, defined, 369
stages of life. See seven stages of life
stories about Adi Da. See Leelas
student, becoming a student of Da
    Avatara International, 336
student-beginner, defined, 370
student-novice, of Adidam, 337-38
Substitution myths, 146-147
subtle dimension, defined, 366
suffering
  the imaginary disease of, 75-76
  life is not, 80
  and sadhana, 230
  as self-caused, 65
  See also "radical" understanding; self-
    contraction

suicide
  of devotee's brother and sister,
    302-303
  killing the heart is also, 303, 306
sunlight, Adi Da as, 38, 41
surrender, to the Master, 195, 196, 202

**T**

tamas
  defined, 370
  described, 227
"Tantric bliss", 228, 228n
Tcha, defined, 57n, 370
therapeutic point of view, critique of,
  234-35
"There is Only God", 127, 135, 316-17
"This is the other world", 328
toxicity, 237
Transmission. See Spiritual Transmission
True Heart-Master, Secret of the, 192-96
Truth. See God; Consciousness (Itself)
Tsiknas, William, 121-22
Tukaram, described, 114n
Tumomama Sanctuary, 345

**U**

understanding. See "radical" understanding
United Kingdom, Adidam regional center,
  348
United States, Adidam regional centers, 348

**V**

Vedanta Temple, Adi Da's Re-Awakening
  in, 20-21, 310-15
Vedanta Temple Event, 20-21, 310-15
vital shock, defined, 370
Vunirarama, defined, 61, 61n

**W**

Way of the Heart
  as a relationship, 53
  becoming a practitioner of, 337-38
  classes, seminars, and special events
    related to, 334-35
  and cultism, 147
  described, 333-48

Way of the Heart *(continued)*
as Distraction by Adi Da, 197-200
financial support of, 371-72
fundamental principle of, 211
how to find out more about, 334-35
an invitation to, 333-48
is not a remedial path, 312-13
life of a devotee in, 341-47
as the "Only-God-Does-it" Way, 201
planned giving to, 372
as present and progressive practice, 72n
as process of "Brightening", 323
purpose of, 213
regional centers of, 348
responsibilities of devotees, 233-37
and sexuality, 253
summarized, 189, 191
transcends Eastern and Western
traditions, 170-72
vs. Great Path of Return, 162
*See also* Adidam
Website for Adidam, 335
Western civilization
as predominant mode in the world,
267-68
*See also* civilization
Western esoteric cults, 181
Western viewpoint
contrasted with Eastern viewpoint and
the Way of the Heart, 180-84
extroverted tendencies of, 182
on orgasm, 257
Western religion compared with
Eastern religion and the Way of the
Heart, 166-72
Western science vs. Eastern views, 106
will, development of, 156
Witness-Position, 84-85, 159, 165, 293
"women and gold", 231
work
and Spiritual life, 236
*See also* service
world, 100-101
"the world is endlessly allowed to be"
(poem), 24
wound of love, 250

**Y**
yama and niyama, 234, 234n
Yoga, defined, 370
Yogis, practices of, 158, 181-82
"You become what you meditate on",
16, 218
"You Do Not Love me", 249
"You don't know what anything is",
113-15, 118-125